URBAN POLICY IN THE EUROPEAN UNION

To the memory of my father, Simos Christou Tofarides

This book is to be returned on
or before the date stamped below

Urban Policy in the European Union

A Multi-Level Gatekeeper System

MARIA TOFARIDES

ASHGATE

Published by
Ashgate Publishing Limited
Gower House
Croft Road
Aldershot
Hants GU11 3HR
England

Ashgate Publishing Company
Suite 420
101 Cherry Street
Burlington, VT 05401-4405
USA

Ashgate website: http://www.ashgate.com

British Library Cataloguing in Publication Data
Tofarides, Maria
    Urban policy in the European Union : a multi-level
    gatekeeper system
    1. URBAN Community Initiative 2. Urban policy - European
    Union Countries 3. Community development, Urban - Great
    Britain 4. Community development, Urban - France
    I. Title
    307.7'6'094

Library of Congress Control Number: 2002109605

ISBN 0 7546 1786 6

Printed and bound by Athenaeum Press, Ltd.,
Gateshead, Tyne & Wear.

Contents

List of Tables

Acknowledgments

This book draws on research for a PhD thesis defended at the European University Institute (EUI) in June 2000. I would like to thank many people for their help in completing the thesis. Firstly, many thanks to Professor Yves Mény as my PhD supervisor and Professor Colin Crouch as my co-supervisor; both were very supportive throughout the period of research providing advice and guidance. Indeed, all the staff at the Robert Schuman Centre, the Department of Political and Social Sciences and the services of the EUI helped make my time there both pleasant and productive. I would also like to thank Professor Michael Keating, Chair of the examining board and Dr. Howard Machin who provided useful suggestions for the book during the discussion at the oral defence of the thesis.

The writing of this book would have been impossible without the cooperation of a wide range of organisations and individuals involved in this policy area. I would like to thank everyone who allowed access to meetings and found time in their busy schedules to speak about their work. Part of my programme at the EUI also involved a traineeship in 1997 at the European Commission. Here too I found everyone very open and helpful, both for my own research and the work related to the training programme.

I would like in particular to thank Mr. Graham Meadows for welcoming me to his team in the Directorate-General for Regional Policy (then DG XVI, Directorate D) and allowing me to examine material for the purposes of this study. Thanks also to Mr. Vittorio Curzi, Head of Unit for organising my work schedule and providing guidance throughout my training period. Mr. Peter Berkowitz was also very helpful in my everyday work. During my time as a trainee, I was also introduced to Dr. Ian Bache, lecturer in the Department of Politics at the University of Sheffield. Our cooperation on URBAN has since been extended to our academic work. A special thank you to Dr. Ian Bache and Professor Colin Crouch for commenting on various drafts of the book as well as earlier versions of the PhD thesis.

Finally, I would like to thank my family and friends for moral and emotional support during the PhD and the work related to this book. A big thank you to my husband Kevin for his love, patience and practical assistance helping me move around Europe between Florence, Brussels, Marseille and London as part of my research; his encouragement throughout made the completion of my book possible. My daughter Julia was born shortly after the thesis defence; although her arrival on 7 October 2000 temporarily delayed work on the book, she has been a source of great joy to everyone. Thanks also to Kris and Stella for helping to look after Julia so I could work on the book. I am also indebted to my parents, Simos and Anastasia who encouraged me to continue my education and pursue opportunities that were not so easily accessible to them in their generation in Cyprus. This book is dedicated to the memory of my father, Simos Christou Tofarides, who suddenly passed away on 16 September 2000.

List of Abbreviations

AGAM	*Agence d'Urbanisme de l'Agglomération Marseillaise* (Urban Planning Agency of the Urban Area of Marseille)
ALA	Association of London Authorities
ALG	Association of London Government
CCAS	*Centre Communal d'Action Social* (Communal Centre for Social Action)
CCLRA	Consultative Council of Local and Regional Authorities
CDF	Community Development Foundation
CEC	Commission of the European Communities
CED	Community Economic Development
CI	Community Initiative
CIAT	*Comité Interministériel à l'Aménagement du Territoire* (Inter-ministerial Committee for National and Regional Development)
CIQ	*Comité d'Intérêt de Quartier* (Neighbourhood Committee)
CIV	*Comité Interministériel des Villes* (Inter-ministerial Committee for Towns and Cities).
COCPUR	*Comité d'orientation du* PIC URBAN (Advisory Committee for the Community Initiative URBAN)
CoR	Committee of the Regions
CURS	Centre for Urban and Regional Studies
DATAR	*Délégation à l'Aménagement du Territoire et à l'Action Régionale* (Delegation for National Planning and Regional Action)
DDE	*Direction Départementale de l'Équipement* (Departmental Office for Infrastructure)
DETR	Department of the Environment, Transport and Regions
DfEE	Department for Education and Employment
DG IV	Directorate-General Competition
DG V	Directorate-General V Employment and Social Affairs
DG VI	Directorate-General Agriculture
DG XVI	Directorate-General XVI Regional Policy and Cohesion
DIV	*Délégation Interministérielle à la Ville* (Inter-ministerial Delegation for Towns and Cities)

DoE	Department of the Environment
DRCA	*Délégation Régionale du Commerce et de l'Artisanat* (Regional Delegation for Commerce and Artisan Industries)
DRIRE	*Direction Régionale de l'Industrie de la Recherche et de l'Environnement* (Regional Office for Industry, Research and the Environment)
DRTEFP	*Direction Régionale du Travail, de l'Emploi et de la Formation Professionelle* (Regional Office for Work, Employment and Professional Training)
DSU	*Développement Social Urbain* (Social and Urban Development)
EC	European Community
ECU	European Currency Unit
EDR	Economic Development and Regeneration
EP	European Parliament
ERDF	European Regional Development Fund
ESC	Economic and Social Committee
ESF	European Social Fund
EU	European Union
EUI	European University Institute
EZ/EC	Empowerment Zones/Enterprise Communities
FAS	*Fonds Action Sociale* (Funds for Social Action)
FF	French francs
GLC	Greater London Council
GO	Government Office
GOL	Government Office for London
GPU	*Grand Projet Urbain* (Great Urban Project, Infrastructure Programme)
GTP	*Groupe technique de Programmation* (Technical Programming Group)
HLM	*Habitation à Loyer Modéré* (Social Housing)
IDO	Integrated Development Organisation
LBA	London Boroughs Association
LDDC	London Docklands Development Corporation
MEP	Member of the European Parliament
MF	Million (s) Francs
MIPPE	*Mission des programmes privés et européens* (Department of the Municipality of Marseille with responsibility for private and European programmes)
MP	Member of Parliament

OECD	Organisation for Economic Cooperation and Development
OJ	Official Journal
PACA	Provence-Alpes-Côte-d'Azur
PIC	*Programme d'Initiative Communautaire* (Community Initiative Programme)
PMC	Programme Monitoring Committee
PS	*Parti Socialiste* (French Socialist Party, 1969–)
RPR	*Rassemblement pour la République* (Gaullist Party, 1976–)
SGAR	*Secrétariat Général pour les Affaires Régionales* (Secretariat General for Regional Affairs)
SME	Small and Medium Size Enterprises
SPD	Single Programming Document
SRB	Single Regeneration Budget
TEC	Training and Enterprise Council
TPG	*Trésorier Payeur Général* (Treasurer and Paymaster General)
UAP	Urban Action Plan
UDC	Urban Development Corporation
UDF	*Union pour la Démocratie Française* (French centre-Right federation, 1978–)
UIDU	URBAN Initiative Development Unit
UK	United Kingdom
UKREP	UK Permanent Representation to the European Communities
UMC	URBAN Management Committee
UPB	Urban Partnership Advisory Board
UPG	Urban Partnership Group
UPP	Urban Pilot Project
US	United States
VAW	Voluntary Action Westminster
VCSF	Voluntary and Community Sector Forum

Introduction

This study seeks to explore the 'aconstitutional' but growing involvement of the European Commission in urban policy matters. There is no Treaty basis for a European urban policy although an urban dimension to the Structural Funds has developed incrementally in the post-1988 period. There are two main sections to the book; the first, chapters one to three, concentrates on answering why, and how, the Commission has ventured into the urban arena. The second section, chapters four to seven, concentrates on the implementation of one specific European programme, the Community Initiative (CI) URBAN in the United Kingdom (UK) and France. Reference is made to the experience of two European cities, London and Marseille. The comparative approach explores the relationship between national and European policies in the two Member States. Chapter eight draws conclusions from the Commission's urban policy experiment and our two case studies.

How has the Commission, often viewed as a remote Brussels bureaucracy, come to be involved in urban policy dealing with small pockets of deprivation in cities? This extension of competences is beyond what could have been foreseen by the Treaties establishing the European Union (EU). Furthermore, the launching of specific urban policy measures is a recent phenomenon, dating back to 1988. In the early stages of this research, there was little material, primary or secondary, relating to this field. The Commission's urban policy experiment was in its infancy. In view of this, we began by seeking other examples where a higher level of government has intervened in local policies. The comparative research focuses on two European states, yet preliminary research involved a curious detour to the United States (US). Here we found a wealth of material on federal initiatives in urban policy. What can we learn from the American experience?

The US federal government has been involved in urban policy measures since the 1930s. Similar to the European case, there had been no formal changes to the Constitution granting the higher level government additional powers. Legally, states are the effective unit of government and every city is subordinate to the state. Why, and how, did the federal government in the US venture into a policy area, beyond its constitutional powers? In the European case, urban policy is not mentioned in the Treaties. Why and how has the Commission entered a policy area where, legally, it has no competence? Understanding the tools of federal expansion helps prepare our framework of analysis for the European case. This is set out in chapter one where we explore the concepts of cooperative federalism and partnership. Another instrument of federal expansion was the federal budget. The financial resources of the federal government influenced relations with the state and municipal levels. Although Europe is not a federal state, the increased budget of the Structural Funds in 1988 impinged on the Commission's relations with Member States and other levels of government.

Lessons from the American experience may provide some initial guidance. This is not, however, sufficient to address the questions raised in this study. Clearly, Europe is not a federal state; neither is there a 'standard' or 'typical' model of EU policy-making (Nugent, 1994). Before examining the empirical material we need to gather additional analytical tools for our European case studies. For this, we turn to existing works on the European policy process. Chapter two reviews the secondary material which is useful for this research. Firstly, we turn to the literature on public policy which helps explain the Commission's 'aconstitutional' intervention in urban policy. Secondly, we focus on concepts that can guide us through the maze of empirical material on the delivery of urban policy measures. Existing studies on European policy-making complement the section on American federalism. This allows us to prepare an original framework of analysis tailored for our individual case studies.

Cities fall within the competence of the Member State rather than the higher level of government, the Commission, in the European case. Chapters one to three seek to explain why Member States would accept the Commission's 'intrusion' into an essentially national policy area. Once the policy is launched, what can the Commission, the supra-national level of government, achieve from its urban policy experiment? Cities may be affected by the policies of more than one Directorate-General. Since this study focuses on urban policy initiatives in the context of the Structural Funds, we concentrate on the work of Directorate-General XVI, Regional Policy and Cohesion (DG XVI). Some of the programmes explored have a European Social Fund element, the responsibility of Directorate-General V, Employment and Social Affairs (DG V). Where relevant this is incorporated into the analysis, although the main emphasis is on the work of DG XVI.[1]

---

[1] This research was conducted prior to the changing of the names of the Directorates-General and Services under President Romano Prodi. Throughout this book, therefore, we refer to the Commission's services as listed during the period covered in this study.

Since we are focusing on the work of DG XVI, we explore the policy from the perspective of the four principles of post-1988 regional policy: concentration, programming, additionality and partnership. The principle of partnership is of particular interest since this may involve the Commission seeking to engage sub-national actors, below the level of elected national, regional and local authorities. The actual recipients of the programmes, at grass roots level, may be involved in delivering the policy.

In an interview in 1997, Eneko Landaburu, Director-General of DG XVI stated the following:

> The referenda in France and Denmark about Maastricht showed us that if we wanted to be successful in Europe, in better integration, better life between member states, we needed to be closer to the citizens. The citizens do not understand Europe – it is too far away. The better way of involving them is through better participation at the local level.[2]

A cynic may view the involvement of local volunteers as the European Commission paying lip service to a policy area in which there has been little actual investment. The sums involved in the Commission's urban policy experiment are small, relative to overall spending on regional policy. The main urban specific programme examined in this study, that is the CI URBAN, had a budget of ECU 885 million for the period 1994-1999 and involved 110 participating cities.[3] Extending the concept of partnership, to include local volunteers, may be a way in which the Commission promotes urban policy measures in a cost effective way. In this way, the Commission

---

[2] Political interview, 'A man for all regions', interview with Eneko Landaburu, Director-General of DG XVI in *Parliamentary Review*, March 1997. The quote was part of a reply to the question of whether Mr. Landaburu would support Scottish devolution, in which case the answer was that this was for the British to decide. The remark can still be interpreted though as indicating that the Commission is seeking closer links with its citizens through different means.

[3] Some cities also benefited from EU assistance within the framework of mainstream programmes, particularly under Objective 2. Further details are provided on this in chapter three. The figures for URBAN are quoted from the OECD, 1998, report. The overall Structural Funds budget for the period 1994-1999 (including the Cohesion Fund) amounted to ECU 27.4 billion (CEC, 1994c, see also Wishlade, 1996). The figures quoted indicate how small a proportion URBAN was to the spending on Structural Funds as a whole during the programming period 1994-1999. Since the period covered by this study mainly focuses on events prior to the introduction of the EURO on 1 January 1999, all figures are quoted in the European Currency Unit (ECU) or, where relevant, French Francs (FF) and £ sterling.

can be seen to be sensitive to the needs of European cities without actually investing large sums into urban policy measures.

Small-scale experiments can also provoke debate about broader issues. One such example is that of subsidiarity – which level of government is considered most appropriate for tackling urban problems encountered, in different degrees, by virtually all Member States of the EU? The residents of the targeted areas, as well as voluntary and community associations who are active there, may consider that they are best placed to tackle the needs of deprived neighbourhoods. Local solutions to local problems may be an effective way of utilising the limited funds available. Can the Commission, a supra-national level of government, succeed in engaging local communities, at neighbourhood level, to actively participate in the delivery of Structural Funds programmes? If the Commission, as the higher level of government, manages to promote local strategies, the processes could be sustainable. If successful, the local communities could continue the regeneration process beyond the duration of any European funding programme.

While the supra-national government may have policy objectives and a budget to achieve these, the Commission depends on the Member State's administration to implement its policies. Any urban policy conceived in Brussels has to go through a number of barriers before it reaches the targeted recipients on the ground. The implementation of European regional policy in the period after 1988 involves a wide range of actors at national, regional and local level. Although each plays a part in the policy process, they may also act as 'gatekeepers' between the conception of the policy in Brussels and its delivery on the ground. This notion of 'gatekeeper', seeking to control the policy process, will be more fully explored in chapter two where we develop our model for the analysis of the Commission's urban policy experiment; this can feature at different levels of government.

The initial 'gatekeepers' may be national government, that is Member State central ministries. Although the European intervention aims to complement the policies of Member States, this should also have its own identity and added value. In this sense, the European funds should not be used purely to co-finance existing schemes operating at national level. Yet within the Member State, regional or local government may also act as 'gatekeepers' by seeking to control implementation of the European policy. Furthermore, given the distance of Brussels to the locality, can 'gatekeepers' also appear in the form of individuals or organisations seeking to assert their own influence on the process at neighbourhood level? This raises a number of issues: Who represents the local community in the targeted areas of the cities concerned? Is this composed solely of residents in the neighbourhood?

Can voluntary and community associations based in, or operating in the area, also claim to be representative of the targeted recipients? This gives a flavour of the types of problems involved when a higher level of government, the Commission in this case, ventures into an essentially local policy area. We now turn to our choice of case studies where the institutional differences are of interest in the Commission's urban policy experiment.

Why conduct a comparative study on London and Marseille? The two cities are different in size, demographic composition and geographical location. Furthermore, the cities are based in two different Member States each with their own administrative systems. Yet, historically, the first specific urban policy measures, financed by Structural Funds, were launched in London and Marseille in 1988; the background to this will be explored in chapter three. The two cities provide an example of the local dimension to European Regional Development Fund (ERDF) Structural Funds policies, whereby the Commission targets pockets of deprivation in a city. Deprived neighbourhoods may, as is the case in London, exist in an otherwise wealthy city or region. Indeed, the problem neighbourhoods may be in close vicinity to the wealthier parts of the same city. Again, London provides an example where the area known as Inner East London is next to the massive wealth of the City of London.

The UK and France are two traditionally centralised states. Following a series of decentralisation laws in the 1980s, France has elected regions. Furthermore, reforms from 1872 in the third Republic in France made the mayor the choice of the popularly elected municipal council (Schmidt, 1990). With reference to the Municipality of Marseille, we find an elected Mayor of Marseille which is part of the elected region Provence-Alpes-Côte d'Azur. This study covers the period following the abolition of the General London Council in 1985 during which London had no single authority to govern the entire city. There are 33 separate London boroughs and London did not have an elected mayor to represent the city as a whole. Moreover, there was no elected regional assembly representing London. This situation changed following the election of the Labour Government, in 1997, committed to an elected Mayor and Assembly for London. Although this was approved by referendum on May 8 1998, the institutional changes did not affect the implementation of the programmes examined in this study.

Following the analytical framework of chapters one and two, this study aims to trace the Commission's urban policy initiative from Brussels down to a very local level in the participating cities. The differences in institutional structures of our chosen case studies allow us to compare and contrast the experiences of two cities in two different Member States. The concept of partnership is essential in the dialogue between the supra-national, national and sub-national levels of government. This interaction between the Commission and its partners can take place at various stages of the policy process – both the launching and subsequent implementation of the European policy. Chapter three aims to explain how, and why, urban policy initiatives were launched while the remaining chapters focus on the delivery of those policies. The notion of 'gatekeeping', as developed in chapter two, will be used to identify the barriers between the policy, conceived in Brussels, and the targeted recipients of that policy.

Chapters four and five deal with the policy process regarding the selection of cities and the administrative framework for the delivery of URBAN, in the UK and France. Chapters six and seven deal with the implementation at grass roots level in London and Marseille. Here the Commission aims to tackle precise areas of deprivation in the cities involved. However, in order to reach the deprived neighbourhoods, the Commission must work with the levels of government in the Member State concerned. In the case of London, the local authorities participating in URBAN for the period 1994-1999 were the City of Westminster, the London Boroughs of Brent, Hammersmith and Fulham (Park Royal area). In East London, the London Boroughs of Hackney and Tower Hamlets were involved. Each London borough has its own elected local council. In Marseille, a single municipality implemented the programme under the elected mayor of the city as a whole.

There are interesting variations not only between the two cities but also, in the case of London, between different programmes within the same city. We will seek to apply the framework of analysis prepared in chapter two in order to account for the differences in outcome in the respective case studies. The findings should bring insights into how the European Commission works alongside national, regional and local systems of government. At time of writing, the programmes were still being implemented and it was not possible to follow the programmes through their entire duration. Analysis of the case of Marseille is up to July 1998. The material on London is followed until April 1999 in order to include the developments relating to the financial responsibility for the funds; this point will become clearer in the course of the analysis.

The empirical chapters of this study are based on a wide range of field work in Brussels, London and Marseille. The aim of this was to gather data and gain the perspective of all levels involved, from the Commission, down to the residents and organisations based in the targeted neighbourhoods. The methods used were observations of the policy process and a wide range of interviews with a selection of partners involved at each level; the emphasis was on acquiring qualitative data from each. Formal interviews of the partners involved were conducted in Brussels, London and Marseille. Some individuals were interviewed more than once in the course of this study in order to take account of the different stages of the policy process.

The research also included a five month training period in the Directorate-General for Regional Policy (then DG XVI) who allowed access to a wide range of internal, unpublished documents. Experience gained while working on the implementation on URBAN in DG XVI between March and July 1997 and informal discussions with colleagues were an essential part of the research for this study. The European Commission, Government Office for London, the Department of the Environment Transport and Regions, the local Urban Partnership Groups, the Municipality of Marseille, the Prefecture of the Region Provence-Alpes-Côte d'Azur all provided access to meetings, documents and data. None of the more sensitive, unpublished material is quoted directly. Any interpretations of the material are the author's and do not represent the official view of the organisations who forwarded information for the purposes of this study.

1   Federal Expansion and Urban Policy: What Can We Learn from the American Experience?

Introduction

The first part of this chapter focuses on the tools of federal expansion in the American experience of urban policy. The second part examines the implementation of urban policies launched by the federal government. Any federal expansion was through a complex mix of programmes and conditions attached by the higher level of government. Through the concept of 'partnership', federal programmes involved a wide range of public and private actors. Turning to the European case, chapters two and three will then refer to the American experience when seeking explanations for the supra-national intervention in urban policy. An understanding of the instruments of federal expansion can help guide our analysis of recent developments in European urban policy measures.

The flexibility of American federalism allowed the higher level of government to expand and contract its urban policy measures at various points in time. Section 1.1 examines the model of American federalism which allowed this federal expansion without any changes in the Constitution. Turning to the European case, could the Commission's urban policy experiment lead to the birth of a European urban policy? On the one hand, Member States may welcome the additional funds from Brussels. On the other hand, the Commission may be accused of interfering in policy areas where, legally, it has no competence.

For the implementation of urban policy, the United States (US) experience provides us with concrete examples of how federal intervention in cities works in practice. As Cappelletti notes, 'comparison is not meant exclusively as a search for models to follow, but also for pitfalls and shortcomings to avoid' (Cappelletti, 1986, p.XII). What are the problems associated with a federal or supra-national institution in the case of Europe, dealing with a local policy area targeting specific neighbourhoods? Could the federal level, in the US, bypass the state level government and establish direct links with the locality? Similarly, could the Commission bypass central and local government and establish direct links with local organisations operating at grass-roots level? In both the US and European cases, 'partnership' has led the higher level of government to seek alliances with organisations below that of elected municipal government.

It is important to stress that this chapter is not intended to be a comprehensive review of American urban policy. Neither do we seek to present a comparative chapter on American and European urban policy. Clearly, the US federal system of government is a different animal to the EU. The major objective here is to capture the processes involved in the American experience of urban policies in order to acquire tools of analysis for the European case. The US provides a wealth of material on how urban policy, involving different levels of government, works in practice. Any European level urban policy, although in its infancy, also involves different levels of government: supra-national, national, regional and local. Understanding the mechanisms of the American federal system can provide a starting point for following the complexities of the Commission's urban policy experiment. Let us begin by examining the model of American federalism.

1.1 What Type of Federalism does the American Model Represent?

Legally, federalism has been defined as an arrangement whereby the central government and the constituent states are each granted a specific set of powers and authority (Riker, 1964, Leach, 1970). In the American federal system, the national government has powers mainly in the areas of commerce, trade and national defence. In order to understand how the federal level could be involved in cities, we need to explore how the American federal system works in practice. Moving away from the legalistic approach, scholars of American federalism have stressed a *cooperative,* rather than *dual* federalism, which the model outlined above would suggest:

> The American system pattern of federalism has been cooperative since its beginning because, since its inception, most powers and competences have been treated as concurrent, shared by the various planes of government (Elazar and Greilsammer, 1986).

One key element to 'cooperative' federalism is the principle of 'partnership'. Elazar and Greilsammer (1986, p.104) define partnership as a principle which guides political relationships that link together institutions, groups, interests and individuals in the American system. Power is distributed between several centres which negotiate cooperative arrangements in pursuit of common goals. Elazar and Greilsammer (1986, p.110) argue that the cooperation between actors enhances, rather than challenges, the cohesion of the political system. In 1986, partnership between private and public institutions is presented as a major element of American federalism which does not feature in Europe.

For the period covered in this study, we can now question whether this public-private cooperation is 'non-existent in Europe' (Elazar and Greilsammer, 1986, p.10). Indeed, 'partnership' as a concept in the 1988 reform of the Structural Funds actively sought to incorporate 'economic and social partners' in the policy-making process – this can also include the private sector. It is not within the scope of this book to fully compare all aspects of partnership in the American federal model to that in the overall development of the EU to date. However, the 'partnership' principle and the idea of 'cooperative arrangements' can be identified as a central theme in the post-1988 period, at least in the area of regional policy of which the implementation, in particular, involves a broad range of actors.

Indeed, the concept of partnership blurs all the usual divisions and distinctions which may exist in the political process – public and private; European, national and local; hierarchy and informality; lobbying and participation. There may be national, or regional, variations in the composition of partnerships within the different Member States of the EU. In the empirical material, we will seek to identify the types of partnerships which have developed around EU urban policy measures, both their launching and subsequent implementation. In this context, the principle may be extended to include non-governmental actors, embracing voluntary and community organisations, as well as residents of areas targeted to receive Structural Funds assistance.

Another aspect of cooperative arrangements in the American system is the concept of the 'marble cake'. Grodzins (1966) described American federalism as a 'marble cake', rather than a layer cake, whereby lines of authority are blurred rather than rigidly defined. This is compatible with the notions of partnership and cooperative arrangements since federal intervention could be justified in policy areas where the participants shared common goals. The flexibility of American federalism allowed the higher level of government to intervene in the affairs of cities. All levels of government shared the common objective of tackling the problems of urban areas. While the federal intervention was in line with cooperative federalism, this also involved more specific instruments, namely the federal budget. Section 1.2 examines the impact of the federal resources on intergovernmental relations in the American system. Furthermore, the 'marble cake' scenario also had a more negative side. Although the actors may have shared common goals, a number of setbacks emerged. Section 1.3 draws on examples from American urban policy which illustrate the problems of coordination and competing political interests among the recipients of federal programmes.

Turning to the European case, can the 'marble cake' metaphor be useful in analysing the Commission's urban policy experiment? Writing in 1986, Elazar and Greilsammer viewed the European Community as resembling more a layer cake than a marble cake. During this period, the most significant spheres of state activity such as foreign policy, economic policy and financial policies remained mainly with the Member States. Since 1986, particularly following the Maastricht, Amsterdam and Nice Treaties, the EU's policy agenda has also, to a certain extent, expanded to some of these areas. A detailed analysis of EU involvement across all policy areas is beyond the scope of this study. This research focuses on the peripheral area of urban policy in the context of DG XVI's regional policy. Since the reforms in 1988, it would be difficult to argue that the implementation of European regional policy resembles a layer cake.

In the empirical chapters, we will examine how the principle of partnership involves a multiplicity of actors in the delivery of the Commission's programmes. In view of this, the 'marble cake' could be an appropriate way of assessing the European policy making process. The lines of authority are not clearly defined between the numerous levels and actors involved. It would be useful, therefore, to highlight the problems encountered in the American federal experience of urban policies. Any European urban policy initiatives may encounter similar hurdles. Firstly we should complete our understanding of the tools of federal intervention. For this we turn to the impact of the federal budget.

1.2 The Federal Budget and Intergovernmental Relations

The major theme is the ability of the federal government to use its financial capacity in order to expand its competences beyond those stated in the Constitution. Historically, Elazar (1984) traces the increase in federal aid from the period 1802 to 1977. A major development after 1913 was the sixteenth amendment which introduced income tax as the major financial resource of the federation. The revenue generated from the fiscal arrangements permitted the federal government to expand, when considered appropriate, federal aid to the state and local levels. As a corollary to this, was the way in which the federal government was able to attach conditions to its programmes of aid to the states (Kempf and Toinet, 1984). In this way, due to the financial resources at its disposal, the federal level was able to intervene increasingly in the states' affairs.

Returning to the European situation, evidently there have been developments in terms of the Community budget: the development of the European Community's 'own resources' and the transfer of a portion of Value Added Tax to the Community have developed certain federal characteristics to the budget. This is not to say that the scale of the EU's budget can be compared to that of the federal level in the US; neither is it within the scope of this study to assess the figures involved. For our purposes, the main point is the existence of financial resources at another level of government to which Member States, and local levels of government within them, can have access. The scale of European regional policy has vastly expanded since the 1988 reform of the Structural Funds. For the period covered by this study, this commands around 35 per cent of all EU expenditure.[1] This presents the scenario whereby a higher level of government, as provider of funds, can further its influence by attaching conditions to potential recipients of those funds.

Cappelleti, Seccombe and Weiler (1986, p.41) refer to the ability of federal governments to 'buy' the loyalty of states by means of financial aid and the conditions attached to this. This allows the federal level to intervene in areas beyond its constitutional powers. Financial tools are also viewed as 'result orientated instruments' which offer incentives to the states to comply with federal policy. This is seen as more effective than judicial remedies to tackle any non-compliance from the state level. At time of writing, Cappelletti, Seccombe and Weiler (1986) presented the above as a fundamental difference between the US and European example which nevertheless was a 'tantalising option' for future Community evolution.

Only two years after the publication of the above assessment, the 1988 increase in scale of the European Structural Funds did herald a period where

---

[1] Figures related to the overall cohesion and Structural Funds budget were ECU 27.4 billion projected for 1999 compared to ECU 7 billion, or just 19 per cent of the budget in 1987 (CEC, 1994c, Eurostat 1992, see also Wishlade 1996).

the Commission played a more pro-active role in implementing regional and cohesion policy. Similar to federal funds, European funds are awarded in accordance with certain conditions and regulations. In this way, the Commission can arguably extend its influence through the 'power of the purse'. Yet this is subject to complex negotiations and bargaining between the actors involved. Before examining the European case, we should learn from the American experience of intergovernmental relations involving cooperative arrangements between different levels of government.

Wright (1988) analyses and develops the concept of 'intergovernmental relations' in the context of American federalism within which it developed. Wright takes Anderson's definition of intergovernmental relations as 'an important body of activities or interactions occurring between governmental units of all types and levels within the US federal system' (Anderson, 1964). As Wright notes while the term is not intended to substitute the term federalism, it suggests the usefulness of a different way of referring to the numerous and complex relationships between different levels of government found in the United States (Wright, 1988 p.39). Indeed, Wright's preferred model of federalism is one of 'overlapping authority' whereby relations between national, state and local government are interdependent and involve bargaining. The impact of the federal budget is a main feature in the example presented by Wright:

> Wide areas of intergovernmental relations involve exchanges or agreements. For example the national government offers scores of assistance programmes to states and localities in exchange for agreement to implement a programme, carry out a project, or pursue any one of a wide variety of activities. *Of course as part of the bargain the recipient of the assistance must usually agree to conditions such as the providing of matching-funds and the satisfaction of accounting, reporting and performance* requirements (Wright, 1998, p.47, emphasis added).

This concept of intergovernmental relations can be directly applied to the European case regarding the implementation of programmes partly financed by the Structural Funds. The Commission grants Structural Funds but the recipients must produce matching funds and comply with the Commission, and Member State regulations, for the accounting, reporting and evaluation of those funds. In this way, the higher level of government can exert influence even without any major changes in the Treaties granting formal competences to the Commission. Similar to American federalism, the European policy process will entail complex negotiations and bargaining between the actors involved. Identifying problems encountered in the American experience can therefore assist in the analysis of the European case. It would be difficult to identify a comprehensive, federal urban policy at any period of American history. The American experience is more one of federal initiatives at specific junctures. The next section selects practical examples from American urban policy which illustrate the means of federal expansion and the problems associated with this. The conclusions to this chapter will then highlight points from this which can be useful in guiding our analysis of urban policy in the EU.

1.3 Policy Examples and Models from the American Experience

The 1930s provided the first example in the US of local actors mobilising themselves in order to demand action from the federal level. Following the scale of the problems caused by the Great Depression, representatives of cities felt that, in view of the resources at its disposal, it was the federal level which could tackle their problems more effectively. The National Municipal League and newly formed US Conference of Mayors pressed the case for a national programme to assist urban areas (Mohl, 1993). The first example of the federal level intervention in American cities was in the 1930s with Roosevelt's New Deal. The Supreme Court initially opposed the New Deal since it involved the federal level going beyond its legal competences as stated in the Constitution. However, once the early opposition was overcome, a period of 'cooperative federalism' began in the US. This interpretation of federalism allowed the federal government to intervene in policy areas beyond its constitutional powers. This early experience of American federal intervention highlights the debate regarding which level of government should tackle specific policy areas:

> In theory, federalism suggests the allocation of powers to the level 'best' suited to exercise them. Which level is indeed best at achieving certain goals? Herein lies the crux of the matter (Cappelletti, Seccombe and Weiler, 1986, p.8).

Clearly, the mayors' lobby in the 1930s turned to the federal level to demand action for cities. Once the legal obstacles were overcome, the federal level could justify its intervention since mayors representing cities had demanded federal aid. Federal intervention could be presented in terms of cooperative federalism where the actors pursued common goals.

The 1950s and 1960s present us with examples of more ambitious federal initiatives. This has been characterised as 'creative federalism' and involved a major expansion of federal programmes (Wright, 1988, p.66). The background to this was the election of a Congress dominated by Democrats in 1958 and the 1964 landslide victory for President Johnson. Kaplan (1990) argues that the origins of specific policy initiatives directed at cities, particularly distressed cities, were rooted in the civil rights and anti-poverty movements of the early and mid 1960s. During this period, federal policy makers felt that the higher level government had the financial resources to tackle long neglected domestic problems (Reischauer, 1990). In the period 1963-1967, Congress legislated over a hundred new programmes. Two programmes, within the framework of the 'Great Society', as expressed by Johnson, were directly targeted at cities: the 'War on Poverty' and the 'Model Cities'.

The federal grants had an impact on intergovernmental relations in the US. Cities were seen as the most deserving level of government as states were considered to have given insufficient attention to their urban areas Reischauer (1990). Federal action therefore sought to bypass the states in order to deal directly with the cities. Local actors responded to the expansion of federal funds by developing increasingly sophisticated techniques to acquire funds: mayors, city managers, county administrators, school officials and governors were all involved in the federal grant 'game'. Indeed, some cities and counties hired professional lobbyists to help secure federal grants. Although the 'Great Society' may have had a central theme, the number of federal grants and agencies made policy implementation a complex process.

By 1970 the proliferation of agencies and actors involved in preparing the grant bids led to severe problems of coordination in American urban policy. Furthermore, some elected and municipal officials applied for grants simply because the funds were available and made commitments to match-fund the projects without due regard for existing priorities (National Journal, Washington DC, 1973). Kaplan (1990) draws attention to how lines of authority in this period were unclear; complicated relationships grew between the various federal agencies, local governments, citizen and non-profit groups. Grodzins' (1966) 'marble cake' metaphor, as described in section 1.1, would appear to accurately represent the policy process during this period of federal expansion.

The lack of clear rules and the multiplicity of actors moved American federalism into a new phase, characterised by rivalry between participants in the policy process. Wright (1988, p.66) categorises the later Johnson period as one of 'competitive federalism'. This period was characterised by competition and conflicts between professional programme administrators, state and locally elected officials involved in acquiring and administering federal grants. When President Nixon came to power in 1969, he had little sympathy for the expensive urban programmes of the 'Great Society' era (Mohl, 1993). Nixon spoke about reversing the hitherto expanding role of government. Using his definition of 'New Federalism', Nixon gradually reduced federal programmes and the special purpose federal agencies which had multiplied under the Johnson Presidency (Brown et al. 1984, p.27). The period of the 1970s to 1980s is categorised as the 'calculative' phase (Wright, 1988, p.66). Local actors estimated the costs, as well as the benefits, of acquiring a federal grant following the experiences of the 1960s. Indeed, the near bankruptcy of New York City in 1975 highlighted the problem of dependency on federal grants. This concept of dependency is more fully explored by Kantor (1995).

Although the rhetoric used may differ, Nixon's successors continued this policy of distancing the federal level from the direct intervention characterising Johnson's presidency. In the Reagan period in particular, direct federal/local links were lessened, leaving cities to cultivate instead their links with the state level. There have been no examples of the mass expansion of federal aid since that of the Johnson era. Even Clinton's federal initiatives in urban policy did not revert to any federal shower of dollars. Indeed, Clinton's policy has been referred to as a 'non-urban urban policy' (Clark, 1997). The main emphasis of Clinton's urban policy was the 'Empowerment Agenda' representing a multi-faceted approach to urban problems in the form of designated Empowerment Zones and Enterprise Communities (EZ/EC). There was no attempt by the Empowerment Agenda to bypass the states. State governments retained a primary role in partnerships to deliver a federal urban policy. States were a part of the EZ/EC initiative and most federal funds were channelled through the states to the participating communities and zones. Furthermore, federal policy was often viewed by states as a complement to their own state level urban policy. Clearly, while the federal level was involved, the major responsibility for cities remained with the state level governments.

1.4 Conclusions from the American Experience

Which conclusions can we draw from the American experience? Firstly, attention focuses on the birth of European urban policy measures. The

American example illustrated how the mobilisation of mayors played a key part in promoting initial action from the federal level. Once the early legal obstacles were overcome, the pattern of 'cooperative federalism' was established whereby the federal government could act beyond its stated competences. Clearly, the mayors' lobby in the 1930s turned to the federal level to demand action for cities. This provided some legitimacy for the federal intervention since elected mayors, representing cities, had demanded federal aid.

Turning to the European case, the Commission does not have a legal mandate for an urban policy. Yet the argument regarding which level is best at achieving certain goals may be used to justify the Commission's intervention in areas where it has no legal competence. The Treaty on European Union introduced the principle of subsidiarity. There are differences in the interpretation of subsidiarity, yet under certain conditions, this may be interpreted to justify action by the supra-national institution:

> The Community shall act either within the limits of the powers conferred upon it by this Treaty and of the objectives assigned to it therein. *In areas which do not fall within its exclusive competence, the Community shall take action, in accordance with the principle of subsidiarity, only and in so far as the objectives of the proposed action cannot be sufficiently achieved by the Member States and can therefore, by reason of scale or effects of the proposed action, be better achieved by the Community* (Article 3B, Treaty on European Union, emphasis added).

Representatives of cities may well view Europe, with an increased Structural Funds budget of the post-1988 period, as an appropriate level to be involved in urban problems. Although Member States have their own policies relating to cities, sub-national actors may feel that the European level should also act. Europe represents an additional source of funds which can be directed at areas perceived to be neglected by national policies. We will seek, in the empirical material of chapter three, to find examples of sub-national mobilisation. Similar to the American case, the mobilisation of representatives of cities could provide some legitimacy for the Commission's intervention in urban policy. The task is then to identify the tools available to the supra-national level. On the one hand, there could be attempts to provide a Treaty basis for a European urban policy. On the other hand, European urban policy measures could 'creep in' through existing programmes such as those partly financed by the Structural Funds. These possibilities will be explored in chapter three.

The interesting point will be to note the reaction of Member States to the Commission's launching of urban policy measures. Under which conditions do Member States accept, or reject, the Commission's intervention? The 'creative' phase of American federalism illustrated the problems associated with federal attempts to create direct links with organisations below the state level of government. The federal level initially sought to establish direct links with cities and public-private actors below the level of the states. Yet Johnson's policy of bypassing the states was relatively short-lived; this was abandoned in the Nixon period and has never been adopted since.

The Commission may seek to forge direct links with sub-national actors at various levels. Dialogue with representatives of cities may, as discussed above, promote European urban policy measures. In the context of partnership, the Commission may seek to engage new partners in the delivery of its policies; this can include voluntary and community organisations, or representatives of residents, in the targeted area. However the supra-national level may encounter barriers, within the Member State, rendering the forging of direct links with the grass roots a difficult task. The conclusions to this study will explore whether the Commission's programmes have changed the balance of power between the partners involved at various levels of the policy process. Even if partners share the common goal of regenerating the targeted area, there can still be differences in opinion regarding how best to tackle urban problems. The implementation of European urban policy can illustrate variations in the interpretation of the principle of subsidiarity in practice.

The central and local levels of government may welcome the additional European funds but challenge some of the conditions attached to these. Central government may not easily adjust to changes in administrative procedures related to the implementation of European programmes. Municipal government may feel that this is the best level to deal with urban problems and reject any 'intrusion' from the central or supra-national government. 'New' partners such as residents, community and voluntary associations active in the targeted areas may feel that they are best placed to find solutions to local problems. Although the Commission's urban policy experiment may be small-scale, this could open a 'Pandora's Box' regarding the debate on which level can best tackle the problem neighbourhoods of European cities. These themes will be explored in the case study material in chapters four to seven.

Another lesson from American federalism is that action by the higher level of government may result in problems of coordination. The 'marble cake' scenario was particularly evident in the Johnson period. Given the wide-ranging partnership in place to deliver Structural Funds programmes, the 'marble cake' could appear in the European case. Unclear lines of authority may cause problems and delays in the implementation of EU sponsored urban policies. One particular problem of urban policy is that the nature of urban problems invariably involves more than one field. Housing, health, education, employment and training, local economic development, crime and security, the urban environment, and transport are all areas which affect cities. Any comprehensive European urban policy would involve numerous Directorate-Generals at Commission level as well as national ministries at Member State level.

This study confines the analysis to the urban dimension of DG XVI's regional and cohesion policy. Yet implementation of the European policy may involve more than one ministry within the Member State. The Commission is dependent on the Member State's administration to implement its policies. Central government operates at different levels since both the UK and France have deconcentrated levels of central government, namely Government Regional Offices and the Prefecture respectively. The involvement of other levels of government, as well as actors operating at the grass roots, increases the complexity of the policy process. The case studies will seek to identify problems of coordination in the delivery of URBAN in London and Marseille. This can raise questions about the effectiveness of the supra-national intervention.

Continuing with the question of practicality, as US federal aid expanded there were problems of dependency on federal grants and costs associated to fulfilling match-funding requirements. We should look for this is in the European case as this could outweigh any added value of the Commission's intervention. Are the additional funds worth the resources involved in acquiring and implementing them? Applying for funds is one aspect of the process; can the recipients fulfil the requirements to actually deliver those policies? In order to qualify for European Structural Funds, the recipients must fulfil 'match-funding' requirements. Can small community and voluntary organisations, targeted as potential recipients of funds, become active partners in the delivery of Structural Funds programmes? Many such organisations have few reserves and are directed to European funding as a way of continuing to survive financially. Whether, or how, such groups manage in the jungle of European and national funding regimes will be explored in the case study material on London and Marseille, chapters six and seven respectively. Before venturing into the field, we should turn to the secondary literature on European policy-making in order to complete our analytical tools.

2 Supra-National Policy in a Multi-Level Government System: Tools for Analysis of Regional Policy after 1988

2.1 Introduction

There is a vast range of literature dealing with both European integration and the EU policy-making process. This chapter is not a comprehensive review of existing works. The aim is to refer to existing research which can be used to develop a framework of analysis for the empirical part of this study. Firstly we examine existing works which focus on the role of the Commission. Similar to the American federal level, the Commission has various means of extending its policy agenda. Since there is no formal Treaty provision for a European urban policy, it is important to understand how the Commission works alongside its partners in the Member State. Studies on bureaucratic politics concentrate on the everyday activities of the Commission. This prepares us for the empirical material in chapter three which seeks to explain how, and why, the supra-national government became involved in the peripheral area of urban policy. Secondly, we seek models which we can apply to our investigation on the delivery of European urban policy presented in chapters four to seven.

A review of Structural Funds programmes of DG XVI reveals differences in implementation arrangements; this depends on the sums involved and the regulation framework for each. The various instruments of European urban policy will be presented in chapter three. Even allowing for such variations, the Commission depends on the national administrations to implement its policies. Both the UK and France are unitary, rather than federal, states. Central government is a key partner in the implementation of EU programmes. We therefore concentrate on the literature emphasising the role of central government in the European policy process. This leads us to the state centric model, sometimes referred to as 'intergovernmentalism'. Much of this research focuses on the everyday work of national administrations rather than the major events at high profile Council of Ministers or European Council meetings. The state centric model is adapted so that this can be incorporated into the analysis. This is set out in section 2.3 where the notions of 'gatekeeper' and 'extended gatekeeper' are introduced.

The implementation of European urban policy involves other levels of government as well as non-governmental actors. In view of this, we refer to studies on multi-level governance and policy networks with specific reference to regional policy. Similar to the American literature on intergovernmental relations, this highlights the interdependence between the actors involved at different levels. The conclusions to this chapter develop the notion of 'multi-level gatekeeping'. While not claiming to present a new theory of European policy-making, the metaphor of 'multi-level gatekeeping' is a useful framework for examining the implementation of URBAN in the UK and France. The conclusions to this chapter will explain how the use of this concept can help identify the barriers between the inception of European urban policy, in Brussels, and its local delivery in London and Marseille.

2.2 The Commission as an Actor: Agenda Setting and Bureaucratic Politics

The Commission's formal position as guardian of the Treaties, based around the 1957 Treaty of Rome and subsequent amendments, is to ensure 'the proper functioning and development of the common market'. Another Treaty obligation of the Commission is that of independence of its action. Yet over the decades, the Commission has increasingly favoured measures at Community level to tackle policy problems in a broader range of areas (Donnelly, 1993). Indeed, it may be argued that the Commission is divided between two contradictory objectives: on the one hand, the Commission's role is to expand its agenda in order to push for a more integrated Europe; on the other hand, it may be accused of having a 'democratic deficit'.

The President of the Commission and the individual Commissioners are appointed following nominations by Member States. The Treaty on European Union established provisions for the European Parliament's approval of the President and the other members of the Commission. However the Commission, as a body, is not required to agree on a manifesto and seek a popular mandate for its programme. This can be contrasted with the political process within Member States. There are variations in the political systems within Member States ranging from German federalism to traditionally unitary systems such as the UK. Yet national, regional and local administrations in the Member States are usually elected on the basis of a particular political programme.

Peters (1992) observes how the members of the Commission, and its bureaucratic nature, may appear remote to both national governments and the mass of ordinary citizens within individual Member States. The Commissioners and the Commission bureaucracy must work with national governments, represented by the Council of Ministers. Furthermore, the Commission is dependent on national administrations to implement its policies. In seeking to expand its agenda, the Commission is aware of the necessity to cultivate coalitions with national politicians and officials whose interests a proposal may affect. We could take this argument a step further by arguing that in certain policy areas, such as regional, there is a need for the Commission to forge coalitions with sub-national as well as national actors.

Chapter three will examine the interaction between the Commission and sub-national levels in order to explain how and why urban policy measures were launched. Similar to the American experience, the supra-national level of government may expand its policy agenda in response to demands for action from the sub-national level. There are numerous tactics which can be used to accelerate the agenda setting process. Possibilities are institutional paths through, for example, the Committee of the Regions. Representatives of cities may seek support from Members of the European Parliament or the Permanent Representation of the respective Member States. Another strategy would be for representatives of cities to seek direct dialogue with key Commissioners, notably the Commissioner for Regional Policy and Cohesion. Chapter three will present the empirical material on the mobilisation of sub-national actors in order to place urban policy on the EU's agenda. Chapters four to seven concentrate on the Commission's attempts to engage non-governmental actors in the implementation of European programmes. The principle of partnership is extended to include local residents and representatives of the voluntary and community sector.

The Commission has various means of placing matters on the Council's agenda. Pollack (1996) highlights the Commission's formal right to propose policies. The Commission's 'expertise, brokering skills and institutional persistence' provide it with additional tools to set the agenda for the Council to make the decisions (Pollack, 1996, p.449). In this sense, the Commission can act as a policy entrepreneur. However there is no Treaty provision for a European urban policy. We need therefore to also focus on the everyday work of officials in DG XVI. Peters (1992, p.80) argues that 'the politics of the European Community is best understood as a bureaucratic politics model' within a complex system of governance. Indeed, Peters (1992, p.80) draws a parallel in this respect with the US federal system:

> The specialisation and differentiation make EC policy-making look somewhat more like policy-making in the US federal government than in most parliamentary governments. The many policy communities or networks appear to exert great influence if not control, over public policy, more than in most national governments in Europe.

The bureaucratic politics model focuses more on the everyday activities of the Commission and its officials in drafting regulations and preparing the groundwork. This is seen to serve as a public policy basis for the integration visualised by the major political acts. One example given is that of public health policy. Under the Treaty of Rome, the Community has no competence in public health policy but it has acquired one through creative bureaucratic use of other powers (Peters, 1992, p.87).

Incremental expansion of the Commission's policy agenda can take place away from the politicised Council and the watchful eye of the media. In a politicised environment, any additions to the Commission's Treaty competences could be opposed by national governments nervous about ceding additional powers to Brussels. The American experience illustrated how the federal level could expand its policy field by funding federal programmes in cities and attaching conditions to these. Officials in DG XVI are involved in drafting and negotiating programmes partly financed by European Structural Funds. Since cities form part of the regions receiving European funding, programmes can involve cities even if the Commission does not have a Treaty basis for action. Chapter three will examine this aspect of DG XVI's work in order to explain the urban dimension which has appeared in European Structural Fund programmes.

2.3 State Centric Models of European Policy-Making: the Notions of 'Gatekeeper' and 'Extended Gatekeeper'

This section seeks to develop an analytical framework to assess the role of central government in the implementation of urban policy measures. The state centric model and the notion of 'gatekeeper' are a useful starting point. There are different presentations of the 'state-centric' model but the emphasis is on a Europe of nation states. The term 'intergovernmentalism' is referred to but not in the same sense as in the literature on American 'intergovernmental relations'. In the American literature the term 'intergovernmental' is used, in the context of American federalism, to explain the interactions between governmental units at different levels in the American system.[1] In the European case, the term 'intergovernmentalism' encompasses the body of literature which focuses on the role of member governments in the European policy process. The section below seeks to summarise the main arguments of the state centric or intergovernmental model. We also refer to some of the major developments in regional policy which the intergovernmentalists seek to explain.

Following the 'empty chair' crisis of 1965-1966, Hoffmann made a major contribution to the state centric model by developing the notion of 'gatekeeper'. Hoffman (1966) emphasises the role of member governments as 'gatekeepers' between their domestic political system and the Community. The model reaffirms the survival of the nation state particularly in the area of 'high politics' regarding matters which could threaten state security or the continued existence of the state (this could broadly be classified as foreign policy). A distinction is made between such 'high politics' and 'low politics' classified as dealing with domestic, functional matters administered by national civil servants (this could broadly be classified as social and economic affairs).

Under this differentiation between 'high' and 'low' politics, regional policy may not at first be identified as a policy area where governments would exercise 'gatekeeping'. Yet Hoffmann's (1966) distinction was challenged by early case study material of policy processes suggesting a more blurred picture between the foreign and domestic arenas (Webb, 1983, p.24). Indeed, regarding European Community (EC) policy-making, the concept of 'gatekeeping' was seen as relevant for domestic as well as foreign policy issues.

> Governments have frequently attempted to play a 'gatekeeping' role monopolising channels of communication between the state and the Community, in a way reminiscent of foreign policy stances even on those *domestic* issues which are likely to prove particularly contentious at home or politically embarrassing in the Community (Webb, 1983, p.6).

The early case study material also questioned the effectiveness of governments as 'gatekeepers' in view of the complex domestic environment

---

[1] The full explanation is in section 1.2 of chapter one.

in which governments operate and the diverse interests within this (Wallace, Wallace and Webb, 1983). This promoted interest in the domestic political process, within Member States, in order to explain the European arena.

Taking the 'domestic politics' approach, Bulmer (1983) emphasised the impact of domestic politics on EC policy-making. Bulmer (1983) highlighted the different procedures for deciding EC policy in each Member State taking account of national political culture, interest group activity, parliamentary bodies, political parties and sub-national government. Moravcsik added to the state centric model by reformulating intergovernmentalism. Moravcsik (1991, 1993) developed a model of 'liberal intergovernmentalism'. This continued to emphasise the role of the Member State although it analysed the Commission's ability to progress with integrative measures along with the policy preferences of national governments. Regarding the birth of the Single European Act, for example, Moravcsik (1991) emphasises the role of the Council of Ministers and the European Council.

There is no doubt that the actions of Member States within the framework of the Council of Ministers or Intergovernmental Conferences produce major decisions regarding, for example, institutional changes or budgetary decisions. Webb (1983, p.25) argues:

> It would appear that the rhythm of Community policy-making can be dominated by governments if, and when, they choose. They may wish to define an issue as corresponding with their national interests – perhaps the Regional Development Fund for the British between 1973-75.

André, Drevet and Landaburu (1989) underline that the accession of Britain and Ireland, both with existing regional problem areas, along with Italy's long-standing call for a regional policy, resulted in the creation of the European Regional Development Fund (ERDF). The establishment of the ERDF was agreed at the 1972 Paris and 1973 Copenhagen summits and its details at the 1974 Paris summit. The Single European Act of 1986 set out the legal basis for the EC's commitment to economic and social cohesion. One explanation for the growth of the Structural Funds in the post-1988 period is that this represented 'side payments' paid by wealthier Member States to the poorer peripheral member states in order to secure their agreement for the proposed 1992 Single Market Programme (Marks, 1992). The next major landmark in regional policy was the Treaty on European Union which established the cohesion fund, the institution of the Committee of the Regions and the principle of subsidiarity.

European urban policy measures cannot be detached from the major developments in regional policy some of which have been outlined above. Yet the Commission does not have a formal urban policy mandate. Our study does not therefore deal with monumental Treaty changes or major events in European integration. The emphasis is on the everyday implementation of a peripheral policy area at various stages: its launching (chapter three), its integration into existing national policies (chapters four and five) and its local delivery on the ground (chapters six and seven). We therefore need a framework of analysis which can help assess the role of central government at these different phases of the policy process, beyond major decisions taken at the high level Council or European Council meetings. Concepts from intergovernmentalism can be adapted in order to relate to our chosen policy area.

Since this study investigates potential barriers to the Commission's attempts to forge links with a broader range of actors, the 'gatekeeper' metaphor, from the state centric model, merits greater attention. Webb (1983, p.6) identified central government gatekeeping in domestic issues which involved the EC. However, as noted above, this notion was applied to explain major events such as the establishment of the ERDF. The empirical section examines whether central government seeks to monopolise channels of communication between the Commission and the other partners involved in European urban policy. Such gatekeeping may make it difficult for the Commission to forge direct links with representatives of cities or the broader range of partners such as residents, local businesses, the voluntary and community sectors who are involved in preparing and delivering programmes. Bache (1996) has developed a framework of analysis which focuses on central government gatekeeping in the implementation of policy. This is more relevant for our research and will be presented in detail below.

Bache (1996) initially adopted the gatekeeper concept from intergovernmentalism in order to theorise the role of central government seeking to achieve its aims throughout the policy process. Bache's approach was to follow, in detail, the role of central government in its efforts to achieve its objectives in two clearly defined areas of post-1988 regional policy: additionality and partnership. These two principles, as well as those of concentration and programming, were formally introduced in the 1989 reform of the Structural Funds. Bache (1996) differentiates between higher profile Commission and Member State negotiations, either at summits or in the general Council of foreign ministers, and implementation. Discussions over regional policy, and allocations to each Member State, take place in high profile summits where the broad framework is decided. Yet Bache's findings suggest that concessions the Commission gains, at this level, can be overruled by Member States at the implementation stage. Additionality provides one example of this:

> When the Commission has not been frustrated by national governments at the supranational level over additionality, it has found the national government gatekeeper difficult to bypass at the *implementation* stage where domestic priorities have been an obstacle. The implementation of the agreement which ended the RECHAR dispute illustrated this (Bache, 1996, p.178, emphasis added).

The empirical evidence in the area of partnership also concluded that central government acted as 'gatekeeper' in the implementation of European regional policy. The Structural Fund regulations designated central government as the main 'competent authority' with responsibility for administering programmes. This gave central government the opportunity to dominate the local partnerships by monopolising key positions in the regional partnerships. Central government officials chaired programme monitoring committees and the technical and sub-regional committees which linked into them. Central government also had the power, within the framework of the regulations, to select the other partners and decide on the frequency of meetings (Bache, 1996, p.181).

Clearly, Bache (1996) does not contest the main argument of the state centric model which identifies national governments as the most significant actors in the regional policy process. However the empirical findings, summarised above, identify certain shortcomings in this approach. The traditional intergovernmental approach concentrates mainly on high profile summits where the broad framework is decided. Yet Bache's contribution is to illustrate how central government may seek to exert control in the everyday implementation of European policies. Furthermore, Bache (1996) highlights the difficulties in assessing the influence of central government in implementation. Bache's conclusions suggest that 'the relative influence of actors fluctuated at different stages of the policy process and over time within the same stages of policy-making' (Bache, 1996, p.185). The original concept of member governments as 'gatekeepers' between the domestic political system and the Community (Hoffmann, 1966) does not take into account these variations at different points of the policy process.

Bache therefore adapts the original notion of 'gatekeeper' in order to construct a model which can incorporate the complexity of European policy-making. While not claiming to present a new theory, Bache (1996) introduces the concept of 'extended gatekeeper' which aims to assess any gatekeeping role of central government at different stages of the policy process. The 'extended gatekeeper' approach focuses on the role of central government in delivering EU programmes within the Member State. In the conclusions of his study on RECHAR, Bache (1996) develops an outline of the 'extended gatekeeper' model that could be applied to other empirical research. This can be adapted for the purposes of our study on the Commission's urban policy experiment.

Bache's (1996) model allows us to assess the role of central government in the implementation of EU urban policy measures. This is relevant for chapters four to seven of this book. Our empirical research concentrates on two unitary, rather than federal, states. In both cases, central government is a key partner in the delivery of European urban policy. Our study is concerned with potential barriers to the Commission's attempts to form direct links with sub-national actors including non-governmental actors. The initial 'gatekeeper', preventing direct links, could be central government. Furthermore, central government may seek to dominate any partnership established to deliver European programmes. The empirical section will refer to one specific instrument of European urban policy: the Community Initiative (CI) URBAN. The origins of the programme are presented in chapter three. The remaining chapters will then refer to Bache's notion of 'extended gatekeeper' in the analysis of the implementation of URBAN in London and Marseille.

The section below presents Bache's model (1996) and highlights points which can be applied to our empirical study. Bache's approach refers to issues rather than entire policy sectors; the significance of this is to narrow the field of analysis given that policy sectors are broad. Furthermore, related issues may cover more than one policy area. The example given is the issue of side payments, granted by larger states to peripheral ones, to secure agreement for the Single Market Programme through the policy of Structural Funds (Marks, 1992). The 'extended gatekeeper' approach also makes certain assumptions as listed below.[2]

> The various stages of the EU policy process are linked and to explain fully government action at one stage of the process may require understanding of government action at others. Thus for the fullest explanation it is less important at which point in the analysis the policy process investigation begins than it is to consider the related stages of the policy process.

---

[2] The small print contains extracts from Bache's model presented in full in Bache (1996, pp.196-197).

For the purposes of our study, in order to explain central government action in the delivery of policy at local level, it would be necessary to understand government action at earlier stages. Chapters four and five assess the role of central government in the higher level Commission/Member State negotiations dealing with the broad framework for the delivery of the CI URBAN in the UK and France. This is then related to the subsequent implementation of the programme at grass roots level (chapters six and seven respectively).

For analytical purposes it is helpful to distinguish between EU-level decision-making and the implementation stage.

In our analysis a distinction will be made between the Commission's decision to launch the CI URBAN, announced in the Official Journal of July 1994, and its subsequent implementation in the Member States.

A member government will seek to defend what is defined as its interests on a particular issue or set of related issues at a given time against unwanted policy developments resulting from EU membership *at all stages of the policy process.*

This is where Bache introduces the notion of the 'extended gatekeeper'. The assumption is that where a Member State is overruled by the EU at higher level negotiations, it will use its resources to seek the most favourable outcome at implementation stage. Our study will concentrate on assessing the Commission's aims and objectives in its urban policy measures. We will then explore how this is interpreted by the national administrations responsible for implementing the programmes. Can tensions be detected between the Commission's quest for a genuine regional policy and Member States seeking to supplement their own national urban policies?

The definition of a member government's interests in any given policy sector may change over time and may be influenced by a range of actors within and outside national government.

The CI URBAN was officially launched to cover the period 1994-1999. Administrative arrangements agreed in Member State/Commission negotiations in the early stages cannot be altered; these are set out in the terms of reference for each programme. Factors such as a change in national government, as in the UK in 1997, and the range of actors which have access to the new administration, could affect policy outcomes. This may occur without any formal changes to the broad framework agreed for implementing the programme. This will be explored in the section dealing with the implementation of URBAN at grass roots level (chapters six and seven respectively).

> The policy networks approach provides the tools to facilitate understanding of how the government's negotiating position is decided on a given issue.

The policy networks approach will be reviewed in section 2.4 of this chapter in order to assess its utility for this study.

> EU policy-making involves a process of bargaining at both the EU level and the implementation stage in which actors exchange resources to secure favourable outcomes. A member government will seek to mobilise the resources it controls to resist unwanted policy outcomes from EU membership at both EU level and during implementation, while recognising other actors will do likewise to achieve their policy objectives.

The bargaining between the Commission/Member State representatives will be observed, both in negotiations for the framework of delivery for URBAN, and subsequent implementation on the ground. The study will seek to identify the key actors involved in the delivery of URBAN in the UK and France. There may be variations in the case studies between what actors perceive to be unwanted policy outcomes; this could also appear at different stages of the policy process for the respective Member States.

> Resource exchange takes place within perceived 'rules of the game' which all participants recognise must be observed if negotiations are to be successful. These rules of the game change over time as the boundaries of what is permissible are continually tested.

This would be particularly important not only for analysing Commission/Member State negotiations, to establish the administrative framework for URBAN, but also for its subsequent delivery on the ground. Here we would seek to assess whether, and how, the participants could seek to adapt the rules to favour their preferred policy outcomes.

> The importance of different types of resources available to governments and other actors will fluctuate across policy sectors and over time.

This can be related to point four of the 'extended gatekeeper' model. The resources available to the member governments, or other actors, can alter the definition of a member government's interests. There could be variations in this throughout the duration of URBAN in London and Marseille, 1994-1999.

> While this research found that political, financial and informational resources were important in the EU regional policy network, and these types of resources may provide the starting point for other case studies, empirical investigation may reveal the importance of additional types of resources in other networks.

The significance of the resources listed will be assessed in each of the case studies. This may affect policy outcomes regarding the delivery of URBAN in London and Marseille. In the case of London, there may be variations in resources available to actors in each geographical area of the city. One example would be the existence of established voluntary and community groups in any given area. In both London and Marseille, the case studies will investigate whether the resources available to the actors involved vary at different points of the policy process. This can highlight differences between Anglo-French policy communities and their relationship to European policies.

> This approach suggests that in order to gain the fullest explanation of the role played by a single national government in the EU policy process, account has to be taken of the influence of factors external to the EU system which influence EU-level bargaining.

Bache quotes the analysis of change in the global political economy as an example of an external factor which may provide a fuller explanation of why the preferences of Members States of the EU converge, at certain times, and diverge at others. Since our own study concentrates on a narrowly defined and peripheral policy, implemented at local level, this point may be less relevant to our particular research.

Bache (1998, p.156) later introduced the metaphor of 'flexible gatekeeping'; this suggests that gatekeeping is a flexible rather than rigid concept. Governments can practise this at different stages of the policy process. Furthermore, the gatekeeping role of national governments at higher level negotiations is flexible over time. One example quoted is that of the 1993 reform of the Structural Funds where Member States reasserted control over certain aspects of regional policy. 'Flexible gatekeeping' is compatible with the earlier concept of 'extended gatekeeper' which focuses more on central government control at the implementation stage. Yet our own research question requires us to go beyond the analysis of central government. Since urban policy involves municipal and possibly regional government, depending on the institutional structures of individual Member States, we need to consider the action of other tiers of government at the various stages of the policy process.

The Commission, in its 'urban policy experiment' is seeking to go beyond not just national, but also regional and/or municipal authorities in order to target the neighbourhood level. The empirical evidence may support the case that central government plays a gatekeeping role in the implementation of European urban policy measures. However other levels of government may also play a gatekeeping role, monopolising channels of communication, between the European and neighbourhood levels. Central government may be the first of many potential 'gatekeepers'. Regional and/or municipal authorities may also seek to dominate the policy process. The supra-national policy may therefore face a number of hurdles before reaching the targeted recipients on the ground. In order to identify such gatekeeping by various levels of government, we should firstly complete our review of the literature on the European policy process. There are numerous studies which portray European policy-making in terms of 'multi-level governance'. This approach, similar to that of the 'extended gatekeeper' brings out the complexities of the European policy process.

Multi-level governance can help explain how various levels of government are involved in European policy. The section below will review some of the existing works relating to multi-level governance. Some of this makes specific reference to Structural Funds policy in the period after 1988. Some studies on multi-level governance refer to the policy networks approach (Hooghe, 1995, p.178). Bache (1996) also uses the tool of policy networks in his 'extended gatekeeper' model. It would be useful therefore to review the policy networks approach alongside that of multi-level governance. This will lead us to the concept of 'multi-level gatekeeping' which can be useful in the analysis of the empirical material.

2.4 Multi-Level Governance and Policy Networks

Since the 1988 reform of the Structural Funds, a number of studies have applied the concept of 'multi-level governance' to explain the European policy process. Marks (1993) presents the following scenario:

I suggest that we are seeing the emergence of multi-level governance, a system of continuous negotiation among nested governments at several territorial tiers – supra-national, national, regional and local – as the result of a broad process of institutional creation and decisional reallocation that has pulled some previously centralised functions of the state up to the supra-national level and some down to the local/regional level (Marks, 1993, p.392).

Marks' approach stresses the significance of the post-1988 period during which DG XVI developed increasing contacts with sub-national governments in order to deliver its regional policy. Another aspect stressed are the transnational networks, the argument being that in the area of structural policy a complex situation is emerging whereby 'sub-national governments interact both with the EC and crossnationally' (Marks, 1993, p.404).

Hooghe (1995) interprets Marks' model as one portraying a Europe with the Regions. This approach emphasises the Commission's dialogue with regional authorities. Yet this is seen to enhance, rather than challenge, the role played by Member States in European policy-making. Sub-national units can interact directly with the supranational level, in a complex system of governance, where each participant brings their own networks and resources at various levels of government:

> Sub-national mobilisation does not erode, but complements the aggregating role of member states. Hierarchical relationships are weak but interdependence is high. Actors are linked through networks, which span several layers and in which each actor brings in valuable resources (Hooghe, 1995, p.178).

Scharpf (1994) develops the idea of multi-level policy making in the EU with reference to both German and American federalism. Our study is based on unitary, rather than federal, Member States. Yet Scharpf's presentation of multi-level policy-making can help explain the Commission's expansion into policy areas not covered by the Treaties. Scharpf proposes a form of multi-level policy-making whereby the central authority, rather than weakening or displacing the authority of Member States, actually accepts and enhances it. Member States, for their part, can exploit central competences to devise their own policies. Such a system does not exclude sub-national units of government:

> The European Union is not, and cannot become, a unitary nation state; it can at best become a multi-level political system in which national and sub-national units must retain their legitimacy and political viability. Thus, while

for (many) states centralisation and political, cultural, and legal unification were (and still may be) considered legitimate purposes in their own right, that is not true of Europe. The legitimacy of European rule making must rest on, and is limited by, functional justifications...At the highest level of analytical abstraction, central government rules in a multi-level system may serve three functions: redistribution of resources among constituent units, coordination for the prevention of negative external effects and for the achievement of collective goods, and coordination for the better achievement of private goods (Scharpf, 1994, p.12).

Scharpf (1994) illustrates the above argument with reference to the areas of technical standardisation and regulation.[3] However, a case could be made for relating this example of multi-level policy making to the area of urban policy. Like other areas of public policy, urban policy could be related to the major objectives of the EU: the guarantee of free movement of goods, persons and services. There are many measures classified under the umbrella of 'urban policy' ranging from those to combat poverty, and improve housing, to the broad range of local economic development strategies. There is no reason why these cannot be linked to the internal market objectives identified by Scharpf (1994). In this way, as in the case of the American federal government since the 1930s, European intervention in urban policy can be justified even without an explicit legal mandate for such action. Member States, hostile to any Treaty changes, could accept the Commission's intervention in the form of European programmes.

Following this line of argument, such a system of multi-level policy-making would not necessarily displace the Member States or sub-national units within them. Indeed, we could argue that the national and sub-national actors would be involved in the policy process along the lines of a cooperative, rather than dual, federalism. The actors involved would share the common goals of tackling the problems of deprived urban areas. Similar to the American case, the policy process will be complex and involve a wide range of participants at different levels. In view of this, we turn to the literature on policy networks which may provide additional guidance in assessing the dynamics of multi-level policy-making. The notion of networks reminds us of the framework of 'intergovernmental relations' as developed by Wright (1988, p.7). Like intergovernmental relations within American federalism, the literature on policy networks refers to interdependence and bargaining between the actors involved.

---

[3] For a more detailed analysis of multi-level policy-making in the EU see also Scharpf (1988, 1998).

There are a variety of approaches and uses of the term 'policy networks'.[4] It is not within the scope of this section to fully analyse all uses, and applications, of the concept. We will select some definitions and applications which can be considered relevant to our research question relating to the birth, and subsequent implementation, of EU urban policy measures. The principle of partnership, in the implementation of European regional policy, requires cooperation between a wide range of actors. The policy networks approach may be useful in understanding the complex interaction between the participants. Identifying networks in our chosen policy area can help explain how, and why, the Commission has ventured into the field of urban policy. Furthermore, tools of analysis from the policy networks approach may help account for differences in outcome in the individual case studies. The following models may assist us in identifying the EU urban policy network.

Marin and Mayntz (1991) present policy network studies incorporating a range of policy areas with cross national, cross sectoral and diachronic comparisons. Marin and Mayntz also stress how policy networks can be defined not only by their structure as interorganizational relationships, but also by their *function* (emphasis added). Policy networks can exist around the formulation and implementation of a particular policy. Furthermore, the term policy networks can apply to both private and public actors. Networking may imply interdependence and interaction amongst participants but this, as Marin (1990) points out, does not exclude antagonistic forms of competition or even cooperation. Another key aspect to networks is that they can be found on different territorial levels: international such as European, regional and local. Networks can evolve over time and across events. Some networks develop around a broad range of issues while others concentrate on a specific issue. Schneider and Kenis (1991, p.41) argue that policy networks are a means of political resource mobilisation in situations where the capacity for decision-making, programme formulation and implementation is widely spread between private and public actors.

Marsh and Rhodes' (1992) model on policy networks in British government was subsequently adapted to characterise policy making in the EU. Of interest to us is the presentation of a policy network as a 'resource dependent organisation'. This concept is developed in the context of the Structural Funds and is related to situations of multi-level policy-making.

---

[4] For a review of major existing models, see Rhodes, Bache and George (1996).

Resource dependence will be high when the policy sector is characterised by the institutional fragmentation of multi-level governance, when the policy is complex, and when the Commission needs information and expertise. The Commission's dependence on other actors can be high because it is small with limited expertise; it is an 'adolescent bureaucracy' (Mazey and Richardson). However, it is important to stress that networks are characterised by interdependence. So, the Commission controls resources – notably, authority and money – which interest groups, local and regional governments and national governments need.[5]

Similar to the situation of American federalism, there is reference to bargaining and cooperation between the actors concerned. The higher level of government provides funds and can exercise some control through conditions attached to these. Yet the Commission depends on the Member State machinery to implement its policies. Furthermore, there could be an element of interdependence between the actors involved in implementing European policies. Central government may depend on information from regional and/or municipal authorities in order to prepare the case for attracting European funds. The other levels of government may depend on more local groups in order to receive information about how best to implement any European funds.

In our case studies on the launching and implementation of urban policy measures, we will seek to assess the resources of each actor at different points of the policy process. Marks (1993) argues that policy networks can be identified at any stage of the policy process, including that of initiation. Peterson (1995, p.402) stresses the utility of the policy networks approach at the policy formulation stage and highlights the informal bargaining between the actors. Hooghe (1995, 1996) refers to networks in European regional policy and the resources actors bring to these. Marks (1993) also identifies policy networks related to the administration of the Structural Funds. For the first time the administrations are creating policy networks that encompass sub-national governments, and private interests, in individual regions. The empirical section in chapter three will aim to identify the networks involved in the initial launching of EU urban policy measures. Chapters four to seven will explore the networks which have developed around the implementation of the European urban policy with reference to the CI URBAN.

---

[5] See also Mazey and Richardson (1993, p.10) to which this extract from Rhodes, Bache and George (1996) refers.

2.5 Conclusions from the European Literature

This review of existing scholars' work on public policy and European integration has complemented that on American federalism. Subsequent chapters will now seek to apply these concepts to the empirical case studies. Firstly, we will focus on the role of the Commission as agenda setter. The Commission is a major actor in both the initiation, and subsequent implementation, of urban policy measures. One aspect of this will be at the intergovernmental Council and European Council meetings. However, since there have been no significant additions to the Treaties granting the EU competence in this area, we will concentrate more on the everyday work of the Commission. Chapter three focuses on how the Commission may engage in dialogue with sub-national actors in order to promote certain policy measures/experiments. Representatives of European cities may, as was the case in the American experience, turn to the higher level of government demanding action for their cities. Models on bureaucratic politics and policy networks can help guide us through the empirical material in order to explain how and why the Commission has ventured into the area of urban policy.

All the recent literature reviewed on the implementation of European Structural Funds indicates that national administrations are key players in the European policy-making process. Our task is to identify the forms of central government influence, beyond any major politicised Council or European Council meetings. DG XVI's urban policy experiment has not, to date, made any major headlines in the national press or reached the realms of prime time national television in the UK or France. Bache's (1996) 'extended gatekeeper' framework is adapted for our purposes. Building on the original 'gatekeeper' concept, the 'extended gatekeeper' model allows us to assess central government action in the everyday delivery of policy. This also takes account of the various stages of the policy process: both the launching and implementation.

In our study, it would be too simple to confine our analysis to that of central government action since we are dealing with a broader range of actors. Combining Bache's extended gatekeeper approach, with the literature on multi-level governance and policy networks, enables us to develop the concept of 'multi-level gatekeeping'. This will feature in the case study material on the implementation of our chosen European programme, namely URBAN. Like Bache's notion of 'extended gatekeeper', 'multi-level gatekeeping' does not claim to be a new theory; it is an analytical tool which allows us to order the empirical material into a meaningful framework. The first step will be to identify the aims and objectives of the European intervention in urban policy.

The perspective of the Commission will be presented in chapter three dealing with the birth of European urban policy measures. From this, we can assess how central government in our case studies seeks to integrate the European policy into the existing national policies and administrative framework. There is a delicate balance between European and national policies. On the one hand, EU initiatives in urban areas aim to complement schemes operating at a national level. On the other hand, in line with the post-1988 principles of regional policy, the European intervention should also provide additional value. Chapter three will briefly examine the principles of concentration, programming, additionality and partnership in order to clarify what the Commission would seek to achieve by intervening in this policy area.

The point is that there may be tensions between the Commission's quest for a genuine regional policy and the policy preferences of the individual Member States. This is where initial gatekeeping at central government level can begin. Chapter three will explore the origins of the Commission's urban policy experiment and identify at which point central government became involved. The remaining chapters will then explore potential gatekeeping by other levels of government. Similar to the American federal government, the Commission can set certain conditions to its programmes which the recipients should respect in implementation. Yet the Commission cannot easily catapult itself into the deprived urban areas which its policies seek to assist. Central government within each Member State must, in turn, work alongside other levels of government such as regional and municipal. The case study material on URBAN will examine how other levels may seek to influence the policy process in line with their own local priorities.

Finally, we turn to the neighbourhood level. Chapter three will examine how, through the principle of partnership, the Commission may seek to engage partners below the level of elected local government. This can include Trade Unions, private business, local residents, voluntary and community organisations. Even with small-scale innovative programmes, the Commission's penetration of the neighbourhood level, subsidiarity at its lowest level, is not a simple process. If there is evidence that central, regional and/or municipal levels of government seek to monopolise procedures, this may present obstacles to a supra-national policy, conceived in Brussels, but directed at local neighbourhoods. Furthermore, do clearly defined local communities exist in our multi-ethnic cities or are we entering the realm of complex local issues, beyond the understanding of a distant bureaucracy such as the Commission in Brussels? The case study material will examine whether certain individuals or groups seek to dominate procedures at the local level.

The models presented in this chapter allow us to identify any multi-level gatekeeping as outlined above. Bache's (1996, 1998) work provides a framework for assessing central government's action in implementation. The literature on multi-level governance and policy networks highlights the complexity of the European policy process. Finally the American experience, explored in chapter one, provides concrete examples of the problems which arise when a higher level of government seeks to intervene in a local policy area. European urban policy is presently in its infancy. Multi-level gatekeeping would arguably render any large scale, interventionist European urban policy problematic. The experience of the Johnson era, from the American literature, highlights the pitfalls of such an approach.

Lessons from American federalism, combined with the models examined of the European policy process, have prepared us for examining the European case. At time of writing, EU urban policy is small-scale and at experimental stage. Lessons from this can provoke further debate regarding the Commission's intervention in this area. The findings of this study also raise questions regarding how effectively the Commission manages its programmes. This theme features in the case study material and will be examined in further detail in the conclusions in chapter eight. Firstly, we turn to the empirical material in order to explain the birth of the EU's urban policy experiment.

3   The Birth of the European Union's Urban Policy 'Experiment'

Introduction

This chapter explores the background to DG XVI's involvement in urban policy measures. We begin with a brief review of the major developments in regional policy since the creation of the European Regional Development Fund (ERDF) in 1975. This will assess the Commission's attempts to create a supra-national regional policy and progress made in this area. In launching urban policy measures, the Commission may encounter similar problems to those experienced in the quest to develop a genuine regional policy. For this reason we can learn from examples whereby Member States have reasserted their role. This can be during negotiations for the broad framework of European regional policy, in a set period, as well as in subsequent implementation. The notion of central government acting as 'gatekeeper', as presented in chapter two, can be applied in seeking to explain events at this level.

It is not within the scope of this chapter to give in-depth analysis of all aspects of European regional policy. Attention will focus on the background information relevant to our research question. Reference to the secondary and primary works quoted can clarify points and provide additional details on the more general aspects of regional policy. Here we concentrate on the impact of developments after 1988, notably the increased Structural Funds budget and the changes in implementation procedures. The analysis covers two specific programming periods, 1989-1993 and 1994-1999.

We explore the different instruments of urban policy as well as the Commission's proposals to gain formal competence in this area. Where relevant, we refer to points made in the earlier chapters to guide us through the empirical material relating to the birth of European urban policy. Following this overview of developments we explain why one particular programme, the Community Initiative (CI) URBAN, was selected for the detailed case studies on implementation in chapters four to seven.

3.1 Developments in Regional Policy: Common Policy or Member State Gatekeeping?

The ERDF was not established until 1975 following the accession of Denmark, Ireland and the UK. The Commission had a limited role in the early period of regional policy. Applications for project assistance were made through the national ministries of Member States. The Commission had some influence over approving applications and it also had responsibility for ensuring that the funds were additional to any planned domestic expenditure of the Member States. Additionality, as a principle, existed at the inception of the European Community's (EC) regional policy although the difficulties of enforcing this also appeared in this early period. Bache (1998, pp.48-49) highlights how problems of enforcement hindered the establishment of a supra-national regional policy:

> Securing the additionality of regional funds would have been a major step towards a genuine supra-national element in EC regional policy. This was recognised by national governments who found convenient ways of circumventing this requirement, much to the frustration of the Commission...A major problem for the Commission in dealing with recalcitrant governments emerged soon after the fund's creation. This was the problem of being able to prove that regional fund receipts had not been spent additionally when the national governments claimed they had.

Proving that Member States had respected additionality was only one of a number of problems characterising the early period. There is a wealth of literature highlighting the difficulties in establishing a common regional policy (Wallace, H., 1977, 1983). In a pessimistic article, Mény (1982, p.374) stated:

> The problems of the present regional policy constitute a restricted but highly illustrative example of the Community's present impasse, which results both from the inadequacy of Community powers and from the excessive nationalisation of procedures.

Developments following the Single European Act involved an increase in resources allocated to regional policy. The Single European Act came into force in 1987 and provided the first Treaty basis for economic and social cohesion (Articles 130a-130e). In 1987 the figure for EC structural actions amounted to ECU 7 billion or 19 per cent of the EC budget. By the end of the 1987 to 1993 period, the Structural Funds budget reached up to ECU 14 billion, approximately 25 per cent of the total EC budget (CEC, 1989, p.16). Following negotiations in 1993, the cohesion fund was established in the Treaty on European Union. The addition of the cohesion fund brought the figure for total Structural Fund actions to ECU 27.4 billion, projected for 1999; this figure represented 35 per cent of the total EC budget (CEC, 1994c).[1] If we compare this to the situation in 1975, when Structural Fund spending amounted to less than 5 per cent of the EC budget, we gain a sense of perspective regarding the significance of the increase in funding.[2]

The increase in resources of the supra-national level provided an opportunity to address some of the problems encountered in the earlier period. Like the federal level in the US, the Commission could attach certain conditions to the receipt of European funds. In this respect, the Structural Funds budget acquired certain federal characteristics. Indeed, the period after the 1988 reform was one where the Commission played a more pro-active role in regional policy. Four principles of regional policy were agreed, at the time of the 1988 reform of the Structural Funds, and accompanied the 1988 budgetary increases. The principles of concentration, programming, additionality and partnership were to guide the implementation of Structural Funds after 1988. Section 3.2 will examine these in further detail. The Commission also drafted five priority objectives in order to guide the allocation of Structural Funds. The objectives for the period 1989-1993 are listed below (CEC, 1989, p.14):

Objective 1: Promoting the development and adjustment of the regions whose development is lagging behind (i.e. where per capita GDP is less than, or close to, 75 per cent of the Community average).
Objective 2: Converting the regions, frontier regions or parts of the regions (including employment areas and urban communities) seriously affected by industrial decline (criteria: average unemployment rate above the Community average, industrial employment rate above the Community average, decline in industrial employment).
Objective 3: Combating long-term unemployment (above the age of 25, unemployed for more than 12 months).

---

[1] See also Eurostat (1992).
[2] For additional factual information, consult CEC (1988) Regulation (EEC) No. 2052/88 of 24 June 1988, *Official Journal* No. L185, 15 July 1988. See also Wishlade (1996), Hooghe (Ed., 1996), Bache (1998, p.70), Allen (1997) and Marks (1992, p.194).

Objective 4: Facilitating the occupational integration of young people (job-seekers below the age of 25).

Objective 5: With a view to the reform of the common agricultural policy:

5 (a): adapting production, processing and marketing structures in agriculture and forestry and

5 (b): promoting the development of rural areas.

Criteria: agricultural employment accounting for a high proportion of total employment; low level of agricultural income; low level of socio-economic development in terms of per capita GDP.

'Mainstream programmes' under the objectives listed above accounted for over 70 per cent of the budget for the 1989-1993 period (Wishlade, 1996, p.57). In addition to this, the Commission allocated almost ECU 4 billion to launch a series of 'Community Initiatives' (CIs) announced in the Official Journal between 1990-1991. The legal basis for these was found in article 5 (5) of the Framework Regulation and article 11 of the Coordination Regulation. Around 9 per cent of the Structural Fund budget was accorded to CIs (Bache, 1998, p.71, p.85). Under these, the Commission could propose that Member States submit applications for assistance regarding measures of significant interest to the Community. The CIs could contain a combination of Structural Funds depending on the problem tackled (ERDF, ESF and EAGGF). CIs for the period 1989-1993 were periodically announced in the *Official Journal* and each was allocated a specific budget. Member States were then invited to present proposals for support, usually through Operational Programmes.[3]

The budget of ECU 4 billion was spread between twelve different CIs for the 1989-1993 period hence the budget for each was modest. President Delors was particularly favourable towards CIs since the Commission played a pro-active role in their launching and subsequent implementation. CIs promoted dialogue and interaction between the Commission, and a broader range of actors, beyond that of mainstream programmes.[4] Indeed, there has been some interesting case study material illustrating this based on the CI, RECHAR, directed at coal mining areas The case studies have been related to the theoretical material over EC policy-making: Marks (1993), Pollack (1995) McAleavey (1992, 1993), Bache (1996). There was no specific CI directed at cities and urban problems in the period 1989-1993; this was launched in the second programming period of 1994-1999. Before

---

[3] A full list of CIs for the 1989-1993 period can be found in Wishlade (1996, p.39). Further details can be found in the Commission's *Guide to the Community Initiatives* (CEC, 1991).

[4] Interview with former Commissioner Millan, January 1999.

examining the background to this, we should complete our analysis of the broader developments in EC regional policy.

In the negotiations for the 1993 reform of the Structural Funds, there is evidence of tensions between the Commission's approach to regional policy and the reactions of Member States. Member States expressed concerns about the way in which European Structural Funds had operated after 1988. Following Council-Commission negotiations, the general aims of the 1988 reform remained unchanged for the period 1994-1999. Apart from the additional objectives following the latest stage of enlargement, the general criteria remained the same. Objectives 1 to 5 were retained although some amendments were made.[5]

However, Bache (1998, p.81) argues that the detail of the 1993 reform challenged the Commission's progress towards a genuine supra-national policy:

> The general thrust of the 1993 reform was one of continuity rather than radical change, with the principles and structures of the 1988 reform remaining largely intact. Yet if the 1988 reform of the Structural Funds suggested the Commission had advanced its regional policy objectives, the detail of the 1993 reform suggested this advance had been halted and the Commission was facing retreat.

An example of this can be found relating to procedures for the designation of areas to receive Structural Funds support. Pollack's (1995) analysis of the 1993 reform emphasises the negotiations over the distribution of funds as national governments successfully pressed the case to include certain regions, not strictly eligible under the objectives of regional policy outlined in the post-1988 period.

Changes in procedures regarding the designation of Objective 2 and 5b areas for the period 1994-1999 provide another example of Member States asserting their influence.[6] After negotiations it was agreed that the Commission would no longer draw up an initial list of areas to be awarded Objective 2 status as had been the case in 1989. The Commission would instead forward to the Member States, individually and confidentially, the basic Community data relating to area designation. From this information,

---

[5] Further details on changes to the objectives can be found in the publication (CEC, 1993a). On the negotiations for enlargement, see also Wishlade (1996, p.57).

[6] Council of the European Communities 1993. Extraordinary Meeting of the Council – General Affairs – Brussels, 2 and 3 July, 1993. Spokesman's service of the European Communities, PRES/93/120.

and criteria in the Framework Regulation, the Member States would forward the list of eligible areas. The Commission and Member States would then negotiate and decide on a final list. The Commission could not include, on the final list, any region that had not appeared on the Member State's proposed list without the agreement of the Member State involved. Bache (1998, p.88) argues that it was the governments of France, Germany and the UK who were most influential in achieving a change in the rules regarding the designation of Objective 2 and 5b regions. Bache (1998, p.88) also highlights the role of the UK government in ensuring that provisions for the monitoring and assessment of Structural Funds operations were strengthened.

The future of CIs was another area which provoked debate around the time of the 1993 negotiations. As noted earlier, CIs permitted a more pro-active role on the part of the Commission and also enhanced dialogue with a broader range of actors. Yet by 1993, CIs had attracted criticism from Member States regarding the bureaucracy associated with them. National governments were also critical of the number of CIs claiming some were too small to have an impact. The Commission proposed that CIs make up 15 per cent of the Structural Funds budget but this was limited to 9 per cent by the Council; a sum of ECU 13.45 billion at 1994 prices.[7] Wishlade (1996, p.45) explains the dilemma of national policy makers who criticised the CIs but did not want to lose out over any potential receipts of funds from them. The Commission was also criticised for not issuing EU wide details of initiatives as national administrations claimed they were often taken by surprise when CIs were announced.

The brief analysis of European regional policy, presented above, illustrates the difficulties the Commission has encountered in establishing a supra-national policy. Following early problems, the increased budget in 1988 presented the Commission with the opportunity to progress towards a common regional policy by attaching conditions to the increased funds at its disposal. Yet by 1993, Member States were reasserting control over certain aspects of the next programming period, 1994-1999. Bache (1998, p.156) presents this as an example of 'flexible gatekeeping' on the part of Member States. Following this argument, gatekeeping is flexible over time. Some of

---

[7] CEC (1994a, volume 2, p.8). In July 1994, the Commission allocated ECU 11.85 billion to these CIs. The remaining ECU 1.6 billion was placed in reserve so that the initial allocation could be adjusted in the light of implementation of the CIs to cover balances between countries and any unforeseen events.

the concessions made by national governments in 1988 were clearly retracted in the 1993 reform.

The other point is the notion of 'extended gatekeeper' (Bache, 1996) highlighting central government control in implementation. This is of particular interest to our case studies, in section two of this book, dealing with the problems of implementation of European urban policy. Similar to the US experience, the policy process involved complex bargaining and negotiation, at various levels of government. Before turning to the national delivery of our chosen programme, we should complete our understanding of the Commission's perspective regarding the implementation of regional policy. We therefore turn to a more detailed review of the four principles of regional policy before examining the origins and instruments of European urban policy in section 3.3.

3.2 Four Principles of Regional Policy

This section seeks to highlight certain key points relating to our analysis of European urban policy measures. As noted in section 3.1, the four principles of concentration, programming, additionality and partnership were included in the 1988 reform of the Structural Funds and retained in 1993.[8] The principles were to guide the Commission in negotiations, regarding the selection of areas to receive support, as well as in its involvement in the management of the programmes. Potential recipients of the funds were also to respect these principles as part of the conditions attached to European funding.

For our purposes, the interesting point is the interpretation of the four principles by the numerous actors involved in European urban policy. On the one hand, there is the technical interpretation of the principles as presented in the formal text; on the other hand, their application in practice may not be as clear as preliminary reading of the texts would suggest. This section aims to highlight issues which can arise in the practical implementation of regional policy. Particular attention is given to additionality and partnership. Here the Commission's intervention in cities raises points that may not have been foreseen in negotiations establishing the broad framework of regional policy.

---

[8] Further details can be found in the publication CEC (1993a).

3.2/1 Concentration and Programming

Concentration involved concentrating the funds in the areas of greatest need. This was the rationale behind the accompanying objectives as presented in section 3.1. In theory, concentration could be determined objectively by facts and figures on specific areas meriting attention under the various criteria. However section 3.1 illustrated that politics enters the field regarding Commission-Council negotiations over the definition of objectives and the subsequent designation of funds to areas seeking eligibility under one of these objectives. Although the 1993 reform retained the four principles of regional policy, national governments reasserted control over the selection of areas to be awarded European funding. For the period 1994-1999, national governments managed to secure European funds for regions not strictly eligible under the principles of regional policy (Pollack, 1995). This was also the case regarding the designation of Objective 2 areas (Bache, 1998).

The empirical section will also explore the principle of concentration in the local implementation of policy. The question is whether other levels of government, such as regional or municipal, also prioritise certain areas over others. In our case studies, the initial designation of areas was agreed between the Commission and central government. Although different districts of a city may be awarded funding, local government may be more committed to improving certain areas. This may be related to the local political situation beyond the understanding of the Commission or even central government within the Member State. In our case studies, we will explore whether there were tensions between the objectives of the European policy and the political situation at local level. The four principles of regional policy should guide the implementation of European programmes. Could there be a conflict of interest between this and local priorities within cities selected to receive European funding. If so, how could the Commission ensure that the recipients of European programmes complied with the conditions attached? This will be explored in the individual case studies.

Programming involved a switch from the project-based approach of pre-1988 regional policy to one of multi-annual programmes. The Commission viewed this as facilitating the administration of programmes and contributing to a more coherent approach (CEC, 1989, p.21). As a principle this was retained at the 1993 reform although some amendments were made. After 1993, Member State authorities were required to submit a Single Programming Document (SPD) which would include a development plan, as well as applications for aid related to this. This was implemented in two programme periods, 1994-1996 and 1997-1999. Community Support

Frameworks, setting out the priorities, funding and forms of assistance, remained.

For mainstream programmes in the UK there were changes to the composition of Monitoring Committees managing programmes agreed in the 1997-1999 period. Following the change in government from Conservative to Labour in May 1997, elected members of local councils as well as representatives of social partners, such as Trade Unions, were permitted to sit on Monitoring Committees for the implementation of the SPD from 1997-1999. Prior to this, only council officers could represent the local authorities on Monitoring Committees. The local authority officers would then brief the elected councillors.

Our detailed case studies concentrate on the implementation of the CI URBAN. For CIs there was only one Programme Document agreed for the entire period 1994-1999. The changes in procedures, outlined above, did not therefore impinge on the delivery of URBAN. The composition of Monitoring Committees for URBAN was agreed while the Conservative party was in government and there were no major changes under the newly elected Labour government. Yet the question of whether elected councillors should be allowed a place on Monitoring Committees for URBAN was a major issue in negotiations between the Commission and the UK national administration. This will be included in the analysis in chapter four.

3.2/2 Additionality and Partnership

As noted in section 3.1, the principle of additionality in EC regional policy dated back to the initial establishment of the ERDF in 1975. As Bache (1998, p.48) points out, the Commission experienced problems in enforcing this principle in the early period. The reform of 1988 and the accompanying expansion of the budget provided the Commission with an opportunity to strengthen the arrangements to secure additionality. This was stated as follows:

> In establishing and implementing the Community Support Frameworks, the Commission and the Member States will have to ensure that the annual increase in the appropriations for the Funds results in at least an equivalent increase in the total volume of official or similar (Community and national) structural aid in the Member State concerned, taking into account the macroeconomic circumstances in which the funding takes place. While the additionality arrangements will be appraised on a case-by-case basis when the Community Support Frameworks are drawn up, a monitoring system needs to

be set up as of now to assess the extent to which the Community effort is matched at national level (CEC, 1989, p.21).

Apart from the new regulations, established to enforce additionality, an interesting development was the involvement of sub-national authorities to implement this. The sub-national involvement was part of the new partnership arrangements to be examined later in this section. Continuing with additionality, we should firstly clarify any changes following the 1993 reform.

The principle of additionality was reinforced in the 1993 regulations which recognised the persistent difficulties of implementing the principle. An addition to the 1989 text was that each Member State was also required to take into account specific economic circumstances, such as privatisations, or unusual amounts of public expenditure taken during the previous programming period and business cycles of the national economy. Under the new regulations, Member States were to submit financial information required to prove additionality when presenting plans to the Commission (CEC, 1993a, p.25).

Like the principle of concentration, additionality may be viewed from a technical point of view in terms of rules and procedures. Yet this does not prevent politicisation of the principle in Commission-Council negotiations. Bache (1996, 1998) analyses the politics of additionality in the 1988 reform of the Structural Funds. Indeed, additionality was particularly problematic in the Commission's negotiations with the UK government.

While other member states had reservations about additionality, only the UK held out on the principle after it had agreed to everything else. Ultimately, the government agreed to the new regulation with the insertion of the clause 'increase in appropriations' when it became clear that the Commission would approve the programmes it had submitted (Bache, 1998, p.78 see also Bache 1996).

The 1988 reform reinforced the role of sub-national actors in the monitoring of additionality. Keating (1998, p.18) notes:

The Commission insisted, more or less successfully, on the principles of additionality and transparency to ensure that the *region* and not state budgets benefited from them. A planning system was set up, with a partnership between the regions, the states and the Commission allowing some direct links between the regions and the Commission. Although the states are still in control of the Community's regional policy, Community interventions have none the less encouraged a strong regional mobilisation, together with the emergence of new actors (emphasis added).

However, the emergence of new actors may not necessarily solve the problem of additionality. Our case study material will explore additionality in the Commission's dealings with sub-national, as well as national, authorities. Structural Funds must be matched by the Member State authorities. In 1993 there was no change to the rules established in 1988 which required any EU contribution to be matched by 50 per cent of the total cost of projects for those under Objectives 2, 3, 4 and 5b. For Objective 1 areas the EU contribution could be up to 75 per cent. However match-funding does not necessarily come from national government budgets, it may be from those of regional and local authorities or even other sources, such as the National Lottery fund, in the case of the UK. Even if the match-funding is forthcoming, this does not always ensure additionality or added value from the EU intervention. Let us present the following situation as an example of the type of problem which may arise in implementation.

A UK local authority may be running a project which is facing financial difficulties, due to overall constraints on local council expenditures and restrictions on raising local taxation. Many local authorities have experienced such problems, particularly since the 1980s.[9] The expansion of European Structural Funds opens up another source of funding hence the employment, by many local councils, of European Officers to exploit these opportunities. These posts are similar to those of Intergovernmental Relations Officers in the American federal experience as discussed in chapter one. Additional funding from Europe can help salvage a project which the local council may, otherwise, not have had the resources to run. The local authority, in this case, would match the EU funding and comply with the rules on additionality in this respect. The question arises over what added value the EU's intervention has brought, other than maintaining the existence of a local project.

As noted above, the reinforcement of the principle of additionality in the 1993 reform addressed the procedures of each national government. Clearly, the Commission requested additional financial information from Member States as proof that regional fund receipts had been spent additionally by national governments. The implementation of urban policy measures would involve local and possibly regional government. Proving that local government spends European funds additionally may be even more

---

[9] For more information on this, please refer to Travers (1989).

problematic for the Commission. Returning to the example presented above, should European funds be used to co-finance an existing project which, arguably would otherwise be funded by the local authority?

The Commission's interpretation of the principle of partnership has also been linked to the enforcement of additionality. As noted above, Keating (1998, p.18) pointed out how the 1988 reform, through partnership, reinforced the role of the region in order to ensure that the region budgets, rather than the state, benefited from the European funds. The planning system established allowed some direct links between the Commission and the region. This model could also be applied to the implementation of European urban policy. The administrative system for managing European urban policy could involve non-governmental actors such as representatives of local residents, community organisations and commerce based in the targeted area. In this way, the Commission could develop direct links with non-governmental actors engaged in implementing European programmes. This could be a step towards ensuring that the European intervention presented additional value rather than finance for existing schemes that the central, or local government was planning to fund anyway.

The individual case studies will examine the practicalities of devolving responsibility for administering funds to the neighbourhood level. Ensuring that European funds benefit the regional or municipal budget, rather than that of the state, is already a complex task. Developing structures for the management of funds at neighbourhood level would be even more complicated. In the area of urban policy, this involved new actors who had not previously been involved in implementing European programmes. Before examining the empirical material we should explore the Commission's interpretations of the principle of partnership in this period. Developments following the 1988 reform opened the door to the Commission's dialogue with a wider range of actors. This is a key element to understanding the Commission's launching of urban policy measures and their subsequent implementation.

Partnership appeared in the early period of the creation of the ERDF. McAleavey (1995, p.167) draws attention to the 'First Annual Report on the European Regional Development Fund' (1976) stating that 'Community regional policy is by nature a partnership between the Community and its Member States with the former at the present stage the junior partner'. As noted in section 3.1, the 1988 reform of the Structural Funds involved an increase in the budget allocated to regional policy. The Commission took the opportunity to give greater prominence to the principle of partnership. This may be interpreted as another step in the Commission's pursuit of a genuine supra-national regional policy. The partnership, between the Community and its Member States, would be broadened to involve other partners in the implementation of regional policy. The example of strengthening the role of partners in monitoring additionality, outlined above, was just one aspect of this redefinition of partnership.

The 1989 'Guide to the Reform of the Structural Funds' (CEC, 1989 p.15) defined partnership in the following way:

> Partnership is the key principle underlying the reform of the Funds in that it determines the implementation of the other principles. The framework Regulation defines it as 'close consultation between the Commission, the Member States concerned and the competent authorities designated by the latter at national, regional, local or other level, with each partner in pursuit of a common goal'. According to the same regulation, partnership also covers 'the preparation, financing, monitoring and assessment of operations'.

The principle of subsidiarity, included in the legal text of the Treaty on European Union signed in 1991, already featured in the Structural Fund regulations of the 1988 reform. This interpretation of subsidiarity extended the principle of partnership to include non-governmental partners in the implementation of European Structural Funds (CEC, 1989, p.15):

> Partnership reflects the principle of subsidiarity. In accordance with that principle, the Commission believes that its structural action should seek to *complement* measures in the field. There needs to be permanent dialogue between the Commission and the Member State concerned to increase efficiency through the sharing of tasks and a pooling of the human resources involved in the Community's structural action (official partnership). But community structural action depends for its implementation, not only on the national and regional authorities, but also on the various economic and social partners (chambers of commerce, industry and agriculture, trade unions, employers, etc.).

The Commission's definition of partnership in the period after 1989 was much wider, and potentially more fluid, than that of 1975. The Member States remained senior partners in that they retained responsibility for designating the partnership. The regulations also allowed for variations in partnerships, both between and within Member States, according to the regional/local situation. Yet the recognition of the broader range of actors in the policy process arguably opened the door for the Commission to engage in direct dialogue with sub-national partners involved in delivering, and monitoring, its programmes. This permitted the Commission to engage in dialogue, and possible alliances, with a wide range of actors.

The 1993 reform also stressed how arrangements, respecting the principle of partnership, should lead to an element of decentralisation in the delivery of Structural Fund programmes.

> The partnership arrangements should also lead to some decentralisation of the Community's structural action, enabling it to be geared more closely to realities in the field, both in assessing needs and implementing measures (CEC, 1993a, p.15).

With reference to the above definition of partnership, the actual residents of deprived urban areas may be the ones who are most aware of realities in the field. In this sense the principle of partnership could be extended, without any amendments in the regulations, to include non-governmental actors such as local residents and members of voluntary and community associations. Following the principle of subsidiarity, such 'new' partners may be identified as being 'closest to the problem' and could therefore be engaged in assessing needs and implementing measures within their locality.

The above interpretation of partnership goes beyond the principle of representative democracy, whereby elected local or regional government represents the neighbourhood level. This does not mean, however, that the Commission would be excluding national, regional or local government. We could argue that the Commission is seeking to bring new partners into the implementation process in order to improve the delivery mechanisms, and effectiveness, of regional policy. Engaging local communities in delivering European programmes may also be presented as a step towards promoting greater awareness about Europe, providing the added value of bringing Europe 'closer to the citizens' in Eneko Landaburu's words.[10]

On a broader level, involving these 'new' partners in the implementation process may be seen as an experiment in local empowerment. Indeed, many residents of deprived areas in France, for example, cannot actively participate in local elections as they are not French citizens. Yet there is nothing to prevent such ethnic minorities, who presently inhabit European cities, from participating in local associations. Furthermore, residents of the targeted areas may mistrust the political system and not exercise their right to vote particularly in local elections (Bache 1997a). The concept of

---

[10] Political interview, 'A man for all regions', interview with Eneko Landaburu, Director-General of DG XVI, Regional Policy and Cohesion, in *Parliamentary Review,* March 1997.

partnership can, in this way, involve the previously excluded and exploit the notion of 'social capital' as developed by Putnam (1993) and Hall (1999).

This is where the Commission's urban policy experiment becomes an interesting case study. Firstly, the principle of partnership opened the door to dialogue with representatives of cities. Secondly, some innovative delivery mechanisms appeared in European programmes, broadening partnership beyond national and regional authorities or institutionalised groups such as Trade Unions. Indeed, in the case of European programmes in the UK, partnership was stretched to involve local residents, as well as voluntary and community associations. There were no major changes to the legal text defining partnership in the 1993 reform. Yet it was in the post-1993 period that this extension of the principle of partnership appeared in the text of European programmes operating in cities in the UK. Before looking at the practicalities of this broad definition of partnership, we should firstly examine the historical development of DG XVI's involvement in urban policy.

3.3 The Instruments of European Urban Policy

For the period of this study, the Commission's intervention in urban policy was through European programmes partly funded by the Structural Funds. DG XVI attached conditions to European funding in line with the principles of regional policy outlined in section 3.2. Individual programmes for geographical areas were negotiated within the broader framework, agreed between the Commission and Member States, for each funding period. There were variations in the rules and regulations for each instrument of European urban policy. Understanding the origins of the different forms of urban intervention can shed light on the Commission's role in the implementation of policy.

We begin this section by reviewing the historical background to the launch of Urban Pilot Projects (UPPs). Particular reference is made to the case of London where we present historical evidence of the Commission's dialogue with representatives of the city. This was a major factor contributing to DG XVI's decision to launch UPPs in London and Marseille. During this early period, we also examine the Commission's proposals for a Treaty basis to European urban policy. Although Member States rejected any changes in the Treaties, a form of European urban policy developed incrementally through the operation of mainstream ERDF programmes in urban areas.

We also examine the background to the Commission's announcement of a specific CI relating to cities, namely URBAN. As noted in section 3.1, URBAN did not exist in the first round of CIs yet was included for those of the 1994-1999 period. How can we explain the Commission's launching of a new CI, directed at cities, when it had faced criticism from Member States after the first round? The birth of the CI URBAN is an interesting case study of how the Commission's interaction with other actors can lead to its involvement in new policy areas. Although CIs are small-scale compared to mainstream programmes, URBAN represents another instrument of European urban policy. The themes developed in this section prepare us for the case study material on the implementation of URBAN.[11]

3.3/1 The Launching of Urban Pilot Projects

The Commission's launching of UPPs can be directly related to developments following the 1988 reform of the Structural Funds. Following the expansion of the budget, agreed at the 1988 reform, a number of European cities received ERDF support as they were part of a region granted Objective 1 or 2 status. In the period 1989-1993, European Structural Funds contributed around ECU 2.5 billion to assist with the regeneration of industrial cities in northern England, Scotland and Wales.[12] The UK received the 'lion's share' of Objective 2 funding in this first period since many regions qualified under the criteria of high unemployment and industrial decline, some of which was found in urban areas (Interview, former Commissioner Millan, January 1999).[13] There were also, however, certain losers in the allocation of ERDF grants. London, for example, received no allocation of Objective 2 money, although some parts of the city were deprived.

The case of London is particularly interesting following the history, in the 1980s, of central-local conflict under the Conservative government. Cuts in

---

[11] The empirical material in this chapter is based on a number of interviews with key actors in this period: the former Commissioner Millan, members of his cabinet, representatives from the Association of London Government (ALG) and officials in Marseille. The interviews took place at various intervals from September 1996 to January 1999 and are listed in the bibliography to the book: names, organisation, dates and place. This is supplemented by information from internal documents provided by DG XVI for the purposes of this study.

[12] Source: internal documents from the Commission regarding Structural Funds allocation within Member States, DG XVI, Brussels.

[13] The Commission divided geographical areas of the UK into regions for the administration of Structural Funds programmes.

local expenditure and restrictions on raising local taxation encouraged local authorities to look for additional sources of finance. Europe, particularly with the increased Structural Funds budget following the reform of 1988, was a potential source of funds. Clearly, this had been recognised by industrial areas in northern England, Scotland and Wales who prepared bids and were awarded funds under the new Objective 2 in the 1989-1993 period. While local authorities in London had long participated in European Social Fund (ESF) programmes, as coordinated by national ministries, the city did not benefit from the share of Objective 2 funds acquired by other cities and regions in the UK.

Other cities in the UK have an elected local council with a leader of the council. The leader is not directly elected but is nominated by the elected majority on the council.[14] Yet the leaders of city councils can represent the entire city when dealing with central government, the European Commission and European networks such as Eurocities.[15] Given the abolition of the Greater London Council in 1985, and the existence of 33 separate London boroughs, how was the city as a whole represented in Europe? In the late 1980s, there were two separate associations of London boroughs: the Labour dominated Association of London Authorities (ALA) and the London Boroughs Association (LBA) whose members were local authorities with a Conservative majority in the council. The two have since merged to form the Association of London Government (ALG) of which all 33 London boroughs are members.

There had been some attempt, coordinated by the ALA, to prepare a bid for Objective 2 funding for parts of the city for the 1989-1993 funding period. The application for Objective 2 funding had not been supported by central government and was unsuccessful. This prompted a delegation from the ALA, led by Margaret Hodge (Leader of Islington Council in this period) to bypass central government and approach the former Commissioner Millan directly. A number of Members of the European Parliament (MEPs), representing parts of London, supported the view that London had been 'neglected by the government' (Interview, former Commissioner Millan, January 1999). Commissioner Millan, with a background in the Labour

---

[14] This refers to the situation prior to the election of a Labour government in 1997 and the subsequent creation of a directly elected Mayor for London and the Greater London Assembly in 1998. There has since been further experimentation with directly elected mayors in other cities and local councils. However these institutional changes did not affect the period covered by this study.

[15] Section 3.3/2 presents more details on the role of cities in lobbying the European Commission.

Party, was viewed by the delegation as someone who would be sympathetic to its cause.

The concept of partnership following the reform of the Structural Funds permitted, and arguably encouraged, such dialogue between the Commission and sub-national actors. Clearly, a number of the representatives from local government were members of the Labour Party in opposition during this period. In the framework of regional policy, 'common goals' and 'partnership' the Commission could engage in dialogue with the sub-national without damaging its relations with the administration of the Member State involved. However, the delegation from London faced an additional problem – that of eligibility. As noted in section 3.1, post-1988 regional policy was focused around the Objectives 1-5. Potential recipients of European Structural Funds were required to fulfil certain criteria to be eligible for the funds as stated in the regulations.

London is a wealthy city with pockets of deprivation. Some northern industrial cities matched the' criteria of Objective 2 regarding high unemployment rates or industrial decline. This could not be extended to cover the specific problems of urban decline and poverty experienced by certain neighbourhoods in London and other cities. While Commissioner Millan was sympathetic to the case of London, the city was simply not eligible for Objective 2 ERDF funds. Yet, in the spirit of dialogue and cooperation, Commissioner Millan proposed a solution to the delegation from London. The Commission's proposal involved experimentation under the provisions of Article 10 of Council Regulation (EEC) No. 4254/88. This provided recognition, by the European Commission, of the problems of deprived areas in an otherwise wealthy city or region. This policy of targeting specific parts of a city was a new aspect of DG XVI's regional policy which had hitherto concentrated on regions as a whole.

Article 10 provides for the use of ERDF resources to finance studies and pilot schemes. Under Article 10, ECU 5.1 million was allocated to a UPP for London to run from 1990-1993. The theme was to find innovative ways of dealing with problem areas of urban deprivation in otherwise wealthy cities. The Commission's UPP only involved small amounts of funding as part of an experiment. Although the sums involved were small, the ALA welcomed the Commission's intervention:

> Millan recognised that there was almost a special case in London that needed help. Therefore, the way that he was able to offer resources were through the own initiative resources of Article 10. So he almost invented the Urban Pilot Projects for London (Interview, ALG official, January 1997).

The Commission announced a UPP for Marseille at the same time as that for London and ECU 4 million was allocated to this. Marseille, like London, had not received any ERDF allocation under the ERDF regulations for the mainstream programmes during the period 1989-1993. Representatives from Marseille had not taken the initiative to go directly to Brussels as had been the case for London. Marseille was not a capital city, neither was it comparable in terms of geographical, or demographic size, to London. The political institutions were completely different in that Marseille had an elected municipal council and was part of the Provence-Alpes-Côte d'Azur Region with its own elected assembly. How can we explain the choice of Marseille for a second UPP?

Commissioner Millan decided to launch a UPP in Marseille during an informal visit the city. This took place around the time that the London delegation had approached the Commissioner to draw attention to certain deprived areas of the city. During his visit, Commissioner Millan perceived that Marseille also had specifically urban problems in parts of the city. Visits are another form of dialogue with local representatives of the city. However, the former Commissioner Millan states that analysis should not exaggerate the importance of lobbying in the Commission's decision to launch UPPs, particularly for the case of Marseille (Interview, January 1999). A major consideration in the choice of Marseille was that that the Commission could not be seen to be making an exception only for the case of London, particularly when the Commissioner for Regional Policy was British! This explains why the UPPs were launched simultaneously in the two cities. Although a delegation from London visited Marseille in the early period, the two cities did not maintain long-term links or establish any future joint strategies.

DG XVI appointed ECOTEC Consulting Ltd. to coordinate the progress of the UPPs.[16] Hooghe and Keating (1994, p.390) make the interesting remark that the Commission often uses such external private agents for management tasks partly to make its own presence less visible. ECOTEC established, on behalf of DG XVI, the RECITE Office to monitor and

---

[16] A full report of the UPP in London was published in 1993: 'The London Initiative. A report to the European Commission on the operation of the pilot programme of urban regeneration projects in London, undertaken under Article 10 of Council Regulation (EEC) No. 4254/88. The report on the UPP in Marseille was entitled: 'Ville de Marseille, Projet pilote, Fonds Européen de Développement Régional, Article 10 du FEDER, Rapport final, Situation au 31/12/93'. The central and local authorities in London and Marseille cooperated with ECOTEC Consulting Limited for the preparation of reports to the Commission. All figures quoted in this section are taken from the final reports cited above.

evaluate the UPPs and Interregional Cooperation projects also financed under Article 10. London and Marseille provided the first pilot projects and the programme for 1990-1993 was extended to include 33 projects from Member States bringing the final ERDF allocation to a figure of ECU 101.04 million.

Although the UPPs originated in DG XVI, which maintained the major responsibility for them, DG V also awarded funding to some of them. The London project was awarded ECU 0.9 million of ESF funding; the project for Marseille contained only an ERDF allocation. Procedures for match-funding were applied also to UPPs bringing the overall spending on the London project to ECU 10.2 million (of which the ERDF component was ECU 5.1 million, ESF ECU 0.9 million) and Marseille ECU 10.0 million (the European element was solely ERDF ECU 4.0 million). On a broader level, the overall percentage of Structural Funds allocated to UPPs amounted to 1 per cent of Structural Funds aid.

In July 1997, the European Commission approved the second phase of the Urban Pilot Programme. The theme continued the original programme's aim of supporting innovation in urban regeneration and planning within the framework of the broader Community policy for promoting economic and social cohesion. Total ERDF allocation to the Urban Pilot Programme in the 1997-1999 period amounted to ECU 63.6 million.[17] Certain London boroughs such as Islington, which had been involved in the first UPP, prepared proposals for the second phase. The Municipality of Marseille also prepared a bid for the Saint Barthélémy neighbourhood of Marseille situated in the 14th district (*14ème arrondissement*). This was backed by a letter to Commissioner Wulf-Mathies, signed personally by the Mayor of Marseille, Jean-Claude Gaudin, Minster of National and Regional Development, Towns and Integration (*Ministre de l'Aménagement du Territoire de la Ville et de l'Intégration*) in July 1996 when the applications for the second round were submitted.[18]

Interestingly enough, neither London nor Marseille were awarded UPPs for the second phase of the programme. As noted earlier, the initial launch of UPPs in each city had been an exception to the rules as neither had been

---

[17] RECITE Office, DG XVI (1995) 'Second Interim Report on the Progress of Urban Pilot Projects funded by the European Regional Development Fund'. See also RECITE (1997) *Urban Pilot Projects*, Autumn and Winter 1997; newsletters produced by ECOTEC Consulting Limited on behalf of DG XVI. The newsletters state that the views expressed are not necessarily those of the European Commission.

[18] Source: internal documents of DG XVI viewed during a training period at the European Commission, DG XVI, February to July 1997.

eligible to receive ERDF programmes in the programming period 1989-1993. Following this early experimentation, the Commission retained and reserved Article 10 for innovative projects. Unlike CIs and mainstream programmes, the allocation of funds for Article 10 remains entirely the responsibility of the Commission. The Mayor of Marseille at the time was also a minister in the central government, yet this did not give greater weight to Marseille's application for a UPP of the second phase. Indeed, the applications from London and Marseille were put aside in favour of other localities judged to have prepared more interesting proposals on this occasion (Interview, DG XVI official, May 1998).

The experience of UPPs soon indicated that it was impossible to bypass central government. Regardless of the origins of UPPs, or even how the cities were chosen, their implementation in the UK and France could not bypass the national administration. In the case of London, although the Conservative Government had clearly not been the motor behind the launching of the UPP, it joined the partnership to deliver this. Central government departments most closely involved in inner city issues worked with the London City Action Team, local authorities and their representative associations, the ALA and the LBA to deliver the programme. The UPP was coordinated within the existing regeneration strategy for the capital and the following London Boroughs were involved in its delivery: Hackney, Tower Hamlets, Lewisham, Lambeth, Haringey, Newham, Camden and Islington. Representatives from the European Commission were also members of the Coordinating Committee overseeing the project. Match-funding was provided by national and local government agencies, established by central government, to manage regeneration programmes and some private sector contributions; sources of match-funding varied according to the project.[19]

In the case of Marseille, there was initial confusion regarding the implementation of the UPP. Local representatives of the French state were not informed about the UPP until the time came for its implementation. Indeed one official stated that he first became aware of the awarding of the UPP reading the newspaper on his way to work showing a picture of a representative of the Mayor of Marseille, of the European Commission's Permanent Representation and Commissioner Millan! (Interview, prefecture

---

[19] An example of this is the Atlantic Road project in Brixton. Here the ERDF contribution was match-funded by an Urban Programme Grant, Local Authority funds (London Borough of Lambeth, Housing Corporation and Private Sector contributions. Source: 'The London Initiative A report to the European Commission on the operation of the pilot programme of urban regeneration projects in London, undertaken under Article 10 of Council Regulation (EEC) No. 4254/88', p.59, Appendix to the report).

official, July 1998). The fact that the local representatives of the state, at the prefecture, had not been briefed led to mistrust that the Municipality of Marseille may have been seeking not to comply with established procedures for the use of European funds (Interview, prefecture official, July 1998).

Once the details of the implementation of the UPP were finalised, it became clear that the European funds would reach the city of Marseille via the central state machinery. There was no financial system in place for the Commission to credit European funds directly to the account of the Municipality of Marseille. Similar to the case of London, the individual projects were match-funded by a variety of partners, reflecting the structures of the Member State concerned. In Marseille, sources of match-funding came from the Municipality of Marseille, the regional council, and the state. Local, regional and national authorities as well as private sector housing companies provided a contribution according to the project concerned.[20] Clearly, the national administration cannot be bypassed in the cases of France and the UK regarding the implementation even of small-scale, innovative projects involving modest sums of money.

We now move from our brief review of implementation to the higher level decision making at European Council level. The launching of UPPs, although welcomed by the cities involved, was not a history-making decision in the evolution of the European regional policy. UPPs were an initial exception to the rules, illustrating recognition of urban problems by the Commission. While urban policy measures are a peripheral part of EU policy, sums allocated to them in the budget are likely to remain limited. We turn to proposals to amend the Treaties to allow for more explicit provision for urban areas. Representatives from London also supported initiatives to include urban policy in the Treaties.

3.3/2 European Urban Policy: Legal or Aconstitutional?

European regions and cities had begun to organise themselves from the 1980s opening offices in Brussels. Eurocities, a network for European cities, was formed in 1986 at the conference 'The city, engine behind economic

---

[20] The full list of partners and match-funding for each project is found in the Appendix of the final report on the UPP coordinated by ECOTEC Limited, 'Ville de Marseille, Projet pilote, Fonds Européen de Développement Régional, Article 10 du FEDER, Rapport final, Situation au 31/12/93)'. Examples of private partners include S.A. D' HLM *Provence Logis* involved in the project *Espaces Extérieurs privés de la Castellane* (improvement of outdoor communal areas in private sector estates in La Castellane neighbourhood of Marseille).

recovery in Rotterdam'.[21] Eurocities subsequently established an office in Brussels. As noted above, London did not have an elected council, or leader of the council, to represent the city as a whole. Since this was a condition of membership, London was ineligible to join Eurocities in the 1980s. Northern cities, such as Manchester, became active players in Eurocities.

European networks such as Eurocities can provide an arena for representatives of cities to engage in dialogue and joint lobbying of the Commission. Organisations such as Eurocities felt that it was appropriate for the supra-national institution, the Commission, to be involved in urban areas. This can be linked to the increase in European Structural Funds following the 1989 reform. Europe was an additional source of funds and sub-national actors responded to this development by lobbying the European Commission. Representatives of cities, which were not members of such organisations, could also approach the Commission directly. This was clearly illustrated by the background to the launching of UPPs in London.

By 1990 the experiment with UPPs, and the awarding of mainstream Objective 2 funds to cities located in declining regions, had placed urban policy firmly on the agenda of the Commission's regional policy. Urban policy was outside the Commission's competences and the existing regional policy had its limitations due to the strict eligibility criteria. Yet there is evidence of increasing sympathy within DG XVI towards the case for more action from the supra-national level. In the 1990 Regional Affairs publication, 'Europe 2000', the Commission stated the following:

> The problems of the urban areas call for more wide-ranging efforts in the 1990s. There is considerable scope for cooperation between cities to exchange information and know-how as part of the effort to raise standards overall. *There is also scope for further action at Community level in dealing with urban problems beyond those of an economic nature currently addressed, in certain cities, under the Structural Funds* (CEC, 1990, p.133) emphasis added).

In the period of negotiations for the Treaty on European Union, the Commission took the bold step of proposing an amendment to the regulations to include 'urban decline' in the definition of objectives of the ERDF. Since urban communities and urban problems *per se* were not included in the Treaty, cities with urban problems that could not be classified under 'industrial decline', were excluded. This explains the

---

[21] Further information can be found from the Eurocities (1997) Conference Publication, 'Tenth Annual Conference, 23-24 October 1997', Rotterdam.

Commission's emphasis on 'urban decline' rather than 'industrial decline' which may, or may not, occur in urban areas.

In the case of London, representatives of the city formed an alliance with the Commission supporting the case for the rules to be amended. An extract from an official publication of the ALA stated the following:

> The European Commission proposed an amendment to the Treaty of Rome at the Inter-governmental Conference on Political Union which would have extended the objective of the European Regional Development Fund (ERDF) to include 'assistance to the areas of urban decline'. This amendment would have provided the basis for London's eligibility for these resources. *London supported the Commission in tabling this amendment.* The Association of London Authorities, in partnership with the London Boroughs Association led a delegation of employers, Trading and Enterprise Councils and Trade Unions to Brussels which argued for support for the Commission's amendment. Unfortunately, this amendment was not agreed at Maastricht (ALA, 1992a, p.16, emphasis added).

Although Structural Fund programmes were operating in cities at the time of the meeting in Maastricht in 1991, the European Council rejected the Commission's proposals for a more formal urban competence in the Treaties. In the former Commissioner Millan's words, the Member States were 'not in the business of extending the Treaty competences' (Interview, January 1999). In a speech at the Eurocities conference in Lisbon in 1993, Commissioner Millan spoke more in terms of the Commission complementing national, regional or local urban policies rather than developing one at European level:

> The Community does not have an Urban Policy as such but cities benefit from Community policies...There is no reference to cities in any of the EC Treaties including the one on the European Union. For the history books, I should mention that the Commission proposed in the context of the revision of the Treaties in 1991, the inclusion of 'urban decline' in the definition of the objectives of the European Regional Development Fund, but this was not accepted by the European Council in Maastricht. In addition, it follows from the subsidiarity principle that most policies to address urban issues are most appropriately carried out by the cities themselves. *We can contribute to the implementation of urban policies developed at the national, regional or local level, but not develop one of our own.* Cities have during the period 1989-1993 increasingly benefited from Community actions, both in financial terms

and policy terms, though sometimes these have not been adequately publicised.[22]

At the time of the 1993 reform, there was a small addition to the Objective 2 criteria to cover 'areas with severe problems linked to industrial dereliction' (CEC, 1993a). This allowed Objective 2 funds to be extended to cities with evidence of such problems such as parts of Stoke-on-Trent. Similar to London, these areas had been ineligible for ERDF support, in the 1989-1993 period, even though their case had aroused sympathy within DG XVI.[23]

In retrospect, the former Commissioner Millan questions the wisdom of the Commission's proposal regarding the amendment to the Treaties (Interview, former Commissioner Millan, January 1999). There is always a danger that extending the Structural Funds support over too wide a geographical area may threaten the effectiveness of any intervention. The Commission may have been flooded with requests for Structural Funds aid under Objective 2 for the programming period 1994-1999. There was, however, a 'safety net' in that the regulations limited Objective 2 support to 15 per cent of the population in a targeted region. In effect, the Commission had to resort to this in its negotiations with the UK government over the granting of Objective 2 to parts of London for the period 1994-1999. London provides an interesting case study of the politics of ERDF allocation.

Following the success with UPPs, representatives of local authorities in London prepared themselves to bid for the larger sums that could be received by acquiring Objective 2 status. The literature produced, in preparation for this, presented the case for London but was linked to the request for European action for urban areas in general.

Although this is a formal submission by London to influence the reform of the funds, it does not seek to put a special case for the capital. This document is intended to give an indication of the types of urban issues which can be addressed *at European level* through the reform of the Structural Funds (emphasis added) (ALA, 1992b).

---

[22] Commissioner Millan's speech to Eurocities Conference, Lisbon, 1993, emphasis added. Source: internal document viewed during a training period at the European Commission, DG XVI, Brussels, February to July 1997.

[23] It is interesting to note that in 1992 Stoke-on-Trent was also awarded a UPP as part of the first round of 1990-1997. This is an additional example of how UPPs were used to illustrate DG XVI's recognition of the problems of certain areas, not eligible for ERDF support, in the first round of Structural Funds allocation following the 1989 reforms.

Initially, the Objective 2 application for the 1994-1999 period of funding involved the following twelve London Boroughs: Barking and Dagenham, Bexley, Enfield, Greenwich, Hackney, Haringey, Havering, Lewisham, Newham, Redbridge, Tower Hamlets and Waltham Forest. London boroughs in the west of London, where much of the Park Royal industrial estate is based, had also been involved in the earlier stages of the bid. However only parts of the boroughs listed above were included in the final submission to the Commission.[24] The Objective 2 bid was firmly backed by both central and local government who had prepared much of the local statistics on unemployment and industrial decline in order to meet the criteria. There was still the feeling in some opposition boroughs that central government was not doing enough for London, yet the regulations required central government support for any bid for funding (Interview, former local authority representative, East London, 1997).

MEPs representing areas in London were involved through asking questions in the European Parliament to place the case of London on the agenda (Interview, MEP, London, 1994). During this period, MEPs in the UK system were based in individual constituencies and this encouraged close consultation with the local authorities in preparing strategies for the bid. The UK's Permanent Representation to the European Communities (UKREP), a central point in Brussels for departmental visits at both official and ministerial level, displayed its support for the case of London to the Commission. Initially, in 1990, UKREP was not particularly responsive to representatives from London who claimed that the city had been neglected in the allocation of ERDF funds. UKREP's position changed once London had gained the support of the national ministries.

Negotiations were at a high level involving senior civil servants, ministers and Commissioner Millan. Although the national government had reduced the size of the original Objective 2 proposal forwarded to the Commission for consideration in the 1994-1999 period, this was still problematic. The Commission rejected London's application since the population coverage of approximately 2.5 million included in this was beyond what the regulations would permit. The UK government attempted to insist that the whole area was included and, at first, refused to recognise the restrictions on population coverage. The Commission offered to mediate to reduce the area, on an objective basis, if the national administration forwarded the data required for this. In practice, it was very difficult to exercise such objective selection in

---

[24] Interviews with local authority officers in the London Boroughs of Haringey, Brent, Hammersmith and Fulham and Newham as listed in the bibliography.

view of the politics surrounding the choice of individual areas. The UK government attempted to maintain its 'all or nothing' approach until the very last minute when it was realised that if the Commission was pushed too far, London would be awarded nothing. The required information was forwarded at the last minute and a compromise was reached. Objective 2 status under urban communities suffering from industrial decline was awarded to parts of the following London Boroughs: Enfield, Hackney, Haringey, Newham, Tower Hamlets and Waltham Forest.

Parts of Marseille were also designated as Objective 2 areas in the period 1994-1999. Similar to London, Marseille had progressed from initial receipt of a UPP to the acquiring of Objective 2 status in the next programming period. Yet there is no evidence of joint cooperation between sub-national actors in London and Marseille to influence Objective 2 allocation. Representatives of each city presented their own case for Objective 2 funds to their national governments. Central government departments then negotiated with the Commission for the final selection of areas. The case of London provides an example of central government seeking to spread Objective 2 funds over as wide an area as possible. The UK government should not, however, be singled out as the only example of this. The Commission also faced great pressures regarding the geographical spread of Objective 2 areas in France and Germany.

This issue of 'spreading the jam too thinly' was a major issue in negotiations to deliver the CI URBAN in the UK and France; this will be explored in chapter four. National administrations have to answer to their own domestic regions and cities seeking maximum gains from European Structural Funds. Yet the Commission aims to promote an effective, supra-national regional policy independent of distributional politics within Member States. The example of the Objective 2 allocation, in the case of London, was a taste of the problems encountered by the Commission in the negotiations to deliver the CI URBAN in the UK and France. Although the sums involved were relatively modest, the allocation could prove as contentious as for the larger-scale programmes.[25] Before exploring this in chapter four, let us examine the origins of the CI URBAN.

---

[25] The precise figures for the allocation of URBAN will be presented in chapter four, section 4.1.

3.3/3 The Birth of the Community Initiative URBAN

Following the 1988 reform of the Structural Funds, the principle of partnership guided the Commission's relations with national and sub-national actors. This could impinge on both the launching and implementation of policy. DG XVI was already engaging in dialogue with the representatives of cities through informal meetings, conferences and in implementing the Structural Fund programmes of the period 1989-1993. After the first round of CIs a more formal consultation process took place. The first step in the consultation involved the Commission publishing a Green Paper entitled 'The Future of Community Initiatives under the Structural Funds' in July 1993 (CEC, 1993b).

The Commission's Green Paper was circulated to a wide range of actors: The Member States, the European Parliament, the Economic and Social Committee (ESC), the Consultative Council of Local and Regional Authorities, (CCLRA), local and regional authorities, development agencies, the economic and social partners and other interested parties, classified as 'organisations concerned by the Community Initiatives' (CEC, 1994e). The Committee of the Regions was not yet in operation. Regions were, however, consulted in the framework of the CCLRA. All the above participants were invited to respond. The departments in the Commission concerned by the proposals outlined above, DGs V, VI and XVI, set up a database to analyse replies. The Commission gave a description of CIs and suggested further action around five themes: cross-border trans-national and inter-regional cooperation and networks, rural development, outermost regions, employment and the development of human resources and the management of industrial change.

It is interesting that the Commission did not propose a specific CI for urban areas. Some elements in DG XVI were keen to promote additional 'urban specific' type measures such as the extension of UPPs or a CI. Other officials of DG XVI preferred the strategy of developing an overall regional policy, from which European cities would benefit, rather than developing a specific urban policy as requested by some representatives of cities.[26] Since the proposal for even minor Treaty changes was rejected by the European Council during the period of negotiations for the Treaty on European Union at Maastricht in 1991, the climate was arguably more conducive to

---

[26] This observation is based on informal discussions with a wide range of officials, employed in different sections of DG XVI, and on overall impressions on the policy process during a training period in DG XVI, February to July 1997.

maintaining and implementing the existing measures rather than venturing into new areas. Yet the responses to the Green Paper, particularly the position of the European Parliament, placed cities on the European agenda.

In the replies to the Green Paper, requests came for additional themes including 'programmes for urban areas with a high rate of unemployment to combat social exclusion' (Northern Member States, the European Parliament, the CCLRA and some ten replies from the other broad category of 'organisations concerned by the Community Initiatives').[27] Indeed, the European Parliament in its Resolution on the Green Paper emphasised the specific difficulties of urban areas, including problems related to social exclusion. It was stated that the European Parliament:

> Believes that apart from the measures envisaged under the 'Employment and the development of human resources' heading which are aimed at countering high levels of unemployment and social exclusion generally, there is a need for a specific integrated development programme, aimed at those parts of the Community's urban areas where unemployment and particularly long-term unemployment are abnormally high; the object of such an initiative would be to stimulate local economic development by facilitating the emergence and harnessing the efforts of local actors whose experience, expertise and commitment are essential to the regeneration of neglected and run-down areas, and to provide ready access to the type of services and systems necessary to support entrepreneurial activity.[28]

Some Member States agreed with the European Parliament in demanding specific urban programmes. However, it was the European Parliament, the ESC, the CCLRA and 100 organisations concerned with CIs, not any Member State, who requested: 'greater participation by territorial bodies and others involved in the local economy particularly the social partners, and the development of a 'bottom-up approach'.

Following the results of the consultation process, the Commission did include a reference to an 'Urban Initiative' in its Communication of March 1994. Indeed the Commission stated that urban problems would need to be tackled in an integrated way by means of concerted action by the national and city authorities.[29] URBAN, as an official CI, was formally adopted on 15 June 1994. The role of the European Parliament, in particular, was seen as instrumental in influencing the Commission to launch a CI specifically

---

[27] COM (94) 46 25. 03. 94 (CEC, 1994e).

[28] European Parliament, Resolution of 28 October 1993, PE 176.537.

[29] COM (94) 46 final 2, 25.03. 1994 (CEC, 1994f, p.4).

targeted at cities. No additional Treaty competences were required as URBAN was within the framework of CIs that had existed since the 1988 reform. URBAN was therefore one of a number of CIs agreed for the 1994-1999 period. At the time of the launching of URBAN, the former Commissioner Millan commented:

> This initiative draws on the experience gained over the last few years through pilot projects and networks of cities. It also responds to a request of the European Parliament and organisations representing large cities for the European Union to contribute to the tackling of some of society's problems found in deprived urban areas. The Commission will seek to put the accent on innovative integrated programmes and the support of the diffusion of experience gained under these programmes.[30]

Chapters four to eight of the book will explore to what extent the Commission succeeded in promoting innovative and integrated URBAN programmes. The Commission had entered a complex policy area that involved more than one ministry at Member State level. The chapters on implementation will examine the Commission's attempts to achieve an integrated approach which incorporated the four principles of regional policy.

3.4 Conclusions

The historical review of European regional policy has highlighted the problems associated with supra-national intervention in this area. From the establishment of the ERDF in 1975, the Commission has encountered difficulties in establishing a common regional policy. Following the 1988 reform of the Structural Funds and the increased budget accompanying this, the Commission played a more pro-active role in regional policy for the period 1989-1993. The Commission attached conditions to European funding in line with Objectives 1 to 5 and the principles of regional policy: concentration, programming, additionality and partnership. Although these were retained in the 1993 reform, the Member States reasserted control over certain areas. The Commission's further progress towards a supra-national regional policy was subject to a continual process of negotiation with

---

[30] Statement made by Commissioner Millan at the time of the launching of URBAN. Source: Internal documentation of DG XVI, D.3, Brussels viewed during a training period, February to July 1997.

Member States over the allocation of European funds and their subsequent implementation.

This is the background to the birth of the EU's urban policy experiment. The material presented in this chapter provides clear evidence of representatives of European cities turning to a supra-national institution, the Commission, to address urban problems. Cities which had been awarded mainstream funding programmes in the period 1989-1993 formed networks, such as Eurocities, and opened offices in Brussels in order to deal directly with the Commission as well as with their own governments. Sub-national mobilisation, in the case of London, contributed to the birth of UPPs. The increased budget of the Structural Funds had clearly impinged on the Commission's relations with Member States and sub-national actors within each.

The UPPs illustrated how the Commission's dialogue with sub-national actors could result in experimentation through small-scale programmes partly funded by the European level. However, the early experience of UPPs indicated that central government, in the UK and France, could not be bypassed at implementation stage. Central government was clearly part of the partnership to deliver experimental programmes, such as UPPs, as well as those financed under the mainstream Objectives. UPPs were arguably viewed as a 'taster' to further Commission intervention in cities. However Member States were reluctant to grant the Commission a formal competence in urban policy. Any further progress towards a European urban policy was therefore confined to the existing framework of regional policy.

Although there were no changes in the Treaties, it was clear in the programming period 1994-1999 that a form of European urban policy had gradually developed. Firstly, the UPPs were extended to other cities and a second phase was announced in 1997. Secondly, the Commission launched a new CI directed at cities, namely URBAN. Thirdly, there was an urban dimension to mainstream Objective 1 and 2 programmes operating in cities. Indeed more cities were eligible to apply for Objective 2 funds in this period following a small addition to the criteria for this at the time of the 1993 reform.

In the case of the UK, the Community Economic Development (CED) element in mainstream programmes introduced new delivery mechanisms in the period 1994-1999. This involved a wide range of partners in the implementation of European programmes in cities in the UK. Both the European policy of CED and national urban policies, running parallel to this, emphasised a bottom-up approach. The CED model was also relevant to the implementation of the CI URBAN in the UK and will therefore be examined in further detail in chapter four. In France there was some experimentation with CED in the Objective 1 programme for French Hainaut.[31] However CED did not feature in French Structural Fund programmes on the scale of those in the UK. This will not therefore be included in the analysis of the implementation of URBAN in France.

It is beyond the scope of this study to examine, in detail, the implementation of all instruments of European urban policy. We therefore concentrate on the delivery of URBAN for the reasons outlined below. In the period 1994-1999, URBAN was a relatively small-scale programme funded under CIs allowing the Commission freedom to promote innovative approaches to implementation. This could permit a more focused application of the principles of regional policy. However CIs have to go through the same procedures as mainstream programmes in terms of negotiations with the Member State machinery. The rules regarding the selection of areas for URBAN were similar to those for Objective 2 in the 1994-1999 period; this involved negotiation with Member State authorities. This was in contrast to UPPs, where the Commission had entire responsibility for selecting participating cities. Detailed analysis of the delivery of URBAN allows in-depth investigation of the possible tensions between the Commission's quest for a supra-national regional policy and the Member States' efforts to control the European intervention. There is a fine line between the Commission's policy complementing that of Member States, and its use purely to co-finance existing projects.

Analysis will focus on the practical problems of applying the four principles of regional policy to the delivery of our chosen programme. The empirical material, presented in chapters four to seven of the book, will develop these themes further. The principle of partnership was clearly a key element in the incremental development of European urban policy. Although the Commission may share common goals with its partners, the implementation of policy may reveal strains in the partnership. We begin with the example of the allocation of European programmes. The Commission aims to allocate these in areas of greatest need in line with the principle of concentration. Due to pressure from domestic politics, national administrations may seek to spread the funds over as wide an area as possible. This could threaten the effectiveness of the supra-national intervention.

Once European programmes have been allocated, regional and/or local levels of government may have the resources to prioritise their own projects

---

[31] COM (97), final, Brussels, 06.05.1997 (CEC, 1997a, p.11).

even if part of a wider European/national programme. In line with the principle of partnership, the Commission can experiment by involving non-governmental actors, based in the targeted areas. This may act as a counterweight to attempts by the regional and/or local government to control implementation at this level. This may also assist the Commission in enforcing additionality by highlighting cases where the use of European funds is proposed to run services that would otherwise be financed by regional or local government. However, the rules and regulations of European funding may restrict some of the ideas presented by the newer partners who do not necessarily have the professional experience of implementing European funds.

Taking the simple example of eligibility, this can be quite contentious when European policy is implemented at local level. Although the rules may appear clear when consulting the legal texts, they can become less so as they filter through the various tiers of government. The policy process may become a 'marble cake' scenario similar to the American experience of federal programmes. Due to the number of actors involved at various levels of government, lines of authority may be blurred. On the one hand, the Commission is seeking active participation to deliver Structural Fund programmes at grass roots level. On the other hand, any ideas proposed from below must fit the eligibility criteria as well as the time scales of the European programmes.

Strict application of the rules on eligibility may cause resentment among the targeted recipients of European Structural Funds aid. Furthermore, rules and regulations of the programmes demand that funds be committed and spent by a certain deadline. Small organisations operating at neighbourhood level may not have easy access to the matching funds required to implement European programmes. Engaging local residents, the voluntary and community sectors may be a complicated, long process in our multi-ethnic European cities. This would be beyond the time scale of a European programme. While programming presents a coherent approach to managing European funds, the process may alienate the very citizens that European regional policy is seeking to involve. Problems may also arise regarding the coordination of European programmes with those existing at a national and/or local level. Lessons from American federalism highlighted the difficulties in coordinating federal and local funding programmes. Our detailed case studies will examine whether we can identify similar problems in the experience of European urban policy.

Chapters four to seven will explore the above themes by using the framework of the 'extended gatekeeper' model presented in chapter two

(Bache, 1996). Gatekeeping by central government may present obstacles to supra-national urban policy measures. This will be examined at the various stages of the policy process from the time URBAN was announced, in the Official Journal of 1994, to its delivery at grass roots level. We will also examine the concept of gatekeeping by other levels of government. Gatekeeping by municipal or regional government may also present hurdles to the implementation of the policy originally conceived by the Commission. In the case of URBAN in the UK, gatekeeping by local councils may interfere with the neighbourhood strategies the CED model aimed to promote. In the case of France, the regional and municipal levels of government could have their own priorities in line with existing urban policy and the local political situation.

Would the CI, URBAN, provide added value once planted in the maze of national regeneration policies? Lessons from the American experience are combined with the models presented in chapter two in order to assess the implementation of URBAN in London and Marseille. Analysis takes place at two levels: firstly, the integration of URBAN into the national administrative system in the UK and France, secondly the local delivery at neighbourhood level in each city.

4   Gatekeeping in a Multi-Level Government System: the Implementation of URBAN in the United Kingdom

Introduction

This chapter seeks to apply the concepts developed in chapter two to the implementation of the Community Initiative (CI) URBAN, in the UK. Firstly, we present facts and figures related to this CI. The previous chapter revealed overall figures relating to Structural Funds in general; here we present details of sums allocated specifically to URBAN. This allows us to gain a sense of perspective of these funds with respect to urban regeneration schemes in place at Member State level. Implementation of URBAN is taken to begin from the date of the announcement of the programme in the *Official Journal* of July 1994.

Following the presentation of facts and figures, we proceed to divide the empirical material into different stages of the policy process. Taking the 'extended gatekeeper' approach, the various stages of EU policy are linked and in order to explain central government action at one stage, we may require an understanding of government action at others.[1] There are differences in procedures for the implementation of European policies in the UK and France. The importance of each stage may vary according to the national framework of the Member State in which the policy is implemented. This will be clearly explained in section 4.1 before we enter the details of the empirical material. Following this, the remainder of the chapter deals only with the implementation of URBAN in the UK.

---

[1] Please refer to section 2.3 in chapter two.

4.1 The Implementation of URBAN in National Systems

The implementation of URBAN took place within the broader framework agreed at the higher level Council/Commission negotiations for the 1994-1999 period where the strategic objectives and regulations regarding European Structural Funds were decided. As explained in chapter three, Community Initiatives (CIs) were launched by the Commission and they only represented 9 per cent of the overall Structural Funds budget for the period of our study.[2]

4.1/1 The Community Initiative URBAN: Facts and Figures

Originally, the total budget allocated to the CI URBAN amounted to ECU 600 million of which ECU 400 million was for Objective 1 areas. Overall priority was for cities in Objective 1 regions. The remaining ECU 200 million was to be allocated to other areas although preference would be given to cities in Objective 2 areas. In May 1996 the Commission decided to allocate some of the reserve fund of CIs to URBAN.[3] The sums for the second, 'reserve' phase of URBAN amounted to ECU 157 million of which ECU 61 million would be allocated to Objective 1 regions and ECU 96 million for other regions (CEC, 1996a). There was no specific quota for each Member State although the number of programmes allocated to each would have to be compatible with the broad allocation between Objective 1, 2 and non-Objective areas.

The limited budget allocated to URBAN clearly did not constitute a global European urban policy, neither was the Commission seeking to promote this. The programmes could only complement existing national, regional and local policies within the Member State (Interview, former Commissioner Millan, January 1999). Moreover, the implementation of European programmes has to comply with the principles of European regional policy namely concentration, programming, additionality and partnership. This would imply a limitation of the number of projects awarded to each Member State in accordance with the Objectives of

---

[2] The Commission had proposed to increase the budget for CIs to 15 per cent for the period 1994-1999 but this was limited by Council to the existing 9 per cent of the total Structural Funds budget.

[3] CEC (1998a, p.8). In July 1994, the Commission allocated ECU 11.85 billion to CIs. The remaining ECU 1.6 billion was placed in reserve so that the initial allocation could be adjusted in the light of implementation of the CIs, to cover balances between countries and any unforeseen events.

European regional policy. The number of programmes the Commission had originally envisaged for the first phase of URBAN amounted to 50.[4]

In view of the limited number of programmes available, the allocation of URBAN would involve an element of competition between cities in the various Member States. Clearly, there would be 'winners' and 'losers' as had been the case regarding the allocation of Objective 2 funds in the UK for the period 1989-1993. Apart from Merseyside with Objective 1 status, all the other prospective candidates from the UK were competing for the smaller pot of funds allocated to Objective 2 or other areas. This was also the case for most of the French cities aspiring to receive URBAN funding. This chapter seeks to illustrate the competition involved in applying even for the smaller sums allocated to CIs. We will concentrate on the negotiations for the allocation of the first wave of URBAN since both London and Marseille were allocated programmes within this.

4.1/2 URBAN – an Innovative European Programme?

The implementation of European policy involves officials from the Commission, national and local government and other partners within the Member State. Taking the case of the UK, central government bureaucracies negotiate the national framework for the delivery of European programmes. Local bureaucracies are responsible for the policy implementation on the ground, in conjunction with representatives of central government as well as the local economic and social partners. The Commission, as the supra-national level of government, is dependent on the national actors to implement policy. As Mény, Muller and Quermonne note (1996, p.7):

> Because European policies are the outcome of complex compromises and interactions, and because the Community institutions have no infrastructure at their disposal, the implementation of policies gives back to the national actors a significant margin for manoeuvre. This is not peculiar to the Community. Everywhere, including a formally centralised state such as France, policy-makers are at the mercy of the implementors.

In the case of URBAN we should take into consideration the way in which Member States criticised CIs during the negotiations to establish the framework for the 1994-1999 period. The implementation of URBAN would

---

[4] Source: Internal documents from DG XVI. Much of this chapter is based on such internal documents to which DG XVI provided access during my period as a trainee February to July 1997.

involve a Management Committee, including Member State representatives, with responsibility for steering the CIs in this second round. Bache (1998, p.85) interprets this as Member States seeking to curtail the Commission's discretion over the nature, allocation and timing of these programmes. While the Commission and Member States share common goals in this policy area, there may be tensions between the Commission and Member States regarding the control of European programmes; this could feature at different stages of their implementation.

In the analysis of the empirical material on the delivery of URBAN, we will refer to Bache's (1996) model of 'extended gatekeeper' as presented in full in chapter two. The application of the concept of 'extended gatekeeper' will focus on the role of central government, in the UK and France, regarding the implementation of URBAN in the respective Member States. For this we adapt Bache's approach for the purposes of our own policy area. The empirical material relating to the implementation of URBAN is divided into different stages. This is set out below and refers to both case studies, London and Marseille. Where relevant, we will apply the notion of 'gatekeeping' to explain the actions of other levels of government as discussed in the conclusions of chapter two.

Stage one The selection of cities to receive URBAN in the UK and France. In both cases, the demand exceeded the supply of programmes the Commission had envisaged for the respective Member States.

Stage two Negotiations for administrative arrangements to deliver URBAN in the UK and France. This section will be more detailed for the UK where a number of unique issues arose in the negotiations between the Commission and central government.

Stage three Negotiations between the Commission officials, central and local authorities regarding the content of the Programme Documents for the targeted areas of the cities selected to receive URBAN. Here, more detail will be given to the case of Marseille where central government took a more active role, regarding the contents of the Programme Document, than was the case for the programmes agreed in the UK.

Stage four Implementation of URBAN 'on the ground' in London and Marseille.

In the case of London, stages one and two are covered in this chapter which deals with central government/Commission negotiations. In the UK the main actors for stages three and four were the local partnerships with responsibility for delivering the programme; this is dealt with in chapter six. In the case of Marseille, central government played a more active role in the negotiations for the contents of the Programme Document; this is explored in chapter five. Chapter seven concentrates on the delivery of URBAN at grass roots level.

Although central government and the Commission were both included in the partnership to implement URBAN, there could still be possible differences in the interpretation of the programme. On the one hand, URBAN could be interpreted by the national authorities as 'business as usual'. This presents the following scenario: selection of cities to receive URBAN is exercised in the same way as for national programmes. URBAN is perceived as another pot of funds to complement what the national authorities are doing anyway. The match-funding principle is respected by the partnership within the Member State and there does not, prima facie, appear to be a problem with this.[5] This may be seen as compatible with Scharpf's form of multi-level policy-making whereby Member States can exploit any European intervention in devising their own policies.[6] On the other hand, CIs are perceived by the Commission to be innovative. In this respect, URBAN should not be viewed purely as a source of extra funds for existing regeneration programmes within the Member State. Although URBAN was to complement existing programmes, any European intervention should have its own identity and added value. Would this be possible or would URBAN be 'hijacked' by Member States and used purely as another pot of funds for what they were doing anyway?

Chapter three outlined how the Commission attached conditions to the increase in the Structural Funds budget agreed at the 1988 reform. Although there were some changes to the detail, the broad Objectives and principles of regional policy were retained in 1993. In our case studies, we will explore whether the Commission's guidelines were sufficient to address the problems of implementation identified in the experience of European regional policy before the 1988 reform.[7] During the period of our study, representatives of

---

[5] In the case of non-Objective 1 areas such as London and Marseille, the rules required any EU contribution to be matched by 50 per cent of the total cost of projects.

[6] Please refer to chapter two, section 2.4 where this line of argument is presented in full.

[7] For details on the problems of the early period of regional policy, please refer to Mény (1982) and Wallace, H. (1977, 1983).

cities demanded more European intervention in urban areas.[8] However persistent problems of implementation can threaten the effectiveness of European policies; this raises questions about whether the Commission should be involved in such local policies. We will return to these issues in the conclusions to this study in chapter eight where we compare and contrast the experience of European urban policy in London and Marseille. We now turn to our first case study dealing with the implementation of URBAN in the UK.

4.2 The Background to Negotiations for URBAN

We begin our analysis of the UK case with a brief review of national regeneration schemes in the UK operating around the same time as URBAN. It is by no means a comprehensive review since this would beyond the scope of this study. An understanding of the existing regeneration policies can help us assess the impact of the European intervention. Of particular interest are the institutional mechanisms in place for delivering national urban policy Can we identify similarities in the national urban programmes of this period and those proposed by the European level? How do the administrative structures for implementing national urban policies differ from procedures for European programmes?

As noted in chapter three, a form of European urban policy developed through the Community Economic Development (CED) priority in mainstream ERDF programmes operating in urban areas granted Objective 1 and 2 status during the period 1994-1999. The origins and features of the CED approach will be briefly reviewed. It is argued here that, in the case of the UK, DG XVI viewed URBAN as an opportunity to experiment with CED in order to better develop this element of mainstream programmes. The interesting point is that there are a number of similarities between the CED approach and that of existing regeneration schemes in the UK. This chapter will examine whether this facilitated the Commission/central government negotiations for the delivery of URBAN in the UK.

---

[8] This refers to the empirical material presented in chapter three. See also Committee of the Regions, 1995, 'Opinion on urban development and the European Union', Brussels 19-20 July, CdR 235/95.

4.2/1 Developments in United Kingdom Urban Policy [9]

Social tensions appeared in inner cities in the UK from the 1960s. In this period, the Urban Programme was launched. This consisted of a relatively small-scale grant-based initiative which focused on funding projects to integrate and develop the skills of targeted groups of the population. The Urban Programme contained some innovative features in that it aimed to promote central government, local authorities and community groups to work together in partnership. Bailey, Barker and MacDonald (1995) argue that the idea of partnership appeared in the late 1970s in a bid to improve overall coordination and delivery of central and local government services. There was an attempt to involve the private sector and the voluntary sector benefited from some additional funding during the 1970s. Yet studies on this period suggest that civil servants in Whitehall, government ministers who chaired the partnership committees and town hall officials controlled implementation of any new policy measures (Barnekov et al., 1990).

Any analysis of urban policy measures in the 1980s must take into account the changes in central/local relations following the election of the Conservative Government led by Margaret Thatcher. As Travers (1989, p.8) notes, the Conservatives' 1979 election programme clearly implied that local government expenditure had to be reduced. Immediately on taking office, the Conservatives announced lower public expenditure plans for local authorities in the period 1979-1980. Many local authorities sought to resist the expenditure cuts by increasing their rates and using supplementary rates; central government responded with legislation. The 1982 Local Government Finances No. 2 Act granted central government power to withhold grants from authorities classified as spending too much and prevented local authorities from raising a supplementary rate at mid-year. The 1984 Rates Act, which introduced 'rate capping' empowered central government to set rate levels by local authorities and reduce those it classified as excessive. In the 1985-1986 list of rate capped authorities all but two (Portsmouth,

---

[9] Although the title refers to UK urban policy the analysis refers to the case of England since our case study from the UK is London. During this period, urban policies in Scotland, Wales and Northern Ireland were administered by the central government representatives there. The analysis does not deal with the details of this throughout the UK since it does not directly affect the implementation of URBAN for the case of London. Some of the general background information for UK urban policy is drawn from an OECD publication (1998). For a more detailed analysis of the concept of partnership in British urban policy and government policy towards this, please refer to Bailey et. al. (1995) which was consulted for this section of the book.

Conservative and Brent, Labour-Alliance coalition), were Labour controlled.[10]

Against the background of the battle over spending came the 1985 Local Government Act which abolished the Greater London Council (GLC). The GLC, at the time, was under a Labour administration which had campaigned against the Conservatives over such issues. Whatever the political motivation, abolition of the GLC gave the Conservative government greater power of control (Hebbert and Travers, 1988). There were further tensions following the abolition of the rates and the introduction of the poll tax, finally replaced by the council tax (1988 and 1992 Local Government Act). Legislation introducing greater privatisation also affected local government powers (Goldsmith, 1993). The 1980 Housing Act privatised council houses to tenants in residence for three years. Under the 1988 Local Government Act, local authorities were obliged to put services such as refuse collection, cleaning vehicle and ground maintenance to competitive tender. The emphasis on limiting public spending, taking powers away from councils opposed to this, and the move towards privatisation guided the Conservatives' urban policy measures of the 1980s.

A number of inner city riots in the early 1980s placed the issue of urban policy on the Conservative government's agenda. Incidents of civil disorder occurred in 1980 in Bristol and in 1981 when more than 4,000 arrests were made following riots in Brixton (London), Toxteth (Liverpool), and Handsworth (Birmingham). Michael Heseltine, Secretary of State for the Environment from 1979-1983, took the initiative of promoting a number of policy changes for the period 1979-1983. The main thrust of the policies was to find ways of involving the private sector in urban regeneration. One example was the establishment of the Financial Institutions Group. This did not involve much new investment to the inner cities yet a House of Commons Environment Committee viewed this as a useful exercise in the context of a policy aimed at increasing private sector involvement on urban questions.[11] Other initiatives involved the use of private sector advisors in the Department of the Environment (DoE). Although the Urban Programme was retained until the mid-1980s, its priorities were tailored to the broader policy objectives of the Conservative government. In the 1980s, the concept of partnership was seen as a way of transferring responsibility for urban policy

---

[10] This refers to the Alliance at the time between the Social Democrat Party, established by former members of the Labour Party, and the Liberal Party. In the case of the London Borough of Brent at this time, the Labour Party formed a local coalition with the Alliance.

[11] House of Commons Environment Committee 1982-3, 'Minutes of Evidence', quoted in Bailey et al. (1995, p. 47) and Deakin and Edwards (1993, p.30).

to the private sector as well as increased centralisation of urban policy (Bailey et al., 1995).

Another feature of the post-1979 period was the growth of 'informal local government' (King, 1993). This term refers to the growth of authorities, established by central government, and granted policy-making powers in specific areas; these were independent of 'formal' local government institutions represented by the elected councils of local authorities (King, 1993). The newly created agencies were run by teams of employees increasingly directed by Westminster; they were complemented by government programmes to re-establish the growing number of public-private schemes in urban policy. Through the creation of 'informal local government', central government could sideline local councils. In this way, urban policy came increasingly under central control although this was coupled with delegation of responsibility to the private sector. Some analysts have viewed the post-1979 events as a redefinition of the partnership between central and local government. This was also to have an impact on the voluntary and community sector. Bailey et al. (1995, p.48) summarise the events as follows:

> The partnership between central and local government, established by the previous Labour Government, was reinterpreted as a partnership between what were presumed to be like-minded interests: central government and the private sector. New initiatives such as Urban Development Corporations, City Action Teams and Inner Task Forces were increasingly staffed and managed by civil servants and private sector employees, with strategic policy being determined by Westminster. Although the voluntary sector benefited to some degree from funding under the Urban Programme, it played no role in the management of, and was rarely consulted about, the individual initiatives or the broad direction of policy. In essence, the voluntary and community sectors were seen as wedded to the outdated dependency culture and thus were largely bypassed along with local government.

Taking the example of Urban Development Corporations (UDCs) these were financed directly by central government to which they were responsible; their aim was to attract private sector investment into areas which had experienced significant economic decline, often de-industrialisation. UDCs were granted powers related to development control and land-use; these had been taken away from local authorities. The aim was to allow UDCs to pursue a more entrepreneurial, business orientated approach to public policy-making. Other legislative changes established Enterprise Zones and Urban Regeneration Grants. Another example of 'informal local government' was the creation of Training and Enterprise Councils (TECs) which replaced the tripartite industry training boards. Rhodes (1988) used the term 'sub-central government' to encompass the range of institutions operating below central government. The case of London was the most extreme example of the new post-1979 structures since, following the abolition of the Greater London Council the capital was to be governed by 33 London boroughs and the newly created agencies. The London Docklands Development Corporation (LDDC) for example, affected the London Boroughs of Tower Hamlets, Newham and Southwark.

In 1990, Michael Heseltine was recalled to the position of Secretary of State for the Environment and a new Conservative government, under John Major, was elected in 1992. Following the peak of the deregulation boom of the 1980s, the value of property fell and continuing recession prompted a further review of urban policy measures. Accompanying this was yet another interpretation of the concept of partnership. In a speech to the Manchester Chamber of Commerce in 1991 Heseltine argued for the competitive approach, linked with that of partnership and citizenship in order to promote successful urban regeneration. This was presented as:

> A sense of *partnership* in our modern cities, it is today's equivalent of that Victorian sense of competitive drive linked with social obligation...competition is the vital catalyst for the new approach...men and women will compete with one another and give of their best. People will set the pace and exercise their discretion. And by enriching themselves, their lives and their communities, they enrich society as a whole (Heseltine, 1991).[12]

City Challenge represented a new integrated approach to tackling the problems of deprived urban neighbourhoods. Areas of urban decay were targeted by independent regeneration agencies which used public money, and the leverage of private sources established, to prepare and deliver action plans over five years. The 'action plans' were required to specify a 'vision' for the area and to outline clear targets for property related and 'people orientated' strategies (Bailey et al., 1995, p.64). Another aspect to the approach of City Challenge was a re-appraisal of the role of local councils, largely bypassed by the previous Conservative government initiatives. Elected local authorities were awarded the task of promoting 'civic leadership' in developing partnerships, utilising existing resources and promoting innovative solutions to problems of urban deprivation (DoE,

---

[12] This quote taken from the report by the Centre for Urban and Regional Studies at the University of Birmingham (CURS, 1995, p.18, emphasis added).

1992, p.6). Partnership therefore incorporated central government, elected local government, the private sector, voluntary and community sector and local residents. Some areas, subsequently awarded URBAN, had already had experience of City Challenge.

The selection of cities for the awarding of City Challenge was through a competitive bidding process. Although presenting new approaches, City Challenge did not represent any major injection of public funds into urban policy. 'No new money was provided and the £83.5 million allocated for 1992-1993 was found by recasting departmental housing and Urban Programme budgets' (Bailey et al., 1995, p.64). In the first round in 1991, 11 out of 15 authorities invited to bid were selected. In the second round announced in April 1992, 57 urban priority areas were eligible to bid for City Challenge Status. Following an assessment based on the quality of bids, innovation, and whether the strategy presented was achievable, central government selected 31 areas for this programme (OECD, 1998, p.94). In some areas, European funding provided additional sources of funding.

Following the strains in central-local relations of the 1980s, 'formal' and 'informal' local government were forced to find new ways of working together. Working in partnership was a prerequisite to qualify for both national and European funding schemes. The principles of European regional policy in the post-1988 period also demanded a partnership approach in implementing Structural Funds. This prompted local authorities, 'informal local government' and central government to present a unified approach. Applications for European funding developed around the partnerships established to bid for, and deliver, national funding programmes. With reference to the Objective 2 bid for London for the 1994-1999 period, reviewed in chapter three, the following partnership was presented for East London:

> We see the Integrated Development Organisation (IDO) as a partnership bringing together public sector funders. Local Authorities, Training and Enterprise Councils, Urban Development Corporations, City Challenge companies together with representatives from key government funding departments: Trade and Industry, Environment, Employment, Transport. The IDO will then work in partnership with the private sector to deliver programmes that enhance the wealth of the region.[13]

---

[13] Quote taken from the following publication: 'The Case for East London Objective 2 Status' (1993), publicity pamphlet, Centurion Press, London.

The interesting point is the balance of power between the partners involved in implementing the national and European schemes. What was the Commission seeking to achieve by its own intervention in this already complex policy area? Could the European intervention bring any significant additional value? By the time URBAN was launched there had been yet further changes to the national urban policy in the form of the Single Regeneration Budget (SRB). There was no departure from the overall principles of City Challenge although there were some important institutional differences. These related to the administration of European, as well as national, regeneration programmes. For this reason, we complete our overview of the national framework by focusing on SRB and the administrative arrangements for its implementation. A new deconcentrated level of central government was created to administer both national and European programmes at sub-central level.

4.2/2 Institutional Change and New Developments in Urban Regeneration

The SRB incorporated resources from four Government Departments – Environment, Transport, Education and Employment and Trade and Industry into a single, flexible budget administered at the regional level by new integrated Government Offices for the Regions. The SRB brought together a number of separate programmes into one set of funding for which the Secretary of State for the Environment was responsible. One report summarised the objectives of the SRB as follows:

> In bringing together the twenty housing, education, economic development and urban regeneration programmes together within the SRB, the intention was to create a flexible regeneration programme that would be more responsive to local needs and give local people much more control over spending priorities (CURS, 1995, p.34).

The Government Offices were established to provide businesses, local authorities and voluntary organisations with a reference point for the annual regeneration budget for England. The new Government Offices were also granted responsibility for administering European funds within the different regions of England listed as follows: North East, North West, Yorkshire and Humberside, Merseyside, East Midlands, West Midlands, Eastern, London, South East and South West. The creation of Government Offices for the Regions should not be viewed, therefore, in terms of any devolution of power to the regions; they were created by central government for the administration of central government policy at deconcentrated, regional level. The Regional Directors of Government Offices are senior civil servants appointed by central government. The civil servants, based in Government Offices, are answerable to central government Departments.

SRB was based on the principles of City Challenge although there were provisions for more flexibility in the use of funds. One difference was that for City Challenge only urban priority areas were eligible to bid for funds, whereas under SRB all areas in the country were eligible to bid. At the launch of the SRB there were some examples of bids from community groups and the private sector, although an OECD study stated that most applications were led by local authorities (OECD, 1998). This reflected the approach favoured by central government in the 1990s encouraging local authorities to display 'civic leadership' in forming partnerships to develop solutions to urban decay (DoE, 1992, p.6).

There are various funding rounds of SRB whereby organisations and local authorities are invited to submit a bid for funding to the Government Office of their region. The allocation of the first round of SRB illustrates how the Regional Offices interacted with other actors in their geographical area. The first stage of this took place just before URBAN was announced in July 1994, and the initial selection process for URBAN was modelled on this process although there were some minor differences. This will become clear in section 4.3 dealing with the allocation of URBAN. Firstly we should review the procedures for SRB and the sums involved in the first round.

The first bidding round for SRB was on September 7 1994, shortly after URBAN was announced in the *Official Journal* of July 1994. Figures indicate the value of the bids in year one was £367.4 million (CURS, 1995, p.50). The available resources in year one were initially estimated at £100 million, although the figure was subsequently increased to £125 million when the results were announced. The first year's allocation was estimated to attract up to 300 per cent overbidding, the total lifetime value of the bids was £2.325 billion which was 200 per cent greater than the £1.12 billion made available.[14] The allocation of the first round of SRB was characterised by five stages:

- Stage 1: April-June 1994. Outline bid preparation.
- Stage 2: October-November 1994. Filtering stage.

---

[14] The term 'lifetime' refers to the duration of the approved projects; this varies from one to seven years. All figures in this section are taken from the CURS report (1995, p.50). See also Clark (1994). For a comparison with France, see Le Galès and Mawson (1994).

- Stage 3: October-November 1994 (continued). Bids checked against policy guidelines.
- Stage 4: November 1994. Final presentation of bids to Economic Development Regeneration – cabinet sub-committee).
- Stage 5: Delivery Plans commence.[15]

The first stage of the process involved the sending of applications by prospective bidders to the Government Office. The next involved selection panels with representatives of the four Departments at Government Office level: the Department for Education, the Employment Service and the Home Office were co-opted on these panels and other relevant organisations such as English Partnerships and the Housing Corporation were consulted. Prior to proposing final recommendations for the bids within their region, the Regional Directors met with the Minister before presenting their final *regional* recommendation to the Economic Development and Regeneration (EDR, cabinet sub-committee).[16] The final representation was by the Minister to the EDR on the basis of regional and local outputs. In November 1994 the successful bids were announced and in January 1995 the DoE held its first meeting on Delivery Plans and began a set of workshops agreed with Government Offices for the implementation of the chosen programmes (CURS, 1995, pp.35-38).

Studies on the SRB suggest that central government took account of any existing European programmes when making decisions on the awarding of funding. For the case of London, in allocating SRB, the Assessment Panel at Government Office took account of the European Commission's London specific regeneration programmes, particularly the Objective 2 designated areas. Furthermore, the bids from Hackney and Tower Hamlets were assessed in the context of proposals made for URBAN funding (CURS, 1995, p.41). Indeed, in Merseyside, the importance of European funding was emphasised yet further: 'Objective 1 funding was central to the SRB in Merseyside: it guided the whole process and was a vital source of match-funding' (CURS, 1995, p.42).

We may expect that areas subsequently allocated URBAN in the two phases (original and reserve) would already have been awarded SRB funds. This was not, however, always the case. The receipt of SRB funding depends on successful bids when each round is announced by central government. Our case studies in London were allocated SRB funding either

---

[15] Adapted from CURS (1995, p.15).
[16] This was in contrast to the approach under City Challenge which entailed a more centralised selection process.

prior to, or following, their selection for URBAN. Indeed, some local government officials involved in applying for both national and European funding schemes stated that the awarding of one set of funds, say European, could strengthen the bid for another such as SRB (Interviews, Park Royal, London, September 1996). Clearly, although national regeneration programmes may provide a source of match-funding for some elements of a European programme, there is not always perfect synergy between the timing of national and European funding regimes.

Apart from problems of coordination with national policies, there is evidence that there was some reduction in national regeneration programmes at the time that URBAN was launched. One report on the SRB presented the following facts and figures on urban policy in the 1990s:

> The peak of property-led regeneration schemes was in 1990/91 after which there was a change of policy focus and a greater role for local authorities, with more emphasis placed on community and social issues through initiatives like City Challenge. It is evident, however, that the expenditure allocated to the projects that make up SRB peaked during the first year of the City Challenge programme. The expenditure on programmes within SRB peaked in 1992/3 and then began to decline. Using the 1993/94 base figures: there is projected to be a 25.5 per cent real reduction of SRB funds by 1997/98 and a 22.7 per cent reduction of 'ring-fenced' monies. Moreover, spending reductions are not confined to SRB, but also apply to other regeneration programmes. This is important as it was the government's intention that SRB resources be complemented by other mainstream funding programmes, as was explicitly stated in the Bidding Guidance. It is estimated that between 1993/4 and 1997/8 £6 billion of public sector expenditure will be removed from programmes which assist the regeneration process. *This means that SRB will operate in a climate where both SRB and other urban regeneration programmes are being substantially reduced* (CURS, 1995, p.34, emphasis added).

While it is beyond the scope of this analysis to include all of the figures of the SRB to the present day, the main point to be drawn from the above discussion is the climate of pressures related to the reduction of funds for programmes. Local authorities, awarded URBAN funding, may have seen its immediate matching with SRB as a logical process. In terms of each £ sterling per ECU, additionality would be respected since the European funds would be matched by funds from a national programme. However as noted in chapter three while the European intervention, through URBAN, could complement existing schemes, the Commission would have its own aims and objectives in this policy area.

Section 4.2/3 below provides further details on the CED priority in ERDF programmes in the UK. We argue that the Commission aimed to incorporate the CED model into the implementation of URBAN programmes in the UK. URBAN represented a small-scale innovative programme, as part of the Commission's CIs. This represented an opportunity to develop a more focused approach to CED. Understanding the CED model can therefore explain the Commission's perspective in negotiations with both central and local government. The interesting point is that the 'bottom-up' approach featuring in the CED model was also advocated by national urban programmes such as SRB. Did this facilitate the negotiations between the Commission and central government regarding the structures for the delivery of URBAN in the UK? Before analysing this stage of the policy process, we should firstly examine the origins and objectives of the CED priority in ERDF programmes.

4.2/3 Community Economic Development in Urban Areas

The bureaucratic politics model presented in chapter two, section 2.2, can help explain the origins of CED in mainstream ERDF programmes. Away from the politicised higher level discussions, ordinary officials in DG XVI work on drafting and negotiating programmes to be delivered within the agreed budget allocated to each Member State. DG XVI's urban policy experiment can be related to the CED priority as it first appeared in mainstream programmes. There is a problem of defining 'community' as there is no single definition of the term. Given that we are dealing here with specific ERDF programmes, of which URBAN is an example, we should seek to understand the Commission's interpretation of the term.

In the case of the UK a preliminary starting point would be the mainstream programmes referring to the 'community'. The origins of the CED priority in mainstream Structural Funds can be found in the Single Programming Document (SPD) for Merseyside, UK. Here we see an example of how the Commission broadened the concept of partnership to include additional players in the UK, beyond those of elected regional and local government or other established agencies active in urban regeneration such as the TECs. Although the SPD was based on the definition of Merseyside as a region, classified as Objective 1, many of the measures were targeted at *urban* areas within the region. The measures of the programme included a 'better quality of life' covering targeted packages of environmental improvement, better community facilities, targeted access for health awareness linked to employment and initiatives related to crime. There was also a whole section of the programme on 'community involvement'. Here we find the origins of 'pathways to integration', the measure in the programme providing a package of economic and social support that was directed at key communities in Merseyside. The pathways initiative was described as follows:

> The success of the pathways to integration initiative is crucially dependent on involvement of local residents and businesses. Local residents and firms should be the key players in designing, setting up and monitoring the initiatives, *with assistance from local councils and other groups* (emphasis added).[17]

ERDF assistance was made available for initial public awareness and start-up costs. ERDF support was also available for a wide range of measures such as facilities to improve access of residents to education and training opportunities, costs of child-care to help people access jobs, community work schemes, and community enterprise development. Specific business support was available for the commercial Small and Medium Size Enterprises (SME) sector in the targeted communities. The ERDF aspect to programmes was complemented by European Social Fund (ESF) measures that were directed at areas such as school-college, school-industry and school-home-community links.

Clearly, the pathways to integration initiative emphasised the role of local residents and firms in promoting the regeneration of targeted areas. The sentence 'with assistance from local councils and other groups' from the SPD for Merseyside has been highlighted in order to indicate the types of delivery mechanism sought by the Commission (CEC, 1994d). It can be argued that the Commission was seeking a 'bottom-up', rather than 'top-down', approach in the implementation of ERDF programmes. While local councils and central government could be included in the partnership, the point is the balance of power between the local partners. Local councils should not seek to dominate the local partnership by adopting a 'top-down'

---

[17] European Commission, DG XVI (1994d) 'Single Programming Document, 1994-1999, No. ERDF: 94.09.13.00. No. ARINCO: 94.UK.16001, Merseyside Objective 1 Region'. It should be noted that there is some debate regarding the origins of 'pathways' since the term is also used in DG V programmes. However, a former official in DG XVI closely involved in the ERDF programmes during this period insisted that 'pathways' was very much the brainchild of DG XVI and presented the SPD of Merseyside, quoted above, as evidence of this (Interview, former DG XVI, official, July 1997).

approach towards the targeted recipients of ERDF programmes. In a later presentation on the subject, one DG XVI official expressed this in terms of 'provider led' and 'demand led' delivery mechanisms.

> *Provider led* integration of projects is driven by the need to manage different streams of funding, reduce unit costs. *Demand led* integration should lead to projects focused around needs of beneficiaries.[18]

Similar to Intergovernmental Relations Officers of the American experience, a number of local councils in the period following the 1988 reform developed specialist personnel to deal with the range of European funding and its coordination with existing programmes at national level. In the European case, council officials are often referred to as European Officers. In developing a strategy to manage national and European sources of funding, a local council may arguably opt for the 'provider led' approach. Indeed, the European Officers employed by local councils have the responsibility to attract European funds, and manage these with other schemes, in order to co-finance council policies.[19] The Commission is arguably making the case for a longer-term vision of regeneration. One DG XVI official explained this as follows:

> Generally capacity building has involved creating mechanisms to consult people or businesses on how the money is to be spent. The problem, is of course, that where the money runs out, the rationale for consultation disappears...It is much better where capacity building involves beneficiaries in the *delivery*, design and implementation of projects. In this way they can always look for money elsewhere and continue to pursue regeneration in other ways.[20]

The point made is that in the longer term, the strategy of involving beneficiaries may be more sustainable as they undertake part of the responsibility for the regeneration of their areas, which can continue beyond the life of the European programme. This may involve acquiring the skills to attract sources of finance in the UK from national regeneration schemes, the

---

[18] Extract from a speech, by official from DG XVI, Peter Berkowitz, 'The Challenges of the late 90s for Economic Development Agencies', Brussels, April 1997. This represented his interpretation of CED rather than an official opinion of the Commission.
[19] The precise job title of European Officers and their specific responsibilities vary between local authorities.
[20] Extract from a speech, by official from DG XVI, Peter Berkowitz, 'The Challenges of the late 90s for Economic Development Agencies', Brussels, April 1997.

private sector and the National Lottery funds. Once the process of regenerating the local economy has begun, there could be a gradual move away from dependence on national or European funding programmes.

The increasing interest of the Commission in the role of local residents, voluntary and community associations in delivering Structural Funds programmes can also be found in its sponsoring of studies and reports to conduct research in this area of local economic development. One study (CEC, 1996b) focusing on the CED priority in European Structural Funds programmes in Great Britain concentrated on the role of the local communities within mainstream programmes in Objective 1 and 2 areas. The 1996 'Lloyd Study' on CED in mainstream programmes was sponsored, in particular, by the UK Unit in DG XVI, Directorate D3.[21] This study may be seen as an example of the Commission seeking the advice of experts in developing new policy areas. While CED had first appeared in the everyday programmes of the Commission, drafted by officials, expert studies could provide the Commission with additional knowledge on how to implement this in practice.

The debate on CED was extended beyond its presence in UK programmes when it was highlighted in the Communication of the Commission 'Towards an urban agenda in the European Union' (CEC, 1997a). Although the CED model may be implemented in cities, the Communication emphasised the contribution this can make to *regional* economic development:

> CED seeks to involve local communities and businesses in the process of regeneration. An essential aspect of the priority concerns capacity building measures which attempt to strengthen individuals and local organisations to implement local development actions. Efforts are also done to create linkages between deprived communities. *It is important to note that CED allows to focus resources in accordance with the desires and needs of the communities themselves.* In attempting to reintroduce the most vulnerable groups into the

---

[21] CEC (1996b), *Social and economic inclusion through regional development. The Community economic development priority in European Structural Funds programmes in Great Britain.* The study is often referred to as the 'Lloyd Study' after Professor Peter Lloyd of Liverpool University who directed the research programme. Indeed, the personal involvement of the Desk Officers from DG XVI, Unit D.3 was acknowledged on page 3 of the report although it is also stated that the research findings are those of the Research Team and do not necessarily reflect the views of the Commission.

regular economy, CED can make a positive contribution to the wider aims of improving regional economic development.[22]

Another section of the above Communication presents the case for 'the need for creating trust based relationships between various actors at the local level in order to promote local empowerment, responsibility and initiative' (CEC, 1997a, p.15).

There is also evidence that CED had spread from Objective 1 programmes in Merseyside to Objective 2 programmes in other cities for the period 1997-1999. Indeed, CED features in the SPD covering Objective 2 areas in London. It is stated that in developing actions to promote an integrated approach, the measures would build on tried and tested models of urban renewal, 'including the approach under the EU funded URBAN Community Initiative'.[23] However, following the announcement of URBAN in the Commission's Official Journal in 1994, there was a delay of two years before implementation at local level. This was due to the lengthy negotiations between the Commission and central government regarding administrative arrangements for the delivery of URBAN. The point is that it was difficult for phase two of Objective 2 programmes to draw lessons from URBAN; by 1997 there had been little progress made at grass roots level. Consequently, URBAN and Objective 2 programmes, both with elements of the CED model, operated in close vicinity during the period 1997-1999. This presented potential problems of coordination although this will not be examined until chapter six.

Section 4.3 will examine how the Commission aimed to incorporate the CED model into the delivery of URBAN in the UK. Before examining the details of the negotiations for the implementation of URBAN, we conclude this section by examining the administrative arrangements for the administration of European programmes in the UK. The Government Offices dealing with SRB at sub-central level also had responsibilities relating to European funding. There were, however, some differences between procedures for national and European regeneration programmes. We examine how this presented potential problems of coordination for the delivery of URBAN in the UK.

---

[22] Extracts from the Commission Communication: 'Towards an urban agenda in the European Union' (CEC, 1997a, COM (97) 197 final, p.11 of Annex, emphasis added).

[23] Extracts from the 'Single Programming Document for Community structural assistance in the region of East London and the Lee Valley concerned by Objective 2 in the United Kingdom' (CEC, 1997f, ERDF: 97.09.13.001, ARINCO: 97.UK.16.001 Text of 7 May C (97) 1126).

4.2/4 Administrative Arrangements for European Programmes

The newly created Government Offices were granted responsibility for administering both the SRB and European programmes within each region. DG XVI also worked on a regional basis in devising its programmes, even in Member States that did not have a regional level of government. Indeed one senior Commission official believed this was a major factor prompting the UK government to reorganise its administration at a regional level as represented by the Government Offices (Interview, DG XVI official, Brussels, July 1997). At this level, the proposed delivery of URBAN appeared compatible with the administrative arrangements for the national programme. The selection of areas to receive URBAN was also closely modelled on existing procedures for SRB as outlined in section 4.2/2. There was, however, one major difference at the level of central ministries regarding the releasing of European funds. This was to have major implications for the subsequent delivery of URBAN in England.

For European funding each central government Department retained responsibility for its own budget and policy interests. There was no pooling of the funding received from the Commission to make URBAN funds the overall responsibility of one Department. This posed an immediate problem for URBAN which contained an ERDF and ESF element. Coordination at Commission level would be required between two Directorates, DG XVI and DG V. DG XVI was mainly responsible for URBAN but would consult DG V on the ESF element of this. Implementation at the level of central ministries in the UK would involve the DoE responsible for ERDF and the Department for Education and Employment (DfEE) responsible for ESF.[24] Hence the ERDF and ESF components of the URBAN programmes would be subject to the procedures of two different Departments at central government level. At deconcentrated, regional level the Government Offices would then have to coordinate with two separate Departments as well as with the partners on the ground.

From the outset, we can identify potential problems of coordination regarding the Commission's urban policy experiment in the UK. Clearly, the Government Offices were dependent on the procedures of the central Departments before being in a position to release the funds to the local

---

[24] Following the election of a Labour Government in 1997, a reorganisation took place which created the Department of the Environment, Transport and Regions (DETR) with responsibility for European Structural Funds (ERDF) in conjunction with the DfEE (responsible for ESF).

partnerships. Vertical coordination would be required between two central Departments, Government Offices at regional level, and the partners on the ground. Horizontal coordination would involve the two central ministries, two Directorates at the Commission, as well the partners at the local level. We are faced with the following paradox: the actual policy objectives of SRB and URBAN, the national and European regeneration programmes, appear compatible. SRB aimed to achieve a flexible regeneration programme involving local people and giving them control over spending priorities. The CED priority in Structural Funds aimed to involve local people in the design, and implementation, of policy. Yet the possible delays caused by the necessity to coordinate the procedures of two central Departments, for such a small-scale programme, posed a potential threat to the innovative, integrated approach which URBAN was seeking to promote.

Clearly, the UK government had recognised the need for a more flexible approach in regeneration initiatives and had adjusted its administrative structures to deliver this. Would there be any adjustment in order to facilitate local delivery of a *European* rather than national urban policy? So far, the analysis has referred to central government as a single entity. Yet in European policy, it would be difficult to view 'central government' as representing a unitary actor. Individual government ministries may be protective of their own policy interests with respect to European funds. In this case, individual Departments could act as 'extended gatekeeper' in the implementation of European policies. Following the model outlined in chapter two, individual Departments could be reluctant to release control of their own policy interests regarding European funds. This would have the following implications.

An innovative European programme, seeking to tackle urban problems, would be faced with the following obstacles: firstly, activities would have to fit within the eligibility criteria of ERDF and ESF programmes. For non-Objective 1 areas this narrowed the eligibility field even further. Secondly, the European funds would have to filter through complex administrative arrangements. Government Offices still faced the problem of coordinating the procedures of two separate Departments. In practice, this implied that even small-scale projects run by local organisations would have to comply with the administrative regulations of two separate Departments. Even if the merging of European funds from two Departments was not a possibility, how else could central government adjust in order to facilitate the delivery of URBAN? This was a major theme in the negotiations to agree the administrative arrangements for URBAN in the UK. This chapter concentrates only on stages one and two of the policy process as set out in section 4.1/2. Any changes in central government policy during the implementation of URBAN, at grass roots level, will be examined in chapter six.

4.3 Negotiations for the Delivery of URBAN in the United Kingdom

This section focuses on the main issues in negotiations for the selection of areas and administrative arrangements for URBAN. The negotiations provide a detailed case study of the tensions between supra-national and national policy-making even for small-scale CIs. The analysis seeks to explain the perspectives of both the Commission and the national administration. In principle, the Commission and Member State shared the same policy objectives in seeking to address the problems of deprived urban areas. How then can we account for the delay of two years before the implementation of URBAN could begin at local level?

There is evidence that local councils sought to influence negotiations for the delivery of URBAN. However the key actors in the early period of implementation were the representatives of DG XVI and central government. The term 'central government' can cover a wide range of actors at different levels; the analysis identifies the key actors representing central government at each stage. The empirical material on Commission/central government negotiations is organised around the adaptation of the 'extended gatekeeper' model set out in section 4.1/2. In the case of the UK, the issues relating to the institutional framework were particularly complex. Section 4.3/2 highlights the difficulties of reconciling the community-led features of the CED model with the administrative arrangements for European programmes in the UK. Firstly, we examine procedures for the selection of cities to receive URBAN.

4.3/1 Stage One: the Selection of Cities

The regulations for CIs in the 1994-1999 required the Commission to negotiate with the Member States regarding the allocation of URBAN. The similarity with Objective 2 allocation for this period is that the Commission could not include, on its list, any city which had not already been short-listed by the Member State. Since our detailed case study concentrates on London, the analysis here focuses on the selection of programmes for England.[25] In England, the initial selection process was similar to that for the SRB. This did not entail, at this stage, any major administrative adjustments for URBAN. Even so, from the launch of URBAN in July 1994, it was not until March 1995 that the final list was agreed. How did the selection take place and which issues arose?

For England, each individual local authority aspiring for URBAN funds directed applications to the relevant Government Office for the region concerned. Individual local authorities in London presented bids to the Government Office for London (GOL) for a slice of URBAN funding. Some London boroughs presented joint bids – indeed such was the case for the ones ultimately chosen from London. The Park Royal area included parts of three local authorities: the London Boroughs of Brent, City of Westminster and Hammersmith and Fulham. The Heart of the East End bid involved the London Boroughs of Hackney and Tower Hamlets. Numerous local authority officers complained about the short notice given to prepare their case. In the case of London, local authorities were asked by GOL to present a bid within one week of the announcement of URBAN in the Official Journal. Certain local authority officers presented the cynical view that such tactics on the part of central government were a way of limiting applications and eliminating weak, unprepared local authorities from making bids.[26]

One response from central government was that it was the Commission that was putting pressure on central government to forward their proposals since DG XVI was keen to begin implementation of the programme as soon as possible (Interview, senior DETR official, January 1999). Although the time scale was limited, GOL worked with the Association of London Government (ALG) to disseminate the information. In London, with 33 separate local authorities, there was already intense competition between boroughs responding to the call for proposals for URBAN. GOL had the initial filtering task of forwarding a short-list to the DoE. Unlike SRB, all applications for URBAN were local authority led either by a City Council

---

[25] Selection of cities for Scotland and Wales was coordinated at the time by the Welsh Office and Scottish Office respectively. Northern Ireland is not included in the analysis since the negotiations there were dealt with by a different geographical unit of the Commission (DG XVI, C.2 at the time, dealing with Ireland and Northern Ireland). The administrative arrangements finally agreed for the implementation of URBAN, as listed in Appendix one, chapter four applied to all programmes in the UK.

[26] These comments are based on interviews conducted as part of an unpublished Masters thesis (Tofarides, 1994). During September 1996, additional interviews were conducted for the purposes of this study. Interviews involved local authority officers from London boroughs awarded URBAN as well as those awarded Objective 2 funds.

or, in the case of London, by the individual boroughs. One official described the process as follows:

> We received quite a lot of them, a file a good couple of inches thick of expressions of interest in the original bid. Internally, there was then a discussion with a variety of colleagues, different people involved in regeneration in different areas, involved in all sorts of things. These were whittled down to at least four projects which we actually put forward to DoE, out of which two were chosen. In England, there was always going to be one programme in Merseyside because it has Objective 1 status, but the rest is up for grabs (Interview, GOL official, September 1996).

Following the forwarding of bids by Government Offices to Whitehall, the DoE decided on a list submitted to the Commission in November 1994. It is interesting to note that the timing also coincided with stage four of the first SRB process: the final presentation of bids made to the EDR cabinet sub-committee. The reports on SRB presented in section 4.1 suggest that there was some consideration taken of European programmes for the SRB allocation. The local authorities in East London had already been awarded SRB funds in the first round in 1994.[27] The UK authorities presented their initial short-list to the Commission. This included the two short-listed from London: the Heart of the East End, involving the London Boroughs of Hackney and Tower Hamlets, and the Park Royal bid involving the London Boroughs of Brent, Hammersmith and Fulham and Westminster City Council. Many of the local authorities involved believed their bid had been successful following the information from Government Offices that they had been pre-selected for URBAN, by the UK government, when the initial list was forwarded to the Commission in November 1994. In fact, there were a number of other hurdles to pass and for this we turn to the perspective of the Commission.

In view of the relatively small sums of the Structural Funds budget allocated to URBAN, the Commission presented the case to Member States for limiting their choice of cities. The Commission's aim was to monitor the innovative effects and impact of its 'experiment'. The Commission was therefore anxious, in its negotiations with the representatives of Member States concerned, to highlight that any over-allocation concerning the

---

[27] The Heart of the East End received SRB funding before URBAN. Other local authorities such as the London Borough of Hammersmith and Fulham received SRB funding after being allocated URBAN. All the URBAN programmes in London received some SRB funding in the lifetime of URBAN and this was a valuable source of match-funding.

number of cities included would risk diluting any impact of the limited resources. Correspondence regarding overall allocations of URBAN to the UK and the number of cities which could receive a programme was between senior civil servants, Permanent Secretary level, and the highest level of DG XVI, that is the Director-General who liaised with the various units concerned within DG XVI.

Although the sums involved were relatively small, allocation of URBAN reached high political salience in the UK. Correspondence was directed by numerous cities stating the case for their city to be awarded URBAN funding. Members of the European Parliament (MEPs) also wrote letters and asked parliamentary questions related to URBAN, its allocation and state of play regarding negotiations.[28] As noted in the earlier section regarding the regulations on CIs, the Commission alone was in no position to decide on any particular city. There was nothing to prevent dialogue and correspondence between the Commission and the local authorities or their representatives in the European Parliament. It would be difficult to argue, however, that the Commission's interaction with the European Parliament or sub-national authorities had any significant impact on the allocation of URBAN.

The major feature of 'high-level' discussions between senior levels in the Commission and high-ranking civil servants in the UK, or even ministers themselves, was one of reduction of bids rather than selection of cities. The Commission does not appear to have contested the choice of cities, leaving this very much to Member States. How was the final choice within the UK made? Again URBAN followed a similar process to the SRB. Ministers made the final selection following presentations from short-listed candidates. For URBAN it was representatives from the local partnership, who made the case to ministers, not the Director of the Government Office concerned as had been the case for SRB. Yet there is evidence that Regional Directors also played an informal role in supporting the case for cities within their individual regions. For URBAN, as for SRB, the Regional Offices provided

---

[28] Questions were either presented by MEPs with a constituency interest in URBAN during this period such as Evans, a London MEP, or else by those participating in regional policy Committees in the European Parliament such as McCarthy. The questions demanded transparency in how decisions were reached but the Commission was unable to give anything other than standard replies since it was a matter for the central UK authorities at the DoE who decided behind closed doors. The lack of transparency does not, however, appear to be an exclusive feature of the UK case (internal correspondence from documents within DG XVI documentation).

additional support vis à vis relations with ministers and the central ministries. One civil servant explained the process as follows:

> One of the things ministers would have been considering at the time is geographical spread, but it is by no means the only one. We in GOL were there to fight London's corner and we were there to try and get as much as we could for London but, in terms of fair decision-making, the geographical spread of things was only one of a number of different issues. I know, for example, our Regional Director spoke to ministers and I am sure that Regional Directors from other regions did the same. They all do their own bit of lobbying and they are there to support the candidates from our side, because by that stage we had looked at them and had said these are projects/programmes that we think we would want to support and would be done well (Interview, GOL official, September 1996).

Following the individual presentations, the 'winners' were announced by the DoE in the manner of a 'beauty contest' where there is no specific explanation regarding why one candidate was chosen in preference to another. The following cities were granted URBAN funding: in England two areas of London were chosen, Park Royal (not a designated Objective 1 or 2 area) and the Heart of the East End (the London Boroughs of Hackney and Tower Hamlets, parts of which had Objective 2 status). URBAN was also granted to areas in Liverpool, as part of Merseyside, which benefited from Objective 1 status. The remaining programmes were allocated to targeted areas in the following cities which already had Objective 2 status: Manchester, Birmingham, Nottingham, Sheffield. Scotland was awarded two programmes, Glasgow and Paisley, both Objective 2 areas. Wales was awarded one programme, Swansea. The programmes for Scotland and Wales were chosen through the Scottish and Welsh offices respectively.

The question still remains: to what extent was the selection of URBAN based on objective criteria? The necessity to choose among a number of applications did involve a political decision. One view from a central government official involved is that the presentations to ministers were a means of allowing decisions to be made at a political level. The process allowed representatives from the local partnerships to present their case directly to ministers who are accountable to Parliament. Yet there were no official explanations given by central government to the Government Offices, or local authorities, regarding why one city was chosen over another from the initial short-list. Interviews with central government officials (DETR, January 1999) suggest that, in addition to the presentation to ministers, civil servants assessed the cases on technical merit based on the local strategy presented and the ability to deliver this. This did not prevent speculation among local authorities that party politics played a role in some cases. Regarding the Park Royal bid for London, this included the City of Westminster one of the few remaining Conservative councils at the time.[29]

The URBAN Reserve fund was announced by the Commission in 1996 (CEC, 1996a) which allowed some new programmes to be chosen from within the UK. The DoE decided that there was no need to call for new proposals for the URBAN Reserve since they already had a pool of applicants from the original round. For the case of London, this meant that the DoE still had two applications from the original four short-listed by GOL. However no new programmes were awarded to London for this second round. Clearly, for this first stage of the policy process, URBAN did not represent a challenge to the existing administrative arrangements in place for the national regeneration programme. The selection process was modelled on the procedures in place for SRB. Although, as in the allocation of SRB, there were 'winners' and 'losers' in the bidding, there were no major problems other than having to finally select among candidates who may have all been judged as presenting a good case. So far, it was 'business as usual' for central government. Negotiations to agree the details for the administration of URBAN proved to be more problematic. A number of issues arose as outlined below.

4.3/2 Stage Two: Negotiations for Administrative Arrangements

The main actors at this stage were the Commission and the European Regeneration Policy Division of the DoE. The administration of programmes already chosen is arguably less openly political than the initial decisions regarding which cities would be allocated URBAN. The key actors involved in the Commission would be the units dealing with Member State programmes rather than the Director-General who would be more involved in higher-level correspondence with ministers or the more senior civil servants at Permanent Secretary level. The civil servants dealing with regional policy at the UK Permanent Representation in Brussels were also involved in liaising between the relevant central government ministries and the UK unit within DG XVI.

---

[29] Interviews with representatives of local authorities in the period September 1996 to September 1997 suggest that some considered that this factor a reason contributing to the success of the Park Royal bid. It should be noted though that although the City of Westminster had a Conservative majority, the URBAN funds were awarded to one of the few Labour wards within the council.

Once the selection of cities had been finalised, no individual programmes could be negotiated unless financial allocations were agreed. This was an area where the Commission could, as distributor of funds, question the UK authorities' allocation of these to individual programmes. However, even though CIs represented only 9 per cent of the Structural Funds budget, central government in the UK could still veto Commission proposals regarding the financial allocation of programmes within the Member State. The matter was resolved in negotiations between the central authorities at the DoE and the Commission, DG XVI. Local authorities were not involved in the process regarding financial allocation and were prevented from implementing any programmes until this was agreed. Following some compromises, the question of financial allocations was settled by October 1995. Hence from the final agreement of lists in March 1995, another seven months delay occurred concerning the settlement of financial allocations to individual areas. The following table presents details of the sums involved for cities in England selected in the first allocation of URBAN.[30]

Table 4.1 Financial Allocation of URBAN in the United Kingdom

CITY	ECU (MILLION) ALLOCATION		
	ERDF+ESF	ERDF	ESF
Birmingham	8.036.000	6.429.000	1.607.000
London-East End	8.036.000	6.429.000	1.607.000
London-Park Royal	7.653.000	6.122.000	1.531.000
Manchester	8.036.000	5.842.000	2.194.000
Nottingham	6.786.000	5.563.000	1.223.000
Sheffield	6.786.000	5.089.000	1.697.000

Source: Adapted from internal document, DG XVI, URBAN, Summary Sheets of Operational Programmes adopted before 31/12/96.

The discussions over financial allocations were minor compared to the long drawn out negotiations over the details of institutional arrangements; these were not finally agreed until July 1996. Officials at the Commission in DG XVI, and those representing central government at the DoE, took time to

---

[30] Clearly there were relatively minor differences in the sums allocated to each city with the exception of Merseyside, allocated approximately ECU million 17.296.000 (ERDF + ESF total); this was the only area in England designated under Objective 1 during this period.

agree the precise wording of the terms of reference to deliver URBAN within the UK. Once a text was agreed, this was inserted as a template within each Programme Document for the geographical areas concerned. The final text therefore set the framework for implementation which would then be interpreted, and put into practice, by each of the local partnerships involved.[31]

A number of issues arose in the Commission/Member State negotiations; in order to understand these we must understand the broad themes in the debate over technical points. One major point of discussion centred on interpretations of the principle of partnership. It is argued here that the Commission was seeking ways of developing partnerships that would facilitate the participation of a broader range of actors, including representatives from grass roots level. Partnership and participation already existed in the SRB programmes. However some DG XVI officials expressed concerns regarding SRB partnerships following criticisms that some of these existed on paper, but did not involve true participation by residents and community representatives on the ground (Interview former DG XVI official, July 1997, confirmed by DG XVI internal discussion papers). Indeed, this view is supported by reports on partnership for the first round of SRB as presented below.[32]

Local authorities were identified as the prominent leaders of regeneration partnerships since bids led by local authorities were awarded 60 per cent of the total SRB funds and a further 15 per cent of funds were awarded to joint bids presented by local authority/TEC partnerships. On a more general level, local authorities were represented in 86 per cent of all bids, the private sector in 83 per cent and the TECs in 76 per cent.[33] The poor representation of the voluntary sector was attributed to poor appreciation by voluntary bodies and local authorities as to how the former could play an effective role. Secondly, the report argued that local government and Government Offices had tended to give low priority to voluntary sector participation. An additional disadvantage was the lack of history of partnership between the voluntary and community sectors and the business community. It appears that the potential of the voluntary and community sectors was not being exploited by the local authorities or the private sector:

---

[31] The full text finally agreed for the implementation of URBAN is in Appendix one, chapter four. Reference to this can help clarify points made in this section.

[32] Information and figures quoted in this section are taken from the CURS (1995) report.

[33] TECs represented one of the new bodies of 'informal local government' (King, 1993) identified earlier in this chapter.

Despite the problems which the voluntary sector have had in securing involvement in the SRB process, it is evident from the analysis of both mega-bids and those bids which have been funded in areas which have not previously been eligible for Urban Programme that there is potential for SRB to develop the capacity of the voluntary and community sector. However, it is necessary for the process to be reformed if a serious attempt is to be made as a national policy objective to involve community groups...Much needs to be done to more fully engage the community and voluntary sectors in the SRB process. They are a major resource which is not being capitalised upon. The private sector bids exhibited diversity, but were characterised by two factors: firstly, a bias toward physical and economic development; and secondly they were based largely on pre-existing partnerships and strategies. There was a low level of voluntary sector participation in the private sector led bids (CURS, 1995).[34]

Returning to the European policy could the Commission, a supra-national institution, achieve any greater success than national regeneration programmes in engaging local communities? It is argued here that the principle of partnership, and how best this could be translated to deliver CED, was a major influence on the Commission's position in negotiations related to URBAN.[35] DG XVI was particularly keen to establish an institutional framework which could nurture such participation of the targeted recipients of programmes. Indeed, the Commission was seeking to go beyond established groups and involve grass roots organisations and ordinary citizens who had never participated before. This was an ambitious task since even the established groups were experiencing problems regarding participation in national programmes such as SRB. What of the perspective of central government in the UK?

In principle, central government was not hostile to the idea of local participation in designing and delivering programmes. Clearly, this had been a feature of recent initiatives at a national level, namely City Challenge and SRB (Interview, senior DETR official, January 1999). Yet the reports on national programmes suggest that, although encouraged, the participation of the community and voluntary sectors was not prioritised as such (CURS, 1995, p.107). DG XVI's proposals for new institutional structures were

---

[34] Extracts taken from the CURS report (1995, p.98, p.107).

[35] The Commission and central government perspectives in negotiations for the administrative arrangements for URBAN are based on my own interpretation of internal documents provided by DG XVI for the purposes of this study. This material was supplemented by interviews of Commission and central government officials involved in negotiations at the time.

seeking to make the bottom-up approach a *prerequisite* for the delivery of URBAN in the UK. The Commission's emphasis on local participation did not contradict the broad policy objectives of the national SRB programmes. There was a problem, however, in finding ways of reconciling the Commission's request with the existing administrative structures to deliver European funds (Interview, senior DETR official, January 1999). The streamlining of procedures at central government level, to facilitate such local delivery, challenged the existing systems whereby ERDF and ESF funds were the responsibility of separate Departments. Other issues emerged relating to differing interpretations of the principle of subsidiarity introduced in the Treaty on European Union.

The concept of federal 'purse strings', as explored in chapter one, can help us understand the Commission's bargaining position with respect to Member States. URBAN, like other European programmes, is partly financed by European Structural Funds. On the one hand the Commission as the supra-national institution can, like the federal level in America, attach conditions to its granting of aid. On the other hand, the central and local governments can argue that they would be the level best equipped to know how to deliver the policy. In this case, the Commission could risk being accused of being over-prescriptive in its demands emanating from Brussels, far away from the realities of the problems experienced in the targeted neighbourhoods. Moreover, the Commission depends on the national bureaucracies to implement the policies. The debate regarding which level of government is most appropriate to tackle urban problems is one which features at all stages of the policy process, from the launching of policies to their subsequent implementation.

Negotiations between the Commission and central government were complex and lengthy. With separate Departments at central government level dealing with European funds, a number of issues arose relating to central government representation on Monitoring Committees and financial accountability, We investigate this below using the metaphor of central government acting as 'extended gatekeeper' between the policy conceived in Brussels and its subsequent delivery within the Member State.

One major issue which arose was that of the chairing of Monitoring Committees for the URBAN programmes. DG XVI's proposals appeared to challenge the existing arrangements for the management of CIs in the UK. Initially, the DoE presented the idea of a central Monitoring Committee composed of Regional Directors, from Government Offices concerned, as well as civil servants from central departments. DoE officials believed that Commission wanted a central Monitoring Committee particularly since the

CI LEADER had been agreed just before the negotiations for URBAN and was to be managed in this way (Interview, senior civil servant DETR, January 1999). Why did the Commission seek alternative arrangements for URBAN?

In order to answer this, we should look at administrative structures within DG XVI for administering mainstream programmes. Structural Fund programmes in Objective 2 areas were managed by regional Monitoring Committees with representatives from central government, the Commission and local partners.[36] A regional Monitoring Committee would make the management of URBAN compatible with procedures for other programmes. Furthermore, DG XVI officials perceived that a more decentralised management would respond to the needs of this programme which essentially targeted local areas within a region. The bargaining between Commission officials and the UK authorities was intense. One view in the Commission was that if 'forced' to have a national Monitoring Committee for all of the UK programmes, they should at least seek to influence the composition of this and ensure that key partners, not just civil servants, were represented on the Monitoring Committee (Interview, former DG XVI official, July 1997). The Commission clearly aimed to ensure that representatives of the local partners would play an active part in the management of the programme.

Following negotiations, the UK authorities did indeed eventually accept a regional, rather than a national, Management Committee basing this on structures already in place for mainstream programmes. An URBAN Management Committee (UMC) would be established for each programme and this would be a sub-committee of the regional Objective 1 or 2 Programme Monitoring Committee (PMC). The Commission also secured agreement on its proposed membership of the Management Committees since this included a wide range of partners, as presented in full in Appendix one, chapter four. Representatives of the targeted groups themselves, such as the local community and the voluntary sector, would have a place on the UMC.[37] The geographical basis and administration was settled, but the

---

[36] It was only for the 1997-1999 SPDs, following the election of a Labour government that central government allowed elected councillors and representatives from Trade Unions to sit on Monitoring Committees for European regional programmes.

[37] There were no changes, however, related to the issue of elected councillors or representatives from Trade Unions who, as in the mainstream programmes, could not sit on Management Committees during the period of negotiations for URBAN.

chairing of these UMCs was another point where the Commission's proposals differed from those of the central government.[38]

Negotiations on administrative arrangements were strictly between the DoE and the Commission yet local councils, involved in URBAN, managed to acquire information regarding the proposed central government chairing of Monitoring Committees. Local authorities, and their representatives in the European Parliament, turned to the Commission for support in this matter arguing that this represented an intrusion into the governance of the city. In this case, subsidiarity could be interpreted in the following terms: any programme impacting on a specific city should be managed at the level of the city concerned. Although sympathetic to such views, the Commission was unable to achieve any major changes regarding established procedures for the chairing of Monitoring Committees.

The DoE stated that since other CIs were chaired by central government representatives, this point was non-negotiable. On the one hand, the position of the UK authorities, regarding Monitoring Committees, may be interpreted as excessive centralisation. On the other hand, we should take into consideration the context of the negotiations which took place within a period of Conservative power, with a history since 1979 of opposition to any devolution of power to elected regional or local levels. As far as the UK authorities were concerned, one official summarised their point of view as follows: 'Any subsidiarity below the Member State is a matter for us' (Interview, senior civil servant, DETR, January 1999).[39]

It was finally agreed that the UMCs would be chaired by the relevant nominee of the Government Office concerned. The Government Office would be responsible for the drafting of minutes and the forwarding of all relevant correspondence to the partners. Since the SRB was also administered at a regional level, this was compatible with existing procedures for the national regeneration programmes. However, the European team at the Government Office is separate to that administering the SRB. It was the responsibility of the local partners, not the Government Office, to coordinate any match-funding received from SRB relating to the local delivery of URBAN.

From the establishment of UMCs at regional, rather than central level, we now turn to the local management of the URBAN programmes. The

---

[38] All references to final agreement refer to the text on URBAN administrative arrangements as presented in full in Appendix one, chapter four.

[39] The official concerned did not feel that there had been any major change in interpretation of the principle of subsidiarity since the 1997 change to a Labour government with devolution on the agenda.

Commission proposed a new institutional framework, not evident in mainstream programmes, the idea of an Urban Partnership Group (UPG) below the level of the UMC, in order to deliver an 'Urban Action Plan' (UAP) within the targeted area. Selection of an individual project for financing under URBAN would involve the Commission part funding a project and the local partners the other part. Such a process would not be unusual and had long existed in mainstream programmes. The idea of having a UAP implies a more strategic approach to tackling the needs of the targeted area since packages of projects would be presented to complement each other.

With reference to national regeneration programmes 'action plans', specifying a 'vision' for the area with targets involving the local community as partners, were a feature of both City Challenge and SRB.[40] The UAP was seeking a strategic approach to the use of European Structural Funds. An example may be a local business venture that would present employment opportunities, and a parallel ESF project providing training, so that local people would have the skills to access the jobs. A package of such projects complementing each other would involve the use of ERDF and ESF funds; these in turn would have to be match-funded by national programmes such as SRB or other sources for example National Lottery funds. Yet the UAP would be the end product of a process involving the targeted groups to prepare and deliver such a plan. The motor behind the perceived UAP was to be the UPG. This may be interpreted as the Commission seeking to ensure that the European intervention would promote processes leading to community-led and integrated regeneration strategies. Arguably, this would protect the European funds being used as extra funding for a set of pre-existing projects presented by more established partners such as local authorities. This could therefore be a way of ensuring added value from the European intervention, beyond the 50 per cent requirement as stated in the regulations for match-funding.

The UPG would be composed of representatives of the local community, taken from residents within the targeted area, the voluntary sector, the local business community, local educational agencies and training bodies. Finally, the UPG would be chaired by one of the local partners and no representatives of the central government authorities would be on this group. Unlike the UMC, elected councillors from the targeted wards could have a

---

[40] See Bailey et al. (1995, p.64). For more specific information on the involvement of the local community in the SRB Challenge fund, see the Community Development Foundation guidelines (CDF, 1997).

place on the UPG; it would have responsibility for building the capacity of the local community to become involved in the regeneration process. Following this, the UPG would present the UAP to the UMC for approval. So far, there was nothing controversial about the Commission's plans to set up this administrative group, at grass roots level, in order to promote the types of processes identified in its CED priority.

The UK authorities did not object, in principle, to the establishment of a locally based institution to manage the programme. The real issue which arose was that of financial responsibility for the funds. Here was the 'bombshell' whereby the Commission, in the context of the urban policy experiment, presented the proposal that the UPG be established as a legal entity to manage URBAN funds. The Commission may have viewed this as an exercise in experimenting with local empowerment. Local ownership of the programme could promote the 'local empowerment, responsibility and initiative' mentioned in the Communication of the Commission published at a later date (CEC, 1997a).[41] Yet how could this fit with the existing arrangements for implementing European Funds in the UK? How would the question of financial accountability for the funds be tackled? There was no mechanism in place for the Commission to award the URBAN funds directly to the UPG. Procedures would have to filter through the Member State machinery. Were the administrative structures of the Member State equipped to deliver an innovative programme, conceived at supra-national level, but destined for locally based delivery?

Clearly, some aspects of the programme presented a challenge to the existing arrangements to manage European funds. A long process of exchange of texts regarding the template for the administrative structures for delivery of programmes took place between the Commission and central government. Furthermore around March 1996, a late stage of the negotiations, it seemed as though the UK government would withdraw previous hard won concessions regarding, for example, a regional rather than a central Monitoring Committee for URBAN. Although the discussions were very technical, we can attempt to interpret some of the broader issues around the text. Some of the points related to the role of the UMC. Normally, this was to be a sub-committee of the higher level PMC that was in place to manage the mainstream Objective 2 programmes. The DoE

---

[41] CEC (1997a) COM (97) 197 final, 'Towards an urban agenda in the European Union', p.15. The negotiations for URBAN took place between 1994 and 1996, they therefore predated this Communication which officially stated the position of the Commission on CED.

agreed that the UMC could endorse UAPs rather than recommend them for agreement to the PMC. Presumably, this would avoid possible delays caused by the UMC having to coordinate its meetings with the higher level PMC which was in place for mainstream funding rather than the smaller CIs.

Other issues raised in negotiations of 1995-1996 were regarding the role of the URBAN Programme Secretariat at Government Office level. The UK authorities proposed that the Government Office Secretariat had responsibility for appraising UAPs while the Commission proposed that the Secretariat would appraise the *eligibility* of the plans. The difference between the two is not immediately apparent. Arguably the Commission was seeking to ensure that the role of the central government, as implementing authority, would be to monitor eligibility rather than direct the UAP towards central government objectives. Yet any match-funding would come from the local partnerships, not the central government Departments; in this respect the UAP would have to be locally driven anyway.

By June 1996, the programme was still 'blocked' at the level of central government and Commission negotiations. The funding period for URBAN was from 1994-1999, all funds would need to be committed by December 1999. It appeared no longer permissible to allow further delays and a compromise had to be reached. The intervention of senior managers from the DoE permitted a final agreement. The DoE agreed, for example, that Government Office Secretariats would only be responsible for appraising the eligibility of projects which could, at the discretion of UPGs, be presented in packages. This may not have been immediately apparent to the local partners since this was not included in the final text of URBAN administrative arrangements inserted in each Programme Document (Appendix one, chapter four). Furthermore there was no clarification, at this stage, regarding how, or when, the UPG would actually access the funds to release to the groups running projects at grass roots level.

In theory, once a UAP was approved, the money to finance individual projects within this could be released from the central Departments to Government Offices. The latter would then forward the funds to the UPG, once it had been formed as a legal entity, or to a lead agency acting on its behalf (Appendix one, chapter four). It was not clear in the text agreed how the problem relating to the involvement of two separate Departments, at central government level, would be overcome. An offer letter would be required from each separate Department – the DoE and DfEE for the ERDF and ESF elements of the UAP; this would then be coordinated by the Government Offices. Given that each Department has their own procedures for European funds, the Commission expressed concerns in 1996 that this would build additional delays into the process. Yet there was no clarification even after the lengthy negotiations, relating to the administrative text, were finally agreed. In the compromise of July 1996, the DoE agreed to explore ways of ensuring the fastest possible payment of grant claims by looking at ways to streamline the process. The matter was left open when the Commission moved to the next stage of implementation, finalising the contents of the Programme Documents with the local authorities and the relevant Government Offices.

4.3/3 Innovative Delivery Mechanisms or the Seeds of Confusion?

There had been two years of painful Commission/central government negotiations in order to select cities and perfect the financial and administrative procedures for URBAN. Yet a number of points regarding implementation had not been clarified. This may have planted the seeds of confusion leading to problems at later stages of the policy process. It was not until November 1996 that central government produced an Efficiency Scrutiny Report on Information Flows between Central and Local Government. The Report, entitled 'Lifting the Burden', was published on 14 November 1996 after consultation with a number of individual local authorities and other interested parties. This highlighted some of the issues debated around URBAN involving the grouping of projects into 'action plans or packages':

> In short, the Review indicated that the current system was not delivering an efficient and effective service to its customers. Moreover, the project by project process did not promote a strategic approach towards the delivery of Single Programme priorities and measures, nor did it encourage integration between the ERDF and ESF alongside domestic regeneration programmes. The Efficiency Scrutiny Report made a number of specific recommendations on how the Structural Fund processes could be improved. It proposed grouping projects into action plans or packages and suggested that as far as practicable, appraisal, monitoring, claims and payments should relate to packages or action plans rather than individual projects.[42]

Following this, DETR issued draft guidance notes and organised seminars for Government Offices on Action Plans (Interview, DETR

---

[42] *European Information Service*, Issue 177, February 1997, 'Streamlining the Structural Funds-Government Reviews Administration in England' by Jeff Jacobs, Head of Regeneration Division at the DoE.

official, January 1999). However, the final version of guidance on Action Plans was not produced until June 1997; a second version followed in September 1997. In anticipation of the definitive version of Action Plan Guidance, Government Offices could not give clear advice to the local partners. Chapter six will examine how this early confusion caused tensions in relations between Government Offices, the Commission and local partners. Furthermore, the published guidelines did not directly tackle the problem related to the involvement of two separate Departments for such a small-scale programme. The only provisions made were that procedures could be streamlined up to a certain delegated limit as stated below:

- For the majority of ERDF projects grant amounts of up to £100 000 grant (revenue) and £250 000 grant (capital) can be appraised and approved by the local Partnership provided that:
- the project contributes to the objectives of the Action Plan and comes under one or more of the measures identified in the SPD;
- the project is appraised following the requirements set out and by the responsible body and
- the project is neither novel nor contentious (if in doubt please contact the Programme Secretariat).
- The same provisions apply to ESF except that for ESF the Partnership can appraise and approve all ESF applications up to the amount approved for ESF in the Action Plan for each Measure.[43]

The Action Plan guidance was mainly geared for the larger scale Objective 2 programmes. It was believed, at the time, that mainstream programmes would go down the Action Planning route and the regulations produced were designed for the larger programmes. However, changes in national government coincided with negotiations to agree SPDs for mainstream programmes.[44] Under the newly elected Labour government in 1997, additional negotiations took place between central government and the Commission. Following these, it was decided that the Action Planning route would be optional. Most regions chose to retain the existing procedures based on approval of individual projects within a programme. This was not

---

[43] Adapted from the following documentation: 'EC Structural Fund programmes in England: Action Plans for European Regional Development Fund and European Social Fund, Guidance Note No. 2' produced in September 1997 (DETR, 1997b, p.30). Guidance Note 1 (DETR, 1997a) was produced in June 1997.

[44] As noted in chapter three, section 3.2/1, the implementation of mainstream Objective 1 and 2 programmes for the period 1994-1999 involved two separate SPDs, the first covering 1994-1996 and the second 1997-1999.

an option for the CI URBAN as the administrative arrangements, finally agreed in 1996, stated that the programme would be delivered through Action Plans (Interview, DETR official, April 1999).[45] DETR circulated an internal note to Government Offices highlighting the main differences between Action Plans for mainstream programmes and URBAN (Interview, DETR official, January 1999). However, there was no specific Action Plan Guidance produced for URBAN. Local partners therefore had to rely on advice from Government Offices and guidelines which been prepared for mainstream programmes rather than URBAN.

In theory, URBAN was a bottom-up, innovative programme. Yet clearly, the language of the administrative documents, and guidance to implement it, were not very 'user friendly'. The innovative nature of URBAN was beginning to be lost in the technicalities involved in delivering a programme, emanating from the supra-national level, but aiming to promote action at neighbourhood level. Furthermore, there was still some confusion regarding the establishment of the UPG as a legal entity to receive URBAN funds. This will be explored in chapter six where we will see variations between areas awarded URBAN in London.

4.4 Conclusions

The review of national urban policy highlighted a number of similarities between regeneration programmes in the UK and the approach sought by URBAN. Both SRB and URBAN aimed to promote partnership and an integrated, innovative approach to tackling the problems of urban neighbourhoods. Taking the approach of Scharpf (1994), the European intervention could enhance the authority of the Member State; indeed, the Member States could exploit the European policy to devise their own policies. Both the Member States and sub-national units could be involved in delivering the European policy in the framework of partnership, as specified in the regulations for the implementation of Structural Funds. However, the empirical material of the early stages suggests that 'extended gatekeeping' by central government made a smooth integration of the European and national level policies problematic. Examples of central government acting as 'extended gatekeeper' are summarised below.

---

[45] Please refer to the administrative arrangements for the delivery of URBAN in Appendix one, chapter four. As noted in chapter three only one Programme Document was agreed for CIs of the 1994-1999 period.

Firstly there were complications related to the Commission's dependence on the national administrations to select the cities. Unlike Urban Pilot Projects (UPPs) central government was involved in the selection of cities to receive CIs in the same way as for mainstream programmes under the Objectives. This caused difficulties within the Member State since the selection of cities reached high political salience. There was tension, in the early stages, between the supra-national approach and Member State priorities. The Commission aimed to limit the number of cities in order to monitor the impact of its intervention. The UK, and other Member State governments, faced political pressure from representatives of their cities and sought to allocate as many programmes as possible, even if the resources were spread thinly between areas. Commission/Member State negotiations over limiting the choice of cities and agreeing financial allocations caused the initial delays.

Central government controlled the allocation of URBAN in the UK and also maintained a monopoly on negotiating the administrative structures to deliver URBAN. There were examples of the local authorities seeking to influence certain points of the policy process but it would be difficult to argue that this had any significant impact on negotiations. The Commission, as grantor of funds, could negotiate concessions regarding, for example, regional rather than central Monitoring Committees but not prescribe the precise framework for the implementation of the programme. Certain issues, such as the chairing of Monitoring Committees, were simply non-negotiable. URBAN also had to fit the national administrative framework for implementing European funds.

Paradoxically, while the Commission's attempts were in accordance with the broad policy aims of SRB, DG XVI's aim to produce a fertile environment for CED fell on barren soil. Although there had been some adjustment at central government level for a more flexible approach in the national SRB programme, this was not achieved for URBAN. Here we see an example of 'extended gatekeeping' by individual government Departments seeking to control implementation of European funds. Each Department jealously guarded its own budget and responsibilities for the European funds. Beyond the drafting of guidelines for Action Plans, central government Departments showed little flexibility in adapting procedures to meet the needs of a small-scale European programme. The involvement of two separate Departments as well as Government Offices resulted in a complex administrative system where the lines of authority and processes were unclear. The marble cake scenario was evident even in the early period of the implementation of URBAN.

The next stages of policy implementation are explored in chapter six. It is at this level that we begin to investigate whether the Commission was more successful, than national regeneration programmes, in engaging a wider range of partners to deliver its programmes. The network of actors at subsequent stages broadened; central Departments remained involved through interacting with the Government Regional Offices. The local authorities, involved in preparing the bids for URBAN, were only one element of the local partnership in place to deliver the programme. In theory, the programme was to be managed by the UPG not the local authority. How could this be reconciled with the civic entrepreneurship encouraging the local authorities to develop their strategy to receive the European funds?

On the one hand, local councils had to show leadership and an entrepreneurial approach to beat competition from other cities for national and European funding programmes. On the other hand, the Commission appeared to be asking the local councils to devolve responsibility, and possible financial control of the programme, to the institution of UPGs which had not even been formed yet. Is there evidence of 'gatekeeping' by local councils seeking to control the policy process in the local delivery of URBAN? In the chapter on implementation on the ground we seek answers to the following questions.

How were the UMCs and the UPGs in the respective areas formed? To what extent did they represent the local community? How was the establishment of UPGs as a legal entity, stated in the administrative arrangements, implemented in practice? Which procedures would satisfy central government for the local management of the funds? Did central government make any further concessions to create more a more flexible environment for the needs of URBAN? If so, at which point of the policy process did central government adjust and how can this be accounted for? Chapter six, dealing with the implementation of URBAN by the local partners in London, will address these questions. Firstly, let us turn to the Commission/central government negotiations for the early stages of the implementation of URBAN in France.

Appendix 1 to Chapter 4

URBAN Administrative Arrangements

1 The URBAN Management Committee

An URBAN Management Committee (UMC) will be constituted as a sub-committee of the East London Objective 2 Programme Monitoring Committee (PMC) to oversee the administration, implementation and monitoring of the East End URBAN programme. The membership of this Management Committee will be drawn from the principal local partners including the Urban Partnership Group (UPG, see 2), local authorities, the private sector, Trading and Enterprise Councils (TECs) the voluntary sector, the local community, the Government, the European Commission and other relevant bodies operating in the URBAN eligible area. If necessary, the PMC may co-opt to this sub-committee additional members based in the eligible area. The UMC will have the following tasks:

- to commission capacity building work including community audits to create or enhance the UPG;
- to invite the UPG to submit a draft Urban Action Plan (UAP, see 3);
- to examine, discuss with the UPG, and agree the UAP;
- to agree the detailed arrangements for the UPG to take forward the UAP;
- to submit to the PMC annual progress reports on the URBAN programme based on UPG reports;
- to agree arrangements for the promotion and publicity of the programme; and
- to make arrangements for the monitoring and evaluation of the implementation of the UAP.

2 Urban Partnership Group

The UPG will include representatives of local community organisations and is likely to include representatives from the voluntary sector, local authorities, the local business community, local educational agencies, and local health and training bodies. It will be chaired by one of the local partners. It will have access to the expertise and support necessary to fulfil its tasks effectively. The UPG must satisfy the UMC that:

• there is widespread community involvement and support for the group and that evidence is provided of this and
• the group has developed capacity building actions (e.g. Community audit, strategy development, training for community participation) to enable the local community to contribute to the development of the area and has developed a UAP to address the area's problems.

The group must be formally constituted as a legal entity and be subject to control for audit purposes in order to manage public funds. A lead agency may receive and manage grants on behalf of the UPG. The group or agency must specify clear and transparent arrangements for financial management and administration including, where appropriate, the nomination of a specific individual to be responsible for the management of public funds provided to it and for reporting to the group and liaising with the UMC. The tasks of the UPG will be to:

• draw up and implement the UAP, following discussion with and agreement of the UMC;
• secure match-funding for the UAP;
• provide to the UMC an annual report describing the implementation of the programme to date, the outputs achieved and expenditure actually incurred, and a six monthly interim financial report; and
• to propose arrangements for the promotion and publicity of the programme.

Where local geography dictates, distinct UPGs may be established each operating in accordance with the above.

3 Urban Action Plan

A UAP is a pluriannual programme conforming with the strategy and measures set out in this document. It should offer an integrated and holistic approach to tackling the problems identified in the area based on strong community involvement. The UAP must meet the following eligibility criteria:

- adequately describe the action intended to be taken;
- occur within the eligible area;
- quantify outputs and detail clear and attainable targets and an indicative financial plan; and
- demonstrate that the UAP would not go ahead, would proceed on a smaller scale or would be delayed without the support of the URBAN programme.

The UAP should also have the following characteristics:

- value for money measured in the context of the conditions applying in the URBAN area;
- job creation and access to employment opportunities for the most marginalised;
- contribution to equal opportunities;
- the inclusion of innovative approaches to addressing problems identified in the programme; and
- contribution towards sustainable development by outlining a forward strategy to continue activity beyond the end of the URBAN programme.

Source: Adapted from an extract of the 'Heart of the East End URBAN Initiative Operational Programme' (CEC) (1996c), DG XVI, Brussels.

5 Gatekeeping in a Multi-Level Government System: the Implementation of URBAN in France

Introduction

This chapter applies the framework of analysis, developed in chapter four, to the delivery of URBAN in Marseille.[1] In this chapter, we concentrate on stages one to three: the selection of cities, the administrative arrangements to deliver URBAN and the negotiations up to March 1996 when the Programme Document for Marseille was agreed by the Commission. Implementation at grass roots level, as in the case of London, is dealt with in a separate chapter. We begin by examining the administrative system in the period following the 1982 decentralisation laws; new administrative procedures emerged for national and European policies. Although urban policy measures date back to 1970, the specific term for urban policy *'politique de la ville'* only began to be used at the end of the 1980s (*Habitat*, 17 April 1997). The Commission did not launch URBAN until 1994, by which time urban policy in France was integrated into a contractual system. A complex range of existing measures were running parallel to URBAN. We therefore invest in a detailed review of the contractual policy as this is essential in explaining how URBAN was implemented in Marseille.

Examination of the contractual process illustrates how the different levels of government, central, regional and local, are involved in the administration of national and European programmes. For the implementation of URBAN, we concentrate on identifying which level of government intervened and at which stage of the policy process. Central government, like that of the UK, was the key actor regarding the choice of cities to receive URBAN in

---

[1] Please refer to chapter four, section 4.1/2 where the stages of implementation are set out.

France. In contrast to the UK, there was little discussion between the Commission, and the French authorities, regarding the administrative structures to deliver URBAN. We will seek to account for these differences in approach in section 5.2 which explores how the administrative procedures, for delivering national and European policies, were adapted for the implementation of URBAN.

Another difference to the case of URBAN in the UK is that the next major intervention of the central authorities was at stage three of the process, the negotiation of the contents of the URBAN Programme Document for the targeted areas of Marseille. The elected municipal and regional authorities, for Marseille and the region Provence-Alpes-Côte d'Azur (PACA) respectively, were also involved at this stage. The negotiations should be placed in the context of the planning contracts (*Contrat de Plan, Contrat de Ville*) which developed in the period following the decentralisation reforms of the 1980s. The financial arrangements related to the contractual process can help explain why each level of government would intervene at this stage. We should not assume that central government was any less significant than in the case of the UK. Even after the series of decentralisation laws, Mazey (1995, p.135) suggests that France remains a unitary state:

> The declared objective of these reforms was to devolve powers and responsibilities from Paris to the directly elected local and regional governments. In short, the French state was to be decentralized and democratized in accordance with the socialists' long-standing electoral promise. However, France was to remain a unitary state and there was no intention to transform it into a federation. Moreover whilst the socialists were anxious to reform the state, they never intended to weaken it. As the then Prime Minister, Pierre Mauroy explained, 'the more one decentralizes, the more necessary it is for there to be a strong state presence'. *Débats Assemblée nationale*, 8 July 1981. Thus political decentralization was balanced by administrative deconcentration.

It would be too simple, however, to explain things in purely legal terms of the post-1982 decentralisation laws, stating the competences of each level of government. The lines between central, regional and local government can become blurred due to the system of *cumul des mandats* – the accumulation of mandates, allowing politicians to hold local and national office. Indeed for part of the period of the implementation of URBAN the Mayor of Marseille, Jean-Claude Gaudin, was also the elected President of the Region Provence-Alpes-Côte d'Azur and a minister in the central government. Jean-Claude

Gaudin became Minister of National and Regional Development (*Ministre de l'Aménagement du Territoire*) in 1996.

With reference to the 'extended gatekeeper' approach presented in chapter two, the importance of different types of resources available to governments, and other actors, can fluctuate across policy sectors and over time. Bache's (1996) notion of central government as 'extended gatekeeper' can be applied to assess the role of the central authorities in the implementation of URBAN in Marseille. For other levels of government, namely regional and municipal, we will use the term 'gatekeeper'. Combining this with the 'extended gatekeeper' model, developed by Bache, allows us to assess potential 'gatekeeping' by different levels of government involved in implementing URBAN in France, with specific reference to Marseille.

We aim to assess which resources were available, to the key actors, at different points of the process. Which level of government was successful, at each stage, in controlling the delivery of URBAN? The City of Marseille would arguably have additional political resources when, for example, the mayor was also a minister in the national government; such factors can help explain policy outcomes. Similar to the case of URBAN in the UK, the Commission's urban policy experiment faced a number of barriers before reaching the targeted recipients on the ground. Although there will be some reference to the case of the UK, in the course of the analysis, more systematic comparison is not presented until the conclusions of the book in chapter eight. We begin with our review of the contractual policy set out below.

5.1 The Background to Negotiations for URBAN

France has a particularly complex system of local government. There are three levels: 22 regions, 96 departments (*départements*) and 36,750 communes. The department and the region were created as administrative bodies to manage state functions. The commune has a longer history dating back to the French Revolution. The three levels of local government all have a role in the system of local administration. The state is represented, at local level, by the prefecture. Furthermore, after 1982 a series of decentralisation laws were passed and this promoted new ways of working between the state and the local administrations. The different levels of government in the French system also adapted to the European environment (Mazey, 1995).

This section will explore administrative arrangements for delivering the state's territorial policies in the post-1982 period.

5.1/1 Institutional Changes in Central/Local Relations: the Contractual Policy of the French Governments

Balme and Bonnet (1995) have conducted a comprehensive analysis of the contractual relations between the state and the regions in France in the period after 1982.[2] Following the law of 29 March 1982, the regions became formally responsible for regional economic development and were granted the legal status which allowed them to negotiate with state representatives. After further legislation, a framework developed in which the regions could draw up regional plans, contributing to the national plan. These would be implemented through the system of planning contracts (*Contrats de Plan*). The implementation of URBAN is within the third generation of *Contrats de Plan*; the first covered the period 1984-1988, the second 1989-1993 and the third 1994-1998. The first regional elections, by universal suffrage, took place in March 1986 and each authority elected their own chairperson, the president of the region. Although the regions have played an active role in the *Contrats de Plan*, their responsibilities and resources are limited in other respects.[3]

Balme and Bonnet (1995) identify three major forces, at the national level, in the *Contrats de Plan*: The General Planning Commissariat (*Commissariat Général du Plan*) involved in planning since 1946, the regional planning body DATAR (*Délégation à l'Aménagement du Territoire et à l'Action Régionale*) which has conducted regional policy in France since 1963, and the Ministry of the Interior involved in implementing the decentralisation reforms of the post-1982 period. The *Contrats de Plan* have been viewed as 'a new institutional mechanism designed to ensure cooperation between actors in a post-unitary state' (Balme and Bonnet, 1995, p.52). Indeed, the first period of *Contrats de Plan* was characterised by bargaining between the centre and periphery. As part of this process, the central and local levels interacted to define the areas suitable for

---

[2] The secondary information on the contractual relations between the state and the regions is largely based on the article of Balme and Bonnet (1995). The material on the subsequent application of this to the *Contrat de Ville* model formally launched in 1988 is taken from Le Galès and Mawson (1994).

[3] For a detailed account of the competences of the different levels of government after the 1982 reforms see Douence (1995), Keating and Hainsworth (1986), Mény (1983) or Mazey (1987).

contractualisation, with territorial policy split between the macro-level of national planning and the micro-level of regional policy. The following section briefly summarises procedures for the first generation of contractual planning; this presented a model for subsequent plans, including that covering the period 1994-1998. By then national planning barely existed so attention was focused on micro economic policy for each region.

In the first generation of contractual planning, the state was represented at regional level by the regional prefects who played a role in identifying regional planning priorities to be included in the *Contrat de Plan* following discussions with the regional councils. The regional proposals would then be reviewed and taken into consideration by the different administrations, at central government level, involved in the national plan. Decisions were finally confirmed in 1983 by the inter-ministerial committee with responsibility for regional planning, CIAT (*Comité Interministériel à l'Aménagement du Territoire*). Although the time scale was limited, 21 metropolitan regions agreed and signed their *Contrats de Plan* in the period between March and July 1984. The process was extended to the 1989-1993 period although the new contracts were to be developed with a more strategic and European focus. Another feature of the post-1988 period was the extension of the contractual process to include municipalities.

Contracts for municipalities (*Contrats de Ville*) were introduced by a central government decree on 28 October 1988. This also led to the creation of an inter-ministerial delegation dealing with towns and cities, DIV (*Délégation Interministérielle à la Ville*). The DIV was attached to the Prime Minister in 1991. The role of the DIV was one of coordination of matters related to towns and cities – this could involve up to forty central ministries (Donzelot and Estèbe, 1994). The approach of the *Contrat de Ville* was to develop an inter-ministerial approach at central government level and coordination at the local level by the state representative, the regional prefect. The *Contrat de Ville* was organised along the same lines as the *Contrat de Plan*; it involved detailed financial negotiation between the central government and local authorities.

The DIV had limited sources of direct funding since its role was to mobilise the resources of central ministries and the local authorities in jointly agreeing programmes of action. Responsibility for monitoring and negotiating the *Contrat de Ville* was with the prefect and the officials representing the field services of the state. The prefect represents the state at local level although Le Galès (1994, p.12) distinguishes between the role of the regional prefect and departmental prefect. The regional prefect is viewed as a more recent innovation with responsibility for facilitating an integrated approach to the local delivery of state services but with particular concern for infrastructure projects, transportation and economic development matters in a region. The departmental prefect represents the government in the department and has responsibility for supervising and coordinating the field services of the state; these include the *Direction Départementale de l'Équipement* (DDE) which provides expertise in housing, town planning and transport at local level.[4]

Further administrative changes were introduced by Mitterrand who created the office of sub prefect for towns and cities (*Sous-Préfet à la Ville*) at departmental level in 1991. The sub prefect for towns and cities was accorded a limited role and functions: responsibilities included the management of local projects and liaising with local elected politicians and field services of the state. The regional prefect still retained overall responsibility for the region although there would be exchanges of information regarding the project development in the *Contrat de Ville* measures with the sub prefect for towns and cities. Following any negotiations at local level, the regional prefect retained responsibility for reporting back to central government. However local politicians who also have a national mandate through the system of accumulation of offices may undermine the prefect in dealings with the central authorities in Paris (Le Galès, 1994).

Similar to recent regeneration programmes in the UK, such as City Challenge and the Single Regeneration Budget (SRB), there was an element of competition between cities seeking to participate in the early *Contrat de Ville* model launched in 1988. Initially, a pilot programme was run whereby the DIV received more than 100 requests from local authorities which were willing to participate in the experiment. From this 13 were finally selected, including Marseille, which signed its *Contrat de Ville* in 1990.[5] Urban policy, both in the UK and France, straddles a number of policy areas and levels of government. In France, as in the UK, the concept of partnership emerged for national as well as European policies.

The contract can be interpreted as a form of partnership in which the state, by offering greater influence over its programmes and some limited additional

---

[4] It is possible for one individual to hold the post of regional and departmental prefect with overall responsibility for both the region and the department (see section 5.1/2 on the case of Marseille).

[5] This is mentioned in the contractual plan covering the period 1994-1998: 'Contrat de Plan, État/Région Provence-Alpes-Côte d'Azur, Politique de la Ville, Contrat de Ville' (Ville de Marseille, 1994, p.2).

funding, demands of the local authority that it is representing the interests of all sections of the population and engages in collaborative action with neighbouring local authorities to tackle urban problems straddling the local authority boundaries. The local authority, in turn, requires of the state the delivery of high quality services either directly, or by providing the means to do so through local authority or other relevant bodies (Le Galès 1994, p.23).

Le Galès (1994) argues that the *Contrat de Ville* was not a general development plan; its objective was more one of addressing specific social and economic problems in urban areas. This involved an inter-agency strategy which aimed to promote a coherent approach regarding the plans of the various ministries and local authorities. Following the initial experimentation in 1988, the *Contrat de Ville* became integrated into the third generation of *Contrats de Plan* for the 1994-1998 period. European funds could provide additional resources to deliver this. The *Contrats de Plan* for the 1994-1998 period consisted of approximately FF 75 billion and the Structural Funds for 1994-1999 represented FF 50 billion (regionalised objectives only). Structural Funds made up about 15 per cent of the overall public aid budget in areas eligible for Structural Funds assistance.[6]

The third tier of local government, the departments, had not been formal signatories in the contractual process. There were regional variations in the extent of involvement of departments. Legally, the regions were obliged to consult constituent departments, as well as cities and towns with a population exceeding 10,000. The means of conferring, however, was at the region's discretion. In practice, the political circumstances of each locality determined the form of consultation and cooperation. Departments requested to be formally included in the third generation of contractual procedures. The government considered the possibility of entering into contracts with departments as well as regions, for the 1994-1998 period, however the idea was not finally pursued. Nevertheless, Balme and Bonnet (1995, p.64) suggest that departments and municipalities, seeking to play a more active role in the planning process, weakened the newly created regions. The section below explores how the City of Marseille was involved in the third generation of *Contrats de Plan* covering 1994-1998. The Commission's

---

[6] The figures quoted cover Structural Funds for all the objectives, 1-5b for the period 1994-1999. Specific sums allocated to URBAN in France are quoted in section 5.2 of this chapter. The figure of 15 per cent indicated an average sum; there were regional variations to this – for 10 out of 26 regions, the figure was above 25 per cent and for 5 out of 10, it was over 50 per cent. For further details on facts and figures for Structural Funds aid in France as a whole, see Lagrange (1997) in Bachtler and Turok (Eds).

Community Initiative (CI) URBAN was implemented in the 1994-1999 programming period. The European programme therefore coincided with the contractual process at national level; this is examined in further detail below.

5.1/2 Contrat de Plan, Contrat de Ville: the Case of Marseille

In the case of Marseille, the *Contrat de Ville* was part of the *Contrat de Plan* for the period 1994-1998. This involved the French state, the Provence-Alpes-Côte d'Azur Region and the Municipality of Marseille. The *Contrat de Ville* was signed on 11 July 1994. The French state, at regional/departmental level, was represented by Monsieur Blanc, Prefect of the Region Provence-Alpes-Côte d'Azur and the Department Bouches-du-Rhône. Central government was represented by Madame Veil, Minister of Social Affairs, Health, Towns and Cities (*Ministre des Affaires Sociales, de la Santé et de la Ville*).[7] The *Contrat de Ville, Contrat de Plan* was also signed by the elected representatives of regional and municipal government: Monsieur Gaudin, President of the Region Provence-Alpes-Côte d'Azur and Monsieur Vigouroux, Mayor of Marseille, Clearly, the highest level of politicians and officials representing each tier of government at the time were signatories in this contractual agreement.

The elected departmental council (*conseil général*) also has some competences regarding elements of social policy. The post-1982 decentralisation laws enhanced the powers of the department in areas such as health, social welfare, education, road maintenance and school bus transport (Wright, 1989, p.296). Although these policy areas affected towns and cities within a department, only half of the departmental councils in France got involved in signing agreements with municipalities (Lelévrier, 1997, p.6). The Departmental Council for the Department Bouches-du-Rhône did not enter any agreements with the City of Marseille. Interviews with local officials suggest this can be attributed to the local political situation where

---

[7] Following the elections in 1993 and the formation of a Balladur government, the DIV was placed under the responsibility of the Ministry of Social Affairs, Health, Towns and Cities under the responsibility of Simone Veil. The integration of the *Contrats de Ville* into the *Contrats de Plan* represented continuity with the previous government although Le Galès (1995, p.268) argues that urban policy was not a priority of the Balladur government. At the same time, Charles Pasqua, Minister of the Interior (*Ministre de l'Intérieur*) was focusing on measures to promote more security in cities as well as passing a series of anti-immigration laws.

differences emerged between the elected representatives of the department and those of the municipality and region.[8]

Central government in France commits some of its own funding to the contractual process as does as the region and the municipality. The signatories of the *Contrat de Plan, Contrat de Ville* commit themselves to funding the various elements of the programme. Through the contractual process, there is a pool of funds already committed to the national programmes which can then be used to match-fund any European intervention. The European funds are directed to the central ministries and then to the regional prefect who liaises with the section in the prefecture dealing with European funds, the *Secrétariat Général pour les Affaires Régionales* (SGAR). At a regional level, the various activities, financed under European programmes such as URBAN, would be match-funded by the existing pool of funds committed to national programmes by each level of government.

In the case of Marseille, the *Contrat de Ville-État-Région* included the following funding package: FF 137.00 million was contributed by the state, FF 127.15 million by the Municipality of Marseille and FF 40.00 million by the region. Each partner committed these funds in order to deliver the various activities to be funded under the programme.[9] Each contributor, the state, the region and the municipality, would arguably seek to ensure that its interests were represented in the European Programme Document for URBAN finally agreed with the Commission. In this case, then each level of government would seek a slice of the European funds to complement its own stake in the *Contrat de Plan, Contrat de Ville* programme. We will test the validity of this observation in the section dealing with the Programme Document for URBAN in Marseille.

Turning to the region, Balme and Bonnet (1995, p.64) found that 'regions are still immature institutions compared with cities or departments and lack

---

[8] A range of officials from the local state, the municipality and the region were interviewed in the period July to August 1998. Since this study focuses more on the implementation of URBAN within the *Contrat de Ville, Contrat de Plan* structures, in which the departments, according to Balme and Bonnet (1995) were not formally included, time constraints restricted further investigation to establish exactly why the Department Bouches-du-Rhône did not enter into any agreements with the Municipality of Marseille.

[9] Source: CEC (1996e, p.12) URBAN Programme Document for Marseille. Annexe II of the document of the contractual plan for Marseille (*Contrat de Plan, Contrat de Ville*) provides more details of this (Ville de Marseille, 1994). The contribution of the state consisted of FF 67.00 million allocated specifically to the contractual plan for the Marseille (*Contrat de Ville*) and FF 70.00 million to the Funds for Social Action (*Fonds Action Sociale*) aspect of the plan aimed at the integration of immigrants in the targeted areas.

the political and legal authority to negotiate effectively with other levels of government in situations of conflict'. While there may not have been conflict in the case of Marseille, we should be aware of this 'weakness' of regions when analysing the case of URBAN in Marseille. In terms of funding committed to the *Contrat de Ville* programme, clearly the main actors were the state and the municipality. The department was not involved; if the region played a minor role, the main bargaining regarding the contents of any European programme would, arguably, be between the state and the municipality. Of course the waters become muddy when one politician, Jean-Claude Gaudin, may be mayor, president of the region and a minister in the national government! For this reason, it is important to identify the stages of the policy process, and which ones coincided with these positions. Following Bache's (1996) application of the policy networks approach to the 'extended gatekeeper' model, the resources available to each actor could vary at the various stages of the policy process.

Before entering the politics of any allocation of URBAN and subsequent negotiations regarding the Programme Document, we should equip ourselves with knowledge regarding the main themes of the *Contrat de Plan, Contrat de Ville* for the City of Marseille. The *Contrat de Plan* was part of the XIth Plan which built on the Xth Plan. There were various elements to the *Contrat de Ville* programme; activities ranged from economic activity, improvements in physical infrastructure and buildings, social and cohesion policy and external relations.[10] We will begin by exploring the social policy aspects around the social and urban development measures (*Développement Social Urbain,* DSU) put in place in 1989 by the inter-ministerial committee dealing with towns and cities (*Comité Interministériel des Villes,* CIV). This was part of the developments following Prime Minster Rocard's creation of the inter-ministerial delegation, DIV, in 1988 and featured in the 13 experimental *Contrats de Ville.*[11] Marseille signed the first *Contrat de Ville* programme in 1990 and had already acquired some experience in this from the pilot project stage.

---

[10] The law of 6 February 1992 allowed local authorities to sign conventions with local authorities in other states provided this was within the limits of their area of competence and respected the international commitment of the French state. Prior to this, the external relations of the locality were limited to town twinning, other areas were monopolised by the central government. Source: Délégation Interministérielle à la Ville et au Développement Social Urbain (1996), 'La coopération internationale dans l'initiative URBAN France, propositions d'actions'. Discussion paper on international cooperation on the URBAN programme (Inter-ministerial Delegation for Cities, Social and Urban Development) viewed during a training period at the European Commission.

[11] Lelévrier (1997) 'Cahiers de l'Aurif,' in 'Repères historiques' section of *Habitat,* no.17.

The social and urban development (DSU) element of the *Contrat de Ville* programme in Marseille for the period 1994-1998 was organised around five priority objectives listed as follows: educational success and literacy, economic action and employment, the prevention of delinquency and the fight against drugs, integration through sport, the improvement of degraded buildings and housing estates. The municipality would have the major responsibility for setting up the grass roots structures to manage the programme although the region and the state financed some of the programme. Interestingly enough, the promotion of citizenship featured in the objectives of the *Contrat de Ville*. This was to be developed through a system whereby a project leader (*chef de projet*) would be based in the targeted neighbourhoods.

The project leader for each area would have responsibility for coordinating a team of officers to promote projects that would tackle problems associated with social exclusion, poverty, drugs, delinquency and feelings of insecurity amongst the local population. The partners of the *Contrat de Ville* encouraged the participation of residents in projects related to improving the social environment and the development of citizenship skills. The *Contrat de Ville* document granted the Mayor of Marseille responsibility for supervising the project leader teams as well as liaising with the state and the regional authorities.[12] Clearly, there were a number of social policy activities in the *Contrat de Ville* programme in Marseille.

Turning to the European perspective, URBAN also sought to promote participation of citizens in economic regeneration. Since this was a part of national programmes, and structures were already in place to deliver this, the European intervention may appear to complement the national programme. There could, however, be a potential problem of coordination once the European intervention was added to that existing at national level. The CI URBAN was under the responsibility of DG XVI dealing with ERDF funds although it contained some ESF elements funded by DG V. Given the amount of social policy activities contained in the *Contrat de Ville* programme we should observe, during negotiations for the URBAN Programme Document, whether the national, regional and local authorities pushed for a greater ESF element than would normally be the case for CIs under DG XVI. If so, what would be the implications for the subsequent operation and coordination of URBAN? Would DG V be as actively

---

[12] This information is taken from the following document: 'XI ème Plan, Contrat de Plan, État/Région Provence-Alpes Côte d'Azur, Politique de la Ville, Contrat de Ville de Marseille' covering the period 1994-1998 (Ville de Marseille, 1994, p.3).

involved in the management of URBAN given that the major responsibility for the URBAN programme was with DG XVI? As in the case of the UK, the implementation of URBAN required both vertical and horizontal coordination at the national and European levels of government.

Furthermore, if European funds were perceived by the national authorities as an additional resource for some of the social policy elements of the *Contrat de Ville*, could issues arise regarding additionality and the eligibility of projects proposed to be funded under URBAN? Some activities in the *Contrat de Ville* were eligible for European funds under Objective 2, and others under URBAN; this depended on the geographical area and the contents of the respective Programme Documents agreed with the Commission. Administrative procedures required the negotiation of two Single Programming Documents (SPDs) for Objective 2; the first for the period 1994-1996 and the second for 1997-1999.[13] For the CI URBAN, only one Programme Document was signed covering 1994-1999, although the contents were only finally agreed in March 1996.[14]

The European funding provided by URBAN could arguably be perceived, by the signatories of the *Contrat de Ville*, as an immediate source of funding to provide additional resources to those committed in the existing programme. Yet it is not clear that the European funds, with their own mechanisms and rules on eligibility, would automatically 'fit' with the *Contrat de Plan, Contrat de Ville* measures. Furthermore, could the European funds provide any added value beyond representing another pot of funds to co-finance existing schemes? 'Gatekeeping' on the part of the signatories of the *Contrat de Plan, Contrat de Ville* could make it difficult to assess the contribution of the European intervention. Before entering the details of the implementation of URBAN, the European programme, we should complete our review of the broader framework of the *Contrat de Plan, Contrat de Ville*.

A broad range of initiatives emanating from central government ministries were incorporated in the framework of the national programme. This illustrates further how the state, itself, is not a unitary actor since various ministries are involved in different types of urban policy measures at

[13] CEC (1994g) 'Document Unique de Programmation (DOCUP)1994-1996, No. FEDER: 94.03.13.042, No. ARINCO: 94.FR.16.019' (SPD agreed for Objective 2 areas in the PACA Region, 1994-1996). CEC (1997e) 'DOCUP 1997-1999, No. Feder: 97.03.13.018, No. Arinco: 97.FR.16.018' (SPD for Objective 2 areas in the PACA Region covering the period 1997-1999).
[14] CEC (1996e) C (96) 644, URBAN Programme Document for Marseille, No. Feder: 94.03.10.048, No. Arinco: 94.FR.16.052.

central government level. Three other centrally led urban policy initiatives were launched in Marseille at around the same time that the European Commission announced URBAN. The first, entitled the *Grand Projet Urbain* (GPU) appeared to directly complement the *Contrat de Ville* measures listed above. The other two, those of *Euroméditerranée* and the *Pacte de Relance pour la Ville* (Urban Renewal Pact) represented a different approach to tackling urban problems.

Euroméditerranée was not officially launched until 1995 however the planning around this formed part of the broader *Contrat de Plan, Contrat de Ville* strategy. Furthermore, although the GPU and *Euroméditerranée* were two separate programmes, they shared the same parent ministry at central government level. Both were answerable to the Ministry of Infrastructure (*Ministère de l'Équipement*) in the central government although they had different management structures at the local level. The Urban Renewal Pact was not launched until January 1996, so was not a formal part of the *Contrat de Plan, Contrat de Ville* signed in July 1994. However, the contractual system appeared flexible enough to allow both existing and new measures to be incorporated into the strategy. Indeed, the major themes of the *Contrat de Plan, Contrat de Ville* programme, outlined below, indicate a vague policy document covering a wide range of areas.[15]

The *Contrat de Plan, Contrat de Ville* (1994-1998) states that its objective is to make Marseille one of the major European cities in the Mediterranean. Four general areas of development are identified in order to achieve this goal. These include:

- Economic activity;
- Infrastructure and city planning;
- Development of a sense of social solidarity and cohesion; and
- External relations.

Within this framework, the economic strategy of the City of Marseille is to be developed in the following vocational fields:

- Maritime and commercial;
- Industrial;
- Scientific and Cultural;
- Tertiary sector; and

---

[15] This information presented is adapted from the following document: 'Contrat de Ville, Contrat de Plan' covering the period 1994-1998 (Ville de Marseille, 1994, p.2).

- Tourism

The *Euroméditerranée* project is seen as a major asset to the future economic development of Marseille and the achievement of the goals of the city. The *Contrat de Ville* is presented as a way of achieving better coordination of sectoral policies, aimed at the city as a whole, and action directed at the level of specific neighbourhoods. By integrating both previous and future initiatives, the *Contrat de Ville* is viewed as a way of promoting a more dynamic implementation of the urban and social policy under the DSU measures put in place in Marseille.[16]

The *Contrat de Ville* document states that both new and previous urban initiatives can contribute to the achievement of objectives within the broad themes listed above. Indeed, a wide range of activities which could be included in the broader contractual scheme are listed without any precise details regarding how each of the different areas could be linked to form a coherent strategy for the regeneration of Marseille. The problem of coordinating the wide range of national and European schemes will be explored further in chapter seven dealing with the implementation of URBAN on the ground.

We now briefly review the three main urban policy initiatives relating to the overall aims and objectives of the contractual process (*Contrat de Plan*, *Contrat de Ville*): GPU, *Euroméditerranée* and the Urban Renewal Pact. Knowledge of the different schemes enables us to put the implementation of URBAN into the broader local and regional strategy. This can also help identify the priorities of each partner that had invested in the *Contrat de Plan*, *Contrat de Ville*. Once we complete our snapshot of the existing activities around Marseille and the PACA Region, we can use the information when seeking to assess the bargaining position of each level of government in negotiations with the Commission for the contents of the URBAN Programme Document. The argument presented here is that each level of government would seek to ensure some European funding for its own stake in the *Contrat de Plan*, *Contrat de Ville*. Firstly, we turn to central government investment in the GPU.

---

[16] This refers to the social and urban development measures (DSU) launched by the central government outlined on p.129.

5.1/3 Grand Projet Urbain: the Case of Marseille

The *Contrat de Ville*, signed in Marseille in 1994, was in the framework of the XIth Plan. The launching of twelve GPUs by the French state in 1994, was also incorporated into the framework of the XIth Plan (*Habitat*, 17 April 1997). This was aimed more at developing building and infrastructure projects in the targeted areas. Although infrastructure was included within the broad framework of the *Contrat de Ville* document, the GPU sites concentrated solely on building and infrastructure. The GPU action was targeted on the whole of the 16th district of Marseille (*16ème arrondissement*) and seven out of 11 neighbourhoods of the 15th district (*15ème arrondissement*) in the north of the city.[17] The GPU represented the greatest single element of state funding in the region since FF 250 million was invested in the GPU element of the *Contrat de Ville*.[18] The following table summarises the funds allocated by each level of government to the *Contrat de Ville* programme in Marseille.

Table 5.1 Financial Planning for the *Contrat de Ville* of Marseille

	Contrat de Ville MF	GPU MF	FAS MF	Total MF
State	67.00	250.00	70.00	387.00
Region	40.00			40.00
City	127.15			127.15
Total	234.15			554.15

Source: Adapted from the *Contrat de Plan, Contrat de Ville* document for Marseille.[19]

---

[17] *Les quartiers nord* of Marseille are classified as anything north of the main street *La Canebière*. The northern part of the city is where most of the poverty and degradation exists whether in social housing, *Habitation à Loyer Modéré* (HLM) or downgraded private housing (*co-proprietés*). Areas south of *La Canebière* are more bourgeois and residential. This was verified by fieldwork in Marseille and is noted in the Programme Document for URBAN (CEC, 1996e).

[18] Source: Annexe II (-11-) of the document for the contractual plan for Marseille, 1994-1998 , Ville de Marseille (1994).

[19] Source: Annexe II (-11-) of the document for the contractual plan for Marseille, 1994-1998 (Ville de Marseille, 1994). FAS represents the social funds (*Fonds Action Sociale*) element of the *Contrat de Ville* aimed at the integration of immigrants in the targeted areas. Figures state the total millions of French Francs committed to each programme.

The municipality employed the project leaders as part of the implementation framework of the *Contrat de Ville*. The role envisaged for them by the sub prefect for towns based in Marseille was one of organising the consultation of residents in order to forward proposals to the Director of the GPU regarding the improvement of the physical environment, that of buildings. The Director of the GPU would then liaise with the various partners in order to prepare a case for the Monitoring Committee (*Comité de Suivi*) to make a final decision. The Monitoring Committee would be chaired by the prefect and include a representative of the regional council and the City of Marseille. Another technical committee had responsibility for implementing the decisions of the Monitoring Committee.

Administrative procedures, agreed for the implementation of URBAN, were largely based on the existing ones for the *Contrat de Ville* and GPU programmes. Prior to this stage were the negotiations, between the Commission and its partners, regarding the contents of the URBAN Programme Document for Marseille. We will investigate how the state intervened, at that point, in order to represent its interest in the GPU area. The state investment in the GPU area was for infrastructure projects. There was a gap, however, in terms of social policy activities. Only part of the GPU areas benefited from the DSU measures included in the framework of the *Contrat de Ville*. Where could additional funding be found to finance social measures to complement the GPU in areas not covered by the DSU strand of the *Contrat de Ville* Programme? This is where the ESF element of URBAN could interest the central authorities since the funds could finance social policy activities to complement the building and infrastructure projects of the GPU. Here, we could predict a possible tension between the principles of regional policy and their interaction with existing policies at Member State level.

Taking the principle of additionality, this can raise the following issues: Does the financing of social policy measures, to complement a building and infrastructure programme of the French State, represent any additional value from the European intervention? URBAN, as a CI, is the responsibility of DG XVI. The URBAN programme in Marseille included ESF measures that could complement the ERDF projects in order to promote an integrated approach sought by DG XVI. The limited funds allocated to such small-scale programmes could provide an opportunity for the Commission to closely monitor the impact of its intervention in the areas selected to participate. However, if the European funds in the programme were 'sliced up' to complement existing schemes, it would be difficult to assess the added value of the supra-national intervention.

Additionality could, therefore, be problematic even where the principle is respected if we measure this purely in terms of French Francs per ECU. Furthermore, it is not clear in the complex maze whether the inhabitants in the targeted areas could differentiate between the European funding element and the programmes existing at Member State level. In France, the institutions to deliver URBAN were modelled on the *Contrat de Ville* system of implementation with a project leader based in each targeted area. There were, however, some variations in procedures due to the involvement of the officials from the prefecture dealing with European policy, the SGAR. This will be explored in section 5.2 dealing with the administrative arrangements to deliver URBAN.

Returning to our review of the existing regeneration initiatives operating in Marseille, the measures explored so far have focused on two specific approaches to tackling urban problems. Firstly, the improvement of the physical environment through infrastructure projects and housing, as represented by the GPU policy and elements of the *Contrat de Ville*. Secondly, the social policy and economic measures which featured in the *Contrat de Ville*. A third strategy that could be pursued is one of business entrepreneurship and strong leadership of the city as developed by Parkinson (CEC, 1993c). Following Jean-Claude Gaudin's election as Mayor of Marseille in 1995, events suggest that the Municipality of Marseille favoured the entrepreneurial approach to urban regeneration. The section below argues that the details of this are essential in understanding the progression from Marseille's initial application for URBAN, submitted to the Commission in 1994, to the actual contents and subsequent implementation of the Programme Document finally agreed in March 1996.

5.1/4 Marseille: a European Entrepreneurial City?

The notion of European entrepreneurial cities was highlighted in a report prepared for the European Commission by Parkinson (CEC, 1993c). This involves marketing and 'civic entrepreneurship' focusing on the role of cities, rather than regions. The emphasis is on broad economic development, rather than policies to tackle specific problems of urban deprivation. In an interview at the time, Parkinson presented the following view:

Cities have to be re-evaluated. They need to be recognised again as the wealth of nations. They are great sources of added value. In Europe, there is an emerging network of cities with similar entrepreneurial outlooks. After 15 years of decline, at some point in the mid-1980s big cities started to grow again, or at the very least, they started stabilising. The trend is solid and is reversing the former outward drift of population. We are developing a Europe of the cities, not a Europe of the regions.[20]

Examples quoted in the Parkinson report of entrepreneurial cities defining themselves in a European rather than regional or national role include Glasgow, Manchester, Birmingham, Rotterdam, Hamburg, Barcelona, Lyons, Lille, Dortmund, Stuttgart, Frankfurt and Milan. Parkinson recognises that the beneficiaries of such a strategy are those who are educated, qualified or trained in specific areas; there may therefore be elements of the population who are excluded from the process:

> You have a polarised labour market, overlaid with the problems of ethnic minorities and immigrants. Some people are being excluded. We found that Hamburg has more millionaires than anywhere else in Europe, but more people on welfare. One of the key challenges of the next couple of decades will be how to improve a city's competitiveness without increasing the social cost.[21]

Clearly, the urban and social development (DSU) elements of the first and second *Contrat de Ville* concentrated on tackling urban social problems and involved small-scale projects rather than a more global economic development strategy. The *Euroméditerranée* and the Urban Renewal Pact initiatives could be interpreted as representing a more entrepreneurial approach around the themes developed by Parkinson (CEC, 1993c). We will examine the main features of both approaches before turning to the implementation of URBAN. *Euroméditerrannée* in particular corresponded to a particular vision the political majority in the municipality had for the future of Marseille as a city.

Euroméditerranée involved a specific development plan whereas the Urban Renewal Pact was more a policy of fiscal incentives to promote the growth of businesses in the targeted areas. The *Euroméditerranée* programme in Marseille bordered part of the targeted area of URBAN and the Urban Renewal Pact included some of the GPU area of URBAN, eligible for the ESF.[22] The launch of *Euroméditerranée* was during the period of the

---

[20] Professor Michael Parkinson, Director of the European Institute for Urban Affairs at Liverpool John Moore's University, quoted in the *Financial Times*, Monday July 12 1993. Professor Parkinson completed a three year study for the European Commission on 24 cities (CEC, 1993c).

[21] Professor Parkinson, quoted in the *Financial Times*, Monday July 12 1993.

[22] This will become clearer in section 5.2 dealing with negotiations for the contents of the Programme Document for the delivery of URBAN in Marseille.

negotiations for the Programme Document for URBAN in Marseille. The Urban Renewal Pact was initiated in January 1996. The French government announced the targeted zones in each city selected to participate in the scheme in March 1996. Marseille, where the authorities had agreed the contents of the URBAN Programme Document with the European Commission two weeks earlier, was also selected for the Urban Renewal Pact.[23] A brief review of both programmes enables us to understand the municipality's approach to urban policy in Marseille. Furthermore, the proximity of *Euroméditerranée* to URBAN raises certain issues in the implementation of URBAN at individual project level. These form part of the analysis in chapter seven concentrating on the local delivery of URBAN.

Euroméditerranée has ambitious long-term aims of making Marseille southern Europe's major metropolis. The origins of the programme date back to the Corfu European Council summit in 1994 where Member States agreed on the need to strengthen the Union's Mediterranean policy and to develop the Mediterranean region into an area of cooperation, to guarantee peace, security, stability and economic well being. In a Communication published in October 1994, the Commission recalled the social, political and economic links between the European Union and the countries of the eastern and southern Mediterranean. Following summits in Essen and Cannes in 1995, the Barcelona Declaration was adopted at the Euro-Mediterranean conference of the Council of the European Union in November 1995. This set the target date of 2010 to establish a free trade area in the Mediterranean region. An increase of EU financial assistance and the implementation of economic cooperation in the relevant areas was another aspect to this.[24]

Following the above developments, the French state launched the *Euroméditerranée* urban development programme in Marseille in December 1995; this has been operational since 1996. The programme was initiated with a FF 1.7 billion injection for ongoing public investment. The main responsibility for *Euroméditerranée* was allocated to the Ministry of Infrastructure (*Ministère de l'Équipement*) at central government level

---

[23] Information taken from a document relating to a joint press conference involving Monsieur Gaudin, Minister of National and Regional Development at the time and Eric Raoult, Minister of Towns, Cities and Integration during this period (*Conference de Presse de Jean-Claude Gaudin, Ministre de l'Aménagement du Territoire et Eric Raoult, Ministre Délegué à la Ville et a l'Intégration, jeudi 28 mars 1996*). Document produced by the Ministry of National and Regional Planning, Towns, Cities and Integration (*Ministère de l'Aménagement du Territoire, de la Ville et de l'Intégration*, Paris, 1996).

[24] For more information, see CEC, COM (94), 427 final and the 'Barcelona Declaration', CEC (1995b).

although the ministries for transport, housing, the Ministry of Finance and the regional planning body, DATAR would also be involved. At local level, a public agency was established to run the programme – the *Établissement Public d'Aménagement Euroméditerranée* consisting of representatives of the French State, the City of Marseille, the Marseille-Provence Metropolitan Area, the Regional Council of Provence-Alpes-Côte d'Azur and the Port Authority. The partners were committed to a long-term, geographical vision of elevating the position of Marseille within a broad European framework. [25]

In 1997, the total package approved for *Euroméditerranée* amounted to FF 280 million.[26] This included the ERDF and ESF funds for *Euroméditerranée* agreed in the Objective 2 Single Programme Document (SPD) for the PACA Region.[27] The geographical area of *Euroméditerranée* covers part of the 2nd and 3rd districts in Marseille (*2ème et 3ème arrondissements*); this bordered the area targeted under URBAN (CEC, 1996e, p.14). The section in the Objective 2 SPD on *Euroméditerranée* places the project at the heart of France's ambitions for pre-eminence in both Mediterranean and EU policy. *Euroméditerranée* is a long-term operation seeking to promote economic development in Marseille and the surrounding area. The aim is to create up to 20,000 jobs in the period of operation of *Euroméditerranée*, estimated at 15-20 years.[28]

One *Euroméditerranée* official explained the vision of the programme in the following terms:

Marseille is a city that has lost jobs, a city that has plunged into a cycle of poverty, a downward spiral. So we have to take advantage of operations that try and change Marseille's image and aim to reverse the downward trend. We have to recapture the city's dynamic qualities. In order to attract new inhabitants and new jobs you have to make your city more appealing.[29]

---

[25] Information from this section is based on an interview with an official employed in the *Euroméditerranée* programme (August 1998). Additional information is taken from documents provided by the *Euroméditerranée* official.

[26] 'Marseille, Euroméditerranée' information pack published by *Euroméditerranée* Public Agency (1997b).

[27] Single Programming Document (SPD), DOCUP, for Objective 2 areas, Provence-Alpes-Côte d'Azur (PACA), 1997-1999, No. Feder: 97.03.13.018, No. Arinco: 97.FR.16.018, agreed in Brussels on 27 June 1997 (CEC, 1997e, p.67).

[28] Information taken from SPD for Objective 2 areas in the PACA region, 1997-1999 No. Feder: 97.03.13.018, No. Arinco: 97.FR.16.018 (CEC, 1997e, p.66).

[29] Extracts from an interview with a *Euroméditerranée* official (August 1998). All interviews quoted relating to the case of Marseille were conducted in French and subsequently translated into English by the author. Although every attempt has been made

Prominent local politicians expressed a similar view on the role of *Euroméditerranée* on the future development of the City of Marseille.

> The state, the city, the local authorities and economic policy-makers are working together on this operation of national interest. In this way, we are creating together the conditions necessary for the expansion of our economy in order to offer a welcome site to attract new investors, develop services and create jobs. *Euroméditerranée* is a major stake for the metropolitan area of Marseille and offers an exceptional opportunity for those who seize it.[30]

The literature produced by the *Euroméditerranée* Public Agency suggests that the programme's long-term objective is to make Marseille a successful European city in the league of those listed in the Parkinson (CEC, 1993c) report. The marketing strategy of *Euroméditerranée* clearly states that the success of the programme should benefit the city as a whole. The major sectors of economic activity identified are telecommunications, information technology, services for international commerce, water, cooperation and training, cultural industries, financial services and tourism.[31] Given that the vision for *Euroméditerranée* extends over a long period it would be difficult, at this stage, to evaluate whether the policy has any substance or is a successful feat of marketing designed to attract funding to the programme.

The section on *Euroméditerranée* in the SPD for 1997-1999 sets targets for each specific measure relating to the programme. This involves economic outputs in areas such as improvement of the environment and the attractiveness of economic sites.[32] Measure number 10 for example indicates that the improvement of 25 hectares of land in the *Euroméditerranée* area can potentially create up to 5,000 jobs on the improved site as well as 350

---

to respect the original transcript, responsibility for interpretation and the quality of translation remains with the author of this book.

[30] Renaud Muselier, President of *Euroméditerranée*, Deputy Mayor of Marseille (*Président d'Euroméditerranée, Premier Adjoint au Maire de Marseille*) and member of the National Assembly during this period representing the Department of the Bouches-du-Rhône (*Député des Bouches-du-Rhône*). This quote is taken from an information booklet entitled 'Marseille Euroméditerranée' published by *Euroméditerranée* Public Agency (1997b).

[31] Internal document produced in October 1997 relating to the marketing strategy of Marseille forwarded by *Euroméditerranée* official for the purposes of this study: '*La stratégie économique et de marketing Euroméditerranée*', *Euroméditerranée* Public Agency (1997a).

[32] This relates to measure number 10 under section 4 of the SPD for 1997-1999 focusing on the area of developing economic and urban dynamic in the *Marseille-Euroméditerranée* area, No. Feder: 97.03.13.018, No. Arinco: 97.FR.16.018 (CEC 1997e, p.149).

jobs relating to the building work involved. A preliminary evaluation report in the Appendix of the SPD underlines how difficult it is to evaluate the programme in its early stages. The SPD presents broad themes and outputs, yet individual actors within the targeted areas need to present projects that correspond to these. Hence it is not possible at the time of drafting the SPD to evaluate the precise impact of individual projects since details on each would not be available at that stage.[33]

It would therefore be impossible, at time of writing, to evaluate the performance of the long-term strategy of *Euroméditerranée*. Furthermore, there remains the problem identified by Parkinson (*Financial Times*, 1993) that the beneficiaries of such programmes may be the educated, qualified or trained segments of the population. Programmes such as *Euroméditerranée* do not directly address the issue of how to reach those who are excluded from mainstream economic and social activity. Interviews indicate that this was recognised by officials at *Euroméditerranée* although they did not see themselves as being directly responsible for this policy area:

> Social policy is another matter that isn't directly addressed by us – it is tackled by the state and the municipality. There are various structures in place to deal with it. We have a role to play, an important role, but it is clear that there are a number of actors already playing a part. These include voluntary associations, the state and the municipality that has its own section dealing with urban and social development measures (DSU). Indeed, there are a lot of people working directly in that specific field (Interview, *Euroméditerranée* official, Marseille, August, 1998).

Euroméditerranée and the activities around the DSU programme both feature in the *Contrat de Plan, Contrat de Ville* document for the period. In principle, the economic and social policy measures under the DSU aspects of the *Contrat de Plan, Contrat de Ville* would complement the activities of *Euroméditerranée*. These are listed as follows:

- Success in school and public literacy;
- Economic action and jobs;
- The prevention of delinquency and the fight against drugs;
- Insertion through leisure, culture and sport; and

---

[33] Extract from Appendix of the SPD for the 1997-1999 period (CEC, 1997e, p.5), No. Feder: 97.03.13.018, No. Arinco: 97.FR.16.018, ex-ante evaluation drafted by the SGAR for the PACA Region, 8 October 1996.

* The improvement of the physical urban environment and of the housing of the most impoverished.[34]

The problem is that the *Contrat de Plan, Contrat de Ville* document, as noted earlier, is a vague all encompassing document. Different sections of the city benefit from a number of national or European funding schemes yet there is no evidence to show that each are linked to one another. It is not clear, for example, whether the beneficiaries of the DSU measures would have the skills required to gain access to employment opportunities under *Euroméditerranée*. Many of the sectors listed, such as financial services, require specific skills.

Another national initiative in France, that of the Urban Renewal Pact, was launched by Prime Minister Juppé's government in 1996. This is one of the few urban policy measures, in the case of France, drawing inspiration from the American experience. In a visit to the United States in April 1996 the Minister for Towns, Cities and Integration. Eric Raoult, visited Empowerment Zones launched by President Clinton: 'Eric Raoult took his hat off to American private companies who don't hesitate to invest in deprived areas of cities' (*Le Monde*, 16 April 1996). The policy was also supported by Jean-Claude Gaudin who was both Mayor of Marseille and Minister for National and Regional Development at the time.[35]

The Urban Renewal Pact did not represent any major injection of public funds since it concentrated more on creating fiscal incentives for economic activity to establish itself in rundown areas. From 1 January 1997, any existing firms or new firms settling in the areas designated as a free urban zone (*zone franche urbaine*) would be exempt from certain taxes and charges related to the business enterprise. This was estimated to amount to around FF 2 billion in tax exemptions to be granted to businesses in distressed urban areas with an additional FF 1 billion to finance urban jobs for young people between the ages of 18 and 25 (OECD, 1998, p.85).

---

[34] Extract translated from the contractual plan (*Contrat de Plan, Contrat de Ville*) for Marseille covering the period 1994-1998 (Ville de Marseille, 1994, pp.5-6).

[35] Some of the information presented on the Urban Renewal Pacts is taken from a document relating to a press conference on Thursday 28 March 1996. The Urban Renewal Pacts were announced jointly by Jean-Claude Gaudin, Mayor of Marseille and Minister for National and Regional Development and Eric Raoult, Minister of Towns, Cities and Integration (*Ministre Délégué à la Ville et de l'Intégration*). The press dossier was prepared by the Ministry of National and Regional Development, Towns, Cities and Integration (*Ministère de l'Aménagement du Territoire, de la Ville et de l'Intégration*, Paris 1996).

The French government had consulted the European Commissioner for Competition at the time, Karel Van Miert and gained the Commission's approval of the policy.[36] There were six main objectives to the Urban Renewal Pact:

- To create economic activity and jobs;
- To re-establish public order;
- To re-establish equality of opportunity by improving minimum standards of schooling and peripatetic education;
- To renovate and diversify housing;
- To reinforce the partnership in urban policy (*politique de la ville*) and
- To establish a geography of urban policy adapted to the gravity of situations.[37]

Three sites in Marseille were targeted under the Urban Renewal Pact: Plan *d'Aou, La Bricarde and La Castellanne*. Parts of these areas were also eligible for European Structural Funds allocated to Marseille.[38] Consequently, DG XVI as well as DG IV and DG V were briefed; for DG XVI this came at the time when negotiations were being prepared for the 1997-1999 SPDs. The main issues which arose related to which activities in the Urban Renewal Pact designated areas would also be eligible for ERDF and ESF support.[39]

5.1/5 Conclusions from the Multiple Initiatives in French Urban Policy

In the case of France, there was a wide array of policies at the national level all seeking to promote regional development and tackle urban decline. On the one hand, there appears to be a coherent scheme in the form of the contractual process; this appears flexible enough to incorporate other government initiatives. The European level can complement existing activities by providing additional funds to those already committed by the national, regional and local authorities. If different parts of the city are

---

[36] *Le Monde*, 3 February 1996, p.9.

[37] List adapted from information released in the press dossier of Thursday 28 March 1996 (see footnote number 35).

[38] The district of *La Castellane, 15ème sud*, for example, was within the GPU site; this area was also eligible for ESF funding under URBAN.

[39] DG XVI, internal information document viewed during a training period at the European Commission.

allocated one of the programmes, Europe can then provide additional resources and there is something for each of the difficult areas of the city.

On the other hand, there may be problems of coordination since the different schemes aiming to tackle urban problems are not necessarily well coordinated. Although the contractual system may suggest an integrated approach, with the different levels of government working together, the reality may be more fragmented; each actor is dealing with their own specific area. Furthermore, the question of how the different European and national funding schemes could be better integrated to complement each other was not directly tackled by the European Commission or the national authorities. If a marble cake scenario is already evident in the national picture, the European intervention may provide additional funds, but exacerbate existing problems of coordination.

While additional funding from any source was welcomed, interviews with local officials in Marseille suggest that the European contribution was viewed more as an additional layer in the cake of existing measures rather than representing any radical changes in the current picture. One official expressed his view in the following terms: 'It's a little bit like the system of the cake with thin layers, you always add a layer but you never remove the previous ones. Europe is yet another layer in the cake' (Interview, senior official, City of Marseille, July 1998). Indeed, this point was raised in a report, presented to the French government, often referred to as the 'Sueur report' of 13 February 1998. The report underlined how procedures of the numerous urban policy initiatives can cause confusion. It is stated that the various schemes often become muddled and are superimposed on existing ones even though each initiative is presented as having a unique and global plan of action.[40] The Sueur report was also critical of the free urban zones (*zone franches*) of the Urban Renewal Pact arguing that there was an absence of reliable statistics to assess their impact.

There have been other sceptical views of the Urban Renewal Pact. Bachmann (1996) argues that the measures in the Urban Renewal Pact did not, in reality, cost the state anything and that, despite all the rhetoric, urban policy was not a priority for the French government. The budget for urban policy in the 1990s was less than that of the 1950s, 1960s and even the 1970s. Bachmann states that in the mid-1990s, the French government

---

[40] Information taken from a summary of the report 'Demain la Ville' (Tomorrow's Town) presented to Martine Aubry, Minister of Employment and Solidarity at the time (*Ministre de l'Emploi et de la Solidarité*) by Jean-Pierre Sueur, Mayor of Orleans, 13 February 1998. Press dossier, summary of two volumes: list of 50 proposals (*Dossier de Presse, Resumé de deux tomes: Liste des 50 propositions*, p. 9).

allocated more funds to Air France than to urban policy. Bachmann points to failings in local democracy identifying a gap between the number of elected politicians in rural communes and the absence of representation at neighbourhood level of urban areas.[41] This appears to confirm an earlier comparative study by Le Galès (1995) who argues that urban policy in both the UK and France had been allocated limited resources and represented a piecemeal approach reacting to crisis. In this respect, urban policy was clearly not a priority for the French and UK government. The issues of urban problems and social exclusion required more attention than that given by existing urban policies. In France, Le Galès found that the post-1995 increase in spending on urban policy measures took place following budgetary transfers from the different ministries rather than an increase in funds allocated specifically to this area (Le Galès, 1995).[42]

Could the European intervention make a difference? Figures, presented in previous chapters, do not represent any major financial allocation of European Structural Funds specifically for urban areas. Did the European funds manage to reach areas neglected by the national schemes or were they carved up to co-finance existing priorities? The answer may be a complex mix illustrating the tensions involved in implementing a supra-national regional policy. We begin investigation with reference to the empirical material where we test the concepts of 'extended gatekeeper', as applied to central government, and 'gatekeeper' for other levels. We follow the strategy of each level of government in order to assess how each sought to represent its interests in the negotiations for the contents of the Programme document in order to ensure that there was a slice of European funds to co-finance its own stake in the multiple initiatives.

The ambitions of the mayor regarding the development of Marseille as a leading European city could also be a factor in explaining the bargaining position of the municipality during the negotiations for URBAN. *Euroméditerranée* was not part of the targeted area for URBAN, however its proximity to the centre of the city influenced the negotiations around the

<hr/>

[41] Christian Bachmann, Senior Lecturer (*maître de conferences*) in political sciences at the University of Paris – XIII quoted in a newspaper article (*Le Monde*, 19 June 1996). Christian Bachmann is co-author with Nicole Le Guennec of a book dealing with urban policy reviewed in the above article in (Bachmann and Le Guennec, 1996).
[42] For more details, please refer to Le Galès (1995, p.267). For the UK, Le Galès (1995, p.253) found that the total sums allocated to urban policy in 1990 amounted to around £1 billion sterling, representing around half a per cent of the total budget of the state. According to the CURS (1995) report presented in chapter four, the SRB actually reduced the overall spending on urban regeneration. Hence, from not being a priority area in the first place, urban policy spending in the UK was reduced even further in the 1990s.

contents of the Programme Document (Interviews, DG XVI officials, May 1998). Yet before any battle over the contents of the Programme Document, the City of Marseille had to compete with other cities in order to ensure selection for URBAN. We now turn to this stage of the policy process; was there any possibility of bypassing central government in order to ensure that the funds came to Marseille?

5.2 Negotiations for the Delivery of URBAN in France

Similar to the case of the UK, the demand for URBAN in France far exceeded the supply of programmes the Commission had envisaged for the Member State. Following initial experimentation, 185 *Contrats de Ville* were agreed for the period 1994-1998; only a restricted number of these could gain funding under URBAN. Given the limited scope of the CI URBAN, the initial number of projects anticipated for France by the European Commission was six. The financial allocation for France as a whole was one of ECU 4.8 million for Objective 1 areas and ECU 50.2 million for non-Objective 1. Was there any element of bypassing the Member State or did the Commission, as was the case in the UK, allow the central authorities to make the selection?[43]

5.2/1 Stage One: the Selection of Cities

There was evidence of Marseille seeking to be an entrepreneurial city even before the ambitious *Euroméditerranée* programme was launched. A Permanent Representation of the European Commission was established in the mid-1980s during Gaston Defferre's period in office as Mayor of Marseille. This was linked to the enlargement of the EU with the accession of Spain and Portugal in 1986 and firmly established Marseille as France's second city (Interview, Commission Official, Marseille, August 1998). Indeed, some local representatives of the French state view the origins of the Permanent Representation as an example of Marseille seeking to bypass central government. However, the European Commission's Permanent Representation does not get involved in the allocation or implementation of

---

[43] This section is largely based on information from interviews of officials in DG XVI conducted in Brussels (April 1998). The figures quoted are also confirmed by internal documents made available to me for the purposes of my research during my period as a trainee in DG XVI, February to July 1997.

Structural Fund programmes in Marseille; this is discouraged by the prefecture officials (Interview, Commission official, Marseille, August 1998). Activities are limited to the diffusion of information about the various programmes.

The events around the launching of the first Urban Pilot Projects (UPPs) are quoted as another example of the City of Marseille pursuing its own agenda (Interview, prefecture official, July 1998). Yet we saw in chapter three that it was impossible for the city to bypass the central authorities in the implementation of the UPP, even if the programme had initially been launched as an exception to the rules. Regarding the application for URBAN, representatives from the City of Marseille actually went to Brussels to make the case for their city to be awarded URBAN. In this sense, Marseille was an exception to the other French cities that had not taken the initiative to contact DG XVI directly in order to promote their application (Interview, Commission official, Brussels, May 1998). Commission officials were willing to engage in dialogue through informal meetings with representatives from Marseille. However, the actual bargaining to choose the number of cities to be awarded URBAN in France was carried out between the Commission and central government. In contrast to the case of the UPPs, the local state officials at the prefecture were informed about the city's bid for an URBAN programme and were supportive (Interviews, prefecture, Marseille, July and August 1998).

The period between July 1994, when URBAN was first launched, and November 1995 was one of intense negotiation between DG XVI and the representatives of central government. France, like the UK and some other Member States, initially presented a list of towns and cities to the Commission exceeding the number of programmes provisionally allocated by DG XVI. In November 1994, the French national authorities had submitted a total of twelve projects to DG XVI. Although a small programme in terms of funds negotiations in France, like in the UK, took place at a very senior level. The dossiers were prepared by officials from DG XVI. Both the Director-General, Eneko Landaburu and the former European Commissioners, firstly Commissioner Millan and his successor, Commissioner Wulf-Mathies, were involved and kept informed of progress.

Negotiations with the French authorities were through senior officials at the regional planning body, DATAR. Both the former Commissioner Millan and Commissioner Wulf-Mathies corresponded with the French ministers in the Balladur government. Simone Veil, Minister of Social Affairs, Health, Towns and Cities and Daniel Hoeffel, Minister for National and Regional Planning were both involved in the negotiations for the allocation of

URBAN. Throughout 1995 the Commission insisted that the number of French projects, like those of other Member States, had to be reduced in number in order to ensure concentration of resources to allow evaluation of the impact of European funds in the targeted area. If resources were allocated to an excessive number of projects in any Member State, this could dilute the impact of the programme and threaten the integrated approach which the Commission sought for URBAN.

Failure by the national authorities to make an early choice of cities in 1994 meant that the allocation of URBAN in France gained increasing political salience as it coincided with the electoral cycle of 1995. Clearly the French authorities did not want to choose in view of the May presidential elections and the forthcoming municipal elections in June. Furthermore, following the elections in May 1995, there was a temporary period where a new government was to be constituted and during this time correspondence was channelled through France's Permanent Representation in Brussels.[44] The Commission compromised with the French authorities by agreeing to accept eight projects instead of the original six envisaged for France. Yet the central government in France was still in a position of having to eliminate four projects from their original proposal of twelve. Given the political salience of the matter, due to the forthcoming municipal elections, the French authorities were not willing to decide. How could the deadlock be broken?

The Commission, dependent on the national authorities to make a decision, considered various possibilities. The first was to wait until after the elections when the French authorities would decide. The second was to yield to French pressure and agree to take on twelve projects. A third option would be for the supra-national institution to select projects on the basis of technical merit as judged by the Commission officials – such had been the solution to the Italian case whereby the DG XVI had to choose twelve cities out of an original thirty three proposed by the Italian authorities. Yet the central government in France rejected any proposals for the Commission to mediate in this way. Similar to the UK, the central government in France monopolised the decision-making regarding the allocation of URBAN within

---

[44] Prime Minister Balladur had stood as a presidential candidate against Chirac causing some divisions within the Right in France at the time. Following Chirac's subsequent victory, Juppé was appointed Prime Minister under Chirac until the legislative elections of 1997. Following the results of the legislative elections, President Chirac, a member of the *Rassemblement pour la République* (RPR) party appointed a Socialist Prime Minister, Lionel Jospin (*Parti Socialiste* – PS). The Socialist government under Prime Minister Jospin worked alongside President Chirac; this is often referred to as a period of '*cohabitation*'.

the Member State. Despite the Commission's attempts to gain an early response from the French authorities, no decisions were reached until November 1995. The following were included in the final selection: Valenciennes (Quartier Dutemple) Objective 1, Mulhouse, Roubaix-Tourcoing, Amiens and Marseille (Objective 2), Aulnay-sous-Bois, Les Mureaux and Lyon (all ineligible for Objectives 1 or 2). Bastia (Objectve 1), Saint-Nazaire, St-Etienne de Rouvray and Châlon-sur-Saône (all Objective 2) were excluded.[45] The first negotiations for the Programme Documents concerned Valenciennes, Roubaix-Tourcoing and Marseille.

In short, it was sixteen months from the Commission's launch of URBAN to the final selection of French cities. In addition to the political sensitivity of the matter, Commission officials also attributed delays to the 'administrative slowness' in the procedures of the French state (Interview, DG XVI official, May 1998). There is always a time lag involved between any Commission correspondence and a formal reply from the Member State; this was evident in the British as well as the French example. The case of France also illustrates how European programmes, although launched by a supra-national institution, can fall victim to the electoral process within a Member State; no decisions were made until the presidential and municipal elections were over. This is evident at different stages of implementation since, even when the programme was agreed for Marseille, there was a period from November 1997 to September 1998 when little progress could be made due to regional elections in France. For the duration of the electoral period, no decisions could be taken for any project which also required a financial contribution from the regional authority for the PACA Region.[46]

5.2/2 Stage Two: Negotiations for Administrative Arrangements

We now progress to stage two regarding the administrative arrangements to deliver URBAN. The Commission, as noted earlier, did not seek to influence the composition of the partnership to deliver the European programme. The Commission depended on the national, regional and municipal levels of

---

[45] This lists the eight initial URBAN programmes chosen in France. It does not cover the URBAN Reserve funds launched in 1996 allowing a second selection of cities to be awarded an URBAN programme.

[46] All major decisions are frozen prior to any regional elections and there follows a period of re-adjustment whereby a new majority may take time to re-establish the team to deal with policies involving the region. The key point for the 1998 regional elections was the disruption caused by the electoral cycle rather than the implications of the change of majority.

government to adapt their administrative structures to implement URBAN. The next section reviews how the *Contrat de Plan, Contrat de Ville* framework was integrated with established procedures for administering European funds. In contrast to the UK, the Commission did not seek to ensure that representatives of the local and community sector would have a place on the Management Committees for URBAN. In the case of France, the Commission relied on the existing partnership to establish the means through which the targeted recipients could channel their proposals. By the time Marseille was actually selected, and negotiations for the delivery of URBAN began, the majority had changed in the municipal elections in Marseille. At this stage, we begin to see 'gatekeeping' by the municipal level of government which will be more fully investigated in section 5.2/3 dealing with the negotiations for the contents of the Programme Document. Firstly, let us review which administrative adjustments were made in order to deliver URBAN in Marseille, part of the PACA Region.

The Commission did not seek alternative administrative arrangements for the implementation of URBAN. The Commission relied on the established contractual system involving the national, regional and local authorities to deliver URBAN. One senior Commission official suggested that it was difficult for the Commission to get involved in the issue of the composition of local partnerships in a Member State with directly elected regional and municipal government. In the case of France, it would be more delicate for the Commission to prescribe the composition of a partnership if elected regional and local authorities proposed their own system based on existing decentralised structures.[47] Other Commission officials stated that a more interventionist approach by DG XVI would go against established ways of working with the French authorities at all levels of government (Interviews, DG XVI officials, Brussels, May 1998).

The section in the prefecture dealing with regional and European affairs, the SGAR, was responsible for the everyday management and administration of URBAN. The SGAR was responsible for the overall organisation of the URBAN programme, the dissemination of information and coordination between the various actors. The Monitoring Committee (*Comité de Suivi*) would normally meet approximately two times a year and deal with the

---

[47] Interview, senior Commission official, Brussels, May 1998. The period referred to is prior to the election of the Labour government, committed to a programme of devolution, in May 1997.

strategic aims and objectives of the URBAN programme.[48] Meetings of the Monitoring Committee were chaired by a designated representative of the regional prefect (*Préfet de Région*) who had ultimate responsibility for URBAN. In contrast to the UK, neither the Commission nor the local authorities raised the issue of whether central government should chair the Monitoring Committee for the programme. The arrangements for the Monitoring Committee for URBAN confirmed those for the contractual process whereby management committees are chaired by a representative of the prefect.

The composition of the Monitoring Committee for URBAN was identical to that for Objective 2 programmes during this period.[49] The representation of the state in the Monitoring Committee indicates that this was by no means a monolithic unified structure but one of national, regional and local representation. The implications of this will be explored in the detailed section on the implementation of URBAN in Marseille in chapter seven. A representative from DG XVI and DG V had a place on the Monitoring Committee. It is interesting to note that Commission officials from the Permanent Representation in Brussels were excluded from the Monitoring Committee even as observers; their role was purely one of public relations and dissemination of information regarding programmes. Any additional presence of Commission officials, beyond that of representatives of DG XVI and DG V who actually provided the funds, was not encouraged by the SGAR (Interview, official from the Commission's Permanent Representation, Marseille, August 1998).

The implementation of URBAN in France raises additional issues, although they were not an individual point of discussion between the Commission and national authorities. URBAN was aimed at deprived areas of cities where certain elements of the population were excluded from participating in the democratic process. In France only French citizens have the right to vote at national, regional and local elections; even legal residents who are not French citizens are unable to vote at these elections. The districts of Marseille allocated URBAN funds have a high percentage of immigrants who are unable to vote. Hence even without entering the debate on voter apathy or abstinence amongst the existing electoral pool, we have the problem that many residents of these areas are completely excluded from

---

[48] There were variations to this depending on the local situation for each programme. In the period covered by this study the Monitoring Committee for URBAN in Marseille had met on an annual basis.

[49] The full list of participants can be found in Appendix one, chapter five.

the democratic process. We therefore need to examine the means through which the targeted population could channel their demands. The *Contrat de Ville* structures had some provision for grass roots consultation, through the system of project leaders to which we now turn.

As noted in section 5.1, a project leader (*chef de projet*) was based in each of the targeted areas of the *Contrat de Ville*. Their role for URBAN, as for the national *Contrat de Ville* or GPU measures, was to consult the local population resident in the area in order to channel their input through the established system. Examples of this consultation process are provided in chapter seven which investigates the delivery of URBAN at grass roots level. Here we concentrate on the overall administrative system in place through which any projects proposed would have to progress. Local associations or residents on the ground would firstly propose projects to the project leader through the existing procedures.[50] For URBAN there was an administrative body, below that of the Monitoring Committee, the URBAN Advisory Committee (*Comité d'orientation du Programme d'Initiative Communautaire* URBAN, COCPUR).

The Commission only participated at the higher-level Monitoring Committee that dealt with the overall steering of the programme. The COCPUR dealt with the selection of projects to be awarded URBAN funding and met more regularly than the Monitoring Committee. Meetings of the COCPUR took place approximately every three months. The precise frequency of meetings also depended on whether sufficient projects had been prepared and were at the stage of final approval to receive funding under URBAN. This would require the dossier for an individual project to be complete including details of the match-funding committed by each partner involved in the proposal for URBAN funding.

The COCPUR was chaired by the sub prefect for towns and cities – the local representative of the state with responsibility for urban policy (*politique de la ville*). A representative of the SGAR attended the COCPUR chaired by the sub prefect for towns and cities and the latter attended the Monitoring Committee chaired by the SGAR. In this way, the existing arrangements for the delivery of the national urban policy were fused with the European and national procedures. The sub prefect for towns and cities had responsibility for urban policy and coordinated the everyday emergence of projects in line with the broader objectives of the *Contrat de Ville* and, where appropriate, the GPU; hence the chairing of the programming

---

[50] In chapter seven, we will see that there were variations in procedures depending on the specific programme and the political majority in the municipality at the time of proposal.

committee – the COCPUR.[51] The higher-level Monitoring Committee dealing with the more strategic aims was chaired by the SGAR, the representative of the state dealing with European programmes. In contrast to the UK, there was closer administrative integration between the European and national urban policies. Yet in chapter seven, we will investigate whether there was sufficient flexibility to allow non-established groups to access the European funds.

Clearly, the only legitimate channel for representation of the targeted recipients of URBAN funds was through the project leader. Interestingly enough, the origins of the URBAN bid in Marseille were through this system. In the following section, we will explore how the original bid for URBAN in Marseille emerged following careful preparation by officials in the City of Marseille operating within the procedures of the already established *Contrat de Plan, Contrat de Ville*. The final contents of Programme Documents could only be decided once a city had secured selection, by the national authorities, for URBAN funding. By the time the final choice was made in November 1995, there had been important changes in both local and national politics.

5.2/3 Stage Three: Negotiations for the URBAN Programme Document

In June 1995 the new majority took office in the Municipality of Marseille. Monsieur Jean-Claude Gaudin belonging to the *Union pour la Démocratie Française* (UDF) became Mayor of Marseille with the support of the *Rassemblement Pour la République* (RPR) party.[52] The period from June 1995 when the new majority took office in the Marseille and March 1996, when the Programme Document was signed, was one of major negotiation at national, European and local level. Jean-Claude Gaudin, the newly elected Mayor of Marseille and President of the Region Provence-Alpes-Côte-d'Azur, also became Minister for National and Regional Development in the Juppé government towards the end of 1995. It is argued in the section below that the changes in the political majorities of the partners involved, namely the state and municipal levels, were to impact on the final version of the

---

[51] This information was provided by documents made available by DG XVI and by the regional prefecture (*Préfecture de la Région* PACA) based in Marseille. The information was confirmed by interviews with local officials in the prefecture and observation of the Monitoring Committee on 9 July 1998.

[52] This was a local coalition of two parties of the French Right, the Gaullist RPR party and the Centre-Right Federation of the UDF.

URBAN Programme Document as well as its subsequent delivery which will be explored in chapter seven.

Once the national authorities had finally selected the cities to receive URBAN, there was a further period of negotiation with the Commission from November 1995 to March 1996 in order to agree the contents and financial package of each Programme Document. Central government and the Commission were the only actors at this stage; this was negotiated between the national authorities, mainly the regional planning body, DATAR and DG XVI. From the overall package of ECU 50 million allocated to non-Objective 1 areas in France, Marseille received ECU 3.938 million of ERDF funds and ECU 3.062 million of ESF funds, a total of ECU 7.000 million as a whole.[53] Given that the ECU 50 million was spread between 7 non-Objective 1 areas, this would appear a reasonable proportion of funds allocated to any particular city. Negotiations regarding the contents of the Programme Document, involved a wider range of actors in line with the French contractual process.

DG XVI had certain guidelines for the Programme Documents for the implementation of URBAN in France.[54] This envisaged projects of benefit to the residents in the targeted areas involved in local regeneration strategies. Operations outside the eligible zone would only receive URBAN funding if this fitted with the regeneration of the area as a whole and was of benefit to the residents or businesses within the eligible area. Guidelines sought to clarify eligibility and aimed to ensure additionality rather than the use of European funds to subsidise projects would normally be the responsibility of local authorities. The refurbishment of public buildings such as the town hall, for example, would not be eligible for funding under URBAN. Yet selected building and infrastructure projects of benefit to the economic regeneration of the area would be eligible. For example the regrouping of public buildings would be eligible, as would administrative buildings, if this was related to training and economic integration of the targeted residents. Additional costs related to innovative or experimental projects aiming to create new services in the targeted areas would be eligible. Examples presented were projects under neighbourhood control (*régies de quartier*) employing local people to run local services.

---

[53] The figures are taken from the URBAN Programme Document for Marseille finally agreed on 12 March 1996 (CEC, 1996e).

[54] This section also draws on internal DG XVI documents recording meetings and consultations regarding the implementation of URBAN in France.

In contrast to URBAN in the UK, the Community Economic Development (CED) priority was not a prerequisite for URBAN programmes in France. At individual project level, the partnership could be broadened to include local associations, the private sector and other socio-professional groups. This was not, however, extended to include representation for the selection of projects or the monitoring of the URBAN programme; the central, regional and municipal authorities stated that procedures for this existed within their own contractual system. Match-funding was left at the discretion of the local authorities. If there was any modification in the amounts given by the national or local authorities within the Member State, this did not concern the Commission provided its total matched the contribution from the European Commission. The Commission allowed the local and national administrations within the Member State to draft the Programme Document.

We now turn to the perspective of the national, regional and local authorities – the signatories of the *Contrat de Plan*, *Contrat de Ville* which provided the match-funding for URBAN. Interestingly enough, empirical evidence suggests that Marseille's bid for URBAN did originate from the grass roots, through the system of project leaders employed by the municipality. However, by the time the initial proposals had progressed through the various tiers of government to reach the supra-national level in Brussels, the final programme agreed and signed presented a different set of priorities. The material below presents the evidence to support the argument that, although a small programme, URBAN was 'carved up' by the various parties to represent their own interests. This is where the concept of policy networks can be combined with that of 'gatekeeping' in order to analyse the processes. Local, regional and national government were already linked into a structure of the *Contrat de Plan*, *Contrat de Ville*. The period from November 1995 to March 1996 was one of intense negotiation between the national and local authorities. Through the contractual process, each of the actors were linked and depended on each other for implementation; each brought their own resources into the network.

Firstly, how was the bid for URBAN originally prepared to ensure selection in the first place? As noted earlier, the *Contrat de Ville* had already been signed in Marseille in July 1994 around the time that URBAN was launched in the Official Journal. As part of the *Contrat de Ville*, a project leader was based in different areas of Marseille. The role of the project leader, as noted earlier, was to liaise with the local residents and businesses to prepare projects for funding under the various categories of the *Contrat de Ville* or the GPU. As part of the *Contrat de Ville* scheme a project leader was based in the St Mauront neighbourhood, situated in the 3rd district (*3ème arrondissement*) of Marseille. St Mauront was at the periphery of the two other major regeneration programmes: *Euroméditerranée* and the GPU.

Although in close proximity to *Euroméditerranée* in particular, St Mauront had not been included in the geographical area where this ambitious programme was operating. St Mauront had also been excluded from the GPU area representing the highest proportion of state spending on building and infrastructure projects. The project leader in St. Mauront and any visitor to this area of Marseille would clearly see the degradation evident in this neighbourhood.[55] The principle of concentration in European regional policy attempts to focus aid on areas of greatest need. It was the central authorities, not the Commission, which decided on the final list of cities to receive URBAN. Yet the decision to grant URBAN to this particular part of the city did not challenge the principle of concentration since the statistics presented in the URBAN Programme Document, and the physical evidence on the estate, presented convincing evidence of the urban decay in St Mauront.

St Mauront is characterised by run-down private estates, often sub-let to illegal immigrants, and with a serious social and drugs problems as well as particularly high unemployment. During the period of negotiations for URBAN, the rate of unemployment in St Mauront was 38.9 per cent compared to that of 20.2 per cent for Marseille as a whole.[56] The area also experienced problems related to the high density of degraded private housing (*copropriétés*). An article in the newspaper *Le Monde* highlighted the difficulties encountered by residents of urban areas with a high density of degraded private housing. The quality of private housing in these deprived urban areas continued to deteriorate although they were hardly mentioned in the latest government initiative at the time, the Urban Renewal Pact. Yet neighbourhoods with a large immigrant population occupying the degraded private housing were described as 'islands of exclusion' where the financial situation gave cause for concern (*Le Monde*, 16 March 1996, p.9). This description fitted the *Bellevue* estate in St Mauront where a project leader was based as part of the *Contrat de Ville* programme. The initial bid for

---

[55] I visited the housing estate as part of my field work in 1998 and interviewed the team of the project leader at the time as well as others involved in preparing the original bid for URBAN. An official from DG XVI had also visited the site in the early stages of the programme, against the advice of officials from the prefecture who felt they could not guarantee the safety of the official concerned in view of the social problems on the estate.

[56] These figures are taken from the URBAN Programme Document agreed for Marseille (CEC, 1996e, p.36).

URBAN appears to have been officer-led since it involved officials employed in this policy area from the Municipality of Marseille. Yet local officials depend on the residents of the targeted areas to assist in the preparation of bids; this feature is evident in both the London and Marseille URBAN programmes. We now explore this grass roots input to the preparation of Marseille's bid for URBAN.

Information is a key element in any network; this was the catalyst to the preparation of the URBAN proposal for Marseille. Officials, employed by the Municipality of Marseille, gained information about URBAN through a network of research centres associated with this policy area. An alliance was formed between local officials employed in the City of Marseille. The project leader worked closely with architects from the municipality's housing department (*Direction d'Habitat*). The local officials prepared a bid to bring URBAN funds to the neglected area of St Mauront. When the process began, the municipality was under Mayor Vigouroux from the *Groupe Majoritaire Marseille*.[57] The officials from the department in the municipality dealing with urban and social policy (*Mission Ville*) worked in alliance with the housing department (*Direction d'Habitat*) with the full support of the elected politicians in the municipality.[58] The local councillor dealing with this policy area was Michel Cristofol, also of the *Groupe Majoritaire Marseille*, with particular responsibility for housing, living conditions and health.

The officials, in turn, relied on information from the grass roots in order to identify the needs of the area and prepare a case for funding. In terms of subsidiarity, it could be argued that the residents of the area were the best placed for identifying the needs of the St Mauront neighbourhood. The project leader organised a number of meetings with local residents in order to prepare the case for bringing European funding to the neighbourhood. One project proposed related to the building of a well-lit pedestrian pathway across the estate to allow safe passage through for adults, and also children, enabling them to reach the school safely. Given the proximity of the

---

[57] Robert Vigouroux became Mayor of Marseille after the death in office of Gaston Defferre; he was then elected in his own right for the period 1989-1995. Although Robert Vigouroux had originally been a member of the Socialist Party (*Parti Socialiste*) there had been some internal wrangles and dissensions among the Left alliance in Marseille at municipal level during his period of office. Robert Vigouroux was supported by the *Groupe Majoritaire Marseille* alliance.

[58] The individual project leaders and their respective teams, based in the targeted, areas are supervised by the Director of the *Mission Ville*, the department in the municipality dealing with urban and social policy.

motorway which dissects the neighbourhood of St Mauront, the residents felt that this pathway would improve economic and social conditions by allowing access through an otherwise closed estate.[59] The pathway was the most significant project proposed which could be eligible for ERDF funding under URBAN. Other projects put forward based on the themes in the *Contrat de Ville*, only some of which were eligible for European funding.

Given that the project leader structures existed as part of the *Contrat de Plan*, *Contrat de Ville* partnership, the Commission accepted the information on the St Mauront district presented by the City of Marseille. In this respect, the proposal fulfilled the criteria of concentration, partnership, additionality and programming and the Commission supported the targeting of this area of this city. The degradation in St Mauront is so acute that a project, such as the proposed pathway opening up the estate, would be immediately visible to the local residents who had participated in the preparation of the bid. Chapter seven will investigate whether or not the project ever came to fruition. Firstly, we should note the incremental changes in the version of the URBAN Programme Document finally agreed with the Commission in March 1996. We begin with the perspective of the majority in the municipality, elected in June 1995.

Jean-Claude Gaudin was the newly elected Mayor of Marseille and President of the Region Provence-Alpes-Côte d'Azur. Towards the end of 1995, Jean-Claude Gaudin also became Minister for National and Regional Development. Although originally conceived by officials dealing with the *Contrat de Ville*, any proposals for URBAN had to be channelled through the section of the City of Marseille dealing with European programmes, the *Mission des programmes privés et européens* (MIPPE). This unit was in direct contact with elected officials and was responsible for the external relations of the municipality. URBAN aroused the interest of the new majority in the municipality. The renewal of the centre of Marseille was one of the broader objectives of the newly elected councillors of the municipality. There was no dispute about the level of degradation of St Mauront, yet the high immigrant population and the inability of many of the residents to vote, due to lack of French citizenship, made the area less of a political prize.[60] Parts of the centre of Marseille were also degraded with pockets of high unemployment; 32.9 per cent in Belsunce and 28.2 per cent in Panier

---

[59] Interviews with officials, the project leader at the time and others in the Housing Department of the Municipality of Marseille, July and August 1998.
[60] See p.150 regarding voting regulations in France.

situated in the 1st and 2nd districts respectively.[61] Addressing the problems in the centre of town, more visible to visitors and potential investors, could also directly complement the activities of the *Euroméditerranée* programme.[62]

One official described how the proposals for the centre of the city were 'implanted onto the projects that had been prepared for St Mauront' (Interview, local official, Marseille, August 1998). Another official explained how the team of the newly elected mayor became involved with URBAN. Officials from the municipality gradually 'seized control of the URBAN programme and prioritised the centre of the city (*centre ville* area) over St Mauront' (Interview, local official, Marseille, July 1998). These assessments were confirmed by numerous local representatives of the state based at the prefecture (Interviews, July and August 1998). The next major area included in the URBAN Programme Document was therefore the centre of Marseille, the first and second districts, some of which had not been covered by the *Contrat de Ville* programme. The process is emphasised in the Programme Document as follows:

> Although the city has already committed itself to significant action in the centre of the city, the lack of finance does not allow acceleration of the regeneration process. The financial assistance of the URBAN CI will be a determining factor to expand and accelerate the steps taken in the 2nd and 3rd districts of the city. It will also be a determining factor promoting intervention in the 1st district which at present is not included in any partnership, local, national or European (CEC, 1996e).

The priority given to individual projects in the centre of Marseille was to become increasingly apparent in the subsequent implementation of URBAN. The tensions this caused between the local representatives of the French state and the municipality will be explored further in chapter seven. We now turn to the role played by of representatives of the French state involved in the negotiations for URBAN.

As part of the negotiating process for the URBAN Programme Document the central ministries, the inter-ministerial delegation DIV and the regional

---

[61] Unemployment figures for the centre of Marseille are taken from the URBAN Programme Document prepared in 1995 and finally agreed with the Commission in 1996 (CEC, 1996e).

[62] An interview with a Commission official, involved in the negotiations for the Programme Document, suggests that the Mayor of Marseille was influenced by the wider strategy of the *Euroméditerranée* programme (Interview, DG XVI official, Brussels, May 1998).

planning body DATAR, insisted that the entire GPU area be eligible for the ESF aspect of URBAN. This was negotiated at regional level by the SGAR which represented the state at local level, regarding European programmes. It appears that the SGAR and the municipality were the key actors regarding the negotiation of the programme. Some officials from the field services of the state felt that there had been insufficient consultation on some of the technical matters relating to European programmes. This could have planted the seeds of some of the problems of implementation encountered at grass roots level; this will be investigated further in chapter seven dealing with the implementation of URBAN on the ground. One official expressed the following view:

> The URBAN Programme Document was truly prepared by officials from the SGAR and the City of Marseille, it then needed to be rescued. I wasn't consulted on URBAN in the early stages, yet I was later consulted on the modification of measures included in the original Programme Document. URBAN is an unusual case as it is a political scheme involving the City of Marseille. The state took some time to get involved in the process; it is a political project of the municipality (Interview, official from the field services of the state, Marseille, July 1998).[63]

How can we explain the bypassing of certain officials representing the state and what were the implications of decisions made? Clearly, there was intense bargaining between the various levels of government. The municipality prioritised the centre of the city with immediate proximity to the *Euroméditerranée* programme. URBAN could complement the activities of *Euroméditerranée* which sought to raise the profile of the city as a whole. By the time the Programme Document was signed, the Mayor of Marseille had also become a minister in the national government. This may explain why, to some extent, the field services of the state may have been undermined.

Yet even with a mayor as a minister, more than one central ministry was involved hence the municipality still had to compromise with the state. A central government representative from the Ministry of Work and Social Affairs (*Ministère du Travail et des Affaires Sociales*) had a place on the Monitoring Committee. The local state service dealing with employment and training was the *Direction Régionale du Travail, de l'Emploi et de la*

---

[63] The modification of the measures of the URBAN Programme Document for Marseille was approved in the Monitoring Committee meeting of July 1998. This will be examined in chapter seven of the book.

Formation Professionelle (DRTEFP). Central government had invested the biggest proportion of funds in the building and infrastructure projects of the GPU programme. However, only part of the GPU area was included in the targeted area of the social policy elements under the DSU dealing with neighbourhood regeneration. This left a gap which could potentially be filled by the European intervention. The ESF could be used to finance social policy measures in the GPU area. This is clearly indicated in the URBAN Programme Document finally agreed in March 1996:

> It should be noted that only part of the GPU area benefits from the DSU programme; thanks to the URBAN programme and measure 4 in particular dedicated to social measures, this type of action will be amplified and extended to cover the entire GPU zone as has been the case for other priority areas included in the planning contract (*Contrat de Ville*) (CEC, 1996e, p.46).[64]

Some officials in the Municipality of Marseille expressed the view that the extension of the ESF element of URBAN to the GPU area had been 'imposed on the city by the French state' aiming to use the ESF to complement its own investment in the targeted area (Interview, City of Marseille official, July 1998). The priority of the municipal authorities was the centre of the city rather than the GPU area. We now turn to the perspective of the regional council of the PACA Region.

The region was a signatory of the *Contrat de Plan, Contrat de Ville* and had a financial commitment to the partnership for the policies which fell under its competences. Clearly, the region's financial contribution was required in order to deliver the programme. The President of the PACA Regional Council (*Président du Conseil Régional*) and the Director-General of the services of the region (*Directeur Général des services du Conseil Régional*) had a place on the Monitoring Committee for URBAN. Interviews with officials from the region suggest that they were not so closely involved in the details of the financial package as presented in the Appendix to the Programme Document agreed with the Commission. Any global financial contributions from the PACA Region were calculated between officials from the Municipality of Marseille and the designated representatives from the prefecture on the basis of what could be expected following the contractual framework of the *Contrat de Ville*. Clearly officials within the City of Marseille were the major actors involved in preparing the financial tables

---

[64] Translation of an extract from the URBAN Programme Document agreed for Marseille (CEC, 1996e), 'Programme Operationnel Initiative Communautaire URBAN, 1994-1999, No. FEDER 94.03.048, No. ARINCO, 94.FR.16.052'.

specifying the contribution from each partner. One official described the process as follows:

> The City of Marseille knows that the region, within the framework of the contract that has been signed, commits itself to contributing significant sums to the process. The city also knows that the region agrees to contribute specific sums to some of the operational areas of the programme. So you can see clearly that they (the officials from the municipality) have calculated the region's contribution by saying if we take into account previous experience, we can count on the region's support in the following areas (Interview, official of the PACA Region, Marseille, July 1998).

In this sense, the Municipality of Marseille may be considered the more pro-active member of the partnership. Yet in terms of political leadership the PACA Region, until March 1998, was presided over by the Mayor of Marseille anyway and the fusion of the two levels of government was taken as given. A leading municipal councillor described the partnership as follows:

> The partnership with the region, when the Mayor of Marseille was at the same time President of the Region, was easy. There were no questions asked; we decided and the region would follow; this helped us save time. Now you have to know what the political climate is like, what direction it is going in, whether the negotiations will come to a successful conclusion. It is much more difficult in comparison to what happened before (Interview, local councillor, City of Marseille, July 1998).[65]

While this can facilitate decision-making, the system of accumulation of mandates raises certain issues. Politicians are democratically elected yet the concentration of power in the hands of a limited number of politicians may have implications, for areas such as St Mauront, which have less political clout since many of the residents are unable to participate in the process. Was there a tension between the public policy launched at European level and the local political situation? In negotiations for the Programme Document, St Mauront could not be squeezed out since this had formed the basis of the bid to bring URBAN funds to Marseille. The principle of

---

[65] This comment was made following the results of the regional elections in March 1998 when the Right lost its majority in the region council. Jean-Claude Gaudin, Mayor of Marseille, had also lost his position in the national government following the Socialist victory in the legislative elections of 1997 and the subsequent formation of a Socialist Government under Prime Minister Jospin.

concentration, and the inclusion of St Mauront in the Programme Document, in theory guaranteed action from the supra-national level of government. In terms of public policy, the Commission could detach itself from the political priorities of the elected authorities at Member State level. Yet, as noted earlier, the Commission depends on the national authorities to implement policies. Chapter seven will investigate whether the Commission did manage to reach the targeted area given that, by the time URBAN began to be implemented on the ground, the district of St Mauront was not a priority for the political majority in the Municipality of Marseille.

5.3 An Integrated Innovative Approach or a Marble Cake?

Compared to the UK programmes, URBAN in France appeared to have an integrated approach. The match-funding was already in place, through a system of partnership whereby each level of government contributed in the framework of the *Contrat de Plan, Contrat de Ville*. The contributions committed by each level of government were included in the Appendix of the URBAN Programme Document agreed with the Commission. Even in areas that had not been directly targeted by a national programme, the contractual partners committed funds to match-fund URBAN as was the case for national programmes. In contrast to the case of the UK, the administrative structures for URBAN did not represent a challenge to existing procedures for national and European programmes. Apart from some administrative adjustment to include the sub prefect for towns and cities in the European programming procedures, normally the responsibility of the SGAR, it was business as usual. Can we anticipate smooth implementation of URBAN in the case of Marseille?

Negotiation of a Programme Document is one part of the process; the ability to deliver is the next stage. One immediate point of interest is the allocation of funds for URBAN in Marseille between ERDF and ESF. During this programming period, URBAN was one of the CIs under the management of DG XVI although DG V was consulted for the ESF elements. Although a DG XVI programme, the ERDF and ESF elements were almost equal (ECU 3.938.000 million and ECU 3.062.000 million respectively).[66] The ESF element of URBAN interested the French state for the GPU area. Yet the municipality was also interested in a greater

---

[66] The London programmes had a much higher proportion of ERDF compared to ESF. The figures for London and other cities in the UK are summarised in Table 4.1 in chapter four.

proportion of ESF than would usually be the case as this could complement some of the DSU measures in the *Contrat de Ville*.

The French state was represented at national and local level by more than one ministry or body. Although the term 'state' (*l'État*) is used an all-encompassing word, the reality was a complex mix of various bodies. As noted in section 5.2, some of the field services of the state were bypassed by the SGAR and the local municipality during the negotiations for the contents of the Programme Document. One such local representative of the French state felt that the equal balance of ERDF and ESF measures was problematic given that DG V was not as actively involved in the management of the programme (Interview, local state official, Marseille, 1998). Although DG V had a place on the Monitoring Committee, it was felt that DG V took a less active interest in URBAN as this was not amongst the CIs under the specific responsibility of DG V.[67] Furthermore, chapter seven will explore problems related to the eligibility of projects presented for European funding; not all of the measures under the DSU element of the programme were eligible for European Structural Fund support.[68]

Moreover, the attempt to 'fine-tune' the Programme Document to reflect the priorities of each level of government arguably did not take into consideration the ability of each level of government to honour its financial commitments. Some officials representing the state in the PACA Region expressed concerns regarding the ability of the local authorities to deliver the match-funding committed to the URBAN Programme Document. This raises the issue of the credibility of programmes if the local match-funders failed to deliver. With reference to the American experience in chapter one, the bankruptcy of New York during a period of expansion of federal funds highlighted the problem of local authorities, seeking funds from a higher level of government, and being subsequently unable to provide the match-funding element.

Officials in DG XVI were equally concerned about the ability of local authorities to deliver the URBAN programme in Marseille (Interviews, DG XVI officials, May 1998). On paper, the match-funding was in place within the *Contrat de Ville* framework. In reality, the impoverished local authorities could find it difficult to find the match-funding. One local representative of the state in Marseille summarised the problem as follows:

---

[67] Indeed, DG V did not send a representative to the Monitoring Committee that I observed on 9 July 1998.

[68] Please refer to section 5.1/2 (p.129) where the DSU element of the *Contrat de Ville* programme is reviewed.

I think that we don't realise that there may well be a problem of delivering the URBAN Programme Document. Up until now, it is the state that has forwarded most of the match-funding. The municipality committed itself to match-funding a number of areas but changed the financial tables when it came to actually respecting the sums indicated. In my opinion, there is a problem (Interview, local state official, Marseille, July 1998).

We will see in chapter seven that there was flexibility regarding which level of government provided the match funding. Yet more than one state official expressed concerns regarding this:

I think Europe at the moment has a problem regarding the credibility or rather the commitment of local authorities – whether it's Marseille or other areas. We (the Commission) have given you the money for that, are you going to be capable of spending it? (Interview, SGAR official, Marseille, July 1998).

While there was a wealth of existing national schemes, and the European funds provided additional resources, it is not clear that there was any coherent integration between the various schemes or the European intervention. Neither is it clear that the match-funding promised could actually be delivered. There was a wide range of actors as well as competing schemes with state representatives at local and central level. Implementation could represent a marble cake scenario with lines of authority blurred, rather than the integrated, innovative approach sought by URBAN. This will be further explored in chapter seven dealing with implementation on the ground.

5.4 Conclusions

The early stages of the implementation of URBAN in the case of Marseille provide examples of 'gatekeeping' by the different levels of government involved. Similar to the UK, the programme was initially paralysed by the failure of the national authorities to select a restricted number of cities for the experiment, as requested by the Commission. Indeed, in the case of France, the programme became a victim of the presidential, and municipal, election process making the choice of cities a matter of high political salience. Unlike the initial UPPs, the Commission was unable to bypass central government regarding the awarding of URBAN to Marseille.

By the next stage of the policy process, it was clear that 'gatekeeping' was not the exclusive domain of central government. The clearest example of this was the negotiations regarding the contents of the Programme

Document. This reflected the priorities of the newly elected mayor and his vision of making Marseille a successful, entrepreneurial city following the *Euroméditerranée* theme. Yet the accumulation of mandates blurs the lines between central, regional and local government in France since, at one stage, Jean-Claude Gaudin held political office at all three levels. While officials may seek to implement programmes objectively, politics can influence procedures. Consequently concessions were made, by central government and the Commission, allowing the municipality to include areas in the Programme Document that had not been part of the original submission to bring URBAN funds to Marseille. The other part of the bargain was for the municipality to honour its commitments to act in areas of low political priority, namely the neglected St Mauront neighbourhood, supported by the Commission and the state in the original bid. The state also depended on the municipality to bring forward projects eligible for ESF funding agreed for URBAN in the GPU area, prioritised by central government.

The state could provide additional funding for the delivery of programmes. Under the decentralisation laws professional training, for example, was the responsibility of the regions; however, in order to tackle the economic crisis and rising unemployment, the state also intervened in this area (Douence, 1995. p.15). The field services of the state could provide specialist advice regarding technical matters such as the eligibility of measures and ultimate responsibility for local implementation remained with the regional prefect. Yet both the central government and the Commission depended on the specialist services of the municipality and the project leaders, based in the targeted areas, to prepare individual projects to receive funding under URBAN.

All the actors involved in the implementation network of URBAN depended on each other at the different stages of the policy process. However the *Contrat de Ville* structures granting the mayor responsibility for the project leaders could potentially give the municipality additional room for manoeuvre with respect to the other participants. Indeed, the complexity of the policy process and the multitude of existing schemes reviewed in this chapter gave powerful local politicians extra leverage in controlling European, as well as national, programmes. We will investigate this 'gatekeeping' in local implementation in chapter seven.

Appendix 1 to Chapter 5

Composition of the *Comité de Suivi* (Monitoring Committee) for the Implementation of the URBAN Community Initiative in Marseille

- *Le Préfet de Région* (Regional Prefect or his designated representative to chair the Monitoring Committee);
- *Le Sécrétaire Général pour les Affaires Régionales* (Secretary General for Regional Affairs);
- *Le Sécrétaire Général de la Préfecture des Bouches-du-Rhône et le Sous-Préfet, chargé de mission pour la politique de la Ville* (Secretary General for Regional Affairs of the Prefecture of the Bouches-du-Rhône and the Sub Prefect with responsibility for urban policy);
- *Le représentant de la Délégation Interministérielle de la Ville* (the representative of the inter-ministerial delegation for towns and cities);
- *Le représentant de la Délégation à l'Aménagement du Territoire et à l'Action Régionale* (the representative of the Delegation for Regional Planning and Regional Action);
- *Le représentant de la mission 'Fonds Social Européen' du Ministère du travail et des Affaires Sociales* (the representative for the European Social Fund from the Ministry of Work and Social Affairs;
- *Les responsables des axes et des mesures du Programme, désignés par le Préfét de Région, Préfet des Bouches-du-Rhône ainsi que le représentant de la Direction Régionale de l'Environnement* (officials with responsibility for the various measures of the programme designated by the Regional Prefect, the Prefect of the Department Bouches-du-Rhône as well as the representative of the regional environmental body);
- *Le Président du Conseil Régional* (The President of the Regional Council);
- *Le Directeur Général des services du Conseil Régional* (The Director-General of the services of the Regional Council);
- *Les représentants des directions générales concernées de la Commission Européenne* (the representatives of the Directorate-Generals concerned from the European Commission);

- *Le représentant de la Banque Européenne d'Investissement* (the representative from the European Investment Bank);
- *Le Maire de la zone eligible* (the Mayor of the eligible zone);
- *Les maîtres d'ouvrage publics concernés* (the Directors of the public works concerned);
- *Le Président du Conseil Economique et Social Régional* (the President of the Regional Economic and Social Committee);
- *Les Chambres consulaires concernées* (the Consular chambers concerned);
- *Le Conseiller Régional, membre du Comité des Régions de l'Union Européenne est invité aux réunions du Comité de Suivi* (the Regional Councillor, member of the Committee of the Regions of the European Union is invited to the meetings of the Monitoring Committee); and
- *Le Trésorier Payeur Général de Région est membre de droit du Comité de Suivi* (the Treasurer and Paymaster General is a member of the Monitoring Committee).

Composition of the Advisory Committee for the Community Initiative URBAN (*Comité d'orientation du Programme d'Initiative Communautaire*, PIC URBAN, COCPUR)

There is only one committee for both ERDF and ESF funds. The COCPUR is chaired by the Sub Prefect with responsibility for urban policy or his representative (*le Sous-Préfet, Chargé de Mission pour la politique de la ville ou son représentant*). The COCPUR includes the following in its membership:

- *Le Sous-Préfet, chargé de mission pour la politique de la Ville* (the Sub Prefect with responsibility for urban policy);
- *Le Sécrétaire Général de la Préfecture des Bouches-du-Rhône* (Secretary General for Regional Affairs of the prefecture of the Bouches-du- Rhône);
- *Le Sécrétaire Général pour les Affaires Régionales* (Secretary General for Regional Affairs);
- *Le représentant de la Région* (the representative of the Region);
- *La cellule Europe de la Ville de Marseille* (the European Unit of the City of Marseille);
- *Les responsables des axes et des mesures* (the officials responsible for the different areas and measures in the URBAN programme); and
- *Le représentant de la Ville de Marseille* (the representative of the City of Marseille).

Any of the members listed above may delegate a representative to attend the COCPUR meetings accompanied by designated officials with responsibility for each area.

Source: Information adapted from the regulations relating to the implementation of the URBAN Community Initiative in Marseille drafted by the *Sécrétariat Général pour les Affaires Régionales* (SGAR), *Préfecture de la Région Provence-Alpes-Côte d'Azur* (Secretariat General for Regional Affairs of the Region Provence-Alpes-Côte d'Azur). Further details of procedures relating to the delivery of URBAN in Marseille can be found in the document entitled: 'Dispositions de mise en oeuvre DOCUP PIC URBAN, 1995-1999' (SGAR, 1997a) from which details on the COCPUR are taken. Additional information relating to the implementation of Structural Funds in the 1994-1999 period can be found in the following pamphlet: 'Vade-mecum de gestion des programmes communautaires en Provence-Alpes-Côte d'Azur co-financés par les fonds structurels européens. Génération 1994-1999' (SGAR, 1995).

6 Implementation of the URBAN Community Initiative in London: the Heart of the East End and Park Royal

Introduction

This chapter seeks to apply the concept of 'extended gatekeeping' to the empirical case study material relating to local implementation of URBAN in London. Firstly, continuing with the framework of analysis developed in chapter four, we examine in further detail how the delivery of URBAN fitted in with existing procedures for delivering national and European programmes. We will explore this in relation to the 'Action Plan' process adopted for URBAN in the UK. As noted in chapter four, certain points remained outstanding when the URBAN programmes began implementation at sub-central level in July 1996. Here, we will investigate 'extended gatekeeping' by central ministries at the next stage of the policy process. Did the central ministries jealously guard their existing procedures for European funds or were any concessions made to facilitate the delivery of URBAN? If so, how could this be accounted for?

The second major theme to be explored in further detail is how the implementation of URBAN reflected the principles of post-1988 regional policy namely concentration, programming, additionality and partnership. Particular attention will be given to the principle of partnership in the context of the Community Economic Development (CED) priority to Structural Fund programmes. Partnership was extended to include local residents, voluntary and community associations and businesses in the targeted area. For URBAN this representation was to be at two levels; firstly that of the URBAN Management Committee (UMC) which was to include members of the Urban Partnership Group (UPG). The former was to be a steering group to oversee the administration of the programme; the latter was to be the main decision-making body regarding the formation and implementation of the Urban Action Plan (UAP).[1] Issues arise around the composition of these groups and their respective roles in the implementation of URBAN.

Would the local authorities emerge as the dominant partners at local level as had been the case in many Single Regeneration Budget (SRB) programmes?[2] In this respect, local authorities could be viewed as 'gatekeepers' at this stage of the process. Finally, how representative were the community and voluntary representatives accorded a place on the management and partnership groups? Could there be 'gatekeeping' at this level whereby certain groups monopolised the policy process? The chapter will seek to shed light on the above issues with reference to case studies of the two areas of London involved in implementing URBAN.[3] Reference is made to the broader themes developed above although the material is organised, for analytical purposes, around the following headings: The management and administration of the programme, representation of the local community, tensions in local delivery mechanisms, problems of coordination and financial responsibility for the URBAN programme.

6.1 The Management and Administration of the URBAN Programme

With reference to the framework of analysis prepared in chapter four, we begin with stage three of the policy process: negotiations between the Commission officials, central and local authorities regarding the content of the Programme Documents for the targeted areas of the cities concerned.[4] As shown in chapter four, the selection of cities for the first wave of URBAN in the UK was finalised by March 1995. Following this, informal negotiations could begin regarding the agreeing of the contents of Programme Documents for the cities selected. The central government reviewed the initial proposals in the submission of URBAN bids, made the final choice regarding the selection of cities and negotiated the administrative arrangements to deliver

---

[1] Please refer to Appendix one, chapter four where the URBAN administrative arrangements for UK programmes during the period 1994-1999 are presented in full.

[2] This refers to the first round of SRB analysed in the CURS (1995) report.

[3] The regulations for the URBAN programmes in the UK during the period 1994-1999 required all URBAN funds to be committed by 1999. The deadline for actually spending the funds was 30 June 2000 for ESF and the end of 2001 for ERDF expenditure. The empirical material in this chapter is based on a series of interviews and observations conducted from September 1996 to April 1999.

[4] Please refer to chapter four, section 4.1/2 which presents the different stages of analysis for the implementation of URBAN.

the programme. Beyond that, it was the regionally based Government Offices which were involved in finalising the contents of the Programme Documents.

Government Office intervention regarding the contents of the Programme Documents was minor. In the UK it was the local partnerships, not the central government ministries, who were involved in finding the match-funding to deliver the programmes. This could explain the relatively 'hands off' approach of the central ministries in the UK at this stage. There was no match-funding forwarded by the central government to deliver URBAN programmes outside the SRB funds which may, or may not, have been awarded to members of the partnership groups involved in delivering URBAN.[5] One UK civil servant made the following observation on UK programmes:

> Well if the government did provide the match-funding, as soon as the European money came in, then we would want the money to be spent, because it was half our money, how *we* wanted it to be spent, and not necessarily how the local authorities or the partnership groups wanted it to be spent (Interview, DETR official, April 1999, emphasis added).

This can explain why central government ministries, for URBAN in the UK, were more concerned with administrative procedures than with the contents of the Programme Documents. In the UK, Government Office officials reviewed the Programme Documents more on technical matters rather than content. At this level, there was direct dialogue between the Commission and the officers from the local councils who had prepared the bids for URBAN funding (Interviews with local authority officers, September 1996). The final details of the Programme Documents were agreed between the Commission, the Government Office for London (GOL) and the participating local authorities. The sums allocated to URBAN amounted to approximately £6 million over the lifetime of the programme.[6]

---

[5] A local authority, voluntary or community sector association could be awarded an SRB bid although the findings of the CURS (1995) report for the first round of SRB suggest that most successful bids were led by local authorities.

[6] Figures taken from the 'Heart of East End UAP, 1997-1999' (Heart of the East End UPG, 1998, p.3). The figures in ECU million allocated to East London are presented in chapter four, table 4.1. The sums in £ sterling were subject to fluctuation in the exchange rate. Indeed this resulted in the actual sums falling in terms of sterling throughout the life of the programme. This was pointed out to the Commission in a meeting in March 1997 (observation of GOL/Commission meeting during my period as a trainee in DG XVI). No provision had been made for exchange rate fluctuations.

Once the central ministries and the Commission had agreed the administrative arrangements in July 1996, there was little delay in the final approval of the Programme Documents. The Park Royal URBAN programme was agreed on 5 August 1996, that for the Heart of the East End on the 16 August 1996. Clearly, at this stage, the local authorities that had prepared the bids for URBAN were the major actors in the negotiations with central government and the Commission. Yet the local authorities were only one of the partners designated by the Commission to manage the programme. Indeed, the administrative arrangements did not necessarily point to local authorities taking the role of lead partners in the management of the programme.[7]

The Government Offices chaired the regionally based UMCs and consulted the local authorities, who had prepared the bid, to find representatives from the relevant organisations operating in each area (Interview, GOL official, January 1999). It would be anticipated that some of the organisations represented on the UMC would bring sources of match-funding to the programme. This explains why the UMC was largely made up of the key agencies that had been active in regeneration programmes in the respective areas of East and West London.

In East London, some of the partners were also involved in implementing Objective 2 funds allocated to the area in 1994. There was some flexibility regarding the membership and attendance of UMCs. Meetings took place, on average, every two or three months at the discretion of the Government Office for London (GOL) who organised and chaired the UMC (Interviews, GOL officials, January 1999).[8] The following tables present information regarding the composition of the respective UMCs in East and West London.

---

[7] Please refer to the URBAN administrative arrangements presented in Appendix one, chapter four.

[8] One example of this is the subsequent attendance of some of the newly appointed staff related to URBAN. Details of this are provided in section 6.2 dealing with representation on the UPG. These additional members were allowed to attend meetings of the UMC as observers.

Table 6.1 Heart of the East End URBAN Management Committee

Organisation [9]	Status	Number
Government Office for London (Chair)	Government	3
European Commission	European Commission	1
LB Hackney	Local Authority	1
LB Tower Hamlets	Local Authority	1
LETEC	TEC	1
Community Rep	Local community	1
BGCC	Local community	1
Stepney Community Rep	Local community	1
Hoxton Hall	Voluntary Sector	1
Hoxton Trust	Voluntary Sector	1
Heart of Hackney	Regeneration Partner	1
Hackney Task Force	Regeneration Partner	1
East London Partnership	Private Sector	2
Total membership		16

[9] Explanation of acronyms: LB, London Borough, LETEC, London East Training and Enterprise Council, TEC, Training and Enterprise Council, BGCC, Bethnal Green City Challenge. The table was prepared from information taken from the minutes of the meeting on 12 December 1996 (Internal documentation, DG XVI). There were some minor changes in the course of the programme reflecting changes in national regeneration programmes running parallel to URBAN. Some national programmes providing a source of match-funding ended during the lifetime of URBAN and their representatives subsequently withdrew from the UMC. Other changes included the representation of community representatives reflecting changes in the UPG as presented in section 6.2 of this chapter.

Table 6.2 Park Royal URBAN Management Committee

Organisation [10]	Status	Number
Government Office for London (Chair)	Government	3
European Commission	Commission	1
White City UPG	Community	3
VAW	Voluntary sector	1
Brent	Local Authority	1
Westminster City Council	Local Authority	1
Hammersmith and Fulham	Local Authority	1
North West London TEC	TEC	1
Kilburn Police	Police	1
Create SRB	Regeneration scheme	1
College of NW London	Educational Sector	1
Total		15

The composition of the respective UMCs reflects differences between national regeneration programmes operating in each area during this period. The London Boroughs of Hackney and Tower Hamlets are located in East London, forming the area known as Inner-East London. Figures presented in the Programme Document indicate that the area targeted by URBAN had a population base of 48,870 and there were problems of structural unemployment. In the early 1990s unemployment in the URBAN area, the Heart of the East End, was measured at 27.6 per cent; this compared to 15.9 per cent in Inner London and 11.6 per cent in 'Greater London.'[11]

Inner-East London is located near areas with wealth generating potential in the City of London, the regenerated Docklands, Lee Valley manufacturing corridor and Thames Gateway. Yet the inhabitants of the URBAN area

---

[10] Explanation of acronyms: VAW Voluntary Action Westminster, NW, North West. This table was prepared from information provided by internal documents of DG XVI (February 1997).

[11] All the information on East London presented in this section is taken from the 'Heart of the East End URBAN Initiative Operational Programme' approved by the Commission in August 1996 (CEC, 1996c). The unemployment figures for London presented in the operational programme (CEC, 1996c, p.8) are based on the 1991 Population census (OPCS Crown Copyright). A differentiation is made between Inner London, and the area of Inner-East London, located in the London Boroughs of Tower Hamlets and Hackney.

encountered difficulties in accessing employment opportunities due to lack of skills/qualifications and language barriers. In 1991, the total non-white population in the Heart of the East End area was 46.1 per cent compared to 20.2 per cent for London as a whole, and 5.9 per cent for England and Wales. The ethnically diverse population was composed of a large number of refugees including Somali, Vietnamese, Tamils, Ghanaians, Zairian, Angolans, Kurds/ Iraqis and Turks. The fabric of the area is largely made up of densely populated flatted estates, run-down surrounding areas with noise and pollution since the area is a major transportation area to and from the City and the regenerated London Docklands.

In view of the problems highlighted above, East London had attracted numerous national regeneration initiatives that recognised the problems of this part of London. This explains a greater presence of representatives from existing schemes on the Heart of the East End UMC compared to that of Park Royal. National regeneration programmes operating in the Heart of the East End URBAN area included the following: parts of two City Challenge areas, parts of two SRB areas and Hackney Task Force. A new SRB bid was being prepared for the City Fringe area in the early stages of implementation of URBAN. Partners involved in existing regeneration programmes represented both formal and 'informal' local government as explained in chapter four (King, 1993). National regeneration schemes were potential sources of match-funding to deliver URBAN in the East End, hence the presence of their representatives on the UMC.

The Park Royal area is in the west of London; the amount of URBAN funds allocated here was also approximately £6 million. In contrast to the East End where the London Boroughs of Tower Hamlets and Hackney opted to pool their URBAN resources into a common programme, the local authorities in Park Royal decided to divide the URBAN resources between the three boroughs. This was permissible since the administrative arrangements allowed for separate UPGs to be established according to geographical areas. From the outset in Park Royal, each of the local authorities concerned, namely the London Boroughs of Brent, Hammersmith and Fulham and the City of Westminster, viewed the £2 million accorded to each as their own pot of funds for their distinct geographical area.[12]

---

[12] The amount in ECU million allocated to URBAN in London is presented in Table 4.1 in chapter four. Exchange rate fluctuations decreased the amount in £ sterling through the life of the URBAN programme. A report on South Kilburn stated the figure of £1.8 million for URBAN in this area: 'A European strategy for Brent. Building on our strengths' (Brent Council: Policy and Regeneration Unit, 1999). Yet the White City, Shepherds Bush, Edward Woods UAP (White City, Shepherds Bush, Edward Woods UPG, 1998) stated the

URBAN in Park Royal covered part of the Park Royal industrial estate and the surrounding urban areas in the three participating boroughs. Similar to URBAN in the East End, the programme targeted the population on high density housing estates, one in each local authority – South Kilburn (Brent), Mozart (City of Westminster) and Edward Woods (Hammersmith and Fulham). As in East London, pockets of deprivation can exist alongside extreme wealth; the Mozart estate is based in the Queen's Park ward, under the City of Westminster, which includes some of the wealthiest districts in London. The Park Royal industrial estate has been a centre of employment in West London since the 1920s employing 70,000 workers at its peak in the 1930s although this figure has since declined to 32,000. Like the East End, Park Royal had received national funding programmes such as Intermediate Assisted Area and SRB. Although Park Royal failed to attract as wide a range of schemes operating in East London during this period, the 1991 census figures also highlighted a number of problems outlined below.[13]

The unemployment rate of the Park Royal area was 19 per cent compared to a Greater London rate of 11.8 per cent. Although this was lower than the 27.6 per cent of the Heart of the East End, the unemployment rate on the estates designated for URBAN funding was more comparable to the situation in East London: 22.2 per cent as a whole, 28.4 per cent on the South Kilburn estate and 24.0 per cent on the White City estate. Similar to East London there was cultural diversity amongst the targeted population. Black or ethnic minority groups made up 34.1 per cent of the population in the area targeted by URBAN. Furthermore, the 1991 census figures showed that over 40 per cent of the unemployed in the area were non-white. In East London, however, there was a wider range of ethnic mixes with language barriers being a particular problem there due to the large number of refugees in the area. Another difference between the areas is the high level of crime highlighted in the Park Royal Programme Document. Representatives from Kilburn Police were involved in preparing the bid to bring URBAN to this area of London.[14] This may explain why the Police had a place on the UMC

---

figures to be £2 million, a three way allocation between the eligible areas. The funds for the Park Royal URBAN programme were divided equally between the three participating areas; hence the variations in figures quoted may be explained by exchange rate fluctuations at the time each respective document was written.

[13] All the information on Park Royal, presented in this section, is taken from the Park Royal Operational Programme, approved by DG XVI in August 1996 (CEC, 1996d, pp.3-5).

[14] Comment made by a representative of Kilburn Police at the GOL URBAN 'Awayday' for the Park Royal area, 29 April 1998. I attended this conference as an observer.

for Park Royal. What is not so clear is whether proposals from the Police would be eligible for funding given the strict rules of eligibility regarding Structural Funds.

The local authority representation on the respective UMCs was that of salaried officers of the council, not elected councillors. The UK government, as highlighted in the section on negotiations, refused to allow elected councillors on the Monitoring Committees of URBAN or mainstream programmes.[15] The local authorities had been the main actors in preparing the bids and agreeing the contents of the Programme Documents with the Commission. Even at the early stages of the programme, some local authority officers indicated that local councils could be seeking a pro-active role in the policy-making process:

> Central government, GOL and to a certain extent local authorities, though not as much, want to keep their hands on the funding and control what is happening (Interview, local authority officer, Park Royal, September 1996).

Yet, as noted earlier, the URBAN administrative arrangements did not necessarily grant the local authorities a prominent role in the partnership (Appendix one, chapter four). We will explore whether, in practice, the local authorities did emerge as the dominant partners, even if the Commission did not intend this to be the case. The Commission did not prescribe how exactly the UPG was to be formed and here there were variations in practice between the programmes in East and West London. Although Government Offices were kept informed of procedures, this was very much for the local partnerships in the respective areas to decide.[16] The Heart of the East End URBAN involved the London Boroughs of Tower Hamlets and Hackney; a joint UPG was established. In contrast to this in the Park Royal area the three local authorities involved, the London Boroughs of Brent, Hammersmith and Fulham and the City of Westminster each formed a separate UPG for their respective geographical areas. Indeed, there was variation not only in the distinct physical separation of the UPGs but also in the procedures relating to the establishment of the respective institutions.

Although there was one UMC for the Park Royal area, the programme rapidly developed almost into three sub-programmes as each local authority devised their own schemes for establishing the UPG and delivering the local

---

[15] See chapter four, section 4.3/2 on the issue of elected councillors.
[16] See the URBAN administrative arrangements for general guidelines regarding procedures (Appendix one, chapter four).

UAPs.[17] London was the only city in the UK with more than one UPG within a single URBAN programme. Following the 1986 abolition of the General London Council, 33 separate London boroughs governed the city. Clearly, the Commission favoured a regional approach to its cohesion policy and this encouraged alliances between boroughs of the type related to the Objective 2 and URBAN submissions. Yet, in implementation, it quickly became evident that each London borough sought to retain control of its own procedures regarding the delivery of European and national regeneration funds.

The role of the UMC related to the strategic management of the programme. However it is the UPG which, according to the administrative arrangements, had the main task of actually delivering the programme (Appendix one, chapter four). Given that the UPG had such a key role, we should focus our attention on this body. The terms of reference accorded responsibility to the UMC to establish the UPG. In practice, it was the local authorities that played the leading role in the formation of the UPG. The following section deals with the varying procedures relating to the formation of the UPG in each respective geographical area.

6.2 Representation of the Local Community: the Urban Partnership Group?

Before venturing into the details regarding exactly how the UPGs were formed in the respective areas, we should briefly explore the role of the voluntary and community sector in local delivery mechanisms. Hall (1999) highlights how British governments have devoted substantial resources to cultivating the voluntary sector, particularly by involving it in the delivery of social services:

> It is commonly assumed that the development of public social programs associated with the welfare state displaces voluntary endeavour directed at the poor and disabled; and indeed, many British reformers sought public social provision precisely in order to free the working classes from dependence on the charity or voluntary efforts of the upper classes. However, from their very inception, many of Britain's social programmes have been designed to preserve a substantial role for voluntary endeavour. To an extraordinary extent, they have used local volunteers, in tandem with public professionals, to

---

[17] There were no formal changes to the contents of the Park Royal URBAN Programme Document (CEC, 1996d); the differences related to its delivery in the three London boroughs.

deliver social services. In addition, a variety of other policies have been adopted over the years to nurture the voluntary sector (Hall, 1999, p.441).

Hall (1999) highlights the Local Government Act of 1972 which authorised local authorities to spend up to 2 pence on rates to finance voluntary organisations. The Volunteer Centre and Voluntary Services Unit was also established in 1972 in the Home Office in order to coordinate and enhance the role of volunteers in providing social services. The Conservative governments of 1979-1997 reinforced the above trend by encouraging local government to contract out a number of services. Prime Minister Thatcher made a declaration, soon after taking office in 1979, stating that 'the voluntary movement is at the heart of all our social welfare provision'. In the period between 1976 and 1987, the income of the voluntary sector from fees and grants almost doubled. In 1994-1995 12.5 per cent of the income of voluntary associations, a total of £687 million was provided by local authorities and central government provided an additional £450 million (excluding funding from housing), a large proportion of which went to organisations which delivered social services in the areas of community care, family welfare, education and recreation. Although some of the organisations employed professional staff as well as volunteers, the government funding did not appear to affect the voluntary nature of the organisations (Hall, 1999, p.443).[18]

The findings of Hall (1999), as presented above, indicate that there is an established voluntary sector in the UK that could be drawn on to promote the delivery of a programme such as URBAN. Indeed, the composition of the initial UMCs reflected the presence of the voluntary organisations already active in the areas targeted by URBAN. On the one hand, the existence of an established voluntary sector activity could be conducive to promoting the types of citizen participation that the Commission was arguably seeking to promote through its experimental Structural Fund programmes. On the other hand, Hall (1999) also finds some distributive issues that are relevant to the deprived areas in which URBAN was operating:

Although aggregate levels of social capital and political engagement in Britain remain high, they are distributed unevenly across the population. For the most part, political activism and the associational life that sustains it have remained middle-class phenomena in Britain and the preserve of those in the middle age. We should not let the relatively good figures for social capital confuse us

---

[18] Hall (1999) draws some of this information presented from the work of other scholars quoted in full in the article.

into summoning up the image of a polity uniformly criss-crossed by organizational networks and participatory citizens. The more accurate image is of a nation divided between a well-connected and highly-active group of citizens with generally prosperous lives and another set of citizens whose associational life and involvement in politics are very limited (Hall, 1999, p.455).

The Commission's URBAN programme, therefore, was operating in a potentially difficult environment. Firstly, we saw in chapter four that in national regeneration programmes, although voluntary and community organisations were involved, the local authorities were the major partners in the programmes. Secondly, URBAN was targeted at deprived areas of cities, also inhabited by a large proportion of ethnic minorities. In areas with high levels of refugees, such as East London, a proportion of the residents were newcomers to Britain as well to the neighbourhood in which they found accommodation. Hall (1999) also found levels of inequalities of social capital relating to class and movement to urban areas:

> In addition, the distinctive friendship patterns and the associational ties of the working class may be especially vulnerable to secular trends. Their friends and organizational memberships tend to be drawn from the local community. Thus, movement to another locality, which the economic restructuring of Britain increasingly demands, can erode the social capital available to them dramatically. All the surveys utilized here indicate that, while movement to a large urban area does not reduce levels of social trust among the middle class, it consistently does among the working class (Hall, 1999, p.456).

While this analysis focused on class rather than ethnic minorities, it is relevant to our study since many of the targeted areas for URBAN, particularly in the East End, were faced with an influx of newcomers who had left their country of origin, as well as their local community there. Was there a notion of community among the ethnically diverse population of the targeted areas?

Bache highlights how the CED priority of URBAN 'was an attempt to reach parts of the community other partnerships did not reach: the so-called "Heineken effect"...' (Bache, 2000, p.581). The Commission sought to include CED in the implementation of all URBAN programmes in the UK by negotiating specific administrative arrangements outlined in chapter four.[19] Could the institutional framework of URBAN, by the creation of

---

[19] Please refer to Appendix one, chapter four.

UPGs, succeed where national regeneration policies had failed? In other words, would the capacity building measures and institutional structures of URBAN, the European intervention, manage to engage the citizens that other programmes had hitherto failed to reach? The first step in evaluating this is to look at the various procedures for establishing the UPGs in the respective areas.

There was little guidance from the Commission regarding how exactly the local UPGs should be established. The only formal terms of reference were the administrative arrangements agreed between the Commission and national authorities inserted into each Programme Document in the areas awarded URBAN (Appendix one, chapter four). DG XVI, in early correspondence with GOL, stressed how URBAN in the UK represented an opportunity for a more focused application of the CED element of the mainstream programmes. In this respect only a community-led approach, in genuine partnership with other organisations in the area, could provide real solutions to the problems. The importance of capacity building in order to promote community involvement and ownership of the programme was stressed. The Commission would be seeking to gain lessons from each of the URBAN programmes with a view to disseminating information throughout Europe.[20]

There were two problems with the Commission's approach: firstly, it was not clearly defined who or what the community is. Secondly, there were no clear guidelines as to how exactly the implementing authorities should pursue a community-led strategy. This would be a sensitive area since, following the principle of subisidiarity, the national and local authorities could argue that they were best placed to develop the community at local level. In terms of how the procedures should be managed, there were initial problems regarding what could be funded under the capacity building measures.

In the Park Royal area for example capacity building was not part of the original submission and was added to the measures, at the suggestion of the Commission, in order to allow local communities to get involved in running URBAN. This led to some confusion in the early stages regarding exactly how much local authorities could spend on capacity building measures. An indicative limit of 10 per cent was set on the resources that could be allocated to this although the Monitoring Committees were allowed some discretion in reviewing and modifying this. This was an early example of the

---

[20] Internal DG XVI/GOL correspondence viewed during my period as a trainee in DG XVI, March to July 1997.

types of issues which arose in the course of the programme. Both East London and Park Royal submitted bids under the capacity building element to recruit additional staff to assist in the task of developing a community based UPG; procedures for this varied.

In East London, one of the early decisions of the UMC was to establish a joint URBAN Initiative Development Unit (UIDU) covering the targeted geographical area of both local authorities, the London Boroughs of Hackney and Tower Hamlets respectively. The proposal for a UIDU had been discussed in shadow meetings from September 1996 and this was formally in place by February 1997. Four posts were created in the UIDU to be financed 50 per cent by the URBAN Programme itself and 50 per cent by the local partners; that is the local authorities and their regeneration partners as listed in the UMC. The URBAN funding element was under the capacity building measures of the programme to enable the formation of the UPG and provide it with the technical assistance in order to fulfil its role.

The main body that had presented the bid under the provisions for capacity building was the London Borough of Tower Hamlets. The administration of the salaries of the employees of the UIDU was through the personnel department of Tower Hamlets. In this sense, the staff of the UIDU served URBAN as a programme and the four new members of staff were recruited following advertising in the national press. The salaried staff of the UIDU were paid through the payroll system of the London Borough of Tower Hamlets, the lead partner in the capacity building bid. Yet by 1999, even though the UIDU had been in operation since 1997, interviews with council officers suggest that that no ERDF funding had yet been received from the Commission (Interview, council officer, Tower Hamlets, January 1999).[21]

An interim UPG was established in 1997 for the URBAN programme in East London. Initially this was formed following a process of public meetings in the targeted areas; these were held in March 1997 in each of the six areas for URBAN: St. Peter's, Stepney, Spitalfields, Hoxton, Haggerston and the Heart of Hackney. This process was organised by the staff of the UIDU which, as outlined above, was in operation by then. Information was distributed to the public through local community groups, Tenants' Associations, newspaper reports and posters. The aim of this was to disseminate information regarding URBAN in order to set up the UPG to

---

[21] Issues related to the payment in arrears of ERDF monies will be discussed in the sections of this chapter dealing with the local delivery of projects and the financial responsibility for the funds.

prepare the UAP and deliver the programme. It was proposed that there should be twelve community representatives on the UPG of which at least 50 per cent would be from local residents, 25 per cent from local small businesses and the remaining 25 per cent from local community groups.[22]

It appears that the community representation on the initial UPG was composed of individuals appointed from existing associations such as voluntary organisations or Tenants' Associations, that the local councils were familiar with. The local councils relied on these groups to select prospective members of the interim UPG formed in May 1997 (Interview with community representative of interim UPG, January 1998).[23] The community representatives on the initial UPG in East London were then subject to a democratic election process, which they themselves had encouraged. Due to the problems of staffing related to the UIDU, no progress was made in this until February 1998.[24]

The interim UPG members worked alongside the existing staff and newly appointed Manager of the UIDU to organise an election campaign. Leaflets were delivered to each household in the targeted area disseminating information about URBAN and inviting nominations for election to the UPG. Twelve community representatives, two from each target area, were invited to participate in the election process. The community representatives could be residents or members of local businesses or community organisations. The leaflets clearly invited anyone, with proof of residence in the targeted area, to participate in the process.

The Heart of the East End URBAN Initiative *Election Machine* wants you to participate in the nomination and election of local people to help manage the URBAN Initiative funding programme. If you are interested and want to know more or discuss what is involved feel free to call for an informal and confidential discussion.

---

[22] Internal document presented to the UMC meeting, February 1997.

[23] During this period, the interviewee was also a member of a Tenants' Association based in the targeted area of URBAN in the East End.

[24] Internal problems in the UIDU resulted in the Manager of the UIDU and one of the Community Development Officers leaving their posts in 1997. A new Manager of the UIDU was appointed around November 1997 and a new Community Development Officer shortly after.

Representatives of other organisations were also included in the final composition of the UPG as listed below:[25]

- 12 community representatives
- 2 local authority representatives
- 1 Training and Enterprise Council
- 2 local regeneration agency representatives
- 4 special interest co-opted members

- Total of 21 members of the UPG

Even though considerable effort had been made to democratise the process, the actual participation for the election of community representatives was extremely disappointing. Firstly, only a limited amount of candidates presented themselves for each of the two places. The area targeted by URBAN in the London Borough of Hackney is known as the 'Heart of Hackney'. In the target area of both the 'Heart of Hackney' and Haggerston, only two candidates actually presented themselves for election as community representatives. Since the two candidates were unopposed, the election was cancelled and they were declared elected. This was also the case in the St. Peters area where the third candidate withdrew, leaving the places open for two others who had come forward.

From the information available, it would appear that the majority of candidates presenting themselves for the community places on the UPG were already involved in some kind of community work through Tenants' Associations, voluntary associations or charity work. Despite the distribution of leaflets to the residents in the targeted areas, there was little wider interest in the programme. The proportion of the resident population who participated in the election process was not a significant proportion of the population of the targeted areas. Interestingly enough, in the two areas where there had been a limited number of votes cast, namely Stepney and Spitalfields, this was more related to internal politics of the resident Muslim community rather than any perception of URBAN as a community-led European programme. Figures presented in the table below indicate the poor

---

[25] Extracts quoted are taken from the *Heart of the East End Urban Initiative Newsletter*, Issue 1, January 1998. The UIDU invited possible participants to contact officers to discuss any matters relating to the election of the community representatives.

turnout to the elections for community representatives for the UPG in East London.[26]

Table 6.3 Heart of the East End UPG Elections

Area	Population	No. of Candidates	Total votes cast
Hoxton	7,200	4	8
Stepney	7,600	6	254
Spitalfields	7,200	6	231
Hackney	20,000	2	-
St.Peters	9,400	3	-
Haggerston	11,878	2	-

Stepney and Spitalfields were the only areas where there was significant competition amongst candidates for the position of community representative on the UPG. In Stepney, 46, 99 and 96 votes respectively were cast for 3 competing Muslim candidates and in Spitalfields 101 and 121 of the votes were cast for two competing individuals from the Muslim community. It appears that the issues between the candidates were related to competition between local mosques in the area with different ideas for the resident Muslim community (Interview, UIDU official, April 1999). The central Stepney area covered one ward in Tower Hamlets. At the time of the elections, within the ward as a whole nearly 42 per cent were from ethnic minority groups with Bangladeshis making up the largest single ethnic minority community (42 per cent). This was also the case in Spitalfields, a culturally diverse area where almost half of all the 7,200 residents during this period were of Bangladeshi origin.[27]

Following the election process, there was a majority of men on the UPG; this was felt to be unrepresentative of the socio-economic composition of the population in the targeted area. In view of this, the elected UPG, in

---

[26] Information presented in the table has been prepared from documents following the election process forwarded to me from the UIDU for the purposes of this study. The figures for the resident population in the targeted areas are taken from the 'Heart of the East End, Urban Action Plan (draft) 1997-1999' (Heart of the East End UPG, 1998, pp.18-20).

[27] Details on the cultural diversity of the targeted population are presented in the 'Heart of the East End Urban Action Plan (draft) 1997-1999' (Heart of the East End UPG, 1998, pp.18-20).

conjunction with the UIDU decided to exercise the option in the constitution of the UPG to co-opt additional members representing ethnic minority women. Some members of the UPG did not agree with this and, in the event, only two out of a possible four additional members were co-opted onto the group (Interview, UIDU official, April 1999). This did not solve the problem of lack of interest in the programme amongst a wider range of the population in the targeted areas. In the London Borough of Tower Hamlets there had been some renewal of UPG membership following the election process. In Hoxton and Haggerston, under the London Borough of Hackney, the community representatives had also been members of the interim UPG.

The Park Royal programme also provides examples of the difficulties of engaging local communities to participate in implementing Structural Fund programmes. Like in East London, the local authorities submitted bids under the capacity building element of the programme in order to recruit additional staff to assist in implementing the programme. Similar to East London, this involved an element of recruiting new staff, not previously employed by the local authorities. Applications were made to the UMC in February 1997 for a Development Worker on the Edward Woods Estate (London Borough of Hammersmith and Fulham) this consisted of £52,409 of ERDF to be match-funded by an equivalent amount of local authority funding.[28]

The London Boroughs of Brent and the City of Westminster also gained UMC approval to appoint new members of staff to run the URBAN Programme. In Brent, there were two new appointments funded under URBAN and match-funded by the council: a Community Development Officer based in the Housing Office of Brent Council, situated on the targeted Carlton estate, and an URBAN Projects Officer based in the European Unit in the Town Hall.[29] The role of the latter two appointments was to fulfil the capacity building aspects of the programme so as to involve the local community. In the City of Westminster, we see a variation in that a voluntary sector organisation match-funded one of two new posts; the Community Development worker was funded under the capacity building

---

[28] Internal GOL/Commission documentation relating to the UMC meeting of Park Royal, 25 February 1997. The match-funding element for the Edward Woods Development Worker was provided by the Housing Department of the London Borough of Hammersmith and Fulham.

[29] The URBAN Community Development Officer represented £54,750 of URBAN funds, match-funded by £54,750 from the Brent Council. A second appointment was the URBAN Projects Officer, allocated £54,875 of URBAN match-funded by £54,875 of council funds. Figures are quoted from internal documents forwarded to DG XVI in 1997 applying for ERDF funding for the posts under the capacity building elements of the programme.

measures of ERDF and match-funded by the council. In the spring of 1997 a second post was created, financed by URBAN, and match-funded by Voluntary Action Westminster (VAW) a voluntary organisation already established in the targeted area.[30] VAW had also been involved in the formation of the Voluntary and Community Sector Forum (VCSF) formed in response to the URBAN funding brought to the area.

Was there any greater success in Park Royal in engaging residents or community groups who had never previously been involved? None of the Park Royal UPGs adopted a process of direct elections for the community representatives as had been the case in East London. Similar to East London, shadow UPGs were initially established which gradually evolved in the course of the programme. Like East London, although new appointments were made related to capacity building measures, problems were encountered in engaging a high percentage of the population resident in the targeted areas. In 1996, the very early stages of the URBAN programme, there was a public meeting in Hammersmith Town Hall; this was for the Park Royal area as a whole rather than this particular geographical area. Some of the participants at the public meeting were from established organisations operating in the area, seeking possibilities for additional funding (Interview, UPG member, Queen's Park, January 1998). In the London Borough of Hammersmith and Fulham, the local council approached known organisations active in the area in the early stages of establishing the UPG.

Similar to East London, there was local authority representation on the UPGs established in each area. Local authority representatives on the White City, Shepherds Bush, Edwards Woods UPG included the following: two local councillors, two officers from the council's urban regeneration unit, two estate strategy workers based on each estate in the targeted area and one manager for the programme as a whole. Although the administrative arrangements did not permit local councillors to be part of the UMC for the Heart of the East End or Park Royal programmes, they were allowed to be members of the UPG within each geographical area.[31] One of the local

---

[30] The URBAN funding for the officers amounted to £59,579. Theses figures are taken from the 'Queen's Park. Urban Action Plan, Draft September 1998' (Queen's Park UPG, 1998).

[31] By the time the UPG was established (January 1998), the Labour Government elected in 1997 had changed the regulations regarding the membership of Management Committees of Structural Fund programmes. Elected councillors could be included on Objective 2 Monitoring Committees for SPDs agreed for 1997-1999. However for URBAN, one Programme Document covered the period 1994-1999 (see chapters three and four). Since

councillors representing the local authority on the UPG, Councillor Sally Powell, also represented London boroughs on the Committee of the Regions during this period. The other councillor was also a member of the White City SRB Board.[32] Both councillors were from the Labour Party which had a majority in the London Borough of Hammersmith and Fulham. The post of URBAN Programme Manager, financed by URBAN and match-funded by the London Borough of Hammersmith and Fulham, was advertised internally within the borough. The former European Officer for Hammersmith and Fulham Council was subsequently appointed as URBAN Programme Manager. By January 1998, the UPG was composed as follows:

Table 6.4 White City, Shepherds Bush, Edward Woods UPG

Organisation	Number of Representatives
Local authority	7
Voluntary/Community organisations [33]	3
Residents [34]	4
Public Agencies	3
(Health Authority	
Local Secondary School	
Local Police Division)	
Total membership	17

Appointments to the UPG were initially made for one year, however the previous year's membership could propose candidates. Questions arose concerning whether the resident representatives on the UPG were

---

the administrative arrangements for URBAN 1994-1999 had been negotiated under the previous Conservative government, local authority officers rather than local councillors continued to represent the local authority at UMC meetings for the duration of the URBAN programme.

[32] A £15 million SRB bid had been approved for the area in December 1996 (minutes of UMC meeting, 25 February 1997).

[33] There was some variation in voluntary/community organisations involved during the lifetime of URBAN. Examples of some of the groups involved include the Fatima Community Centre, Community Networks and the Third Age Foundation.

[34] Three representatives of the local population were from the Tenants' Associations of the White City and Edward Woods Estates. The fourth representative was a local resident in a council ward included in the area targeted by the URBAN programme.

representative of the local community. This point had been raised in a community audit conducted in the area. In terms of representation both the Edward Woods and White City Tenants' Associations were concerned that their committees did not reflect the make-up of their diverse community. Both associations included a high proportion of white and older residents on the estate who had been involved for a number of years.[35] Yet the members of the Tenants' Association, invited to participate on the UPG, were drawn from this group.

Attempts in 1998 by the Estate Strategy worker to broaden the membership of the Tenants' Association were largely met with apathy on the Edward Woods Estate. Although 89 residents appeared at the Annual General Meeting of the Tenants' Association, a larger number than was usual at such meetings, this was minimal in relation to the 2,000 people living on the estate. Furthermore, the majority who appeared were those who already supported the existing procedures. Although there were some additions representing the Afro-Caribbean element on the estate, there were no changes to the Chair and Vice Chair levels of the Tenants' Association that also represented residents on the UPG. Furthermore, events suggested that the new additions to the Tenants' Association were motivated by their own agenda, relating to events around the estate, rather than any specific interest in URBAN or other regeneration programmes in the area (Interview, local official, London Borough of Hammersmith and Fulham, January 1999).

The UPGs, within the City of Westminster and the London Borough of Brent, were drawn from Tenants' Associations and voluntary/community groups already active in the area. In this respect, although the UPG was to be the level at which the local 'community' was to be most highly represented, its composition in these areas almost mirrored that of the Park Royal UMC. One difference in the City of Westminster was the involvement of one opposition councillor, a Labour member of the council, who was also very active in voluntary sector organisations in the area.

Although the Conservatives held a majority on Westminster City Council, the Queen's Park area awarded URBAN was in a Labour ward of the borough. Jill Selbourne, a Labour Councillor, played a key role in disseminating information about URBAN to the voluntary and community organisations active in the targeted area (Interview, UPG member, Queen's Park, February 1997). Indeed, the organisation VAW also match-funded one

---

[35] 'The Community Audit of White City and Edward Wood Estates' (Consultants' report written in conjunction with the London Borough of Hammersmith and Fulham).

of the capacity building posts funded under URBAN.[36] The events in Westminster, in these early stages, were also to impact on the final structures for the local management of the programme; this will be examined in the section dealing with financial responsibility for URBAN funds. The Queen's Park UPG, formally constituted in February 1997, was composed as follows:

Table 6.5 Queen's Park UPG

Organisation	**Number of Representatives**
City of Westminster	4
Voluntary Sector	5
Residents	5
Education Sector	1
Business Sector	1
Total membership	16

The four representatives of the City of Westminster were elected councillors. The councillors were not necessarily drawn from the Queen's Park ward, the targeted area for the funds. The Conservative majority in the City of Westminster decided that there should be three Conservative councillors, and one Labour, in order to mirror the Conservative/Labour party proportion in the council at the time (Interview, City of Westminster official, January 1999). The voluntary sector representatives were elected from the VCSF established to disseminate information about URBAN to groups in the targeted area. A constitution was drafted for this forum in order to clarify procedures and ensure bottom-up input into the proposals. The voluntary sector representatives were elected on an annual basis by members of the forum to represent the organisation on the UPG. The VCSF was an open forum which any voluntary or community organisations delivering services in the Queen's Park or north Paddington area were free to attend; it met on a monthly basis. The Education Sector was represented by a local Head Teacher, not a local authority officer, and the voluntary sector representatives included a wide range of groups from Age Concern to

---

[36] Councillor Jill Selbourne was also a member of VAW.

Westminster Race Equality Council (Interviews, Queen's Park UPG members, January 1998).

In a similar process to that of the London Borough of Hammersmith and Fulham, the resident representatives on the Queen's Park UPG were drawn from the existing framework of Westminster City Council. Resident panels existed on the targeted estates to deal with tenants' issues and engage in dialogue with the local authority. Some of this consultation was also related to national regeneration projects such as the Estates Action Programme. The resident representatives on the UPG were drawn from those forwarded by the resident panels already in place in the targeted estates. Like the London Borough of Hammersmith and Fulham, it was difficult to get beyond residents who were already involved anyway in these types of issues. This can be embodied in particular individuals who may even be seen as 'community gatekeepers':

> I think it is crucial on these things to try and avoid getting the usual faces but it is difficult because a lot of people don't want to give their time. I mean we actually made an attempt to keep one of the 'usual suspects' off this partnership group but she carried on turning up to every single meeting and eventually the group said we should invite her on because she is always there, and she does have a valid local opinion, but you can start to think that her opinion is the opinion in Queen's Park (Interview, City of Westminster official, January 1999).

The neighbouring South Kilburn area, under the London Borough of Brent, had a less well-established voluntary sector than was the case in the City of Westminster. Given the Commission's emphasis on a community-led approach, council officers initially turned to an established voluntary organisation for some early capacity building work. The London Voluntary Sector Training Consortium (LVSTC) was initially involved in setting up a Voluntary Sector Forum in the Brent area. There had been a history of poor relations in the past between voluntary sector representatives and Brent Council (Interview, LVSTC officer, September 1997).

In the early period of the programme during autumn 1996, LVSTC was working with local groups who were seeking to appoint an outreach worker in the area (Interview, LVSTC officer, January 1997). Like the other URBAN areas in East London and Park Royal, the initial UPG was composed of groups or individuals who were already active in the area either through existing regeneration schemes or through membership of established organisations. The existing Create SRB board nominated a residents' representative to attend the UPG. The South Kilburn UPG, formed in December 1996, was composed as follows:

Table 6.6 South Kilburn UPG (Carlton Ward)

Organisation	Number of Representatives
London Borough of Brent	4
Voluntary Sector	4
Community Groups	4
Further/Higher Education Sector	1
Business Sector	1
Environment Association	1
Create SRB	1
Health Authority	1
Training and Enterprise Councils	1
Metropolitan Police	1
Residents	2
Total membership	21

In 1997, the URBAN Community Development Officer held public elections in the targeted estates in order to democratise the selection process and seek to involve new members. As in East London, little widespread interest was shown in these elections; indeed, two people came forward on the day and these were declared elected (Interview, URBAN officer, January 1999). Furthermore, the resident representatives who appeared were those who were already active in the established Tenants' Association anyway.

A South Kilburn Community and Voluntary Sector Regeneration Forum was formed in November 1997; this met on a monthly basis. Similar to the case of the City of Westminster, this forum was formed as part of the URBAN programme with a view to bringing together local residents, voluntary and community associations who were active in the targeted area. Elections were held for the community and voluntary sector representatives on the UPG. However, there is little evidence that any of the initiatives managed to reach a wider audience beyond those already active in organisations or Tenants' Associations. One UPG member expressed the following view:

On the higher density estates it is very hard to get people out and the only time you get them out is over housing, because their landlord is invariably the council. So you have got a picture of South Kilburn invariably not having a voluntary or community sector; it just doesn't have it and so in some ways yes, the local council were forced to hand-pick or select people who they knew would be interested or able to take part but, at the same time, there was no attempt to make sure that the message of URBAN and what it could do and when it was coming and all that to the wider community...there was never any attempt to do that. So, you know, you were just forced into a tunnel with which it was just those people who knew that got involved (Interview, South Kilburn UPG member, January 1999).

Clearly, the URBAN programmes in both East London and Park Royal encountered problems in developing the community-based approach demanded by the Commission, the funder of the programmes. Each area of London experimented with different methods yet there is little to suggest that any of the UPGs managed to get beyond those who were already involved in some form of voluntary or community work. On a more positive note, there is evidence that representatives of the voluntary and community sector were able to influence local delivery of URBAN programmes in other areas of the UK. In the case of the URBAN in Sheffield, Bache (2001) found the Commission was more successful in ensuring that the community representatives played a more active role than had been the case on the national SRB programme in the city. Comparing the procedures for URBAN with SRB, Bache (2001, p.356) concludes:

By contrast [to SRB] the precise requirements for community involvement in the URBAN programme contract made it clear what the Commission expected the roles and responsibilities of the various actors would be. As one Government Office official with a knowledge of both programmes put it: 'The Commission model *makes* you have to stick with it. There's no hiding place' (Government Office Yorkshire and Humberside civil servant, interview 1998).

In London although the problem of representation was an issue throughout all the URBAN programmes, it was felt that the UPG as an institution, promoted dialogue and new ways of working among the participants from the resident, voluntary and community sectors. The UPG and was therefore viewed in positive terms (Interviews, East End and Park

Royal UPG members, 1998-1999).[37] However this did not prevent tensions arising in the actual implementation of policy.

The Commission had stressed the community-led approach in its negotiations for the administrative framework for URBAN and in subsequent correspondence with the local partners. Yet the Commission depended on the national and local authorities to implement the programmes. There could therefore be opportunities for 'gatekeeping' by national and/or local authorities at later stages of implementation. Indeed, in the local delivery of URBAN there was evidence of potential tension between the entrepreneurial approach, shown by local authorities in order to beat competition for the funds, and the Commission's insistence on a local strategy, led by local people. The two approaches, coupled with problems of eligibility related to European funds, caused strains in relations between the local partners, Government Offices and the Commission.

6.3 Tensions in Local Delivery Mechanisms

One tension which emerged early in the programmes was the dilemma between the 'provider led' and 'demand led' integration of projects as discussed in chapter four.[38] Some local authorities officers, particularly in East London where a wide range of national regeneration schemes were running parallel to URBAN, favoured the former approach. The Heart of the East End Programme Document clearly stated all the current regeneration activity present in the area:

- Bethnal Green City Challenge Company (1992-1997);
- Dalston City Partnership (1993-1998);
- Hackney Task Force (1991-1998);
- London East and City and Inner North Training and Enterprise Councils and
- The two local authorities, which are also Single Regeneration programme managers.[39]

The London Boroughs of Tower Hamlets and Hackney were, in the initial stages, 'considering whether to manage the process in-house between the

---

[37] For a comparison of the experience of URBAN in Sheffield and London see Tofarides (2003, forthcoming).
[38] Please refer to section 4.2/3 of chapter four where this is set out in full.
[39] Adapted from the 'Heart of the East End, URBAN Initiative Operational Programme' (CEC, 1996c, p.12).

local authorities' (Interview, council officer, January 1999). Early signals from the Commission and Government Office for London discouraged such an approach in view of the CED emphasis to URBAN. This explained the setting up of the UIDU in premises actually based in the targeted area.

Eligibility was another problem that appeared at the implementation stage of URBAN. Representative issues aside, the UPG was the main decision-making body from which projects would emanate. Yet some of the projects proposed were simply not eligible under the strict criteria for European funding. One such example is that of Closed Circuit Television. This problem occurred in the South Kilburn URBAN area where one official stated the following: 'the community were crying out for it, the Police wanted it, even at Management Committee level the Police wanted it, and it is not eligible' (Interview, Brent Council official, April 1999). Another area which beneficiaries identified as representing need was that of child-care. Yet the regulations specified strict criteria about eligible expenditure on these areas. Ineligible ERDF activities, set out in Department of the Environment, Transport and Regions (DETR) guidelines included the following:

> Establishments providing generalised further education. However specialised activities involving technical education or vocational training, even at university level, may be eligible. Provision of local social welfare facilities e.g. hospitals, nursing homes, fire stations, day nurseries, child-minding facilities, sports facilities, parks, public libraries *when these are not linked to activities of an economic nature specifically related to Single Programme objectives.*[40]

The Commission was keen to resist URBAN being swallowed up as a match-fund for existing regeneration programmes. At the same time any projects proposed, even in the framework of the UAP, had to fulfil the strict eligibility criteria related to European funding. This caused some initial resentment amongst some participants who perceived a contradiction between a programme seeking input, from the targeted beneficiaries, but not able to accommodate their requests in view of the rules and regulations (Interviews, UPG members East London and Park Royal, 1998-1999).

The Commission's attention focused on the UAP. Firstly, ensuring processes were in place to carry out the capacity building required to

---

[40] Extract from 'EC Structural Fund Programmes in England: Action Plans for European Regional Development Fund and European Social Fund, Guidance Note No. 2'(DETR 1997b, p.36) emphasis added. Further details of ineligible activities can be found in the above document.

empower the local communities to participate. Secondly, an evaluation of the contents so that the final drafts of UAPs reflected the priorities of the programme and incorporated the principles of European regional policy. One way of ensuring this was to develop a different focus to the URBAN programme and this was linked to the idea of preparing baselines within the UAP. The notion of baselines consisted of local indicators showing the current situation in an area which could be used as a mechanism to assess the success of URBAN. This was linked to the principle of programming, aimed at developing well-focused local strategies, linked to objectives and measures. The Commission encouraged a strategic approach to the UAP. Given the small-scale of CIs, the UAP represented an opportunity for exemplary programming, which could possibly be transferred to larger programmes.[41]

6.4 Problems of Coordination

Following the delay of two years in the central government/Commission level negotiations, the local partners in both East London and Park Royal were eager to launch projects to be funded under URBAN. The Commission, however, was keen to ensure the processes were in place to achieve the 'integrated holistic approach' based on community involvement.[42] Throughout 1996 and 1997, local authority officers had already produced draft UAPs circulated to Government Offices and the European Commission. Even at this early stage, there were problems related to coordination and lack of guidance. Government Offices could comment on the drafts but had no clear instructions from the Commission, or central Departments, regarding detailed requirements for the approval of Action Plans. There was also a problem of timing since, according to the terms of reference, it was the UPGs that would draft the UAP. Yet in late 1996-1997,

---

[41] This section is based on internal discussion documents prepared around 1995 at the Commission level in preparation for negotiation of Programme Documents and administrative arrangements for URBAN. Some information is also based on observation of meetings and experience of reading early UAPs, prepared for UK programmes in 1997, during a period as a trainee in DG XVI. Any interpretations of the process are my own and do not reflect the official position of the Commission.

[42] This quote is taken from the URBAN administrative arrangements presented in full in Appendix one, chapter four. Reference to this can clarify some of the points made relating to the decision-making process for the local delivery of URBAN.

the UPGs were still in the process of being formed and only existed in shadow form at that stage.

The Commission and Government Offices faced initial pressure to agree projects proposed initially by local authorities. The first projects agreed, but only in Park Royal, were for the new posts for capacity building relating to the establishment of UPGs. The URBAN Programme in East London was more problematic as the Commission and GOL did not agree to any initial capacity building projects for this programme. This may be explained by early differences in approach between the partnership in East London and the Commission. Established local partners in East London initially favoured a strategy in line with the existing regeneration schemes in the area; yet the Commission stressed that URBAN had its own aims and objectives with respect to the CED emphasis of the programme. This resulted in strained relations between the partners in East London, GOL and the Commission.

With reference to the UIDU, one local authority officer stated the following:

> We provide the premises free of charge, which are part of the package. The East London partnership and the private sector leadership team provide advice, which is free of charge. The local authorities and other agencies co-finance some of the cost. ERDF should pay the remaining 50 per cent of the cost. To this date, I haven't had a penny from Brussels (Interview, local authority official, London Borough of Tower Hamlets, January 1999).

The agreeing of the capacity building projects in the Park Royal area did not alleviate the pressure on GOL to approve projects proposed by the local partners. In theory, the projects should have been integrated into the strategic focus of the UAP and additional drafts were sent to the Commission via GOL throughout 1997. However none of the UAPs could be presented as the product of any of the UPGs since they were still being formed between 1997-1998 as explained in section 6.2. The Commission wanted to be certain that the processes, ensuring a truly bottom-up approach, were in place before agreeing any UAPs. Numerous problems of coordination emerged in the local implementation of URBAN.

In early 1997, Government Offices were the initial targets of blame from the local partners although no clear guidance had yet been provided by central ministries. There had been draft guidance notes and seminars for Government Offices on UAPs in 1997. The DETR produced a definitive version of guidance notes in June 1997 and a second version followed in September 1997 (Interview, DETR official, January 1999). The guidance notes referred to the regulations for ERDF and ESF funds in the UAPs (DETR, 1997a, 1997b). However this also raised a number of issues relating to financial responsibility for the funds, which were not actually resolved until 1998.

In the meantime, local partners in the London programmes increased the pressure on GOL and the Commission to agree certain projects that would ultimately be incorporated into the final version of the UAP. The lack of clarity, in the early stages, led to tense exchanges between the partners and GOL, initially blamed for all of the delays. In East London, by early 1998, no projects within the UAP had yet been approved. Yet GOL was powerless to act in the absence of agreed UAPs; these required approval from the European Commission and also raised issues regarding financial responsibility for the URBAN funds, to be examined in full in section 6.5. The delays in the programme caused disillusion among some of the community and voluntary groups hoping to access URBAN funds:

> Everyone who has applications for money is saying where's our money? URBAN is supposed to be a fast track form of funding, community-led, and every time we have tried to make a move forward either GOL or Brussels have said no (Interview, UPG community representative, East London, January 1999).

Delays in the approval of URBAN also caused problems with match-funding that some of the individual projects had secured. While the Commission did not want URBAN to be driven by national funding regimes, they did offer a valuable source of match-funding. Some of this disappeared as the delays in URBAN meant that some projects were no longer synchronised with the match-funding source (Interview, UPG member and local authority officer, January 1999). Smaller community organisations, which URBAN was seeking to engage, did not have the resources to weather the storm and some projects originally proposed collapsed. Indeed in East London some of the new members of the UPG, elected in February 1998, were soon frustrated with URBAN. Ironically, it was the representatives from the Muslim community, the highest turnout in the UPG elections, who stopped attending meetings once they realised that URBAN was not a fast stream source of funding for the projects they had in mind, which may not have been eligible anyway (Interview, IUDU officer, April 1999).

The Park Royal URBAN had more success than East London in gaining agreement for the approval of some projects before the UAP was officially approved. In addition to the capacity building appointments to run the programme, in June 1997 GOL and the European Commission made concessions to agree some projects in the Park Royal area on condition that these were incorporated into the final UAP. However, since there were questions about whether there had been sufficient capacity building in the first place, this 'success' still aroused criticisms among some members of the UPGs who felt that the local authorities were using URBAN to drive through showpiece projects.

One such example was the case of a large-scale project proposed by the Edward Woods, Shepherds Bush, White City UPG, supported by the London Borough of Hammersmith and Fulham. This involved a major project of £275,000, the Community Enterprise and Opportunities Centre and Development Fund.[43] The project was approved by the GOL but, at a local level, there were concerns by some smaller groups about whether they would have access to its facilities.[44] Some concessions were subsequently made to include these organisations as tenants in the Opportunities Centre building, which was formally opened by the Minister for Regeneration at the time, Richard Caborn MP, in June 1998.

Issues around local authorities producing 'showpiece' projects also emerged in the course of 1998 in the South Kilburn URBAN where Brent Council proposed a walkway on the targeted estate to be financed by ERDF and match-funded by the council:

> The big project now is the idea of building a walkway. Again that is interesting but it doesn't come out of the community even though I suspect the community probably think it is a good idea. It is a council-led initiative which will mop up a lot of the funding (Interview, South Kilburn UPG member, January 1999).

Another point which emerged in the implementation of URBAN in South Kilburn related to the preparation of projects from individual members of the UPGs. While there were procedures in place to ensure that individuals could not vote to adopt their own projects, this still raised questions about representation. As one observer noted:

> What is interesting in this last round is that a lot of initiatives are community-led initiatives that have been formulated by people on the board; so yes, they

---

[43] The European funds allocated to URBAN in the London Borough of Hammersmith and Fulham area amounted to approximately £2 million (see note 12 of this chapter).

[44] Internal document presented to at Capacity Building Focus Group meeting of White, Shepherds Bush, Edward Woods UPG, 20 January 1998.

are 'community' projects but in essence they are becoming professional projects of vested interest groups, of people on the UPG. The selected few are empowered but to the point that they become part of the system, either to the point that they start to work in the system or they become officers in the system or they have projects which are endorsed and then they have a vested interest in just maintaining those initiatives (Interview, UPG member, South Kilburn, January 1999).

The initial emphasis on perfecting UAPs and systems to develop a community-led approach also raised problems regarding the actual delivery of the URBAN programme. Concerns were raised as to whether delays and the initial confusion would result in a shortage of projects ultimately presented for URBAN funding. All ERDF and ESF funds for URBAN had to be committed by the end of 1999; this put pressure on local partners to actually prepare proposals for funding within the specified period. Officials from the DETR had expressed their concerns to local partners regarding a possible under spend on the programme but had been assured that this problem would be overcome. One official from DETR stated the following:

It all comes down to timing really because URBAN obviously has to be committed by the end of the year, so whether the programmes will be up and operating in time to actually provide match-funding comes down to timing. I am assured that all the money will be committed but whether in practice it really is, I don't know (Interview, DETR official, April 1999).

Problems clearly existed in coordinating the European funding with the schemes in place at national level. We now turn to examine exactly why there were delays in the approval of UAPs, only finally agreed in late December 1998. One major issue was related to the question of financial responsibility for URBAN funds; this had also plagued the initial Commission/central government negotiations for the administrative arrangements of the programme.

6.5 Responsibility for URBAN Funds

By 1997 the DETR guidelines aimed to streamline the payments of ERDF funds, within delegated limits as part of the Action Plan process.[45]

---

[45] Please refer to chapter four, section 4.3/3.

From 1 April 1997 all ERDF payments, with the exception of the DTI's co-financed measures, will be accounted for by DETR and recorded against a single DETR vote. This will enable Government Offices (GOs) to issue action plan approval letters on behalf of the DETR and to process claims, removing the need to transfer documents and funds between GOs and departments and will speed up the payments process (DETR, 1997a, p.3).

However, there were no concessions regarding the payment of ERDF was in arrears:

ERDF grant must be claimed only for expenditure which has been defrayed. Partnerships must be able to support grant claims with evidence of purchases made or invoices paid (DETR, 1997a, p.16).

This meant that it would be difficult for a non-established organisation, without adequate resources, to take on the 'lead agency' role to receive URBAN.[46] There would clearly be a time lag since any institution would require resources to cover the period between paying for the projects and receiving the ERDF funds. Furthermore, there were no changes regarding any pooling of resources for URBAN from the two separate Departments. ESF monies were still dealt with separately by the Department for Education and Employment (DfEE) which maintained its own procedures.

ESF is funded on an annual basis and the arrangements for payment are significantly different from those of ERDF. Before any payment is made, the Accountable Body must provide one or more of the completed Match-Funding Certificates for each approved measure to confirm that the necessary match funding is in place. As soon as the Measure has been approved (or when the first project in the Measure has started if later) and the Public Match-Funding Certificate provided, Accountable Bodies will be able to claim the first advance of 50 per cent of the amount approved for each of the calendar year in question. A second advance claim for 30 per cent of the support can be made as soon as the first half has been spent. The final claim is made in arrears on the actual cost of the activity in the Measure for the year. The balance is paid to the Accountable Body as representative of the partnership where the DfEE ESF Unit has received payment of the Programme final claim from the European Commission and is satisfied that the applicant's claim is correct (DETR, 1997b, p.67).

---

[46] Please refer to the URBAN Administrative Arrangements presented in full in Appendix one, chapter four.

Clearly, although the central ministries had adjusted to some extent by allowing the local partnerships responsibility for projects up to certain delegated limits, there was no real addressing of the issue of merging the two sets of funds together to be administered at Government Office level. The local partners had to deal with the Government Offices who would then deal with two separate government Departments. Furthermore, as noted above, ESF was managed on an annual basis; this did not appear to be conducive to producing the longer-term strategy of a 'pluriannual programme' sought by the UAP process.

As noted earlier, the first stage for any partnership was for the UAP to be approved. For URBAN in London, this did not take place until December 1998. Regarding a 'lead agency', the term used in the administrative arrangements for URBAN, this was referred to in the DETR guidance as the 'accountable body'. In the first edition of DETR guidance notes, the following provisions were made before central Departments could release any funds.

> Departments can only enter in a funding agreement with a legal entity capable of meeting the liabilities that flow from the conditions of grant. This Accountable Body can be the partnership itself if it has the legal personality or one of the members of the partnership acting on behalf of the rest. Normally the partner leading the Action Plan will become the Accountable Body: but it will be for the partnership to decide how to meet this requirement (DETR, 1997a, p.4).

There was no specification in the DETR guidance that the accountable body should be the local authority. Neither did the administrative arrangements for URBAN indicate that the lead agency, or accountable body, should be the local authority. Yet, as has been shown, it was the local authorities that had emerged as lead partners in the preparation of URBAN bids, the recruitment and match-funding of capacity building staff, as well as the establishment of the UPGs. Local authorities also presented an argument for being the accountable body for the URBAN funds even though the administrative arrangements did not necessarily designate them to take on this function. In all UK URBAN programmes, with the exception of London, the local authorities took on the role of accountable body. In the case of London, there was variation in the outcome regarding who should act as accountable body for the URBAN programme. We begin with the case of East London before examining that of Park Royal.

Throughout 1998 the newly formed UPGs were establishing themselves and agreeing the contents of the UAPs drafted by the officers employed by the local authorities and URBAN. Apart from some of the individual projects which GOL had agreed to approve, the remainder had to await the approval of the UAP and the appointment of an accountable body. In East London, there was no real discussion of whether the UPG, or an organisation independent of the local authority, could become the accountable body for URBAN. The regulations stated that ERDF funds would be paid in arrears hence the case was made that the local authorities should be the accountable body as they had the resources to forward fund projects if necessary. This would alleviate any short-term problems until the European funds could be released from the central ministries. One officer involved in implementing URBAN in East London explained the local authority's case in the following way:

> It will be interesting to see how things play out in practice because they (the local authorities) have won the whole argument that they must be the accountable bodies because they say we can forward fund. If any project goes down, we have got the money to bail it out whereas you (the UPG) would never have it. I know some UPG members are not particularly happy with that (Interview, UIDU officer, London, 1998).

During this period, there was growing impatience felt by local authority officers working on URBAN who were keen to administer the programme, at local level, and were becoming increasingly frustrated with central government (Interview, local official, London Borough of Tower Hamlets, January 1998). In the event, the UAP was not approved until January 1999 and the final appointment of local authorities as accountable bodies ran parallel to the agreeing of the UAP. For URBAN in East London, two separate accountable bodies were established: one for projects operating within the London Borough of Tower Hamlets and a separate one for projects in the London Borough of Hackney. Some members of the UPG in East London were disappointed that there had not been local management of URBAN with the UPG playing a more prominent role (Interviews, UPG members, East London, January 1999).

What of URBAN in Park Royal? Here we see an element of variation. The local authorities could have argued the same case as East London for being the accountable bodies in view of the complexity of the funding mechanisms, the possible delays in acquiring funds and the range of actors involved. This was the case in the London Borough of Brent where, as in

East London, the local council became the accountable body. Again this caused some resentment among some members of the UPG who felt that they had not been adequately consulted on the matter (Interview, UPG member, South Kilburn, January 1999). However, the cases of the London Boroughs of Hammersmith and Fulham and the City of Westminster provide some interesting variations.

The White City, Shepherds Bush, Edward Woods UPG was initially established as an 'Unincorporated Association' in 1996.[47] In 1997, the UPG decided to became a Company Limited by Guarantee. This decision was taken before the UAP had actually been officially approved. The UPG was supported by the Labour Party majority in the London Borough of Hammersmith and Fulham. The support of the councillor who was also Deputy for Regeneration in the borough was a major factor that contributed to the UPG's decision to take this path (Interview, UPG member, January 1999).[48] Interestingly enough, there was additional adaptation of the administrative arrangements as agreed by the Commission and central government ministries.

Following the decision to become a company limited by guarantee, the White City, Shepherds Bush Edward Woods UPG began to be run along the lines of a private company with a Director, employed by the partnership, administration and finance officers.

> It is the Urban Partnership Advisory Board (UPB) which will have responsibility for developing and approving the Action Plan, approving project applications and for taking strategic decisions on the delivery of the programme in the target area. The UPB will report all aspects of the progress of the programme to the Park Royal Urban Management Group via the programme secretariat in the Government Office for London. The UPG will be the Accountable Body for the delivery of the aims and objectives of the Action Plan and for the financial management of the programme. It will do this on behalf of the UPB. The trustees will not have the power to override the

---

[47] 'The White City, Shepherds Bush, Edward Woods Urban Partnership Group, Urban Action Plan, 1999-2001', final version approved by the European Commission (White City, Shepherds Bush, Edward Woods UPG, 1998).

[48] Councillor Powell, Deputy for Regeneration in the London Borough of Hammersmith and Fulham at the time, also played a high profile role as a representative for London on the Committee of the Regions. Councillor Powell was the author of the 1995 Committee of the Regions 'Opinion on urban development', Brussels 19-20 July (CdR 235/95).

decisions of the board unless there is an adequate reason for doing this (e.g. it may result in legal or financial difficulties).[49]

In the above case, we see yet another variation of the text of administrative arrangements for URBAN so painfully negotiated by the Commission. The argument presented in favour of establishing an Urban Partnership Advisory Board (UPB) was that this would make the management of the programme more strategic (Interviews, UPB members, January 1999). However this also introduced additional administrative tiers in an already complex process. Furthermore, while there were attempts to increase the representation of certain ethnic minorities on the UPG, representation still remained an issue given the persistent apathy of the targeted population on estates such as Edward Woods. Although the establishment of the limited company was an achievement, there was still some question regarding whether this fully reflected the CED vision as originally conceived by the Commission.

The case of Queen's Park UPG in the City of Westminster provides the only other example of a UK URBAN programme where the local council did not become the accountable body. Here we have a different political picture to that in the London Borough of Hammersmith and Fulham. During this period the Conservative Party had the majority in the City of Westminster Council, yet URBAN had been awarded to a minority Labour ward in the borough. The Conservative councillors enjoyed a political majority on the City of Westminster's representation on the UPG. However, this was counter-balanced by the members of the VCSF who were not necessarily active in a political party.[50] Similar to other areas in London, by early 1998 the UAPs had still not been formally agreed. However in 1997 GOL had agreed, in the interim, to approve certain individual projects in Queen's Park and other areas of the Park Royal URBAN programme. These included, for example, the early capacity building projects for the URBAN support workers and Paddington Arts Development Plan.[51]

---

[49] Extract from the 'White City, Shepherds Bush, Edward Woods, UPG Annual Report' presented at the first Annual General Meeting of the UPG, 19 January 1999. Although the URBAN administrative arrangements used the term 'URBAN Management Committee' (Appendix one, chapter four) the local partners in London often referred to this as the 'Urban Management Group'.

[50] As noted earlier it was a Labour Councillor, Jill Selbourne, who initially established the VCSF although the members of this represented local organisations, not political parties. Please refer to Table 6.5 which gives details of the membership of Queen's Park UPG.

[51] The URBAN funding for the officers amounted to £59,579 and the Paddington Arts Development Plan, a capital development of arts and media training status, consisted of

Parallel to the developments relating to URBAN was the establishment in 1998 of Paddington Development Trust as a company limited by guarantee. The Paddington Development Trust listed a number of social policy objectives in its memorandum of association.[52] The Paddington Development Trust was independent of any local authority. Part of the rationale for establishing the Trust was to ensure that any benefits from private sector redevelopment around the Paddington Basin area would also be extended to the more vulnerable groups of society living in the area (Interview, local official, City of Westminster). There were links between the founders of Paddington Development Trust and the Labour party. Support was also forthcoming from a Labour MP, Karen Buck, who had also been involved in the founding of the Trust. Although the Paddington Development Trust was not based within the area targeted by URBAN, it was in close vicinity to this. Furthermore, the founders of the Trust also had links with the VCSF of which certain members were part of the Queen's Park UPG.

The Paddington Development Trust expressed an interest in becoming the accountable body for the Queen's Park URBAN programme. This was formally proposed to the UPG meeting of June 1998. In this case, although councillors from the City of Westminster had a formal place on the UPG, the council did not express an interest in becoming the accountable body for URBAN. One explanation for this is that the URBAN programme was operating in an opposition Labour ward; URBAN was peripheral to City of Westminster's agenda which gave more priority to other areas in the borough (Interview, local official, City of Westminster, January 1999). The UPG was presented with two options:

Option 1: the UPG itself becomes a Company Limited by Guarantee and then is financially liable for URBAN expenditure in Queen's Park, in accordance with the Queen's Park Urban Action Plan.
Option 2: The North Paddington Development Trust is financially liable for URBAN expenditure in Queen's Park in accordance with the Queen's Park Urban Action Plan. All decisions on expenditure are made by the UPG as outlined in a written agreement between the UPG and its Accountable Body.

£162, 215. Other projects approved are listed in the 'Queen's Park Urban Action Plan, Draft September 1998' (Queen's Park UPG, 1998, p.9). The budget for the Queen's Park area of the URBAN programme was approximately £2 million (see note 12 of this chapter).
[52] 'Draft Memorandum of Association of Paddington Development Trust' (Paddington Development Trust, 1999, p.1).

Any monies received by the development Trust on behalf of the UPG shall be spent exclusively for the benefit of residents of Queen's Park.[53]

The Conservative representatives of the City of Westminster on the UPG preferred the former option, even though the council itself was not be willing to actually become the accountable body. Although option 2 stated that the URBAN monies would only be spent in the targeted area, a requirement of the European Commission anyway, some councillors presented arguments that option 2 implied the UPG was 'selling' its programme to the Trust. The opposition of Conservative councillors may best be explained in terms of local politics.

Firstly the Conservative majority of the City of Westminster was not keen to see a European programme, albeit a small-scale venture, under the control of an independent Trust with some links to the Labour Party. Secondly, some of the founders of the Paddington Development Trust had played a part in the exposure of the Dame Shirley Porter affair of the late 1980s.[54] The UPG meeting of June 1998 was a tense affair, yet there was a narrow vote in favour of Paddington Development Trust becoming the accountable body for URBAN in Queen's Park. Local politics aside, there remained the hurdle of acceptance by central government, to take on the task of accountable body, and the gaining of concessions from central ministries. The Paddington Development Trust, as a newly established organisation, did not have the resources of a local authority to survive the cash flow problems caused by the payment of European funds in arrears.

In September 1998 Paddington Development Trust wrote to GOL and expressed an interest in becoming the accountable body for the URBAN programme in Queen's Park.[55] GOL was still in the process of agreeing the UAPs with the European Commission. At the same time, GOL entered a process of negotiations with the central ministries, namely the DETR and the DfEE regarding the proposals. Although there had been the precedent of the White City, Shepherds Bush Edward Woods UPG establishing itself as an

---

[53] Internal documentation from the Queen's Park UPG meeting of 2 June 1998.

[54] Dame Shirley Porter, Leader of the Conservative controlled City of Westminster Council, was involved in a 'homes for votes' scandal in the late 1980s. The scandal centred on Dame Shirley Porter ordering the designation of eight wards for council home sales so that the Conservatives could prevent Labour winning control of the City of Westminster Council in 1990. The resulting homeless were moved to hotels like Clarendon Court Hotel, exposed in a report by the local government Ombudsman in 1998. Dame Shirley Porter has since lived abroad, dividing her time between Israel and the US.

[55] This section is based on correspondence between GOL and Paddington Development Trust forwarded to me for the purposes of this research.

accountable body, this was a different case. The former had the support of the local authority which was part of the established partnership and match-funded some of the programme. Hence, although the local authority was not the accountable body, it was fully supportive of the process.

The case of the Paddington Development Trust was different since the City of Westminster did not support the case of the Paddington Development Trust seeking to become the accountable body. The City of Westminster would not, therefore, forward fund the programme should problems arise with cash flow problems while European funds filtered through central ministries. GOL agreed, in this case, to enter into negotiations with the central government departments in order to try and facilitate the process for a newly established organisation, without the resources of a local authority, to be able to take on the role of accountable body. There were also meetings between GOL, officers from the Queen's Park UPG and the Labour MP, Karen Buck who supported the Paddington Development Trust.

In negotiations with the DETR and the DfEE, GOL gained the following concessions: In November 1998 DETR agreed certain procedures based on those for the SRB Challenge Fund. DETR would give an advance of ERDF grant provided the accountable body supported their application by providing information on the projects on which the grant would be spent. Secondly, the amount requested was to be as small as possible and had to be spent within thirteen weeks. Finally, these concessions only applied to ERDF grants not to ESF projects. This concession to forward fund, even small amounts to a charitable Trust, destroyed any potential argument presented by local authorities that they were best placed to be the accountable bodies for URBAN. Local authorities could no longer argue that with respect to less established partners, they alone had the resources to run the URBAN programme and overcome problems related to ERDF being paid in arrears.

However, since the DETR'S decision was made at a late stage of the URBAN programme, in response to the proposal from Paddington Development Trust, it came too late to influence the debate in areas where the local authorities had already made successful a case for taking on the role of accountable body. The forward funding concession for ERDF was also granted to the White City, Shepherds Bush, Edward Woods UPG where the local authority, although supportive, was not the accountable body. At subsequent meetings with central government local authority officers from other URBAN programmes complained about the concession made to these two cases even though the whole argument for local authorities taking the lead was based on the fact that they had the resources to forward fund projects if necessary![56]

The DfEE showed far less flexibility than DETR. There were no changes to the arrangements as detailed in the Action Plan guidance. DfEE insisted that all match-funding be in place before any funds were released in line with the Action Plan Guidance notes 1 and 2 published in June and September 1997 respectively (DETR, 1997a, DETR, 1997b). The only concession made was at Government Office level which, from 1 January 1999, would be responsible for all ESF payments. GOL undertook to give priority to processing claims from the Trust given that it was a newly formed organisation without the resources of a local authority.

6.6 Conclusions from the Implementation of URBAN in London

The implementation of URBAN at local level, in the respective areas of London, raises a number of points. A major problem experienced in both areas of London was the concept of 'community'. URBAN aimed to be a bottom-up process, with local solutions to local problems. Yet in our multi-ethnic cities, the concept of 'community' is not simple to define, particularly where the population is fluid due to arrivals of refugees at different times. All areas encountered difficulty in engaging local residents, or organisations, beyond the 'usual suspects' who were already active anyway. The concept of 'community gatekeepers' monopolising the process appeared in both Park Royal and East London.

Problems of representation aside, there were also difficulties in reconciling local demands with the procedures for European funding. Not all projects proposed were eligible for funding. Furthermore, the Member State machinery was not prepared for the rapid payment of European funds to the grass roots. Attempts in 1997 to streamline the process, and delegate some responsibility to Government Offices, failed to tackle the problems related to the involvement of two separate Departments, at national level, each with their own regulations. The local management of funds, the original conception of the Commission, was also problematic. Further adjustment was required relating to the establishment of accountable bodies to manage the funds. In all but two cases in the implementation of URBAN in the UK, the accountable body was the local authority.

---

[56] Observation of technical procedures meeting between DETR, DfEE and officers from UK URBAN programmes, London, 16 April, 1999.

While the local authorities negotiated with other partners on the UPGs in order to prepare projects within a UAP the local ownership, as conceived by the Commission in the negotiations for URBAN, was never really achieved. Lack of resources and the payment of European funds in arrears made it difficult for local organisations to undertake responsibility for the funds. The Commission had engaged in lengthy negotiations to secure the terms of reference for the delivery of URBAN (Appendix one, chapter four). Yet ultimately, the evidence suggests that the local authorities emerged as the dominant partners in the European, as well as national, regeneration programmes.[57] Furthermore, the complicated processes relating to the administration of European Funds within the Member State made the 'integrated and holistic approach' that was 'based on strong community involvement' difficult to achieve in practice. The reality was closer to the marble cake seen in the American literature. Lines of authority were blurred among the layers of government involved.

Government Offices were the immediate targets of blame yet they had the task of implementing a programme, negotiated by a central department, the Department of the Environment (DoE) at the time. Moreover, Government Offices were dependent on the procedures of the central Departments which, until a late stage in the programme, did not become involved with the partners on the ground.[58] The local councils were leading partners in all the URBAN programmes in London with the exception of the Queen's Park URBAN. Interestingly enough, it is at this late stage that the DETR made concessions to forward fund some of the ERDF. How can this be explained?

With reference to Bache's 'extended gatekeeper', model as set out in chapter two, 'the definition of a member government's interest may change over time and may be influenced by a range of actors within and outside the government'. By the time the issue of accountable bodies came to be finalised, a Labour government was in power. While the administrative arrangements could not be altered, procedures to implement them could become more flexible. Support from a Labour MP, willing to speak to ministers and GOL, arguably assisted the case of the Paddington Development Trust. There would appear to be a form of 'picket fence' alliance between specialists of the policy area at the different levels of

---

[57] Please refer to chapter four where the findings of the CURS (1995) report on the SRB are reviewed.
[58] Some officials from the DfEE had attended a seminar for the Park Royal partners run by GOL in April 1998. More direct dialogue between central departments and the local partners did not begin until 1999, towards the end of the programme.

government – from the local partners, to the Government Offices who would then speak to the central Departments.

At this stage, one of the two leading Departments, the DETR, made concessions to forward fund ERDF monies to non-local authority accountable bodies based on the procedures for the SRB Challenge fund. It would be interesting to speculate whether more UPGs would have voted for non-local authority accountable bodies had these concessions been made at an earlier stage of the implementation of URBAN Another point which would have favoured the Commission's approach was if there had been more time to implement the initial capacity measures in the areas where, in contrast to Queen's Park, there was a less well established voluntary and community sector. The initial two years delay due to the lengthy negotiations between the Commission and central government had stifled URBAN at birth. However, in view of the problems in defining community in multi-ethnic European cities, the processes URBAN was seeking to promote would arguably require a longer-term vision, and investment, beyond the means of a small-scale European programme.

7 Implementation of the URBAN Community Initiative in Marseille

Introduction

This chapter continues to apply the model of 'extended gatekeeper' to the local implementation of URBAN in Marseille, stage four of the policy process.[1] We enter the details of implementation in order to assess further the distribution of power between the key partners involved in implementing URBAN. The final Programme URBAN Document signed in March 1996 focused on the following themes:[2]

- Economic development and employment;
- Social development;
- Renewal of urban areas;
- Exchange of experience; and
- Local implementation of the programme

This chapter concentrates on the politics and policy of the implementation of URBAN at grass roots level. On the one hand we have a Programme Document, negotiated, signed and agreed by the Commission and the established partnership within the Member State. On the other hand, the

---

[1] Please refer to chapter four, section 4.1/2 where the stages are set out in full. As explained in the introduction to chapter five the term 'extended gatekeeper' refers specifically to central government as developed by Bache (1996). For other levels of government, regional and municipal, we will refer to the notions of 'gatekeeper' and 'gatekeeping'.

[2] Summary list from the original URBAN Programme Document signed on 12 March 1996, summary of contents (CEC, 1996e, p.3). There were no amendments to these themes, only the measures within them and financial plan, as outlined in section 7.3, and presented in the revised Programme Document approved by the European Commission on 12 March 1997 (CEC, 1997d).

analysis in chapter five highlighted how central and local government prioritised different geographical areas within the agreed programme.

The scenario for implementation on the ground can be presented as follows: the European Commission, following the principle of concentration, would seek to ensure action in the areas of most need. St Mauront (3rd district, *3ème arrondissement*) formed the basis of the original bid to bring URBAN to Marseille. Yet by March 1995 the newly elected municipality, whose mayor also became a minister in the national government in 1996, emphasised the needs of the centre of the city, the 1st and 2nd districts. The municipality would arguably give priority to projects for these areas, in line with its overall strategy of making the centre of Marseille more attractive to potential tourists and investors.

The 1st and 2nd districts are more visible on arriving in the city; St Mauront in the 3rd district is peripheral to the immediate city centre. The French state, as chair of the Monitoring Committee (*Comité de Suivi*) was responsible for the overall implementation of the URBAN programme. Yet, as shown in chapter five, the central government intervened to ensure that some of the European funds would be accessible to areas where the state had invested heavily. This was reflected by the extension of the European Social Fund (ESF) to co-finance social policy projects in the GPU (*Grand Projet Urbain*) area where the state had launched an ambitious infrastructure programme. The question is to what extent were the final agreements, following negotiations in the Programme Document, implemented in practice? This chapter investigates the forms, and methods, of any 'gatekeeping' exercised by the municipal level of government.

Chapter five outlined how national and European programmes in France have formal contractual commitments agreeing broad areas of action and the funding, from each level of government, to finance these. What is less clear is whether the French state as the implementing authority or the European Commission, as grantor of the funds, can ensure that all areas of an agreed programme are respected by the local authorities. Venturing into the intricate web of local administration can help explain how it may be possible for a local authority to circumvent the national and European levels of government even though the contents of the programme agreed are not openly challenged. It is important, among the mass of details, to remember the peculiarities of the French system of accumulation of mandates (*cumul des mandats*). During part of the period of implementation of URBAN, the Mayor of Marseille was also President of the Region Provence-Alpes-Côte d'Azur (PACA) and a minister in the national government. Mény (1992, p.62) points out that there are few democratic countries nowadays where so much power is concentrated in the hands of a few individuals. This is the case at all levels of the political process. Power is almost monarchical: the Head of State, presidents of regions and departmental councils and mayors are 'emperors of their realm' (*'empereurs de leurs royaume'*).

The concept of a possible conflict of interest due to the accumulation of mandates is not perceived as an issue in the French case (Mény, 1992, p.29). Taking the example of Marseille, local councillors, from the majority parties viewed it as convenient that the President of the Regional Council of Provence-Alpes-Côte d'Azur (PACA) was also the Mayor of Marseille up until March 1998. One local councillor described this period as follows: 'we decided and the region would follow; this allowed us to save time' (Interview, municipal councillor, Marseille, 1998).[3] In this respect, local and regional authorities viewed the accumulation of mandates as an efficient mechanism since it facilitated the decision-making between the various tiers of government. As Mény (1992, p. 63) notes, it is as if the advantages of the accumulation of offices dispelled any ethical drawbacks of the system: its problem solving capacities appeared to override any potential conflict of interest.

Returning to the example of URBAN in Marseille the practice of accumulation of mandates could, to some extent, facilitate the coordination between the various tiers of government. This raised the possibility, however, of neglected implementation of policy in areas not prioritised by the local authorities. The case of URBAN in Marseille also raises wider issues regarding local democracy in France. The Mayor of Marseille, with his team of councillors and officials, represented the City of Marseille in the local delivery of URBAN. Yet how could the potential recipients of URBAN funds, many of whom were excluded from voting in national, regional and local elections due to not having French citizenship, participate in the policy process?

A review of formal procedures reveals a number of mechanisms by which residents and associations in the targeted area could channel their demands to the mayor. However, closer examination of how the system of local consultation works reveals that URBAN in Marseille, as well as London, experienced difficulty in reaching non-established groups. The empirical material presented on the implementation of URBAN in Marseille is organised around the same themes as that for London: The management and

---

[3] This comment was made with reference to the situation before March 1998 when the Right lost its majority in the regional elections following which Jean-Claude Gaudin, Mayor of Marseille, was no longer President of the Provence-Alpes-Côte d'Azur Region.

administration of URBAN, representation of the local community, tensions in local delivery, problems of coordination and responsibility for URBAN funds. While, at certain points of the analysis, developments are contrasted with the case of London, there is more systematic comparison of the two cases in the conclusions to the book.

7.1 The Management and Administration of the URBAN Programme

The administrative structures to implement URBAN in Marseille are reviewed in chapter five.[4] Here we concentrate more on the role of the field services of the state and the services of the municipality. These were the main actors involved in the preparation of projects to be funded under URBAN. The sub prefect for towns and cities (*Sous-Préfet à la Ville*) and his team were also involved at this level; as chair of the Advisory Committee, the COCPUR (*Comité d'orientation du* PIC URBAN) his role was to coordinate the field services of the state with the specialist teams at the municipality. The field services of the state, each attached to a parent ministry at central government level, played a major part in the programming process for the delivery of URBAN and other European and national policies of this period as outlined in chapter five. The specialist services provided technical advice on projects proposed for European funding.

Investment or infrastructure projects were the responsibility of the state infrastructure department, the DDE (*Direction Départementale de l'Équipement*). The parent ministry of the DDE, the Ministry of Infrastructure (*Ministère de l'Équipement*) also had responsibility for some of the infrastructure projects of the GPU and the Public Agency *Euroméditérranée*. For the European Social Fund (ESF) elements of URBAN, specialist advice would be given by regional representatives of the field services of the state dealing with employment and training: the DRTEFP (*Direction Régionale du Travail, de l'Emploi et de la Formation Professionelle*) supported by the departmental representation, the *Direction Départementale*. A representative of the parent ministry of the DRTEFP, the Ministry of Work and Social Affairs (*Ministère du Travail et des*

---

[4] Please refer to the section 5.2/2 of chapter five and Appendix one, chapter five which lists the membership of the Monitoring Committee and the Advisory Committee (COCPUR) for the implementation of URBAN in Marseille.

Affaires Sociales) also had a place on the Monitoring Committee for URBAN.

The local services of the state also provided specialist advice on sections of the Programme Document dealing with specific fields of economic and commercial development. The state's regional delegation for commerce and artisan based industry, the *Développement Économique du Commerce et de l'Artisanat* (DRCA) and that dealing with industry, research and the environment (*Direction Régionale de l'Industrie de la Recherche et de l'Environnement* (DRIRE) provided expertise for projects in these areas. With such a strong state presence in the policy process at local level how could a local authority, such as a municipality, manage to circumvent the national and in this case European authorities?

The remainder of this section explains how it was possible for the services of the municipality to exercise 'gatekeeping' at various points of the policy process. Section 7.4 presents more details of the tensions this caused in the partnership, particularly between the municipality and the local representatives of the state. Like the state, which created the SGAR (*Secrétariat Général pour les Affaires Régionales*) to deal with European policy, some larger municipalities also developed specialist units to deal with European affairs and their coordination with national policies. The Municipality of Marseille granted responsibility for European policy to a specialist body, the MIPPE (*Mission des programmes privés et européens*) under the direct control of the mayor. One senior official from the Municipality of Marseille suggested that the MIPPE had originally been conceived as the lobbying arm of the city:

> When the municipality developed the MIPPE, it was for lobbying Brussels. The MIPPE doesn't present a case directly to Brussels; this has to go to the state and it is the state that presents our proposal to Brussels; this procedure is obligatory. Yet it is not the state that will lobby on our behalf as the state is not always the best defender of our interests. Cities like Marseille can do this because they are big enough. This isn't the case for most French towns, they can't all have a specialist service to go and lobby Brussels (Interview, senior official, Municipality of Marseille, July 1998).

We saw in chapter five that representatives of the city did indeed go directly to Brussels to lobby for URBAN to be allocated to Marseille. Yet the importance of such dialogue, should not be over estimated since it is the central government which decided on the final allocations. At the implementation stage, however, the municipality could exert influence through its specialist services that were involved at different points in the policy process. Chapter five highlighted how the first evidence of this was in the negotiations for the URBAN Programme Document. In the local delivery of the agreed programme, the MIPPE had three main roles. Firstly, to brief the mayor through his designated representatives on the municipal council. Secondly, to forward any completed dossiers relating to individual projects to the field services of the state. Thirdly, to attend the Monitoring Committee as an observer and the Advisory Committee (COCPUR) as an active participant. One local state representative emphasised the 'gatekeeping' role of the MIPPE as follows:

It is true that the MIPPE has certain claims to power in Marseille, it stems from a desire to control everything that may benefit from European funds whether it is private or public programmes. If the MIPPE, at any particular moment, doesn't consider a project to have priority, you will never see it emerge (Interview, prefecture official, Marseille, July 1998).

The MIPPE followed instructions from the elected councillors; in this respect, there could be political pressure to give priority to projects in areas backed by the governing majority in the City of Marseille. The influence exerted by the MIPPE was likely to be greater in policy areas which came under the direct legal competence of the municipality. The main area was that of building and infrastructure where projects could be financed under areas of the programme dealing with the renewal of buildings and infrastructure in urban areas (*requalification urbaine*). For this, the elected councillors also dealt directly with the specialist services such as the department in the municipality responsible for preparing some of the infrastructure and building projects eligible for funding under the ERDF element of URBAN (*Direction Générale de l'Urbanisme et de l'Habitat*). Dossiers relating to individual projects were only sent to the MIPPE once they were complete. However, the specialist services of the municipality could only work on files related to projects that had been authorised by the elected councillors (Interview, local official, Municipality of Marseille, July 1998).

There was potentially less margin of manoeuvre for ESF projects since, under the decentralisation laws, training is not a direct competence of the municipality. Training is the responsibility of the region although, as we saw in chapter five, the state is also involved. It was not therefore necessary for the specialist teams of the municipality to work on specific dossiers as was the case for infrastructure projects applying for ERDF funding. The municipality's role for ESF projects was purely one of coordination; projects applying for ESF funding would be forwarded to the MIPPE which then directed them to the specialist services of the state. A local official from the state services dealing with employment and training, the DRTEFP explained the process as follows:

> The MIPPE sends us projects when they have them, but they're not involved in ruling any out. The MIPPE plays a role as secretariat for the technical groups of the Advisory Committee, the COCPUR, but they don't get involved in the technical preparation. Any ruling out of projects on technical points is done by the services of the state; we're the ones who are responsible and who provide advice. The municipal authorities have no competence in ESF matters; they may intervene but they don't really have any legal competence. However in projects dealing with buildings and infrastructure, it is not the same, the municipality does have legal competence (Interview, local DRTEFP official, Marseille, July 1998).

On the one hand, the municipality had less of a filtering role in areas, such as professional training, which did not fall within its competence. On the other hand, the European Commission and central government still depended on the services of the municipality to coordinate the work of the project leaders on the field. As noted in chapter five, the project leaders involved in implementing URBAN were under the direct control of the Mayor of Marseille. Officials from the prefecture and the state services were not responsible for actually going out on the ground to develop projects, they relied on the project leaders based in the targeted areas. In this sense the municipal level of government, in charge of the project leader teams, still played a major role in delivering all aspects of the European policy. Any projects aspiring for URBAN funding had a complicated path, through several levels of government, before they actually reached the Advisory Committee, the COCPUR, to be finally selected for funding.

Even at the stage of the COCPUR, processes were lengthy and involved a wide range of actors. The COCPUR was scheduled to meet once a semester although it could only meet if there were sufficient dossiers to merit a meeting. Both ESF and ERDF measures were included in the COCPUR meetings which were organised at the initiative of the sub prefect for towns and cities who also chaired the meetings. Prior to any COCPUR meeting, there would be yet another meeting of a group with specific responsibility for programming, the GTP (*Groupe technique de Programmation*). This met one week before any scheduled COCPUR meetings and dealt with technical aspects of the programme relating to the eligibility and finance arrangements for each project.

The GTP had no actual decision-making power but expressed an opinion on the dossiers presented for projects requesting financing. There were representatives of the different tiers of government at local level. State representatives included the Treasurer and Paymaster General, TPG (*Trésorier Payeur Général*), the main agent of the Ministry of Finance. The section dealing with European affairs, the SGAR was also represented as well as the field services of the state responsible for each measure of the programme (*Secrétaire Général des Bouches-du-Rhône, responsables de mesures*). The region was represented by the specialist services of the regional council (*services du Conseil Régional*) and the municipality by its own European section (*Cellule Europe de la Ville de Marseille*).[5]

Another responsibility granted to a service of the municipality, for URBAN in Marseille, related to the monitoring and evaluation of the URBAN programme. The Monitoring Committee for URBAN in Marseille, which first met on 8 October 1996, appointed an agency of the municipality, the AGAM (*Agence d'Urbanisme de l'Agglomération Marseillaise*) to fulfil the role of technical assistance of the programme; part of this involved undertaking an independent evaluation of URBAN in Marseille. Some officials from the services of the state felt undermined by this decision. One local state official expressed the following view:

> They (the Monitoring Committee) gave the responsibility for technical assistance to the municipality whereas in all the other programmes, it is the state representatives that deal with technical assistance. We spent a lot of time telling the municipality that this programme (URBAN) is managed like other programmes. It is also true that the AGAM was appointed to evaluate the (URBAN) programme; that is another particularity of this programme. Normally, we have an external evaluation service but the Commission agreed to it. DG XVI accepted a situation whereby a service of the municipality would evaluate a programme implemented by the municipality. It's clearly against the rules (Interview, local state official, July 1998).

In October 1996 Jean-Claude Gaudin, Mayor of Marseille, was also Minister of National and Regional Development as well as President of the

---

[5] Original terms and information taken from an internal document produced by the SGAR (1997a) 'Dispositions de mise en oeuvre DOCUP PIC URBAN 1995-1999', drafted on 16 June 1997. The section dealing with European affairs in the City of Marseille is also often referred to as the MIPPE. For a full list of members of the Monitoring Committee and the Advisory Committee, the COCPUR, please refer to Appendix one, chapter five.

Region Provence-Alpes-Côte-d'Azur (PACA). These multiple points of influence may explain why in this case the Commission was more flexible regarding the granting of responsibility for technical assistance and evaluation to the services of the municipality, under the control of the mayor. In the case of Marseille, the Commission did not question the leading role of the municipal authorities in delivering the programme within the established structures of the national policy under the contractual process (*Contrat de Plan, Contrat de Ville*).

So far, we have explored the management and administration of URBAN from the point of view of formal procedures established in the programme. Clearly, these committees excluded local residents and associations operating in the URBAN area. The next section explores the means by which the targeted beneficiaries could be represented in the decision-making process. In France the Commission followed the models existing within the Member State. Under the existing procedures, local residents and associations were not included in the formal partnerships established to deliver national or European policy. Any input into the decision-making processes would be through the existing channels of local democracy and state interaction with interest groups to which we now turn.

7.2 Representation of the Local Community

Jean-Claude Gaudin, Mayor of Marseille, represented the municipal authorities and had a place on the Monitoring Committee for URBAN. In practice it would be unlikely that a mayor, who was also a leading national politician, would attend such meetings in person. The mayor would generally delegate attendance at technical meetings to one of his councillors. The elected list of councillors were ranked in order of importance after the mayor. Each in turn would replace the mayor in the event of, for example, his death in office as occurred with Gaston Defferre, replaced by Robert Vigouroux, who was subsequently elected in his own right in 1989. During the period of implementation of URBAN some of the councillors from the ruling majority of the UDF or RPR coalition were accorded portfolios with responsibility for the various urban policy measures.[6] The MIPPE, dealing with the European programmes briefed each of these four councillors.

---

[6] Jean-Claude Gaudin, Mayor of Marseille belonged to the *Union Pour la Démocratie Française* (UDF, French Centre-Right Federation). The UDF and the *Rassemblement Pour la République* (RPR Gaullist Party) coalition had a majority on the municipal council.

Attendance at the URBAN Advisory committee, the COCPUR, was generally delegated to one of the technical services of the municipality and the MIPPE who subsequently briefed the councillors.

Clearly, there was a system in place whereby the democratically elected mayor, or one of his councillors, represented the inhabitants of the City of Marseille as a whole. It is interesting to note that the elected councillors, to whom the mayor had delegated responsibility for urban policy measures, did not necessarily have their electoral base in the specific neighbourhoods targeted by URBAN. In Marseille, any representation on the formal management committees (Monitoring Committee or COCPUR) would be drawn from entrusted councillors or officials under the direction of the mayor. There would be little window of opportunity for opposition councillors to direct a European programme away from the line taken by the mayor and his ruling majority. The list of councillors, delegated responsibility for various aspects of urban policy by Jean-Claude Gaudin, Mayor of Marseille, is presented below.

Renaud Muselier (RPR, *1er Adjoint*) had responsibility for economic policy, professional training, economic development zones, science parks and *Euroméditeranée*.[7] Bernard Leccia's portfolio (RPR, *3ème Adjoint)* covered urban policy, relations with the HLM (*Habitation à Loyer Modéré*) organisations and the GPU project.[8] Two other councillors, without any specific rank, were granted specific responsibilities for urban policy measures: Monsieur Roland Blum (UDF, *Conseiller Municipal Délégué*) was responsible for social affairs in the municipality. This included relations with numerous voluntary groups and associations such as the CCAS (*Centres Aérés, Centres Sociaux-Jeunesse et Vie Associative*) and responsiblility for social welfare measures under the DSU programme such as those dealing with the prevention of delinquency. Finally, Gérard Chenoz, (UDF, *Conseiller Municipal Délégué*) had responsibility for the initiatives taken to improve the centre of the city of Marseille (*Projet Centre-Ville*).[9]

---

[7] The term *Adjoint* refers to the ranking of the most senior councillors. The position of *1er Adjoint* is therefore the highest rank in the municipal council following the Mayor of Marseille.

[8] HLM refers to low cost or rented housing (also referred to as social housing); this may be may be communal or departmental (see Le Galès, 1994, p.9). Councillor Bernard Leccia was present at the Monitoring Committee for URBAN I observed in Marseille on 9 July 1998.

[9] Source: Internal document, Ville de Marseille (1995) 'Délégations Accordées par M. le Maire (Code des communes – ART.L.122-11), Secrétariat du Conseil Municipal' (City of Marseille, Delegations accorded by the Mayor, Secretariat of the Municipal Council of Marseille).

Some of these senior local councillors were also involved in national politics. Roland Blum, a practising lawyer in Marseille, was a Deputy in the National Assembly as well as a local councillor during this period.

Officials of the municipality also referred to the system of the geographically based mayors (*maire d'arrondissement*) as an example of how local democracy works in the larger cities in France. This is another aspect of the complex decentralisation laws during Defferre's reforms after 1982 and applies to the larger cities such as Paris, Lyon and Marseille. Each district has a local mayor who represents the population for a specific geographical area. In Marseille, the local mayors are involved in implementing national urban policy measures through participation in local consultation committees and liaison with the project leader. These local structures, which we will investigate in this section, were not extended to the implementation of the European programme URBAN. For the delivery of URBAN, the role of the district mayor was restricted to the reporting of local information to one of the delegates of Jean-Claude Gaudin, Mayor of Marseille as a whole.

The district mayor who was actually based in the targeted areas did not therefore have any decision-making power regarding, for example, which projects the services of the municipality should be preparing for approval for the Advisory Committee (COCPUR) meetings of the URBAN programme. Neither was there any dialogue between district mayors and the European Commission. Representatives from the European Commission were only involved at the higher-level Monitoring Committee meetings. At this level, the position of the municipality was presented by one of the councillors delegated by the Jean-Claude Gaudin, central Mayor of Marseille, to attend in his place. Close examination of the targeted areas reveals that many of the districts allocated URBAN had a district mayor who did not belong to the governing majority. The following table presents details of the population of each neighbourhood (*quartier*) within the districts targeted by URBAN.

Table 7.1 Population of Districts Targeted by URBAN in Marseille

1st district	Quartier Belsunce	8, 551 inhabitants
	Quartier Chapitre	2, 682 inhabitants
2nd district	Quartier Hôtel de Ville, Grand Carmes (Panier)	5, 078 inhabitants
3rd district	Quartier Saint-Mauront	14, 995 inhabitants
Total		31, 306 inhabitants

Source: URBAN Programme Document for Marseille (CEC, 1996e, p.33)

In the area targeted by URBAN, only the district mayor from the 1st district belonged to one of the parties of the governing majority: Jean Roatta, UDF (*Maire du 1er groupe d'arrondissements, 1er et 7ème*). The other local mayors represented opposition parties: Jean-Nöel Guérini (*Unité 13 Marseille, Maire du 2ème groupe d'arrondissements, 2ème et 3ème*).[10] Finally, the ESF elements of URBAN were extended to the GPU area operating in the 15th and 16th districts. Here too, the local mayor was in opposition to the governing majority: Guy Hermier, PCF (*Parti Communiste Française, Maire du 8ème groupe d'arrondissements, 15ème, 16ème*).

Interviews with local councillors indicate that there was some recognition of a possible democratic deficit regarding the representation of the targeted areas on the Monitoring Committee for URBAN. However, in the period covered by this study, no concrete action was taken to remedy this situation. One local councillor, with a portfolio for urban policy, made the following comments regarding the composition of the Monitoring Committee but did not elaborate further.

Of course there is a prefect, a mayor and a president of the region. We did note that there should possibly be a mayor from the targeted area, someone involved in local matters or the project proposed, even if the district mayor happens to be a councillor from a party of the opposition (Interview, senior local councillor, Marseille, July 1998).

---

[10] The information on district mayors was taken from an internal document of the City of Marseille (Ville de Marseille, 1995). *Unité 13 Marseille* represented a Socialist alliance in the Municipal Council of Marseille.

The MIPPE produced briefing notes for the attention of the councillors delegated responsibility for urban policy measures rather than for each district mayor based in the areas targeted by URBAN.[11] The latter could have access to the reports but would not be directly involved in the decision-making regarding the implementation of the programme and projects prepared for final selection. Any voluntary and community associations operating in the targeted areas were also excluded from direct representation on the formal committees. We need therefore to delve further into the system of local consultation and interaction with interest groups in France in order to explore whether there were any means by which the targeted recipients could actually make an input into the decision-making process.

The figures from the URBAN Programme Document indicate that the highest proportion of residents, concentrated in a single district covered by URBAN, were based in St Mauront where the district mayor was in opposition to the ruling UDF/RPR coalition.[12] Furthermore, the population figures for the targeted areas reveal a high population of immigrants who, as non-French citizens, were excluded from participating in any of the local elections. The proportion of non-EU citizens in the URBAN area of Marseille is presented as follows: 15.7 per cent of the population of the area targeted by URBAN originated from non-EU countries as opposed to 6.9 per cent of the population in Marseille as a whole.

Population figures since 1982 had registered a decrease in the percentage of non-EU citizens resident in Marseille. Even so, there was a particularly high concentration of non-EU citizens in some of the districts targeted by URBAN: On the Parc Bellevue estate in St Mauront (3rd district) 40 per cent of the population were non-EU citizens, in Belsunce (1st district) the figure given was 45 per cent, in La Canebière area, 35 per cent and in Panier, 18.8 per cent. Furthermore, non-EU citizens experienced greater difficulty in finding employment. Unemployment amongst the non-EU population resident in the 1st district was measured at 36.5 per cent in this period; on the Park Bellevue estate 38.9 per cent of the population was registered unemployed.[13]

---

[11] Internal document of the City of Marseille: 'Ville de Marseille, MIPPE, Rapport au Conseil Municipal, Programme d'Initiative Communautaire "URBAN" Rapport d'étape, 9 juillet 1998' (Ville de Marseille, 1998).

[12] This is excluding the GPU area of the 15th and 16th districts that was only eligible for ESF measures under URBAN. Please refer to Table 7.1 indicating the number of residents in each district.

[13] Population figures for non-EU citizens are taken from the URBAN Programme Document approved by the Commission in 1996 (CEC, 1996e, p.25). Unemployment

For URBAN in Marseille, any consultation and participation was closely integrated into the existing systems in place for the national urban policy under the contractual process (*Contrat de Plan, Contrat de Ville*). Much of this centred on the work of the project leaders. It is necessary to explore further the experiences under this framework in order to understand which channels of communication existed between the targeted recipients of the programmes and those representing the municipality on the formal committees. By which means could the mayor, his entrusted officials and councillors, communicate with the targeted recipients of the programme whom they claimed to represent at the formal Monitoring Committee and Advisory Committee (COCPUR)?

Mény (1998) provides us with an analytical framework with which to assess the interaction between groups and the state; three models are presented. In seeking to apply any model, it is stated how both interest groups and the state can be represented by a wide range of structures. The state in France may be represented at central, local or sectoral level as illustrated in previous sections of this chapter. Mény's analysis can be applied to our policy area since the state, represented at local level by the regional prefect, was the major implementing authority for URBAN in Marseille. However, given that the City of Marseille was a major actor in the partnership to deliver URBAN, we can extend the model to include the municipal authority. Mény's three models (1998, p.11) are briefly summarised below. Of the three, the one most pertinent to our analysis is the third, that of cooperation/interpenetration (*'coopération/interpénétration'*) between the state and other actors.

The first model presented is that of exclusion; there are variations to this model. In some cases both the state and groups reject any dialogue and cooperation, in others the state denies legitimacy to a group; alternatively a group refuses the right of the state to intervene. In this scenario, there is a clear exclusion of the groups from the interaction with the state. One example quoted is the case of relations between Catholic groups and the state following the laws of separation of church and state in France. In the period covered by our case study in Marseille, a high number of associations were officially registered at the prefecture. The state intervened in the area of urban policy and interacted with these groups in the implementation of some of the measures presented in chapter five. The exclusion model would not therefore appear representative of the situation in Marseille.

---

figures are also taken from the URBAN Programme Document (CEC, 1996e, p.25, p.36); the Parc Bellevue estate is situated in the St Mauront area.

The second model is characterised by protest or opposition to the establishment (*'le modèle de la contestation'*). This could be through group manifestations of violence or conflict as shown, for example, by the nationalist groups in the Basque area or Corsica. There have also been examples of violence in French cities; these include the incidents referred to as 'hot summers' (*'étés chauds'*) in certain cities such as Lyon where groups of youths behaved violently in the 1980s and 1990s. This promoted action by the French national and local authorities in the launching of programmes in the framework of urban policy measures as discussed in chapter five.[14] Such a model does not appear representative of the situation in Marseille in the period covered by this study. There was evidence of problems related to unemployment, drugs, delinquency and degradation of certain parts of the city such as the St Mauront district. There had not, however, been any major incidents of more widespread violence or conflict between inhabitants of the targeted areas and the local authorities or representatives of the state. One local state official emphasised the role of local associations in providing an element of stability in the areas experiencing social problems due to deprivation and unemployment:

> There are problems in individual neighbourhoods but there haven't been any organised riots. There have been some incidents of protest on specific sites but not actual riots to cause criminal damage, more a case of individuals trying to get firms to hire them. I think we have a population where there are family links, a network of associations that is very strong at neighbourhood level. There are various layers of immigration that go back a long way; they make a positive contribution to stabilising the social fabric of these areas (Interview, local state official, Marseille, August 1998).

Local councillors also emphasised how local associations, often formed around ethnic or religious lines, were a way of integrating newcomers to Marseille. The City of Marseille was viewed as more welcoming than some of the northern cities due to its port and long history of ethnic diversity (Interviews, local councillors, Marseille, July-August 1999). Even the local football team, *Olympique de Marseille*, was cited as a federating element! Indeed, the Mayor of Marseille, Jean-Claude Gaudin would often attend

---

[14] See Begag Azouz, Delorme Christian (1994) also *Le Monde*, 11 May 1995, p.24, 'Une <<culture des cités>> se développe contre l'exclusion' (An 'inner-city culture' develops against exclusion).

home games and attract media attention in his role as the local leader supporting the city's team.[15]

The third model Mény (1998, p.15) presents is that of cooperation/interpenetration between individual groups and the state; this appears the most relevant for our case study of Marseille. In this model, the state's relations with recognised groups may alternate between periods of intense cooperation and others of protest/disagreement. There are various strategies to achieve this although one main feature is the registering of the groups which, in certain cases, involves the according of a specific status referred to as '*l'agrément*'. This is a form of official approval or recognition of a group that may be accorded to a professional group such as doctors or to issue groups. One example of this process is the law of 1976 regarding the granting of this status to associations concerned with the defence of the environment.

According to Article 1 of the law of 1901, an association is the convention whereby two or more persons have in common their knowledge or activities for a purpose excluding that of sharing profits.[16] All recognised associations in Marseille should be registered at the prefecture declaring the name, assets and premises as well as the name, profession, residence and nationality of each of the two Directors. The declaration is published in the French Official Journal. In Marseille, many associations registered are subsidised by the state, regional and local authorities in the framework of the projects funded by national programmes such as measures under the planning contracts (*Contrat de Plan, Contrat de Ville*). A senior official in the Municipality of Marseille, interviewed in 1998, quoted the following figures relating to implementation of the planning contract at the time: 600 associations were subsidised and up to 800 projects presented by the different associations which varied in terms of numbers of members.[17]

Another aspect of the Mény's cooperation/interpenetration model focusing on the state's interaction with groups helps guide the analysis of recent experiments in this area in Marseille. Mény (1998, p.16) presents a scenario whereby the state engages in the active consultation with specific groups referred to as integration/cooptation ('*intégration/cooptation*'). In

---

[15] Feature on the role of mayors in French towns and cities (France 2, television lunch-time news, 17 November 1998).

[16] For a survey of associations in Europe, see 'Promoting the role of Voluntary Organisations and Foundations in Europe', (CEC, 1997b) COM (97) 241 final, Brussels, 06.06.97. Some details here are quoted from the section on France (CEC, 1997b, p.51).

[17] These figures were quoted by a senior official dealing with urban and social policy in the Municipality of Marseille; the interview took place in July 1998.

this case, state recognition is through the nomination of interest groups in the form of consultative organisations such as committees or commissions relating to certain policy sectors. On a national level, this had not yet stretched as far as actually involving interest groups in the negotiations around the urban policy measures in the planning contracts (*Contrat de Plan, Contrat de Ville*) for example. In the late 1990s, Prime Minister Jospin promoted a high-profile conference for voluntary associations. This raised a number of issues regarding the role of voluntary sector associations in the economy as a whole:[18]

> Why is it that voluntary associations, creators of one job out of every seven, haven't taken part in the conference on jobs in the same way as employers and the unions? Why is it that although the voluntary sector directly tackles the question of youth employment, it is never consulted on the subject? Why is it that although voluntary associations are involved in innovative action on the ground, they don't participate in the development of planning contracts between the state and regions? These questions can be summed up into one: why is it that this sector, which plays an important part in social development, doesn't have the status of formal intermediary in the same way as political parties and unions? (*Le Monde*, 20 February, 1999).

Clearly, any possibility of more formal relations and consultation between the state and voluntary associations was still at discussion stage in the period of implementation of URBAN. Yet there were ample examples of the Municipality of Marseille engaging in formal dialogue, at local level, with groups and associations. Only the central, municipal and regional levels of government were included in the framework of the contractual process (*Contrat de Plan, Contrat de Ville*). However the municipal authorities engaged in various forms of interaction with a wide range of groups through the system of district mayors established following Defferre's decentralisation reforms.

Experiments with local consultation committees (*commissions locales de concertation*) date back to 1989, the early period of urban policy measures in Marseille during which Robert Vigouroux was Mayor of Marseille. In this period, the local committees were headed by the district mayor. Indeed the St Mauront neighbourhood, later targeted by URBAN, provides an example

---

[18] This extract is translated from an article in *Le Monde*, 20 February 1999, which provided details of a conference, the *Assises nationales de la vie associative* organised for the 20 and 21 February 1999, at the *Arche de la Défense*. This was organised following the initiative of Prime Minister Jospin. Seven ministers or secretaries of state were scheduled to attend this conference, the first organised on such a scale.

where the local committees had been quite active and well attended by the local residents. Following discussion, projects proposed for funding under the urban policy measures would go before the district mayor who would make the final decision. A former project leader from the Municipality of Marseille described the decision-making process for projects proposed for funding during the pilot period of urban policy (*Contrat de Ville*) between 1989-1993.[19]

> Local consultation committees existed in St Mauront; there was a committee dealing with jobs, a women's committee and a health committee. They all worked on projects (that had been proposed for funding). They discussed each project between themselves, if two similar projects had been proposed, they would point this out and make it clear that it wasn't possible to finance two identical projects. By the time things were brought before the district mayor, all the discussion between people was over; we could tell the mayor which projects had been proposed and everyone knew anyway. There wasn't any confrontation between people (Interview, former project leader, Marseille, August 1998).

The local committees encountered problems related to political conflicts within the elected majority in the municipality rather than within the neighbourhood. During Robert Vigouroux's period in office as Mayor of Marseille, there was internal dissent in the Robert Vigouroux majority caused by Bernard Tapie forming an alternative group of Socialists; this ultimately affected this system of district mayors. Robert Vigouroux who represented the central administration of the Municipality of Marseille, barred any dissidents amongst the local district mayors from presiding over the consultation committees that had been established for the implementation of urban policy measures. Although the work of the committees continued, the district mayor, with knowledge of the area and its constituents, would no longer chair the meetings. One former project leader summarised events as follows:

> Our local committees continued the work but, politically, the results no longer went before a district mayor. A councillor from the central administration of the municipality would come along, and he knew nothing about the neighbourhood (Interview, former project leader, Marseille, August 1998).

---

[19] For an overview of the experience of the pilot phase of French urban policy (*Contrat de Ville*) during the period 1989-1993 see Le Galès (1994).

For the remainder of his period in office local officials, working at grass roots level in the area of urban/social policy, were forbidden to speak to any elected district mayor who had opposed the list supported by Robert Vigouroux – the existing Mayor of Marseille. Such had been the case of the district mayor in St Mauront, hence his exclusion from the committee meetings for urban policy as outlined above. Once Jean-Claude Gaudin became Mayor of Marseille, in 1995, he re-established the right of local officials to speak to the district mayor but the decision-making power remained with the central administration of the Municipality of Marseille. In the absence of local decision-making, all the local elected district mayor could do was to present local demands to the central administration of the Municipality of Marseille, particularly to those with a portfolio for urban policy.

The *Pacte de Relance pour la Ville* (Urban Renewal Pacts) launched by Prime Minister Juppé's government in 1996 re-established the local consultation committees incorporating residents. In this case, the district mayors were invited to meetings but the decision-making power was with senior councillors who had been appointed by the central Mayor of Marseille (this would be a *Conseiller Municipal Adjoint* or *Conseiller Municipal Délégué*). One local councillor with responsibility for urban policy stated that, although there was a process of consultation, the demands of the groups were not necessarily understood or taken on board: 'we don't always follow them; we listen to them but we don't necessarily understand them' (Interview, senior councillor, Municipality of Marseille, August, 1998).

Experiments in local consultation were part of the national and local policies in the framework of national urban policy. However, in contrast to the case of the UK, they were not integrated into the delivery of URBAN in Marseille. With reference to the implementation of URBAN in the UK the above process, described in the local consultation committees in St Mauront, resembled that sought by the Commission in the establishment of Urban Partnership Groups (UPGs) whereby local residents, associations and businesses to select projects for funding. However for URBAN in Marseille, apart from the initial consultation by the project leader in order to prepare the URBAN bid, there was no evidence of any wider discussion regarding projects proposed for URBAN. Programming for projects for URBAN in Marseille was very technical and no residents were involved in the COCPUR stage, let alone at Monitoring Committee level. Interaction was limited to the project leader who then communicated with the specialist services of the municipality including the European Unit in the MIPPE. Since the latter were under the control of the Mayor of Marseille's entrusted officials, there was a possibility of filtering so that projects represented the priorities of local politicians rather than any demands rising from grass roots level.

Even if the Commission had insisted on some kind of presence of the voluntary and community sector on the formal decision-making structures, there is evidence to suggest that issues would arise regarding to what extent the selected groups represented the targeted population as a whole. Some, like the consultation committees described above, appear to have been composed of local residents who were willing to get involved and allocate time to attending meetings organised by the project leader However, there are no figures available to allow analysis of exactly what proportion of the targeted population left their home to actively participate.

The concept of 'community gatekeepers' also appears in the case of Marseille. Apart from the experiments in the committees for local consultation, specific groups claiming to represent the local community were already established in each neighbourhood – the *Comités d'Intérêt de Quartier* (CIQ). The CIQs claim to stand for the general interests of each neighbourhood; they consist of associations of local residents, originally promoted by a former Mayor of Marseille, Gaston Defferre, in order to develop greater links between residents and elected officials. Although CIQs are still recognised by local councillors, questions arise regarding the extent to which these groups represent a wide range of the population in the targeted neighbourhoods.

The locally elected politicians present the CIQs as an example of how the system of local democracy works in Marseille: local councillors have regular contacts with the CIQ representatives in order to maintain contact with the grass roots of the city (Interviews with local politicians and project leaders involved in urban policy, Marseille, July and August 1998). The CIQ of each neighbourhood in Marseille is included amongst the associations formally recognised by the municipality. One municipal councillor described the process as follows:

> There's another aspect to this system – it's that of the CIQ; these are part of the voluntary associations that operate in different areas within each district of the municipality. There is a list of all recognised associations, including the CIQs closely associated with the municipal council, to whom we present certain projects. There isn't always an open discussion but there is an exchange of views (Interview, senior councillor, Marseille, August 1998).

There are, however, problems of representation related to the restricted membership of CIQs. Membership of a CIQ is through a process of invitation and final selection by existing members of each CIQ. This causes some local residents to resent the CIQs as they are seen to be unrepresentative of the multi-cultural community in these areas. Residents from some ethnic groups equate the CIQ with individuals sympathetic to the National Front (*Front National*) party of the extreme Right (Interview, local resident, St Mauront, July 1998). Interviews with officials involved at grass roots level in the area of urban policy confirmed the views expressed by some residents, particularly of Arab or African origin, that a typical CIQ member would be predominantly white European and often middle aged (Interview, local official, Municipality of Marseille, July 1998). An in-depth study of the sociology of members of CIQs is beyond the confines of this study. However, it is clear that membership is not open to all who live in the neighbourhoods that CIQ members claim to represent.

Mény (1998) argues that it is difficult for new groups to emerge in French society in view of competition from established interlocutors. Groups with new ideas or interests may encounter difficulties in participating in a political process in which institutionalised groups are already well placed. Established groups enjoy recognition and financial resources; this allows them to play the role of 'gatekeepers' of the agenda and to impose their veto on any decisions that contravene their interests. Such factors make it difficult to change French society (Mény, 1998, p.19). In the case of recognised associations in Marseille, such as the CIQ, it would be too strong to say they can apply a veto. Interviews with municipal councillors (July and August 1998) indicate that the CIQ's demands are not always met. Even so, it is evident that during the period of this study, established groups had more privileged access to decision-makers than any new ones. In this sense, the concept of 'community gatekeepers' appeared in the case of local regeneration policies in France as much as in the UK. There is no evidence to suggest that the implementation of URBAN in Marseille had any major impact in promoting wider mobilisation among the targeted recipients of the programme.

The next section assesses the progress of the URBAN Community Initiative (CI) in Marseille. In theory all areas of action, finally agreed in the Programme Document, were to be respected. In practice, there were strains during implementation in the relationship between the state, the main authority responsible for implementing the programme, and the newly elected municipal council which had its own priorities. The Commission, although present at the Monitoring Committee, depended on the national and local machinery for the delivery of the URBAN programme; this is investigated further below.

7.3 Tensions in Local Delivery Mechanisms

This section examines tensions which arose during the implementation of URBAN in Marseille. The formal documentation suggests an integrated approach, whereby the central, regional and local authorities were working in partnership to match-fund and deliver the European programme. However results of implementation in the period covered by this study provide evidence of priority being given to areas targeted by the municipality.[20] The President of the Regional Council of Provence-Alpes-Côte d'Azur (PACA) up to March 1998 was the same person as the Mayor of Marseille; no major issues arose regarding relations between the regional and municipal levels. Furthermore, chapter five illustrated how the region was very much the junior partner in the negotiations for the Programme Document.

Implementation on the ground replicated this situation whereby the region remained involved as a match-funder for certain aspects of the programme, but was not intensely involved in the major details of management. Neither the Monitoring Committee nor the Advisory Committee (COCPUR) were chaired or organised by the region which, nevertheless, had a place on both. In implementation on the ground, as well as in negotiations for the Programme Document, the two main actors within the Member State were the state and the municipality. From the end of 1995 to June 1997 Jean-Claude Gaudin, Mayor of Marseille, was also a minister in Prime Minister Juppé's government. It would be difficult though to argue that the municipality could expect the state, as well as the region, to simply follow its policy. Clearly, the state as an actor in this policy area was not a unitary actor. More than one central ministry as well as representatives of the deconcentrated state were involved; this included the regional prefect, the sub prefect for towns and cities and the field services of the state. Although Jean-Claude Gaudin was Minister of National and Regional Development, other ministries were also involved in implementing URBAN. So while the Mayor of Marseille could exert influence in some matters, there would be questions raised by other representatives of the state.

Finally, the Commission was both a partner and grantor of part of the funding to deliver the programme agreed. Although not involved in everyday implementation, attendance at the Monitoring Committee meetings provided

---

[20] The CI URBAN was implemented during the programming period 1994-1999, with an additional period for the realisation of projects under the ESF and ERDF elements as specified in the regulations. This chapter focuses on the main aspects of the implementation of URBAN up to the summer of 1998, the date of the Monitoring Committee observed as part of the field work relating to this study.

a means for the officials representing DG XVI to raise issues related to the implementation of the programme. By 1997, it became clear that both the state and the Commission, major partners in the funding of URBAN, were concerned about the progress of some aspects of the programme. There was a definite correlation between the priorities of the governing political parties in the municipality and the emergence of projects. By 1997 it was clear that there was a poor record of implementation in areas not prioritised by the municipality, on whom the state and the Commission depended for the grass roots delivery of URBAN. Firstly, we draw attention to the progress regarding ESF measures before focusing on the continuing tensions relating to the St Mauront area.

At the Monitoring Committee of July 1997, the representative of the SGAR expressed particular concern with the under spend of the ESF part of the programme. By March 1997, of the FF 45 million URBAN funds allocated to Marseille, FF 3,119, 388 million of the ERDF had been spent, but only FF 824 490 million of ESF.[21] During the meeting, the sub prefect for towns and cities confirmed that it would be necessary to rectify this balance. With reference to chapter five, the municipality felt that the extension of ESF to cover the GPU area had been 'imposed' by the state (Interview, MIPPE official, July 1998). In implementation, we then see that there was a problem regarding the emergence of ESF projects in the GPU area which had not initially been prioritised by the municipality. A senior official from the Municipality of Marseille made the point, at the Monitoring Committee of 1997, that although training was not strictly the competence of the commune, the city would honour its commitments in the framework of the planning contract (*Contrat de Ville*).[22]

There remained a problem in actually converting such commitments to action on the ground. Another explanation for the lack of ESF projects from the GPU area could be lack of coordination or dissemination of information to the project leaders employed there, or even their reluctance to participate due to the sheer complexity of the European funding process. One project leader employed in the GPU area saw little point in looking for URBAN funding since it would be simpler to look for national funding for the small

---

[21] Internal document provided by officials from the SGAR and the European Commission, DG XVI, for the purposes of this research: SGAR (1997b) 'Relevé de conclusions du Comité de Suivi du 9 juillet 1997' (Summary of the conclusions of the Monitoring Committee meeting of 9 July 1997). As noted in chapter five, even through URBAN was mainly the responsibility of DG XVI, the programme in Marseille had almost equal ERDF and ESF elements.

[22] Internal document, SGAR (1997b, p.2).

projects dealt with. Another project leader was more enthusiastic about seeking to use URBAN as complementary funding for GPU projects although it was considered as just another source of funds rather than any ambitious European, innovative project (Interviews, project leaders employed in the GPU area, Marseille, July 1998). The concept of URBAN as a catalyst to engaging European citizens had clearly not filtered down to the grass roots delivery mechanisms.

Another problem arising in the case of Marseille, as well as London, was the issue of eligibility. Any projects proposed for ESF funding would be developed through the system of project leaders in place for existing urban policy measures, mainly those agreed under the contractual process (*Contrat de Plan, Contrat de Ville*). The specificity of European funding mechanisms required specialist knowledge. Such teams existed at the level of the SGAR, the field services of the state and within the municipality's specialist European Unit, the MIPPE. It is questionable how much of this knowledge actually filtered down to the project leaders on the field, employed primarily in the framework of the contractual programmes (*Contrat de Plan, Contrat de Ville*). Lines of communication were blurred as those based at grass roots level in Marseille spent time and resources on ineligible activities. One project leader mounted a series of projects, in consultation with local residents, only to be told that many of these were not eligible for URBAN funding (Interview, project leader, Marseille, August, 1998).

Some state officials complained that officials from the Municipality of Marseille failed to respect eligibility restrictions attached, for example, to the European Social Fund. One official from the field services of the state expressed the following view:

> Those involved in urban policy in the municipality only knew about URBAN but they never linked this to any (European) regulations; so we had to explain to them that everything had to be within the rules. What was ineligible under the European Social Fund may have been eligible under URBAN but they would have to find someone else to finance it; they couldn't get that into their heads! They wanted finance for extra training in schools, for the children. You can't do it in non-Objective 1 areas, it is not legal, it doesn't conform to the regulations (Interview local state official, Marseille, July 1998).

Questions of eligibility also led to disagreements between the representatives of the deconcentrated state. The section dealing with urban policy measures, under the direction of the sub prefect for towns and cities, would be keen to promote projects in order to improve the performance regarding the spending of European funds. Yet the field services of the state were responsible for their own individual policy area and were also answerable to their parent ministry. This caused tensions between the various actors, all of which represented the French state. Differences were resolved by negotiation and consensus, rather than conflict, but the process took time as correspondence moved laterally or vertically to the national ministries. One official from the state services stated: 'We are answerable to the ministry but we are also answerable to the regional prefect, so we are a little bit torn between the two' (Interview, local state official, Marseille, July 1998).

Another issue raised at the Monitoring Committee meetings related to whether the local authorities could deliver match-funding which had been promised at the stage of the negotiation of the Programme Document. At the stage of implementation on the ground, there was some modification of the financial tables regarding the financial contribution of the municipality. One major decision at the second meeting of the Monitoring Committee in July 1997 was the modification of the ESF tables for measures 3 and 4. The global sums for measure 3 remained unaltered at a total of ECU 1,779 million however there was a change in the balance of funding provided by the national and local authorities: For measure 3, dealing with training and professional qualifications (*formation et qualification*) the contribution of the state was raised from the initial ECU 0,106 million to ECU 0,779 million ECU; the contribution of the Municipality of Marseille was reduced from ECU 1,703 million to ECU 1,000 million.

There were also modifications made for measures in the Programme Document dealing with the development of human resources.[23] The total amount of ESF remained unaltered at ECU 1,283 million. Alterations were made so that contributions from both the French state, and the Municipality of Marseille, were reduced. The state contribution was reduced from ECU 2,361 million to ECU 0,600 million and the contribution from the Municipality of Marseille was reduced from ECU 1,736 million to ECU 0,362 million. The remaining match-funding required, regarding the ESF funds, was to come from private sources calculated to provide ECU 0,321 million.[24] The decision was ratified by the European Commission on 21

---

[23] This was measure 4 under the second broad theme of the Programme Document focusing on Social Development (*Axe 2: Développement Social: mesure 4, développement des resources humaines*).

[24] CEC (1997d), revised edition of the URBAN Programme Document agreed for Marseille. The preamble of the programme states that the European Commission approved the changes on 21 October 1997.

October 1997 and a new URBAN Programme Document with the above modifications was produced by the MIPPE on 22 December 1997 (CEC, 1997d).

Clearly, the Municipality of Marseille had reduced the amount of match-funding originally anticipated for the European Social Fund (ESF) contribution for measures in the programme dealing with areas of social development. Points were raised in chapter five regarding the amount of the ESF element in the URBAN programme that had been agreed for Marseille, a far greater proportion than that for London.[25] The situation of Marseille raised issues relating to the ability of local authorities to produce match-funding to actually deliver European programmes. Although the financial tables had been altered, numerous state officials were not convinced that the municipality would be able to deliver all areas of the Programme Document (Interviews with officials from the state services, the regional and departmental prefecture, July and August 1998).

By 1998, the situation regarding the emergence of ESF projects appears to have been rectified to some extent. A review of the actions validated in the 1997 to 1998 included two major ESF funded projects in the GPU area.[26] These projects focused on the revival of neighbourhood groups in the St Antoine district (*Animation du noyau villageois de St Antoine*) and training related to a cultural project (*Formation de médiateurs culturels/Atelier de rue*); each project received FF 540 000 and FF 300 000 of ESF funding respectively. Four ESF projects were also approved in the St Mauront district. The remaining 19 projects validated by the COCPUR summary for the 1997 to 1998 period related to ESF or ERDF funded actions for the '*centre ville*' area classified as the centre of Marseille or its immediate proximity.[27] Overall, the implementation rates had improved since the situation in 1997. The above developments, particularly the emergence of

---

[25] The financial tables showing the amount of ESF/ERDF funds allocated to the various programmes in London are presented in Table 4.1, chapter four.

[26] Information in this section is taken from the following document produced by the AGAM, the unit of the municipality with responsibility for technical assistance and evaluation of the URBAN programme: AGAM (1998) 'Assistance technique du PIC URBAN, Comité de Suivi du PIC URBAN du 9 juillet 1998. Actions validées par le COCPUR de juillet 1997 à juillet 1998'.

[27] There was one exception among the 19 projects, that relating to expenditure for an operational team of the URBAN Programme (*Dépense équipe operationnelle du PIC URBAN*). This project had been proposed by the MIPPE, the European Unit of the Municipality of Marseille. The project related to the financing of a post with responsibility for implementing the jobs and training related to the social development measures of the URBAN programme as well as subsequent monitoring and evaluation.

ESF projects in the St Mauront area, promoted a positive response from the SGAR at the meeting of the Monitoring Committee in July 1998.[28]

It would be difficult to assess whether the improvement in implementation rates would have occurred in the absence of the changing of the financial tables agreed in 1997. By 1998 DG XVI did not oppose a proposal by the national authorities to increase the targeted area of intervention of the ERDF to the GPU area as well. Prior to this the GPU area, prioritised by the state, had only been eligible for ESF funds under URBAN.[29] After 1998, projects in the GPU area under the measures in the Programme Document favouring the creation or improvement of sports or leisure centres, improvements in the urban environment and quality of life were also eligible for ERDF funding. Furthermore, the national authorities proposed additional changes to the financial tables at the Monitoring Committee of 1998 regarding the ESF element of the programme.

The above events illustrate that the Commission allowed some flexibility during the implementation of the URBAN Programme Document originally agreed. Some officials from the state had reservations about the changing of financial tables in the course of the programme. However the SGAR allowed this flexibility to continue in order to increase the number of projects presented in the parts of the programme where there had been a poor record of implementation. Pressure due to the requirement in the regulations to commit the European funds by 1999 may explain this strategy. Other state officials expressed the view that, although DG V had a place on the Monitoring Committee, DG V took less active interest in the URBAN programme than DG XVI (Interview, local state official, Marseille, July 1998).[30] We now turn our attention to the case of the St Mauront district

---

[28] This comment is based on personal observation of the Monitoring Committee meeting of 9 July 1998.

[29] This decision extended ERDF funds under Measures 5 and 6 of the URBAN Programme Document to the GPU area where projects had previously been restricted to Measures 3 and 4 under ESF. This information is taken from internal documentation provided by European Commission and the SGAR relating to the meeting of the Monitoring Committee of 9 July 1998: SGAR (1998) 'Relevé de Conclusions, Comité de Suivi, 9 juillet 1998'.

[30] Indeed, DG V did not send a representative to the meeting of the Monitoring Committee which I observed on 9 July 1998. This may have been due to the pressures on the time of Commission officials. Priority may have been given to CIs which were the direct responsibility of DG V. Although programmes of this period also contained an ESF element, the CI URBAN was mainly the responsibility of DG XVI (see chapter three for the historical background to the launch of URBAN). By September 1998 it was still not clear whether the Commission, DG V in particular, had agreed to the change of financial tables proposed in 1998 (DG XVI/SGAR correspondence to which DG XVI allowed access).

which promoted tensions, between the municipality and the state, even in the early stages of the local delivery of URBAN. St Mauront was not part of the GPU area and had also been excluded from the *Euroméditerranée* programme operating on the border of this district. Officials involved in the original preparation to bring URBAN funds to Marseille were concerned that the newly elected municipality, committed to its policy of revitalising the city centre, may neglect the needs of St Mauront. The main contentious issue regarding the implementation of URBAN in Marseille was the area of the Programme Document that focused on the renewal of buildings and infrastructure (*requalification urbaine*). Indeed some local officials from the municipality, who had prepared projects for St Mauront in anticipation of URBAN funding, turned to the local state as a means of ensuring that the newly elected majority in the municipality would honour any existing commitments to the area:

> We had a kind of power struggle over St Mauront where we finally managed to convince the state that St Mauront is important. Even though, politically, this district is not of strategic importance for the municipal council, the dossiers were much more advanced than was the case for the central area of the city (Interview, former official, Municipality of Marseille, August 1998).

Documentation from Monitoring Committee meetings has confirmed this version of events. An official from DG XVI had already visited the St Mauront district in 1995 when Marseille was first selected for URBAN funding. During this period, the municipal authorities had presented the Bellevue estate in the St Mauront neighbourhood as a priority site and the dossiers were in an advanced state of preparation.[31] As the newly elected team at the municipality became established, the priorities changed. The files for projects proposed for URBAN funding could only reach the Advisory Committee (COCPUR) stage once the services of the state and the specialised departments of the municipality had completed the preparatory stage. Yet officials employed by the municipality could only work on files as instructed by the central Mayor of Marseille and his team. One local official explained how priorities changed following the results of the municipal elections in 1995:

---

[31] Interview, DG XVI official, May 1998. In the minutes of the Monitoring Committee of 9 July 1997, it is noted that the above official referred to the visit to Bellevue, St Mauront in 1995 (SGAR, 1997b).

The proposals for the centre of the city were added on at a later stage. However since the project for the centre of the city carries much more political weight with the mayor, at the moment this is the only area which has used up any funds. For the time being, the municipality hasn't got involved in ERDF projects in St Mauront; since 1995, we haven't been asked to work on these files at all. It is still in the programme, in terms of provisional sums that have been committed, but there haven't really been any completed dossiers presented in this area. I'm only here to implement policy; you have to leave the decisions to the elected councillors (Interview, local official, Municipality of Marseille, July 1998).

The sub prefect for towns and cities and the services of the state responsible for infrastructure, that is the DDE, had raised the matter with the municipal authorities on a number of occasions between 1996 and 1997 (Interviews, officials from the DDE and the prefecture, Marseille, July and August 1998). One local state official described the process as follows:

The state, that is the services of the state, acted as a mediator between the local authorities and the European Commission. We were highly involved in this matter. The priority shown by the municipal authorities was to put everything into the centre of the city. The state intervened several times through its dealings with the municipality, in some ways the sub prefect for towns and cities got quite tough when it came to the programming for European credits in general, but particularly those relating to the CI URBAN. We (the services of the state) also intervened quite strongly, on several occasions, regarding the necessity to get projects out in the St Mauront area but this hasn't been followed so far (Interview, local state official, Marseille, August 1998).

Indeed, at the Monitoring Committee meeting of 1997 the representative of DG XVI highlighted the fact that, although the dossiers for St Mauront had been in an advanced state of preparation in 1995, by 1997 only the files on the centre of the city appeared to present an integrated approached sought by URBAN. The sub prefect for towns and cities also confirmed, at this meeting, the necessity to maintain a balance of action between projects on the Bellevue estate in the St Mauront neighbourhood, as well as the centre of the city. Neither the Commission, nor the state, objected to the progress of projects approved in the centre of the city since this had also been agreed in the URBAN Programme Document. The points raised related to the necessity to achieve a balance in the programme, that is effective implementation in all areas, not just those accorded political priority by the ruling majority of the municipality at any particular time (SGAR, 1997b).

By 1998 although some progress had been made regarding ESF projects in St Mauront, there was still a distinct gap particularly for infrastructure projects under the areas of the Programme Document dealing with the renewal of buildings and infrastructure. The representative of DG XVI again raised the matter at the Monitoring Committee meeting of July 1998. There was a positive verbal response from the local councillor representing the Mayor of Marseille who confirmed the commitment of the Municipality of Marseille to the St Mauront district. Subsequent correspondence from the Commission to the SGAR further reminded the national authorities of the statement made at the Monitoring Committee.[32] Interviews in 1998 indicated that the local state, in alliance with DG XVI, was considering applying subtle pressure on the local municipality through suggestions that they would not be fully supportive of the municipality's proposed projects for the centre of the city unless some evidence of projects from St Mauront also emerged (Interview, SGAR official, Marseille, July 1998).[33]

The question remains how was it possible for the municipal authorities to circumvent both central government and the Commission? The evidence so far has pointed to a number of factors. Both the Commission and central government depended on the municipal authorities for the grass roots implementation of policy. This dependence was even greater in some policy areas, such as buildings and infrastructure, where municipalities had acquired additional competences following the decentralisation laws of the 1980s. Officials employed by the municipality could only work on files as instructed by the elected councillors, or their senior officials, who would be based in the cabinet of the mayor or a specialist unit of the municipality. There was therefore the possibility of neglected implementation in areas with low political salience such as St Mauront, Bellevue, not immediately evident to potential investors arriving in the city and not offering a strong electoral base to the elected councillors.

Central government and the Commission had no means of effectively addressing the problem of poor implementation of some areas of the URBAN Programme Document. The state and the Commission could raise points at meetings and in correspondence but, short of actually withdrawing the subsidy, it was difficult to enforce effective implementation in areas of low political salience. Whereas a subsidy could be withdrawn in cases of

---

[32] Internal Commission/SGAR correspondence, September 1998 forwarded for the purposes of this study.

[33] This was confirmed by observation of the Monitoring Committee on 9 July 1998 although the partnership worked within a consensual rather than aggressive style of decision-making.

fraud, or misappropriation of funds, it would be difficult to see this happening if the elected authorities were making verbal commitments for action in certain policy areas. The complexity of this policy area also made it difficult for central government and/or the Commission to tackle problems of implementation.

As shown in chapter five there were numerous programmes with similar objectives running alongside one another in Marseille. Apart from the problem of coordinating the wide variety of actions, there was that of coordinating the wide variety of actors and processes of each level of government. This could make it difficult for the Commission, or central government, to manage even small programmes such as URBAN. The European intervention was another programme among the panoply of measures as described in chapter five. This could provide the municipal authorities with legitimate reasons to justify lack of action in areas that were not a political priority; this is explained more fully in the section below.

7.4 Problems of Coordination

The variety of programmes operating in the area made it difficult for the French state to coordinate the actions under each. Local politicians could use the existence of other programmes in order to justify to the European Commission, and the French state, why implementation of some parts of the URBAN Programme Document appeared to have been neglected. The area of St Mauront targeted by URBAN also bordered the ambitious projects of the *Euroméditerranée* area. A senior local councillor, with responsibility for urban policy measures in Marseille referred to the problems of coordination in order to explain the lack of action in certain areas. A major example of this was the pathway project, prepared by the project leader in the St Mauront area, following consultation with local residents. The local councillor gave the following explanation for the lack of progress of the project:

> The state stressed on several occasions that it was necessary to take action in a particular neighbourhood; by the way, this was also the will of the European Commission. It is not that we had neglected the area but if you take into account the fact that there was some interference between projects, we got behind schedule; there is therefore some delay with the process in St Mauront. Why? It's simple; we had planned a walkway, improvements to a square; the motorway entering Marseille cuts the neighbourhood in two, we're on the

borders of *Euroméditerranée*. Then *Euroméditerranée*, on this very site, has plans for the development of an interchange. Well, I'm not going to ask for the development of a walkway that would cost Europe millions of francs when I find out that *Euroméditerranée* is in the process of considering building pavements on this very site! That's the problem of coordination, everyone follows their own logic; *Euroméditerranée* don't consult anyone regarding projects in their area. So what do I do about our project – wait for six months until they present us with their completed project? (Interview, senior local councillor, Marseille, July 1998).

On paper there was a senior elected official from the municipality of Marseille, Renaud Muselier (*1er Adjoint*) with responsibility for *Euroméditerrannée* within his portfolio.[34] Indeed, representatives of the municipality were also included on the *Euroméditerranée* Administrative Council. Yet the above comments from the councillor involved, who was part of the governing majority in the municipality, suggests that there was room for improvement in the coordination between European and national programmes. Interviews with local state officials also suggest there were problems of coordination between the actors representing the French state.

The local state services dealing with infrastructure and buildings, the DDE, staunchly defended the projects. DDE officials had devoted much time to preparing the dossiers for St Mauront that were lying dormant in the administrative machinery of the municipality of Marseille. Officials of the local state also acknowledged that projects proposed by the Ministry of Infrastructure, the parent national ministry of both the DDE and *Euroméditerranée*, could affect projects that had been prepared. Even if no formal decisions were taken, any uncertainty could affect proposals in nearby areas. With reference to the walkway, proposed for the St Mauront neighbourhood, one local state official stated the following:

One of the explanations that could be given for the fact that the project has been delayed is that there's the problem with the motorway that is being considered, but it isn't a project that has been decided on. It's about making an urban boulevard at ground level. It's the state's competence as it is related to the motorway, but it hasn't yet been decided on (Interview, local state official, Marseille, August 1998).

---

[34] The ranking of *1er Adjoint* indicated that Renaud Muselier would be the first councillor to replace the Jean-Claude Gaudin, Mayor of Marseille, if the latter for any reason was unable to continue in office during his term of election.

Information to each of the actors became blurred as it filtered through the system. Even if there had been no official deliberations regarding such an ambitious infrastructure project the state official, quoted above, confirmed that mere discussion of the project could be used by the municipality in its case against engaging in any infrastructure projects under URBAN in the St Mauront area. Since the European funds had to be committed by 1999 there was the possibility that central government would later agree to the local partners spending the funds on projects that had already prepared rather than risk an under spend in the programme.[35]

Other problems of coordination were related to the multitude of actors in the policy process. Although the terms for the municipality (*'Ville de Marseille'*) and the state (*'l'État'*) were used in documents and discourse, it is difficult to identify a single actor for either category. Politicians could operate both at national and local levels through the accumulation of mandates. Politicians aside, the implementation of URBAN had to filter through complex administrative systems. Even if conceived from below by the project leaders working in the targeted areas, all projects proposed for URBAN funding had to pass through the administrative channels of the municipality as well as the state machinery. The process in itself involved inevitable delays. One local state official, with experience in other regions, felt that procedures in Marseille were particularly cumbersome:

> I have the impression that here everyone works through a form of patronage (*'clientèlisme'*) that has developed because Marseille is so big, procedures are so cumbersome; this develops suspicions amongst those seeking funds, you get the impression that they pass from one to another. They say: "I've seen this one, then I saw someone else, then someone else told me such and such…" but in Marseille, there's a lack of coordination by the municipality itself, by the services of the local authority, therefore any dynamic action loses a lot because it is not well coordinated. As I said at the meeting, we are capable of bringing together thirty people in a Monitoring Committee in order to evaluate the real work of three or four people on the ground. It's not normal. We have to reverse the tendency: thirty people on the ground and three people for coordination (Interview, local state official, Marseille, July 1998).[36]

Regarding the contribution of the regional or local authorities, the fate of proposed projects could also be affected by the electoral cycle. The regional

---

[35] It would be beyond the period covered in this study to find the answer to this question.

[36] The official was referring to comments made at the meeting of the Monitoring Committee on 9 July 1998.

elections of March 1998 delayed action on many of the projects proposed for URBAN funding. From November 1997 to September 1998 no decisions could be taken regarding any major project which also required a contribution from the Regional Council of Provence-Alpes-Côte d'Azur (PACA). All major decisions are frozen prior to any election and there follows a period of re-adjustment whereby a new majority may take time to re-establish the team to deal with policies involving the region.[37] The key point for the 1998 elections was the disruption caused by the electoral cycle rather than the implications of the change of majority. Local officials and politicians indicated that the *Contrat de Plan, Contrat de Ville* framework required a consensual style of working given the match-funding committed by all parties. Changes in the majority at regional level could involve more lengthy negotiations with the municipal authorities in Marseille. However, the contractual commitments of the *Contrat de Plan, Contrat de Ville* that had been negotiated for this period required all the partners to continue working together.[38]

7.5 Responsibility for URBAN Funds

Procedures for the CI URBAN were identical to those for the mainstream Objective 2 programmes of this period. The European funds were initially allocated to the central administration which then directed them to the relevant national ministry. The regional prefect (*Préfet de Région*) had ultimate responsibility for the funds as well as the management of the programme. Additional responsibility was allocated to the Treasurer and Paymaster General (TPG) who played the same role as for other state credits. The principle was one of dual responsibility for public funds: the regional prefect had the power to authorise payment following evidence of correct administration of the funds, yet it was the TPG who would actually release the funds. Additional controls of the system allowed the regional prefect to consult the TPG regarding the interpretation of certain rules. The latter could also grant legal, economic or financial advice to the regional prefect.

---

[37] The above information was confirmed by all interviewees, both officials and local politicians.

[38] Interviews with officials based in the Municipality of Marseille as well as the offices of the PACA Regional Council in Marseille confirmed this view.

In the implementation of URBAN in Marseille the regional prefect was assisted by the specialist unit of the prefecture that dealt with European affairs, the SGAR, as well as the sub prefect for towns and cities with specific responsibility for urban policy. The individual ministries were represented at local level by the field services of the state. The match-funding had already been committed by each partner in the framework of the contractual process (*Contrat de Plan, Contrat de Ville*). Financial control was exercised by the TPG. The system in place appears well integrated. Did this mean, therefore, that the targeted beneficiaries on the ground could access the European funds more easily than those in the UK who fell victim to the confusion over action plans, accountable bodies and responsibility for the funds? In fact, the empirical evidence suggests that the same problems emerged for the targeted recipients of URBAN funds in Marseille as in London. Individual projects could encounter problems related to eligibility or, if based in a non-priority area, neglect due to the lack of political clout of the local district mayor. These problems aside, there remained that of the length of the bureaucratic process related to applying for URBAN funds.

Firstly, there were the complex procedures involving the various partners in the policy process. In view of the financial responsibility involved, the TPG was a member of both the Monitoring Committee and the Advisory committee (COCPUR) for URBAN. Returning to the earlier section on problems of coordination, the involvement of the TPG added yet another actor to the already complex system regarding the implementation of URBAN. Under normal procedures, representatives from the team of the TPG would receive the relevant documentation around fifteen days before any COCPUR meeting. Due to problems with the external or internal postal system, or ones of general coordination, some officers from the TPG's office complained about the late receipt of files before meetings, allowing them little time to prepare meaningful comments. This was a lively topic of discussion at the working group prior to a meeting of the Monitoring Committee observed in Marseille.[39]

Secondly, as in the UK, payment of European funds was in arrears. Any proposed projects had to survive the long administrative process described in sections 7.1 as well as the problems of coordination discussed in section 7.4. Even then, swift payment to the beneficiaries of the funds was not guaranteed. The European Commission paid its contribution to the URBAN programme in annual stages. Apart from the first payment of 50 per cent on approval of a programme, the rest would be paid in arrears on receipt of

[39] Observation of the Monitoring Committee, 9 July 1998, Marseille.

evidence for the appropriate spending of funds. Such information on the state of progress was coordinated by the SGAR following consultation with the local state services, and the sub prefect for towns and cities. The local state services also liaised with the national ministries in Paris.

Match-funding emanating from the partners involved in the contractual process (*Contrat de Plan, Contrat de Ville*) could only be released from regional and local authorities following deliberation and agreement in the respective regional and municipal councils. Communication was both vertical and horizontal and no allowances are made for smaller CIs such as URBAN. Any small organisation, without sufficient reserves, had to seek crippling bank loans to survive or else cease its activities. For URBAN in France, there was no specific adjustment of procedures to facilitate the process for smaller groups seeking to access funds. While the URBAN funds were delegated to the regional prefect, there had been no action taken to adapt administrative procedures to the specific needs of the non-established groups hoping to access URBAN funds. Neither the administrative nor financial procedures were conducive to involving non-established groups.

7.6 Conclusions from the Implementation of URBAN in Marseille

The delivery of URBAN at local level has highlighted the complexities of the decentralisation measures of the post-1982 period in conjunction with European policy making. The European intervention, URBAN, was added to the intricate mix of existing urban policies in Marseille reviewed in chapter five. From the point of view of the Commission the implementation of URBAN, and other Structural Funds policies, should respect the four principles established at the time of the 1988 reforms. Yet the experience of the local delivery of URBAN in Marseille suggests that the Commission is still struggling in its quest to develop a coherent regional policy.

Following the principle of concentration, the information provided in the original bid suggested that St Mauront was the area of most need in Marseille. In implementation, the low political salience of the district resulted in the neglected delivery of URBAN in the targeted area. Programming aimed to develop a consistent programme of action through the period of funding. Yet we saw that it was possible to change both the application of the measures of the programme and financial tables in the course of implementation. Whereas originally only ESF funds were destined for the GPU area, some ERDF funds were also subsequently extended to this area prioritised by the state. The process involved constant bargaining between the main actors involved, mainly the state and the municipality for this particular programme.

Furthermore, URBAN and other European programmes can fall victim to the electoral cycle involving the different levels of government in the Member State. The progress of the programming period was impeded during the process of regional elections in March 1998. On the one hand, additionality was respected by the match-funding element, the details of which were agreed in the Programme Document. The integration of URBAN into the existing procedures facilitated the delivery of the programme since the match-funding was provided by the national programmes. On the other hand, it is difficult to assess the added value of the European intervention beyond providing extra funds for the existing regeneration schemes operating in Marseille.

Finally the principle of partnership did not allow for any experimentation in the delivery of URBAN in Marseille. This was restricted to the formal partnership in place for delivering the larger European programmes and other national programmes. The targeted beneficiaries had a very limited role to play since their only point of influence was the project leader. Some groups, such as the neighbourhood CIQ committees, had more privileged access to the elected officials, yet there is little evidence to suggest that this had a major impact on the implementation of URBAN. The dominant partner that emerged at the stage of local implementation was the municipality, as represented by Jean-Claude Gaudin, central Mayor of Marseille. The priority of the elected majority was to improve the centre of the city. Representatives of central ministries, the local state and the European Commission were involved at various points of the policy process. However the dependence on the services of the municipality which controlled the project leaders operating at the grass roots, and the problems in coordinating the various schemes, allowed the municipality additional room to manoeuvre.

This chapter has illustrated how, within the established framework, the municipality could legitimately exercise 'gatekeeping' by steering the implementation of the URBAN programme to its stated priorities. This was particularly evident in policy areas where the post-1982 decentralisation laws had granted additional competences to municipalities, namely infrastructure and buildings; this affected projects eligible for ERDF funding. The state and the Commission depended on the project leaders directed by the central Mayor of Marseille, to bring forward projects to be funded by the European and national funds. Initial implementation problems regarding ESF in the GPU area were rectified in the course of the programme. The situation was far more problematic in areas falling under the competences of the municipality.

The files for building/infrastructure projects in St Mauront did not reach the surface of the complex programming system in place related to the delivery of URBAN in Marseille. No amount of verbal or written correspondence, from the central government or the European Commission could rectify this gap in implementation. The complexity of the system, and the vast range of programmes operating in the city, made it difficult for the central government or the Commission to directly tackle this problem in the framework of the partnership established to deliver the programme. At time of writing, powerful local politicians had hitherto managed to circumvent both central government and the Commission, a supra-national institution.

8 Lessons from the European Union's Urban Policy 'Experiment'

Introduction

This study has followed urban policy in the EU from initial birth to the implementation of the Community Initiative (CI) URBAN in London and Marseille. This chapter seeks to draw certain conclusions from the empirical study. Lessons from the EU's urban policy experiment can be useful in understanding the current implementation of EU regional policy as well as future developments. Firstly, we review what we have learnt about how the Commission expands its policy competences beyond what could have been foreseen by the founders of the European Community (EC).

Following this, the analysis compares and contrasts the experience of URBAN in the two case studies. The implementation of URBAN in London and Marseille involved a complex web of governmental and non-governmental actors operating at different levels. We conclude that the notion of multi-level gatekeeping may be more useful than that of multi-level governance in understanding the limits of EU urban policy. Finally, we discuss some broader issues raised by the EU's urban policy experiment. These include the part played by the Commission in policy delivery, the problems in assessing the impact of the supra-national intervention and the difficulties of mobilising citizens.

8.1 The Expansion of the Commission's Policy Agenda

Although the European Regional Development Fund (ERDF) was established in 1975, there is no legal basis for urban policy in the EU. Before venturing into the empirical material for the European case, we turned to the American experience in order to prepare our conceptual framework. Initially, this detour could be questioned since the EU is clearly not a federal state. However, lessons from American federalism were useful in developing a framework of analysis for the birth and subsequent implementation of EU urban policy. In this section, we concentrate on points that can help explain the expansion of the Commission's policy agenda.

A key word in the American experience was that of partnership; the American case illustrated how this can be interpreted in terms of cooperation between a wide range of actors, including non-governmental. The principle of partnership, formally adopted by the Commission following the 1988 reform of the Structural Funds, is a key element in explaining DG XVI's initial launch of urban policy measures. Another useful concept from American federalism was that of the 'federal purse strings' explored in chapter one. Figures presented in chapter three illustrated how the Structural Funds grew in the post-1988 period. The increased Structural Funds budget presented the Commission with the opportunity to expand its programmes. However, similar to the American federal government, the supra-national institution attached certain conditions to its granting of funds. The Commission introduced formal Objectives to its Structural Funds and emphasised how the implementation of European funding after 1988 was to follow the four principles of regional policy: concentration, programming, additionality and partnership. In this section, we concentrate on that of partnership in order to explain the expansion of the Commission's policy agenda.

Partnership can help legitimise the Commission's intervention in policy areas where it has no legal competence. Chapter three illustrated how the principle of partnership was a major factor contributing to the initial birth of urban policy measures. Similar to the American experience of the mayors' lobbying of the federal level, there was evidence of sub-national mobilisation in the European case. One example of this was informal dialogue between DG XVI and representatives of local government from London. The Commission responded by launching small-scale Urban Pilot Projects (UPPs) in London and Marseille, financed under Article 10 of the ERDF. Although the sums involved were minor, this showed that the Commission recognised the problems of cities even in areas ineligible for Objective 1 or 2 programmes at that time.

The Commission's dialogue with national and sub-national actors was a continuous process. National, local and regional authorities were part of the partnership to deliver programmes granted to cities within areas awarded Objective 1 or 2 status in the period 1989-1993. Networks, such as Eurocities, lobbied the Commission to take further action in addressing urban problems. Representatives of local authorities and other economic and social partners in London pressed for greater Commission intervention in urban areas.[1] However, the Commission's attempt in 1991 to include a formal urban competence in the Treaties was rejected by Member States. Following this failure to acquire a Treaty basis for action, EU urban policy developed through a number of instruments within the existing framework of regional policy. The Commission introduced urban policy measures in programmes under CIs and mainstream objectives for the period 1994-1999.

In line with the principle of partnership DG XVI undertook a formal process of consultation regarding the second phase of CIs for the period 1994-1999. Through this, the European Parliament became involved in the debate on EU urban policy and pressed for more specific measures for cities. This, in conjunction with the response of some Member States and sub-national actors, contributed to DG XVI's decision to announce a new CI directed at cities. Although this involved modest sums, as part of the framework of CIs agreed for this period, URBAN represented another aspect of EU urban policy. The Commission also extended the experiment of UPPs to other cities; a second phase was announced in 1997.

The bureaucratic politics model, explored in chapter two, provides another explanation for the incremental growth of EU urban policy. Similar to the American experience, this involved negotiations and bargaining for programmes within the existing legal framework rather than any formal competences for the Commission. In the case of the UK, urban policy measures were introduced in the mainstream Objective 1 programme for Merseyside in 1994-1996 through the Community Economic Development (CED) Priority. The Commission also aimed to incorporate the CED approach into the implementation of the CI URBAN in UK programmes. By 1997, CED had spread to Single Programming Documents (SPDs) negotiated for other cities in Objective 2 areas including London. The extension of the principle of partnership to include a wider range of actors in the delivery of European programmes was an integral part of the CED model. This embraced local business, community, and voluntary sector groups as well as ordinary residents in the targeted areas. In this way, a form of EU urban policy, seeking innovative delivery mechanisms, developed incrementally without any changes in the Treaties.

---

[1] The delegation led by the Association of London Authorities (ALA) supporting the Commission's proposal in 1991 to amend the Treaties to grant the Commission a formal competence in urban policy included representatives of employers, Trading and Enterprise Councils (TECs) and Trade Unions (ALA, 1992a).

The CED model was less evident in France during the period 1994-1999. CED was not incorporated into the implementation of URBAN in Marseille. In view of this, there was less experimentation with local empowerment than was the case with the delivery of URBAN in London Even so, an increasing number of cities gained experience of administering European Structural Funds through the receipt of European programmes. In the period 1994-1999 local government in Marseille, as well as in London, was involved in implementing European programmes partly financed by URBAN or Objective 2. Similar to the UK, the experience of URBAN in France revealed some interesting points about how the delivery of European regional policy works in practice. Before turning to the comparative analysis on the implementation of URBAN, we conclude this section by briefly examining the issue of sub-national organisations circumventing the Member State. Although there has been much emphasis on the Commission's dialogue with sub-national actors, the expansion of the Commission's policy agenda does not necessarily entail any significant bypassing of the Member State.

The American experience illustrated how any attempt of the federal government to bypass the states, during the Johnson period, was relatively short-lived. Nixon abandoned such a policy and this has never since been adopted. Federal programmes for cities, even under Clinton's Empowerment Agenda, were channelled through the state level governments. Turning to the European case, the early experience of UPPs involved an element of local actors circumventing the Member State. The delegation, in 1988, was led by the Labour dominated ALA against the background of a Conservative government that had been in power since 1979. Bruce Millan had been the Labour Party's choice as Commissioner. In the context of partnership, the former Commissioner could interact directly with sub-national actors from London and Marseille. Discussions with representatives from London were followed by an informal visit to Marseille. In view of the small sums involved under the provisions of Article 10 of the ERDF, the Commission was able to initiate UPPs in London and Marseille without consulting the respective national administrations.

Once the implementation of UPPs began, it became clear that it was not possible to bypass the national administrations in the UK and France. Indeed, the implementation of all EU urban policy instruments, examined in this study, involved central government at different stages of the policy process. The precise point, and degree of central government intervention, depends on the individual programme examined. Variations in central government intervention can also be explained by differences in the administrative procedures of each Member State. The empirical material revealed a complex implementation framework, involving other levels of government, as well as non-governmental actors. The section below explores how the notion of a multi-level gatekeeper system has emerged from this study.

8.2 Multi-Level Governance or Multi-Level Gatekeeping?

The literature on multi-level governance, reviewed in chapter two, presented an explanatory framework for European policy-making involving a wide range of partners. This complemented the analytical tools acquired from the experience of urban policy in the American federal system. Taking the approach of Scharpf (1994), national and sub-national actors could be part of a system of multi-level policy-making. Participants at different levels would be involved in the policy process along the lines of cooperative rather than dual federalism. The actors involved would share the common goals of addressing the problems of urban areas.

In our case studies, the empirical material on the origins of urban policy instruments illustrated how this involved a complex network of actors at supra-national, national, regional and local level. In this respect, the concept of multi-level governance was relevant to our policy area. However, it was also clear that the implementation of EU urban policy in the UK and France could not bypass central government. Indeed, the empirical study aimed to identify barriers between the Commission's urban policy, its conception in Brussels and the local delivery on the ground. As the main implementing authority, central government in the UK and France would play a major part in the national delivery of EU urban policy. It was therefore necessary to find a framework of analysis that could help assess the role of central government throughout the policy process.

The state centric model and the notion of 'gatekeeper' developed by Hoffmann (1966) was a useful starting point. However Bache's (1996) concept of 'extended gatekeeper' was more relevant to our policy area since this focused on the role of central government in the *implementation* of policy. In chapter two the 'extended gatekeeper' model, developed by Bache (1996), was adapted for the purposes of our own policy area. Bache (1998) found that in the area of regional policy, central government control at the implementation stage could restrict the emergence of a multi-level system of governance:

On occasions, the consequence of national government gatekeeping is a political arena characterised less by multi-level governance than by multi-level participation: actors from sub-national and supranational levels participate, but do not significantly influence decision-making processes. In short, multi-level governance needs to take greater account of the gatekeeping powers of national governments, across all stages of policy-making, over time and across issues (Bache, 1998, p.156).

The experience of URBAN in London and Marseille provided empirical evidence that supported some of the above points. We saw how local actors could participate in the launch and local delivery of urban policy measures. However, in both case studies on URBAN, there was evidence of central government gatekeeping at different stages of implementation. There were similarities and differences in the two cases. In both the UK and France, central government played a major part in the selection of cities and the agreeing of the financial allocation to each programme.

In both London and Marseille subsidiarity, regarding the implementation of URBAN, was decided by the national administration. In each case, representatives of central government, not the local authorities, chaired Monitoring Committees. The Commission was sympathetic to the Leaders of City Councils in the UK who viewed central government chairing of the Monitoring Committees as an intrusion in the governance of their city. However, central government insisted that the chairing of Monitoring Committees was non-negotiable. In the case of France, the Commission accepted the administrative structures based on existing procedures for European and national policies. Central government chaired both committees and this was not even a point of discussion in the negotiations for the delivery of URBAN in France.

Bache (1998) also developed the notion of 'flexible gatekeeping' whereby central government 'gatekeeping' could vary across issues, at different stages of the policy process, or over time:

> It is argued that gatekeeping is a *flexible* concept that may be practised by governments at different stages of the policy process. Moreover, the gatekeeping role of governments is flexible over time: the renationalization of aspects of regional policy in 1993 provided evidence of this. Finally, gatekeeping is flexible across issues: while the UK government accepted the bulk of the Commission's 1988 reform proposals, it did not compromise on additionality (Bache, 1998, p.156).

The case of URBAN in London and Marseille provided examples of 'flexible gatekeeping' by central government in the course of the implementation of the respective programmes. In the case of London, we saw flexibility in the procedures regarding the administration of funds, particularly towards the end of the programme. DETR agreed to forward fund ERDF to non-local authority accountable bodies. This aimed to facilitate the case for non-local authority organisations, without financial reserves of local authorities, seeking to be responsible for the URBAN funds. This would give a non-local authority accountable body a margin of manoeuvre to survive any delays related to receiving European funding. There had been no discussion of such concessions in the early Commission/central government negotiations to establish the administrative framework for the delivery of URBAN.

Central government also displayed flexibility in the implementation of URBAN in Marseille. This was evident in the negotiations regarding the contents of the URBAN Programme Document. The original submission to bring URBAN funds to Marseille highlighted the case of the St Mauront district. The newly elected municipality in 1995 prioritised the centre of the city (*centre-ville* area) and this was reflected in the Programme Document finally agreed between the state, the region, the municipality and the European Commission. Similar to the UK, central government in France controlled procedures for administering European funds. However in the course of the programme, central government showed some flexibility in Marseille regarding subsequent amendments to the financial tables originally agreed to co-finance URBAN.

An interesting variation between the two cases relates to the point of the policy process at which central government exercised 'extended gatekeeping'. This can be explained by the differences in procedures relating to the match-funding of the respective programmes. During the period covered by this study, central government in the UK did not provide any match-funding from central government budgets to deliver the European programme. In contrast to this, each level of government in France committed match-funding to the European programme through the contractual process. This can explain why central government intervened, at the stage of the negotiations of the Programme Document, in Marseille rather than London. Some local partners in the UK complained about the lack of central government support to match-fund European programmes.[2] Yet the lessons from France indicate that central government co-financing of the European intervention also involves the targeting of areas that may be prioritised by central government, rather than the local authority. Such was the case regarding the extension of the ESF aspect of URBAN to cover the GPU area (*Grand Projet Urbain*) prioritised by the French state in the case of URBAN in Marseille.

The empirical evidence in this study also supported Bache's findings that the gatekeeping powers of national governments can limit the influence of the supra-national level. The Commission participated in the decision-making processes for URBAN in various ways. Similar to the American federal government, the Commission attached conditions to the receipt of URBAN funds such as the match-funding requirement. The Commission was a member of the Monitoring Committees for the programme in both London and Marseille. In the case of the UK, the Commission pursued a more interventionist approach in negotiations to establish an administrative framework conducive to the approach sought by the CED priority. Despite such provisions, in both London and Marseille the programme evolved in a way beyond what could have been foreseen by the Commission at the launch of URBAN. In this respect, the supra-national level participated but did not significantly influence the decision-making processes (Bache 1998, p.156). Part of this may be explained by the gatekeeping powers of national governments. However, the findings of this study present a more complex picture of the European policy-making process.

While Bache's analysis of central government alludes to tensions within the centre, and suggests the core executive approach as a way of analysing these, this theme was not fully developed (Bache, 1996, 1998).[3] This study highlights the complexity of central government structures in both the UK and France. In the implementation of EU urban policy, it is difficult to view central government as a single entity. The implementation of URBAN in the UK illustrated how different central government Departments jealously guarded responsibility for European funds and their own procedures for dealing with them. Furthermore, in both the UK and France, central government is represented at different levels. In the UK, Government Offices dealing with specific regions have been in place since 1994; these are

---

[2] This comment is based on interviews/observations as part of this study rather than any systematic survey of local partners involved in implementing European Structural Fund programmes in the UK.
[3] See in particular Bache (1996, pp.51-54).

responsible for national and European funding programmes. In France, even after the decentralisation laws, the state has a strong presence at local level (Mazey, 1995, p.135). Indeed, the involvement of the local state was extended to cover new areas, such as urban policy, with the creation of the sub prefect for towns and cities (*Sous-Préfet à la Ville*) in 1991.

Urban policy straddles a number of policy areas. In both case studies the European intervention, added to existing measures and procedures in place for national policies, resulted in a marble cake scenario reminiscent of the American experience. Lines of authority were blurred and there were problems of coordination. In the UK, local partners blamed Government Offices for administrative problems such as delays in accessing the European funds committed to the programme. Yet Government Offices had not actually been involved in negotiating the administrative arrangements for URBAN. Moreover, Government Offices were dependent on the procedures of the central Departments before releasing any funds to the partners on the ground. In the case of Marseille, there were differences in opinion between the SGAR (*Secrétariat Général pour les Affaires Régionales*), the field services of the state and the sub prefect for towns and cities.

The complexity of central government structures accentuated the problems of coordinating the supra-national intervention in urban policy. Furthermore, the lack of clarity over certain issues could give local actors room to manoeuvre. This leads us to another variation from the findings of Bache; the concept of 'gatekeeping' exercised by other levels of government, not just the central government. In stages one and two of the delivery of URBAN, central government monopolised negotiations with the Commission. By stages three and four of the policy process, there is evidence that local authorities played a more dominant part in both the UK and France.[4] In both cases, the influence exercised by local government resulted in policy outcomes that could not have been foreseen by the Commission.

At the stage of the local delivery of URBAN in London, the empirical evidence in chapter six revealed that, in all but one case, the local authority emerged as the dominant partner. This, as noted in chapter four, was not the original model that the Commission had conceived for URBAN. The CED approach sought active participation of a wider range of actors, particularly at grass roots level in the targeted areas. Moreover, URBAN aimed to experiment with local management of the programme through the institution

---

[4] Please refer to chapter four, section 4.1/2 which sets out the four stages of implementation of URBAN for the purposes of this study.

of the Urban Partnership Group (UPG) being established as a legal entity to manage URBAN funds. In reality, this was the exception rather than the rule. Although Bache (1996) prepared the 'extended gatekeeper' model for the analysis of central government in implementation, certain points are relevant in identifying gatekeepers operating at other levels of government. The model can help explain why local authorities emerged as the leading partners in the implementation of URBAN in the UK.

Point nine of the 'extended gatekeeper' approach (Bache, 1996, p.198) listed political, financial and informational resources as important in the EU regional policy network. Local authorities are established partners in administering European funds. Similar to American cities, which employed 'intergovernmental relations officers', local authorities employ European Officers some of which have their own team depending on the size and resources of the local authority. Officers with responsibility for European affairs are answerable to the local councils that employ them. The specific responsibilities of European Officers generally include complementing the European strategy with the funding mechanisms existing at national level, such as the Single Regeneration Budget (SRB) in the UK.[5] Some representatives of non-governmental groups in the UPGs felt that European Officers monopolised information relating to the URBAN programme. It was felt that this 'filtering' of information by council officials limited, to some extent, the role of non-governmental groups in the decision-making processes.[6]

Local authorities in the UK also have greater financial resources than the representatives of local residents or the voluntary and community sector. The case study material from both the UK and France illustrated that European funding has a complicated path before it is released to finance projects at grass roots level. This was a major point in the argument in the UK that local authorities should be the accountable bodies for URBAN. Indeed, some local authorities also had ready sources of match-funding, to deliver the programme, through successful bids in national regeneration programmes such as SRB. The URBAN administrative arrangements referred to the UPG's constitution as a legal entity to manage URBAN funds. It was also stated that a lead agency could receive and manage funds

---

[5] There are variations between local authorities regarding the specific duties of European Officers.

[6] This comment is based on selective interviews with representatives of UPGs involved in implementing URBAN in London for the period of this study.

on behalf of the UPG.[7] Yet in areas where the voluntary and community sector was less established, such as South Kilburn or the East End, there was little prospect of the UPG being constituted as a legal entity to manage URBAN funds.

In both Park Royal and the East End, there was representation of local residents, the voluntary and community sectors on both the URBAN Management Committee (UMC) and the individual UPGs. However the UPGs in South Kilburn and the East End were not in a position to enter the debate regarding local management of URBAN. By the time the decisions had to be taken regarding accountable body status, the local authorities had already made their case to take on this role. The increased financial and informational resources of local authorities allowed them to take responsibility for accountable body status without any major debate amongst other partners. In negotiating the URBAN administrative arrangements, the Commission did not foresee that local authorities would take a dominant position in the partnership to deliver most URBAN programmes in the UK. In this respect, gatekeeping by local authorities significantly influenced the decision-making processes in the implementation of European programmes. There were, however, variations to this pattern in the case of the two other UPGs in London.

The implementation of URBAN in London provided the only cases in the UK where the local authority did not become the accountable body for URBAN funds. Two of the UPGs forming part of the Park Royal URBAN programme in London opted for non-local authority accountable bodies. In the case of White City, Shepherds Bush, Edward Woods UPG, the London Borough of Hammersmith and Fulham did not seek to be the accountable body for managing URBAN funds in this area. However, the council fully supported the UPG's formation as a limited company to undertake the role of accountable body. Indeed, the local council's support in this matter was a major factor influencing the UPG's decision to form itself as a limited company (Interview, White City, Shepherds Bush, Edward Woods UPG member, January 1999).

In the case of Queen's Park UPG, the council did not seek to take on the role of accountable body for URBAN in the Queen's Park area. Since the URBAN funds were allocated to a Labour ward, the Conservative majority in the City of Westminster was not sufficiently committed to the programme to take on the role of accountable body. The councillors proposed instead

---

[7] Please refer to the URBAN Administrative Arrangements presented in Appendix one, chapter four.

that the UPG formed itself as a company limited by guarantee similar to the White City, Shepherds Bush, Edward Woods UPG. However in contrast to the situation in the London Borough of Hammersmith and Fulham, some members of the UPG in Queen's Park were less willing to follow the local council's proposals. The 'homes for votes' scandal of the Dame Shirley Porter affair of the 1980s had left a legacy of distrust between some residents of council estates and the City of Westminster.[8] Furthermore, from the early stages of local implementation, some members of the UPG had expressed concerns about the responsibilities involved in the local management of funds:

> I don't want to be responsible for the money and have people coming to me for it...All I know is that the council does not want to be the accountable body, but that is only one part of the argument. I don't want to be responsible for the money if the criteria for giving the money is laid down by somebody else as all the indications are. I don't mind giving out the money, providing that I know that we can make some mistakes (Interview, Queen's Park UPG member, January 1998).

The comments quoted above indicate that representatives of the local voluntary and community sector were nervous about managing a local entity, subject to control for audit purposes, as stated in the URBAN administrative arrangements. The Commission may not have foreseen the practical problems related to empowering local communities to assume responsibility for management of URBAN funds.

One solution to the problem was the proposal by Paddington Development Trust to undertake the role of accountable body for URBAN funds. Since there were links between the Labour Party and some members of Paddington Development Trust, the Conservative majority in the City of Westminster opposed the offer made by Paddington Development Trust. As noted above, some members of Queen's Park UPG had reservations about its formation as a legal entity to manage URBAN funds. However, Queen's Park UPG was sufficiently empowered to vote against the views of the Conservative majority in the City of Westminster regarding the appointment of the Paddington Development Trust as accountable body. The result was a unique case in UK URBAN programmes of the period 1994-1999 whereby a non-local authority organisation, without the support of the political majority in the local council, undertook responsibility for the management of URBAN funds.

---

[8] Please refer to chapter six for more details on this.

Point eight of the 'extended gatekeeper' approach states that 'the importance of different types of resources available to governments *and other actors* will fluctuate across policy sectors and over time' (Bache, 1996, p.197 emphasis added). Firstly, the voluntary and community sector involved in Queen's Park UPG was more established than in other areas such as South Kilburn or the East End. The change in national government to a Labour government in 1997 granted additional resources to the voluntary and community sector. The support of Members of Parliament, as well as Labour party sympathies among some members of the Paddington Development Trust, could have been the vital political resources contributing to a non-local authority steer. This arguably helped gain flexibility from the central government Departments, particularly the Department of the Environment Transport and Regions (DETR) at the later stage of the programme. The decision by DETR to forward fund ERDF to non-local authority accountable bodies destroyed the argument that only local authorities had the financial resources to survive delays in receiving European funds.

Another consideration was the appointment of an URBAN officer, a new position partly funded by the European Commission under the capacity building measures of the programme. Such posts were created to serve the URBAN programme and the UPG, rather than the local authority, even though the local councils match-funded the appointments. There was an element of independence in such posts since they were created specifically for the European programme. Yet the impact of such appointments varied according to the local circumstances of each UPG. Some members of the Queen's Park UPG were positive about the trust that could be built up between the group and an individual not seen to be part of the existing council machinery. This could also counter any suspicions regarding the local authority filtering of information relating to the URBAN programme. One member of the Queen's Park UPG expressed this in the following terms:

The local authority is the enemy, as far as the local community goes, and in order to build up a partnership it has got to be based on trust. And there has been no trust there at all...all the suspicion, it was all there in the beginning, you lot are blocking it, you are stopping URBAN, where is the money, you are making excuses...It took a lot of hard work...he (the URBAN officer) got so much stick visiting groups...his whole personality is suited just for the job because he doesn't play any games, he doesn't take information back from the community and benefit local councils, he does what he does from the heart. And that is a big difference, that is where the trust has come on board because he is not going to sit in one meeting and tell us one thing and then go to another committee and say something else. He is consistent and he has tried to hold off the councillors and not been swayed by what *they* have wanted.[9]

In the case of Queen's Park, the relationship with the URBAN officer was seen as a factor enabling a newly created body, such as the UPG, to develop its confidence and capacity to make collective decisions. The appointment of Paddington Development Trust as accountable body allowed the members of Queen's Park UPG some distance from the responsibilities involved in undertaking this role. The UPG could therefore concentrate on selecting projects as part of the local Urban Action Plan (UAP). Although the local authority in this case did not emerge as leading partner, the policy outcome was still not that originally envisaged by the Commission. Even in an area where the voluntary and community sector was well established, individuals were nervous about the responsibilities involved in the UPG's constitution as a legal entity to manage public funds.

The case of URBAN in Marseille provided an even clearer case of 'gatekeeping' by local authorities. Here, the newly elected majority in the municipality managed to alter the contents of the original submission for URBAN. The newly elected Mayor of Marseille enjoyed additional political resources since the accumulation of mandates system (*cumul des mandats*) allowed him to hold more than one office. During part of the period of the implementation of URBAN, the Mayor of Marseille was Minister of National and Regional Development (*Ministre de l'Aménagement du Territoire*) in the central government and President of the Region Provence-Alpes-Côte d'Azur (PACA). Specialist officers in the European department, the MIPPE (*Mission des programmes privés et européens*) were directly accountable to the Mayor of Marseille and provided assistance to local politicians forming part of the governing coalition of the Right.[10]

At grass roots level, the URBAN programme was delivered by the machinery of the municipality under the framework of the *Contrat de Plan*, *Contrat de Ville*. In contrast to the appointments of URBAN officers of UK programmes, the project leaders (*chefs de projet*) were firmly under the control of the elected Mayor of Marseille. Both the Commission and central

---

[9] Extracts from an interview with a member of Queen's Park UPG, January 1998, emphasis added. Similar views were expressed by other members of the UPG interviewed during this period Observation of UPG strategy days and meetings also confirmed the positive relationship between the officer concerned and the Queen's Park UPG; dates are listed in the bibliography.

[10] This refers to the coalition between the Gaullist *Rassemblement pour la République* party (RPR) and the French Centre Right Federation, the *Union pour la Démocratie Française* (UDF).

government depended on the services of the municipality to deliver the programme through the project leader system. Even if the project leader had an excellent relationship with non-governmental groups in the targeted area, it would be extremely unlikely that any minority group would be able to steer the URBAN programme in a direction not favoured by the political majority in the municipality as had been the case with the Queen's Park UPG in the City of Westminster. It was clear that in stages three and four of the implementation of URBAN, the local Municipality of Marseille had considerable opportunities to influence the decision-making processes.

Gatekeeping by the local municipality resulted in poor implementation of certain areas designated for ERDF projects as agreed in the Programme Document with the Commission. This was the case in the St Mauront district of Marseille, an area of low political priority for the local municipality. This provided the best example of how the complexity of central government structures granted local politicians a window of opportunity to influence the implementation of URBAN in Marseille. The Programme Document identified St Mauront as a priority area and made provision for infrastructure projects. However local councillors presented *Euroméditerranée* as a legitimate reason to block the project of the pathway prepared for ERDF funding. The Departmental Office for Infrastructure, the DDE (*Direction Départementale de l'Équipement*), had prepared the dossiers for the pathway and pressed the sub prefect for towns and cities for action. Although the DDE shared the same parent ministry as *Euroméditerranée*, that is the Ministry of Infrastructure (*Ministère de l'Équipement*) in Paris, this did not provide a solution to the problem.

All projects seeking URBAN funds would go through the MIPPE and other specialist departments of the local municipality. The Mayor of Marseille controlled representation of the municipality on the Monitoring Committee (*Comité de Suivi*) and the Advisory Committee (COCPUR). Following the decentralisation laws, the municipality had legal competence in policies regarding local infrastructure. The local municipality therefore had powers to delay projects in this policy area. Verbal and written communication from the Commission and the representatives of central government failed to make infrastructure projects emerge in the St Mauront area.[11] Neither the Commission, nor the local state, could rectify this gap in

---

[11] This was the situation in 1998 when the fieldwork for the Marseille case study was completed. Given the delays, it would be unlikely that infrastructure projects would subsequently emerge as all funds had to be committed by 1999. The correspondence between central government, the Commission, the SGAR, the sub prefect for towns and cities and the Municipality of Marseille had continued since the early period of

the implementation of the Programme Document agreed for URBAN in Marseille.

The implementation of URBAN, in both London and Marseille, revealed new bureaucratic hurdles that may not have been foreseen at the launch of the CI URBAN. The sums involved were relatively small, yet URBAN was exposed to the full bureaucratic machinery at all levels of government. It would be difficult to conclude that policy-making was characterised by a wide range of actors in pursuit of clearly defined common goals. In reality, the two case studies revealed a complex system of 'multi-level gatekeeping'. Each level of government had entrenched interests and exercised these at different points of the policy process. Although there were variations in the degree and nature of gatekeeping, there were a number of similarities in the cases of London and Marseille.

In both the UK and France, central government was the initial gatekeeper. Central government in both cases monopolised the early stages of negotiations regarding the selection of areas and financial allocations of URBAN. Central government departments in both the UK and France jealously guarded responsibility for their own policy area. This caused problems of coordination which challenged the integrated approach sought by URBAN. In its aim to mobilise the grass roots in deprived areas of cities, the Commission encountered difficulties in bypassing not only central government but also other established gatekeepers in the Member State.

Local authorities in the UK played a leading role in local implementation even though the Commission's original model for URBAN involved the empowerment of non-governmental actors. The only exception to this was the case of Queen's Park, although this variation was only possible due to the change to a Labour government in 1997. It would have been unlikely that central government Departments under a Conservative government would have made the concessions required to allow the Paddington Development Trust, with links to the Labour party, take on the role of accountable body. Local politicians in the case of Marseille prioritised certain areas of the city and neglected others included in the URBAN Programme Document agreed with the Commission.

In both the UK and France there was evidence that gatekeeping, by central and local government, resulted in policy outcomes that differed from the original objectives set by the Commission. There was little evidence of non-established groups in London or Marseille significantly influencing the

---

implementation. However, by 1998 there was still no evidence that any progress had been made regarding infrastructure projects in St Mauront.

local delivery of URBAN. The case studies provided numerous examples where the supra-national and non-governmental actors participated in URBAN, but did not significantly influence the decision-making process. In both cases, the gatekeeping powers of central and local government hindered the emergence of multi-level governance in the decision-making process. The notion of multi-level gatekeeping may therefore be more relevant in understanding the limits to EU urban policy than that of multi-level governance. The case of URBAN has illustrated that in seeking a 'bottom-up' approach, the Commission has exposed itself to new problems in the management of such programmes. The next section examines, in further detail, the problems related to the Commission's dependence on national and sub-national government to implement its policies.

8.3 The Role of the Commission in Policy Delivery

The impact of the increased resources following the 1988 and 1993 reform of the Structural Funds presented the Commission with new possibilities for experimentation. The empirical material presented in this study has illustrated how, without any changes in the Treaties, the Commission can venture into new policy areas. Section 8.2 explored how the notion of multi-level gatekeeping can help identify the obstacles faced by a supra-national policy directed at local areas. This section assesses the role of the Commission in policy delivery with specific reference to the practical application of the four principles of regional policy. The analysis then turns to some more general points about the Commission's management of European policies.

The four principles of regional policy, concentration, programming, additionality and partnership were to guide the implementation of regional policy in the period 1994-1999 (CEC, 1993a). This also applied to the delivery of URBAN as this represented a local dimension to DG XVI's regional policy. In view of the complexity of this policy area, this was not a simple process. Although URBAN was a small-scale CI involving limited sums, the Commission encountered numerous problems in the delivery of policy. There is evidence of the Commission forging alliances with a wide range of actors in order to improve policy implementation. This was through the Commission's interpretation of the principle of partnership rather than any formal provisions. However the persistent difficulties in implementing EU urban policy raises questions about the effectiveness of the supra-national intervention in this area. The analysis compares and contrasts the case study material from London and Marseille. Each principle of regional policy is examined separately although a number of points are inter-related.

8.3/1 Enforcing the Four Principles of Regional Policy

The Commission experienced difficulties in persuading Member States to respect the principle of concentration. Even for a small-scale programme such as URBAN, we saw how Member States' proposals far exceeded the number of projects envisaged for each. National politicians faced political pressures from within the Member State to award European programmes to as many cities as possible. Yet an excessive number of projects risked diluting the impact of the resources allocated to each Member State. The example of URBAN in France illustrated how external factors, such as municipal and presidential elections, can raise the political salience of matters such as the allocation of a European programme. The effects of this would be beyond the control of the Commission.

The Commission stressed the principle of concentration and negotiated with Member State administrations, to decide on a final list. The necessity to limit the choice of cities resulted in lengthy negotiations between the Commission and central government in both the UK and France. Other Member States also had to be persuaded to limit their choice of cities to be awarded URBAN. In both London and Marseille, local delivery of URBAN was hindered by the initial negotiations between central government and the Commission. Under the regulations for URBAN, all funds had to be committed by 1999. The early delays therefore put pressure on partners involved in the local delivery of URBAN in both London and Marseille.

The Commission encountered problems enforcing the principle of concentration at all stages of policy implementation. In the case of Marseille, the original submission to the Commission focused on action in the St Mauront district which local indicators, and the original bid for URBAN, had portrayed as an area of great need. Despite making concessions to the local municipality, the Commission's efforts to realise projects in St Mauront were frustrated by local political priorities and the complexity of existing schemes. In the UK programmes, resources were allocated to the 'capacity building' measures of the URBAN programme so that the targeted communities could identify areas of need. However time pressures, due to early delays and the requirement to commit funds by a certain date, gave the more organised groups easier access to URBAN funds. In this respect, the Commission failed in its attempt to 're-introduce the most vulnerable groups into the regular economy' through the experiment with CED (CEC, 1997a).

Lessons from URBAN also highlight the practical difficulties of implementing multi-annual European programmes. Since URBAN was a small-scale programme, seeking innovative delivery mechanisms, the Commission aimed for exemplary programming. Through experimenting with URBAN, the Commission aimed to transfer lessons to mainstream programmes.[12] The Commission's emphasis on the Urban Action Plan (UAP) process in UK programmes stressed this strategic approach:

An Urban Action Plan is a *pluriannual programme* conforming with the strategy and measures set out in this document. It should offer an integrated and holistic approach to tackling the problems identified in the area based on strong community involvement.[13]

The case study material on the implementation of URBAN illustrated how differences in procedures, between central government Departments, could jeopardise the integrated approach sought by URBAN. In the UK, local voluntary and community groups had to comply with procedures of two separate Departments in order to receive URBAN funds under the ERDF and ESF measures. Furthermore, since local implementation only began in 1996, this eliminated the first two years of the programme from any pluriannual strategy relating to UAPs.

In the case of France, the principle of programming fell victim to the frequency of elections during the period of implementation of URBAN. The initial delays, as noted above, related to the municipal and presidential elections of 1995. From November 1997 to September 1998 no progress could be made due to regional elections in France. The state, municipality and regional authorities had committed match funding to URBAN through the contractual process. Although any change in political majority would honour sums that had already been committed to the contractual process, the regional authority was unable to release funds to the URBAN programme during the period around elections. All major decisions were suspended prior to any election and there was a period of adjustment following appointments made after the election results. The elements of the programme requiring a financial contribution from the Provence-Alpes-Côte d'Azur (PACA) Region therefore suffered additional delays. The Commission has no means of

---

[12] Internal Commission discussion documents relating to negotiations for the implementation of URBAN in the UK.

[13] Extract from the URBAN Administrative Arrangements quoted in full in Appendix one, chapter four (emphasis added).

tackling implementation problems related to the electoral cycle within the Member State.

Changes in procedures, following a change in national government, could impinge on the Commission's longer-term strategy for the implementation of policies within a Member State. In London, as noted in chapter four, the Commission aimed to transfer lessons from URBAN to the extension of CED in the mainstream Single Programming Documents (SPDs) negotiated for the period 1997-1999. Delays in the early stages of the implementation of URBAN meant only limited progress had been made in the area of UAPs by the time of negotiations for the Objective 1 and Objective 2 SPDs of 1997-1999. Furthermore the additional negotiations following the change to a Labour government gave local authorities the opportunity to opt out of the Action Plan process for Objective 1 and 2 programmes.[14] Most local authorities preferred to maintain the existing project based approach. The Commission did not therefore have the opportunity to extend the UAP process, painfully negotiated for URBAN, to mainstream programmes of this period.

The application of the principles of additionality and partnership in the delivery of URBAN also revealed some interesting points regarding the Commission's role in policy delivery. From the early establishment of the ERDF in 1975, the Commission has encountered problems enforcing the principle of additionality. DG XVI strengthened the arrangements to secure additionality in the 1988 and 1993 reforms. However, empirical studies to date indicate that the Commission has made little progress in this area.[15] Lessons from the implementation of URBAN suggest that the enforcement of additionality remains a complex matter beyond the control of the Commission. One variation from existing studies is the revelation that the Commission has experienced problems in ensuring that regional and local government, as well as central ministries, respect the principle of additionality. The analysis goes beyond the simple assessment of matching funds and raises the issue of assessing the 'added value' of the supra-national intervention.

In the case of France, match-funding for URBAN was clearly set out following the framework of the contractual plan (*Contrat de Plan, Contrat de Ville*) agreed for Marseille. Each level of government, national, regional

---

[14] Most UK regions receiving mainstream ERDF programmes in the period 1994-1999 were classified under Objective 2, with the exception of Merseyside which had Objective 1 status (please refer to chapters three and four which provide more detailed information on this).

[15] See Marks (1993), McAleavey (1992, 1993, 1995), Pollack (1995) Bache (1996, 1998).

and local committed some match-funding to various parts of the URBAN programme. Bache (1998, p.108) refers to a Department of the Environment (DoE) report suggesting that in the case of France, commitments of national resources are made before levels of ERDF receipts are known (DoE, 1992). In this respect, the French authorities could claim to respect additionality within the framework of funds committed to the multi-annual contractual system. This does not, however, solve the problem of assessing the precise impact or added value of the Commission's involvement in this policy area.

Chapter five illustrated how the national, regional and local authorities allocated a portion of URBAN funds to complement various aspects of the existing *Contrat de Plan, Contrat de Ville* programme in Marseille. The Commission accepted that European funds were additional to those already committed by the national authorities to the contractual framework. In this way, URBAN could be seen to complement existing initiatives within the Member State. The question is whether the European funds, allocated to URBAN, actually reached the targeted recipients in the designated areas. The Commission, as a supra-national institution, is independent of party politics within the Member State. The Commission was part of the partnership to deliver the programme and had a place on the Monitoring Committee. The supra-national intervention, formally agreed in the Programme Document for Marseille, should not have been affected by the local political situation.

As noted earlier, problems arose regarding the implementation of ERDF projects in the St Mauront district of Marseille. Had URBAN reached areas neglected by national/local politicians, this could be a form of added value; the projects would not have occurred without the supra-national intervention. The case of St Mauront exposed the extent to which the Commission depended on the national, regional and local authorities to realise projects under the areas covered by the Programme Document. The case of Marseille is peculiar since the Mayor of Marseille, in the earlier stages of the programme, commanded power at national, regional and local level as part of the accumulation of mandates system in France.

In the early stages, it was difficult to see how the Commission could influence the decision-making processes without drastic action such as the suspension of the programme. Yet the municipality's delaying powers were legitimate in the context of bargaining, negotiation and the complexity of existing schemes. The only way the Commission could possibly influence policy outcomes was by forming alliances with other partners involved in delivering URBAN. In contrast to the UK, the Commission had not experimented with new administrative structures for the delivery of policy.

Consequently, the Commission could only operate within the institutional framework that had been decided by the national, regional and local authorities as part of the contractual process. In the later stages of implementation of URBAN, the Mayor of Marseille only held local office. This presented the Commission with more opportunities to influence policy delivery.

At the time of launching UPPs, the Commission had initially bypassed central government and engaged in direct dialogue with the Municipality of Marseille. In the delivery of URBAN the Commission followed a different strategy. We saw how the Commission forged alliances with the local representatives of the state, rather than the local municipality, in order to tackle problems of implementation. However only areas in the URBAN programme prioritised by the national authorities, particularly the municipality, had a good implementation record in the period covered by this study. There is also little evidence that non-established groups managed to access URBAN funds for ESF or ERDF projects. Although URBAN was aimed at the most deprived neighbourhoods of European cities, the programme failed to reach the most vulnerable citizens in the selected areas of Marseille. It would be difficult to conclude that the European intervention had genuine added value since any impact was lost in the complexity of existing schemes.

Evaluating the principle of additionality in UK URBAN programmes is equally complicated. Firstly there was the background of the longstanding debate on additionality between the Commission and national government in the UK. Bache (1996) presented evidence suggesting that the UK government found ways of substituting central government spending by the use of ERDF funds. Bache (1996) found that the UK government introduced Supplementary Credit Approvals to local authorities for European grants after 1992, however this was compensated by a reduction in the existing spending consents from central government (Basic Credit Approvals). Despite certain administrative changes following the dispute over RECHAR, the evidence suggested an element of substitution on the part of the UK government. The effects of this would have been spread across all local authorities in the UK:

> The administrative arrangements had changed, but the UK government view of ERDF payments as reimbursement for its contribution to the EU budget had apparently not, and all the evidence suggested that the government had continued its policy of using ERDF payments to displace its own spending in the regions (Bache, 1998, p.107).

The above findings also had implications for the assessment of additionality at local level. Did local authorities seek to use ERDF payments to displace their own spending within the locality? It would be impossible for the Commission to monitor the maze of local funding in order to determine which funds local government would have committed to the targeted areas before knowing the amount of European funding received. Similar to the case of France, there is the question of whether the provision of match-funding by the national/local authorities is sufficient to comply with the principle of additionality.

In the case of the UK, there were certain contradictions between the Commission's aims and the selection criteria applied by central government regarding the allocation of URBAN. One factor considered by central government in the selection of cities to be awarded URBAN was the local partners' ability to deliver the programme (Interview DETR official, January 1999). Part of this assessment included whether sources of match-funding were readily available through successful bids in, for example, SRB programmes. Yet this 'provider-led approach' did not represent the delivery mechanisms the Commission sought to promote through URBAN.[16]

Studies on the implementation of regional policy in the UK have focused on the Commission's partnership with local authorities in order to enforce additionality (Bache, 1996, McAleavey 1995). In the case of URBAN, the Commission's extension of partnership to include a wider range of actors may be viewed as an attempt to monitor additionality. Through the CED element of URBAN the Commission aimed to empower local residents, community and voluntary organisations with no previous involvement in European funding programmes. The Commission could request evidence that there had been some input from the targeted recipients through community audits, the operation of the UPG and the preparation of an Urban Action Plan (UAP). If successful, URBAN funds would be used to co-finance a community-led UAP rather than projects that had already been selected by local authorities. In practice, it was very difficult for the supra-national institution to manage the complex process of community-led regeneration strategies.

Similar to the case of Marseille, the Commission forged alliances with local representatives of central government in the implementation of URBAN. The Commission looked to Government Offices to assist in ensuring that UAPs represented the integrated, community-led approach

---

[16] Please refer to section 4.2/3 in chapter four explaining the differences between 'provider-led' and 'demand-led' delivery mechanisms.

sought by URBAN. Yet through its experiment to empower local residents/voluntary and community organisations, the Commission risked alienating its traditional partners. Prior to the experience with URBAN, local authorities had been the Commission's allies in its dealings with central government, particularly over the issue of additionality. Having experienced delays in the early stages of the programme, local authorities complained about constant setbacks in implementation. The Commission had entered the complex area of local politics where there was often a history of distrust between the local community and the council.[17] This led to tensions in the partnerships established to deliver URBAN at local level. Many of the new partners, that the Commission was seeking to engage, became disillusioned with the complexity of the policy process.

Although the Commission pursued numerous strategies in seeking to promote community-led delivery mechanisms, the experience of URBAN in London still revealed examples of projects promoted by the local authority. Questions remained regarding whether the projects backed by the local authority represented added value. On the one hand, the use of European funds to co-finance a project that the local authority would have funded anyway may be viewed as a form of substitution at local level. On the other hand, in areas such as South Kilburn where the local community groups were not well established, there was a risk of under spending the funds committed to URBAN. This gave local authorities the opportunity to make a case for large-scale projects such as the pedestrian walkway proposed by Brent Council. Since representatives of the local authorities also had a place on the UPGs in the respective areas, it was possible to influence the programme at this level. The projects promoted by the local council could be included in the local UAP and the local authority provided match-funding. It would be extremely difficult for the Commission to ascertain whether the local authority would have funded the projects proposed by other sources if the European funds were not available.

On a more positive note, in areas where URBAN and Objective 2 funds operated in close proximity, there is some evidence that representatives of the voluntary and community sector differentiated between the CI and mainstream programmes. In the case of Marseille, URBAN encountered problems in establishing its own identity as procedures were almost identical

---

[17] There was an element of council distrust among some elements of the local community in all areas of London included in this study. However the case of URBAN in the City of Westminster with the background of the Dame Shirley Porter affair represented the most extreme example of this (please refer to chapter six).

to those for the larger scale Objective 2 programme that also contained urban policy measures (*politique de la ville*) for selected areas in the city. In the East End of London, there was a section dedicated to CED in the 1997-1999 SPD for areas that had been allocated Objective 2. Despite the problems discussed in chapter six, members of the voluntary and community sector, with experience of URBAN and CED under Objective 2, did perceive a difference between the two. Some made the observation that the council dominated yet further the Objective 2 programme:

> Certainly under Objective 2 a lot of projects put forward by the council are being funded. In my opinion, sometimes to the detriment of the voluntary sector and the long-term viability of the voluntary sector (Interview, UPG member, Heart of the East End, 1999).

The institution of the UPG in the URBAN programme was seen as more conducive to the emergence of projects other than those supported by the local council:

> The pathways regeneration initiative that is coming in is basically on the same lines as URBAN but it has got an extra tier in it where the council and consultants vet, after everybody else, before it actually goes to GOL for approval. *URBAN, as it has been set up by the UPG members doing the Action Plan, has managed to get rid of an extra vetting tier…it goes as far as it possibly can towards partnership* (Interview, UPG member, Heart of the East End, 1998, emphasis added).

In Park Royal, there was no experience of Objective 2 in the area however a number of UPG members interviewed viewed URBAN as a genuine attempt to involve the local community:

> I think, the way that I understand it, this programme is innovative and new in its attempt to involve the community all the way through. But of course, it is like democracy, you cannot define it just from a dictionary, so it is a complex thing. I think the UPG is a good and representative quango. I think it has been interesting, it has been a learning experience, I have no regrets about being on it. I think we have got a long way to go before we can say how successful the whole thing has been …We are part of a process that is three parts democratic and seven parts bureaucratic, what I am constantly trying to do is to recognise

what our role is and what agendas other people have (Interview, UPG member, Queen's Park, 1998).[18]

Although both case studies presented examples of the Commission forging alliances to promote effective implementation of its policies, there is little evidence that the Commission sought to change the balance of power in intergovernmental relations. The Commission was part of the partnership to deliver its policies within the Member State. The alliances can therefore be viewed as part of the continual process of negotiation and bargaining for the delivery of policy. In each case, there were limits to the Commission's intervention. In the case of the UK, the Commission had negotiated administrative arrangements that included non-governmental groups on the decision-making bodies. Yet the Commission did not seek to challenge the role of central government as the main implementing authority. In the early stages of the negotiations for URBAN in the UK, the Commission had been supportive of the claims by local authorities that central government chairing of Monitoring Committees intruded on the governance of the city. At the same time, the Commission did not pursue the matter once the national authorities indicated that the chairing of Monitoring Committees was non-negotiable.

In the case of Marseille, the Commission pursued a less interventionist approach in negotiations for the administrative structures to deliver URBAN. Although the Commission entered an alliance with the local representatives of the state, this strategy was ineffective in the area of local infrastructure where the municipality had formal powers following the decentralisation laws. In the case of London, despite the involvement of non-governmental groups, the local authorities still dominated the policy process at local level. The only exception was the case of Queen's Park UPG, although this was related to a change in government at national level rather than any intervention of the Commission.

There were no examples of the Commission forging alliances with non-governmental actors to challenge the position of central or local government in the UK or France. The Commission's involvement in this policy area added to the complexity of central-local relations but had no major impact on intergovernmental relations within the Member State. In the case of London, there was little direct interaction between the Commission and

---

[18] The term 'quango' is an acronym for quasi-autonomous non-governmental organisation. For a comparison of SRB and URBAN programmes see Bache (2001). For a comparison of community-led regeneration strategies under URBAN in Sheffield and London, see Tofarides (2003, forthcoming).

UPGs. Officials from DG XVI occasionally attended seminars relating to URBAN and also had informal meetings with partners. However, the Commission's involvement remained mainly at the level of attendance at Monitoring Committees and correspondence with Government Offices. Although there were periods of tension in the delivery of URBAN, in both London and Marseille, the Commission aimed to promote consensus amongst partners. We conclude the analysis of the Commission's role in policy delivery by examining more general issues relating to the management of programmes.

8.3/2 The Commission as Policy Manager

The expansion of the Commission's policy agenda has raised questions about whether the supra-national level can manage an increasing number of programmes. Laffan (1997) examines the 'management deficit' of the Commission:

> The central theme of this article is that the Commission must augment its role as a 'policy entrepreneur' by paying equal attention to the management of EU programmes. The Union's management deficit is now more acute than it was in the past because of the expansion in its policy scope, the spread of regulatory regimes, and the range of spending programmes financed out of the Union's budget (Laffan, 1997, p.436).

This study has illustrated how representatives of cities, some Member States and the European Parliament supported the Commission's intervention in the area of urban policy. However the empirical material on the implementation of URBAN highlighted the problems related to the Commission's dependence on national and sub-national actors to deliver EU programmes. There were numerous examples in the case studies where the Commission had no effective means of tackling problems of implementation. This Committee of Independent Experts also raised this point in the final remarks of their report:

> Throughout this report, the Committee has sought, in accordance with its terms of reference, to analyse the specific, everyday management problems of the Commission. Nevertheless, now that it has completed its work, it feels obliged to say that the political and institutional dimension of the Commission's weaknesses are lurking just beneath the surface; often the Commission is only able to take half measures because it does not have the means, in particular the statutory means, to perform its responsibilities in full.

It was not the Committee's task to suggest any institutional reforms that might be undertaken, yet it goes without saying that the Commission must have the means to perform its duties.[19]

This study has illustrated that national, regional and local authorities welcome the additional resources from the Structural Funds. However the failure of the Commission to include an urban provision in the Treaties indicates that Member States have reservations about granting formal competences in this area. Furthermore, the principle of subsidiarity makes the Commission's management of policy a sensitive matter. On the one hand, if the Commission is over-prescriptive in the regulations attached to the implementation of policy, the supra-national institution may be accused of not respecting the principle of subsidiarity. The issue of the chairing of Monitoring Committees in UK programmes was a clear example of this. On the other hand, if there are variations in procedures, the Commission may be criticised for inconsistency in the management of programmes:

> The demanding Commission rules and procedures do not seem to be implemented consistently throughout the EU. Every country has difficulties but they seem to be standardised and consistent. Part of the difficulty lies with the generality of these views, which lead to different interpretations: in some cases they tend to stem from the training and culture of the civil servant in charge of the problem rather than from any well founded policy (Lagrange, 1997, p.335).

There were clear examples of the differences of approach in the Commission's management of URBAN in the cases of London and Marseille. In the case of Marseille the Commission granted technical assistance and responsibility for the evaluation of the programme to the *Agence d'Urbanisme de l'Agglomération Marseillaise* (AGAM), a body forming part of the administration of the Municipality of Marseille. This was not supported by some of the local representatives of the state who were concerned about how independent the evaluation would be. Apart from the appointments under the capacity building measures in the programme, the Commission did not provide for a budget for technical assistance for URBAN in the London programmes. Local partners in London felt that insufficient explanation had been given regarding this. There was also

---

[19] Committee of Independent Experts, 1999. Final remarks of the 'Second report on the Reform of the Commission. Analysis of current practice and proposals for tackling mismanagement, irregularities and fraud': 10 Septermber, 1999.

confusion as to whether other cities within the UK had received different treatment:

> There was no budget for a staff team, it all had to come out of the capacity building so it meant that the staff resource on the ground suddenly became bigger than was expected. The Government Office said that there was very little technical assistance to be spent on the programme as a whole, not that we have ever really seen any of that. I have not had an adequate explanation for it. It probably wasn't sufficiently taken into account in the beginning either by government or by the people who were bidding for it although I think that Strathclyde and some of these European executive bodies that had had some experience of this put it into the SPD as a dossier with a specific heading in that (Interview, local authority official, Park Royal, April 1999).

The experience of URBAN has illustrated that the Commission has a difficult task. National and sub-national actors demand a coherent approach from the Commission. At the same time, the Commission is expected to allow for local variations according to the institutional structures of each Member State. It is clear that the Commission does not have the means to undertake a more interventionist approach in policy delivery. Although there may be a Commission Permanent Representation office in cities, such as London and Marseille, these offices do not have the resources to be involved in the local implementation of policy. Indeed in the case of France, the SGAR discouraged participation of officials from the Commission's Permanent Representation at management meetings since representatives of DG XVI and DG V already had a place on the Monitoring Committee for URBAN.

The experience of URBAN also indicates that the Commission may need to develop a sense of perspective regarding the possible impact of EU programmes. This would involve an assessment of the aims and objectives of each programme in relation to the budget allocated to each. URBAN represented a small-scale, experimental programme targeting pockets of deprivation in European cities. Studies of national urban policies in the UK and France, for the period preceding the launch of URBAN, indicate that this was not a major priority for the national authorities (Le Galès, 1995). In the case of the UK where the Commission aimed to engage the local voluntary and community sector, studies indicated that the national programmes such as SRB had made little progress in this area (CURS, 1995, p.98). Furthermore, URBAN was launched at a time when SRB, and other regeneration programmes, were being reduced (CURS, 1995, p.34).

The Commission had ambitious proposals in areas where national policies had hitherto failed to deliver.

This case study material on the implementation of URBAN in the UK suggests that the resources allocated to the programme were not in proportion to the magnitude of problems the Commission aimed to address.[20] Achieving innovative, integrated local regeneration strategies involving governmental and non-governmental groups is not a simple task. Since grass roots implementation was also delayed by two years of negotiations between the Commission and national administrations, this imposed additional pressures on local partnerships. Engaging citizens with no previous involvement in voluntary activities would arguably require greater investment, beyond the life and resources of a small-scale European programme such as URBAN. The Commission may be accused of raising expectations with policies that could only tinker with finding possible solutions. The URBAN programme in Marseille is open to similar criticism.

The Bellevue estate in St Mauront was characterised by a concentration of degraded private housing, high unemployment (38.9 per cent), drugs and social problems. Similar to the UK, the Commission was seeking results in areas where national policies had failed to deliver. The national and local authorities had failed to tackle the specific problems of these privately owned estates.[21] In view of the high concentration of immigrants in these areas who were ineligible to vote, local politicians did not prioritise districts such as St Mauront. The Commission's venturing into this policy area raised expectations amongst local residents in St Mauront. The project leader had disseminated news about the URBAN programme and involved some representatives of the local community in the preparation of the bid to bring URBAN funds to Marseille. The Commission's failure to promote action for the delivery of the projects in the area was not a positive example for any future EU urban policy initiatives in Marseille. This arguably exacerbated feelings of disillusion and distrust in a neighbourhood that had already been neglected by the national, regional and local authorities.

There may therefore be a case for the Commission to review its role in the delivery of policy. The Commission could distance itself from the everyday implementation of policy but still act as facilitator for decisions taken closer to the problem. This could mean relying on Member States as the main partners, with the interpretation of subsidiarity as a matter for each

---

[20] Please refer to chapters four and five for the precise figures in ECU million accorded to the URBAN programmes in London and Marseille.

[21] This refers to the problem of *copropriétés*, see *Le Monde*, 16 March 1996.

to decide reflecting the political/administrative system of individual Member States. If the Commission becomes less involved in policy delivery, there may be concerns about the misuse of European funds. However the European Court of Auditors could continue its work relating to the audit of public funds. The European auditors could also strengthen links with national auditors.

The Commission could concentrate on areas where the supra-national level could make a more visible contribution. The Commission could, for example, focus on the promotion of networks and the dissemination of information. Although this would not provide immediate solutions to the problems addressed, the European intervention could draw attention to issues that may have been neglected by national policies. The experience of implementing European programmes may also be a catalyst to further experimentation within the Member State. Although there are variations in the institutional framework of each Member State, lessons from innovative programmes such as URBAN can highlight common themes such as the difficulties of mobilising citizens; this is examined in section 8.4 below.

8.4 The Difficulties of Mobilising Citizens

The case of URBAN in the UK highlighted the practical difficulties of involving a wider range of partners in the delivery of EU urban policy. Although some URBAN funds were allocated to measures to promote 'capacity building', engaging citizens to deliver European policies was a complex task. In Marseille, the formal partnership was not extended to the voluntary and community associations based in the targeted areas. However the local and national authorities perceived that citizens could be involved in URBAN in the framework of local democracy and the project leader system. Common themes emerged from the experience of URBAN in London and Marseille.

The case study material on the delivery of URBAN in both London and Marseille indicated that programmes aiming to involve local citizens often encounter apathy amongst the targeted recipients. Some studies of civic engagement looked to the directly elected Mayor of London as a way of making progress in this area:

> Our objective is to ensure that the new mayor uses his or her substantial powers and leadership to enhance the participation of all sectors and communities in London's governance and decision-making, and ensure

Londoners play their part in moving towards a sustainable future. London needs a new politics: specifically, a new distribution of rights and responsibilities and a fresh definition of citizenship. It cannot face tomorrow's pressures in a culture of sectional interests competing for favour. Sustainable development requires advanced citizenship. It cannot be delivered on the basis of a coerce-and-command political culture (ALG: The London Study, 1998, p.51).[22]

Comparison between the cases of URBAN in London and Marseille highlights how the existence of an elected mayor may not necessarily guarantee any greater participation by the targeted beneficiaries of such programmes. In Marseille, the established groups monopolised access to the local politicians. The experiment with alternative administrative arrangements in the UK URBAN programmes may have given non-governmental groups greater opportunities to influence the decision-making process for URBAN. However, it would be difficult to conclude that URBAN managed to engage a wider range of citizens than national programmes such as SRB.

In the majority of cases, the voluntary and community representatives on the UPG or the Monitoring Committee were already involved in voluntary and community groups or Tenants' Associations. Attempts to involve a wider range of citizens were often met with apathy. In East London where there had been experimentation with directly electing the UPG representatives, turnout was almost non-existent. Participation was only significant in Stepney and Spitalfields although this related to rivalry amongst local mosques rather than issues related to the URBAN programme. Attempts to broaden the representation of the Tenants' Association on one of the targeted estates in the London Borough of Hammersmith and Fulham had limited success.

The experience of voluntary and community representatives involved in URBAN did little to promote positive publicity for the programme. It was clear in both London and Marseille that there was no simple definition of the local community. Both cities are multi-ethnic and the deprived areas within them often have a high concentration of immigrants some of whom are illegal. Inhabitants of the targeted areas in both London and Marseille experienced social and economic exclusion due to common problems such as difficulties with language and lack of skills including, in some cases, literacy and numeracy. Other problems related to lack of child-care and fear of

---

[22] The 'London Study' was partly funded by the European Commission. Local authorities in London provided match-funding through the Association of London Government (ALG).

crime. One common theme that emerged with the experience of European funds was the problem of eligibility. In the case of London, citizens involved through the UPGs often requested action in areas that were ineligible under the regulations for ERDF funds. In Marseille, residents and associations who had participated in meetings with the project leader also found that many projects proposed were ineligible for European funding.

In both London and Marseille, many of the targeted recipients who were initially mobilised were perplexed by the specific requirements and regulations relating to European funds. Problems of coordination amongst central government ministries in both the UK and France exacerbated the situation at local level. Lines of authority were unclear and the 'marble cake' scenario resulted in disillusion amongst potential beneficiaries of URBAN funds. In the East End URBAN programme, the elected representatives stopped attending UPG meetings once they realised that this was not a fast track route to funding projects requested by the local Muslim community. The experience of URBAN in London also illustrated that devolving responsibility to the neighbourhood level may be a sensitive matter.

Some members of UPGs resident in the targeted areas suggested that being in close vicinity to groups, whose applications for URBAN funding had been turned down, was problematic. Following the regulations in the URBAN administrative arrangements, the UPG was responsible for drawing up and implementing the UAP. Following the principle of programming, the regulations for UAPs required projects included to quantify outputs, details on targets and a financial plan.[23] Some representatives of the voluntary and community on UPGs were nervous about the responsibilities involved in delivering a UAP:

> You can't guarantee the delivery of outputs. We are doing it all voluntary. My view is as valid as anybody's and I know what is going on as much as anybody and therefore I am prepared to help make those assessments about what projects should be supported and shouldn't. But it is a different kettle of fish to say I am responsible as a UPG member for outputs. It is ridiculous! (Interview, UPG member, Queen's Park, January 1998).

In both London and Marseille, non-established groups encountered difficulties in accessing URBAN funds. Small-scale associations did not have the resources to survive the delays in receiving European funds. On a more positive note, the experience of URBAN promoted debate about the

---

[23] Please refer to the URBAN administrative arrangements in Appendix one, chapter four.

financial resources available to the partners in the EU network. This led to other experiments in the UK seeking ways of addressing such problems. One such example was experimentation through the Key Fund Project in South Yorkshire. This aimed to simplify procedures for targeted groups, namely the community based organisations that found it too difficult to access Structural Funds support under mainstream programmes. The pilot project in South Yorkshire was pre-matched by the ERDF and local partners' contributions. The structures were as follows:

- The setting up of a Fund, whose task is to provide grant-aid to community based organisations.
- The establishment of a fund management and support unit, whose task is to assist community groups and voluntary organisations to access and maximise the use of funds for regeneration purposed (their tasks will include financial and project management appraisal; locally based marketing, pre-application advice and guidance, post-application support and mentoring).
- The commitment to independent evaluation of the Fund implementation process and the effectiveness of the Support Unit.
- The three components are subject to separate approval procedures (i.e. three offer letters) but to all intents and purposes they form part of a single project. The offer letters will lay down the conditions of operation of the fund including guidance provided to applicants, monitoring and financial control mechanisms.[24]

URBAN programmes in London, namely the White City, Shepherds Bush and Edward Woods UPG as well as South Kilburn UPG experimented with a 'community chest', a fund set aside for smaller-scale projects proposed by less established groups. In this way, small-scale projects could avoid the bureaucratic hurdles of the process to access European funds.

In the case of Marseille, we saw that although all match-funding was committed by the various levels of government, procedures were still complicated. This was often due to circumstances beyond the control of individual groups applying for funds. In the case of Marseille, problems arose when it was not clear whether the municipality could actually deliver the funds promised to match-fund URBAN. This problem was rectified following the renegotiation of the financial tables finally agreed in December 1997. However groups seeking to access funds would have experienced delays while the implementing authorities revised the financial contributions

---

[24] Extract adapted from a summary report – 'The Key Fund. Project Description' (1999) circulated by the UK URBAN network at the technical meeting for URBAN officers, organised by the DETR, which took place on the 16 April 1999.

from each level of government. The situation was not as extreme as the case of the near bankruptcy of New York in 1975. Yet, similar to the American experience, the implementation of URBAN highlighted the problems of a city's dependency on external grants. The failure of local authorities to deliver commitments would have a negative effect on mobilising citizens for any future regeneration initiatives.

Some officials in France expressed the view that the principle of programming, introduced to the implementation of Structural Funds after the 1989 reforms, actually worked to penalise the better-organised projects. Following the initial payment of 50 per cent on agreement of the Programme Document, some individual projects failed to progress and this could delay payment of others within the same programme:

> I think this aspect of solidarity between the proposers of individual projects is difficult and I believe that it would be better if we go back to the system before the reform of the Structural Funds because each was responsible for his/her own dossier but not responsible for the good fortune or misfortune of the others. Now there is a kind of solidarity because the money isn't allocated project by project, it is allocated as a whole. If within that batch there are a few missing because some projects haven't made sufficient progress, then they penalise those who are ready. So there's no point saying that it takes a long time to get the money from Brussels or from Paris, that's no longer a good enough argument to explain matters (Interview, SGAR official, Marseille, July 1998).[25]

These observations were made by an official with long experience of European programmes since the inception of regional policy in the post-1975 period. Local officials recognised that delays in accessing European funds could promote a negative image of Europe:

> It is necessary to lighten procedures, to make things simpler, if not we discourage people and this also puts off the residents who are going to be the beneficiaries of any action; they have to wait three or four years before anything develops and people end up no longer believing in the reality of the policy led. And it's clear, if you get into people's minds, that this isn't favourable towards Europe. Those proposing projects say to themselves:

---

[25] Details on the arrangements for the payment of European funds in the PACA Region for programmes in the period 1994-1999 can be found in the following information sheet published by the regional prefecture: 'Vade-mecum de gestion des programmes communautaires en Provence-Alpes-Côte d'Azur, co-financés par les fonds structurels européens. Génération 1994-1999' (SGAR, 1995, pp. 14-21).

"French sources of finance are very complicated but if I get finance from Europe, that's worse than the rest..." So there you are, in terms of the image of Europe, this isn't favourable (Interview, senior official, Municipality of Marseille, July 1998).

Local politicians in Marseille were aware of the problems encountered by non-established groups. Yet, at time of writing, there was no evidence of experimentation with projects such as the key fund or community chest of URBAN in UK programmes. The lengthy procedures were seen as a necessary part of the administration of such programmes. Local councillors in Marseille expressed an interest in the establishment of a local fund for smaller projects. However in contrast to the UK, local councillors looked to representatives of the local state rather than the local partners to take responsibility for a locally based fund:

Well I think these are procedures that are, after all, codified; they can seem rigid, even so I think they are necessary even if it slows things down a bit. Well, the state is to some extent responsible for procedures and is also often the co-financer of projects. The ideal situation would be a mutual benefit fund at the disposal of the regional prefect (Interview, senior local councillor, Municipality of Marseille, 1998).

The experience of URBAN in Marseille and London has illustrated that although there are differences in political and administrative structures, potential beneficiaries in the targeted areas of both cities encountered similar problems. Cities in France could learn from the diverse experiences of URBAN in London: attempts at elected UPGs in the East End, experiments with local management of URBAN in Park Royal and local initiatives to facilitate access to URBAN funding for less established groups. In Marseille, the local politicians with a political majority were firmly in control of the *Contrat de Ville, Contrat de Plan* process. While there is no doubt that local politicians enjoy democratic legitimacy from the electoral process, there is no representation for those who are denied the right to vote.

There have been experiments in local democracy in Marseille, as reviewed in chapter seven. However, it was also clear that residents who are not French citizens are unable to vote in France. The political system therefore excludes some of the targeted beneficiaries resident in the areas selected for URBAN. Even if areas such as St Mauront were not a political priority for the local councillors, any long-term neglect of selected neighbourhoods would have serious implications for economic and social cohesion of the city's population. Alternative institutions, such as the UPG, may represent a way in which such previously excluded groups can be represented on such committees. Experiments with local funds may enable a broader range of voluntary and community associations to access some of the funding available under programmes such as URBAN.

In the case of London, there has been experimentation with a directly elected mayor. Yet lessons from Marseille indicate that this does not necessarily guarantee any widespread mobilisation of citizens. Indeed, the experience of URBAN indicates that local empowerment and sustainable development are complex long-term issues. Following the devolution programme of the Labour Government, the UK could learn lessons from the French contractual process. In this way, some central government support may be secured to alleviate problems of match-funding European programmes. Local and central government could negotiate and agree on committing funds to guarantee match-funding to deliver some aspects of European programmes. National administrations could also aim to be more flexible, particularly for the needs of the smaller-scale experimental programmes such as URBAN. In the case of URBAN in London, we saw that DETR made concessions for the specific needs of URBAN, albeit at a late stage of the programme.

While the European intervention may not necessarily solve all the problems of our cities, this can be a forum for pooling ideas in the search for local solutions and sustainable development. The Commission has already attempted to promote networks to exchange information and ideas under the URBAN programmes.

8.5 The Commission as Promoter of Networks

The first international URBAN conference took place at The Hague on 13-14 June 1997. This was specifically aimed at bringing together local residents involved in URBAN programmes throughout Europe. The theme of the conference was *Pas d'Europe sans nous* – 'No Europe without us'. The conference newsletter clearly indicated that this was a forum for ordinary residents to express themselves:

Politicians are important and they are welcome but this time it is the residents who find themselves at the centre of debates, Europe is impossible without us.

It's for this reason that in the future, we will have to participate well in its construction.[26]

Participants in Marseille and London expressed mixed feelings about the message of the conference at The Hague. In the case of Marseille, a group of youngsters from an association benefiting from URBAN funds and based in the central area of the city (*centre-ville*) were granted finance to attend the above conference. The funding package for the conference required that local residents, rather than officials, attend the conference. However, this could not guarantee any dissemination of the knowledge acquired at the conference to those involved in URBAN in Marseille. In Marseille, there was no follow up to the youngsters' attendance at the URBAN conference in order to disseminate information about the way in which URBAN was implemented in other cities. While the Commission can provide some funding for such conferences, it is arguably the responsibility of central and local government to ensure that there is an exchange of information amongst partners within the Member State.

Local officials dealing with URBAN, interviewed in the City of Marseille, predominantly presented the view that participation of local residents was not a major concern of the programme. The funding from URBAN was, however, welcomed in that it provided additional funds for urban policy projects which may not otherwise have taken place (Interviews, project leaders, Municipality of Marseille, July and August 1998). This view was confirmed by a senior official who also made the point that European funds are purely perceived as another layer to the panoply of measures. While the extra funds are welcomed, this does not appear to promote any mass Europeanisation of citizens since it is not clear to beneficiaries what exactly Europe represents:

> People know very well what a city is and what is a mayor is; they also know what a president of the departmental or regional council is. But who or what is Europe? Who does it go through? You have to recognise that it is very ambiguous in terms of images and communication; it's not really the easiest thing to get people to accept that Europe is a strong partner for the development of projects at neighbourhood level. Who is Europe? It's not Members of the European Parliament are going to represent Europe; they are drawn from national lists. Which French citizen knows their Member of the

---

[26] Cees v.d. Veur, Membre de la LBA Groningen. Quoted in the newsletter of the conference 'No Europe without us' in The Hague, 13 and 14 June 1997 (*Pas d'Europe sans nous*, 13 et 14 *juin* 1997, *La Haye*).

European Parliament since they are drawn from a national list? (Interview, senior official, Municipality of Marseille, July 1998).

In the case of London, it is interesting that the conference in The Hague provided the first opportunity for some members of the respective UPGs to actually meet even though they were representing the same city! Some participants felt that in some cases, officials from European cities had hijacked the conference and used it as a venue to present showpiece projects financed under URBAN. On a more positive note, the conference provided participants with an opportunity to exchange information and discuss common problems with those involved in other URBAN programmes in the UK (Interviews with UPG members of Park Royal and the Heart of the East End URBAN programmes who attended the conference at The Hague). The Commission, from an early stage of the programme, encouraged dissemination of information and exchanges of experience within the UK.[27]

UPGs in the UK pooled resources and established a UK URBAN Network in 1997; its inaugural conference took place in June 1998. The Network later employed a Network Coordinator with responsibilities for producing a regular newsletter and organising conferences hosted by each participant in turn. There were some differences in opinion, amongst local partners, regarding the role of the URBAN network. Some argued that its role should be to disseminate information about good practice and to act as a forum for addressing common problems. Others stated that the Network had sought to go beyond such a role, seeking to lobby for the next stage of Structural Funds, reform rather than concentrate on actually implementing the existing programmes (Interviews, local community representatives, URBAN officers and government officials, 1998-1999). It is interesting how the URBAN Network promoted debate about the roles and responsibilities of the diverse partners involved in implementing Structural Funds programmes.

The URBAN Network generated lively discussion amongst participants; officials from DG XVI also attended some meetings in order to gain feedback on programmes in the UK. Network meetings helped identify common problems and disseminated knowledge about attempts to tackle the difficulties encountered. One example of this was the information relating the South Yorkshire Key Fund Project distributed to UK URBAN officers attending a technical meeting, organised by central government, in April 1999. The URBAN Network newsletter aimed to keep members informed of

---

[27] Observation of GOL/Commission meeting at DG XVI in March 1997 during my training period in the European Commission, DG XVI.

developments in the different geographical areas as well as the wider context of URBAN. Another function was to draw attention to regeneration initiatives at national level such as the 'New Deal for Communities' announced by the Labour government:

> The focus of the New Deal on themes of Worklessness, Health, Crime, and Educational achievement are also similar to URBAN. The lessons we have learnt in the Network (many of them hard lessons) are surely ones we need to share with communities in the New Deal areas. Round One of the New Deal will make available between £30 million and £50 million per area over a 10 year programme. The chosen communities are small – a maximum of 4,000 households, so the effect could be dramatic.[28]

On a broader note, the Commission also took initiatives to disseminate information on urban issues and generate further debate in this area. This involved the launch of web sites including the European Urban Forum Site, the URBAN Community Initiative site, the Urban Pilot Projects site and the European Urban Audit site. The schemes, and the urban elements of mainstream programmes, represent current forms of the Commission's urban intervention; this type of action will continue in the 2000-2006 programming period. We now conclude our study of the EU's urban policy 'experiment' with some final remarks.

8.6 Final Remarks

The experience of URBAN has revealed a number of points about the European policy process as discussed in this chapter. At time of writing, there is little evidence to suggest that the Commission's urban policy experiment, in the form of URBAN, has brought Europe any closer to its citizens. Apart from the problems of actually defining who the local community is, the participants in both London and Marseille were quickly disillusioned by the complicated procedures and the intricate systems. The complexity of the policy process was not conducive to the bottom-up approach URBAN sought to promote. The Commission is geographically and psychologically far from the European citizens it is seeking to engage in its urban policy experiment. The Commission's urban policy experiment may be presented as a step in bringing Europe closer to its citizens. However, the reality appears to be a complex multi-level gatekeeping system

---

[28] *URBAN Networker*, Issue no.1, March 1999.

that could arguably appear in federal as well as the unitary states reviewed in this study. URBAN has highlighted a number of problems associated with a supra-national level of government, the Commission, seeking to involve itself in a local policy area.

It is interesting to note that the Commission proposed to reduce the number of its CIs in the Agenda 2000 proposals of 1997. The three to be retained related to cross-border cooperation, rural development and human resources. This would have excluded URBAN where some of the measures could have been incorporated into mainstream programmes. Yet the 1999 regulations retained URBAN as a CI.[29] It is beyond the scope of this study to investigate why URBAN was finally retained as a CI, even though Member States complained about CIs and the Commission had proposed to mainstream its urban intervention. Even so, the conclusions to this study suggest that the Commission can play a role in urban policy measures even if this policy area remains predominantly the domain of individual Member States.

The Commission, as a European civil service, simply does not have the resources to deal with a wide range of actors. Neither is it necessarily best placed to know about local issues or who the local community is. The European intervention should provide added value, beyond the co-financing of existing schemes at national level. Even if funds allocated to this area remain limited, innovative programmes launched by the Commission may highlight common problems to all parties. Networks, forums and further studies can stimulate debate about, for example, the transferability of models tried and tested in different Member States.

In April 2000 the Commission published guidelines for URBAN II, a CI concerning economic and social regeneration of cities and of neighbourhoods in crisis in order to promote sustainable urban development.[30] The new CI has two main aims:

- to promote the formulation and implementation of particularly innovative strategies for sustainable economic and social regeneration of small and medium-sized towns and cities or of distressed urban neighbourhoods in larger cities and

---

[29] OJ L161Volume 42, 26 June 1999, p. 20 lists the CIs retained. The former President of the European Commission, Jacques Santer, presented the proposals of Agenda 2000 to the European Parliament in Strasbourg on 16 July 1997.

[30] CEC (2000) Brussels, 28.4.00, C (2000) 1100-EN.

- to enhance and exchange knowledge and experience in relation to sustainable knowledge and experience in relation to sustainable urban regeneration and development in the Community.
- The pursuit of these objectives can facilitate the transition from innovation into the mainstream with the programmes in the urban areas accredited as demonstrative, flagship actions.

URBAN II was designed for 50 urban areas with a minimum of 20,000 inhabitants in each designated area although this minimum could be reduced to 10,000 in cases where this could be justified. In accordance with Article 20(2) of the General Regulation, the Commission fixed the total ERDF contribution to EUR 700 million at 1999 prices. Similar to URBAN, the ERDF contribution would be 75 per cent of the total cost in Objective 1 regions and 50 per cent elsewhere.[31]

Any changes in the Treaties granting the Commission additional competences appear unlikely in the immediate future. This study does not conclude that the Commission's involvement in urban policy should be abandoned. However, it is clear that similar to the experience of American federalism, the higher level of government can only play a distant role. A more interventionist approach would arguably fall victim to yet further problems of coordination, as was the case with the early urban policy expansion of the federal level in the US. At the same time, central and other levels of government within each Member State would need to display flexibility in order to meet the needs of the innovative, integrated approach sought by European programmes. All participants involved in delivering European urban programmes should respect the spirit of partnership in order to find solutions to the problems experienced by European cities.

---

[31] CEC (2000) Brussels, 28.4.00, C (2000) 1100-EN, p.10. Full details of the Commission's proposals for URBAN II are provided in this document.

Bibliography

Agence d'Urbanisme de l'Agglomération de Marseille (AGAM) (1998), *Comité de Suivi du* PIC URBAN *du 9 juillet 1998*: *Actions validées par le COCPUR de juillet 97 à juillet 98*, AGAM, Marseille.

Allen, D. (1997), 'Cohesion and Structural Adjustment' in Wallace, W. and Wallace, H. (Eds), *Policy-Making in the European Community*, Third Edition, Oxford University Press, Oxford.

Anderson, M. (1964), *The Federal Bulldozer*: *A Critical Analysis of Urban Renewal, 1949-1962*, MIT Press, Cambridge, Massachussets.

André, C., Drevet, J. F. and Landaburu, E. (1989), 'Regional Consequences of the Internal Market', in *Contemporary European Affairs*: *1992 and After*, Vol.1, pp.205-14.

Association of London Authorities (ALA) (1992a), 'Urban Areas in Decline: Eligibility under the European Community's Structural Funds. A Submission to the Regional Affairs Commissioner', Association of London Authorities and the London Boroughs' Association, London.

Association of London Authorities (ALA) (1992b), 'A Presidential Agenda for London. London's place in the new Europe', Association of London Authorities and London Boroughs' Association, London.

Association of London Government (ALG) (1999), *The London Study*: *the future of the city*, Association of London Government, London.

Bache, I. (1996), 'EU Regional Policy: Has the UK Government succeeded in Playing the Gatekeeper Role over the Domestic Impact of the European Regional Development Fund', Unpublished thesis; University of Sheffield, Sheffield.

Bache, I. (1997a), 'Report on the URBAN Programme for Sheffield (Governance Dimension)' Reproduced in part contribution to the interim report for the Sheffield URBAN Management Committee by JISER (Joint Initiative on Social and Economic Research), Sheffield Hallam University/University of Sheffield, Sheffield, November 1997).

Bache, I. (1997b), 'The Extended Gatekeeper: Central Government and the Implementation of EU Regional Policy in the UK', Paper presented at European Community Studies Association Conference, Seattle.

Bache, I. (1998), *The Politics of European Union Regional Policy, Multi-Level Governance or Flexible Gatekeeping*? Sheffield Academic Press, Sheffield.

Bache, I. (2000), 'Government within Governance: Network Steering in Yorkshire and the Humber', *Public Administration*, pp.575-592.

Bache, I. (2001), 'Different Seeds in the Same Plot? Competing Models of Capitalism and Incomplete Contracts of Partnership Design', *Public Administration*, vol. 79 (2), pp.337-359.

Bachmann, C. and Le Guennec, Nicole (1996), *Violence Urbaines: Ascension et chute des classes moyennes à cinquante ans de politique de la ville*, éditions Albin Michel, Paris.

Bailey, N., Barker, A. and MacDonald, K. (1995), *Partnership Agencies in British Urban* Policy, UCL Press, London.

Balme, R. and Bonnet, L. (1995), 'From Regional to Sectoral Policies: The Contractual Relations Between the State and the Regions in France' in Loughlin, J. and Mazey, S. (Eds), *The End of the French Unitary State? Ten Years of Regionalisation in France (1982-1992)* Frank Cass, London.

Barnekov, T., Boyle, R. and Rich D. (1990), *Privatism and urban policy in Britain and the USA*, Oxford University Press, Oxford.

Begag, A., Delorme, C. (1994), *Quartiers sensibles*.

Benz, A. (1995), 'German Regions in the European Union: From Joint Policy-Making to Multi-level Governance', Working Paper, Martin-Luther-Universität Halle-Wittenberg, Institut für Politikwissenschaft.

Brent Council (1999), 'A European Strategy for Brent', Internal Paper, Policy and Regeneration Unit, Brent Council, London.

British Management Data Foundation (1992), *The Maastricht Treaty in Perspective. Consolidated Treaty on European Union*, British Management Data Foundation, Gloucestershire.

Brown, Lawrence D., Fossett, James, W. and Palmer, Kenneth, T. (1984), *The Changing Politics of Federal Grants*, Brookings, Washington D.C.

Bulmer, S. (1983), 'Domestic Politics and European Policy-Making', *Journal of Common Market Studies*, vol. 21(4) pp. 349-63.

Cappelletti, Seccombe and Weiler (Eds) (1986), *Integration Through Law. Europe and the American Federal Experience, Volume I, Methods, Tools and Institutions, Book I, A political, legal and economic overview*, Walter de Gruyter, Berlin.

Centre for Urban and Regional Studies (CURS) (1995), *The Single Regeneration Budget – The Stocktake*, Report prepared for the Association of County Councils (ACC), Association of District Councils (ADD) and Association of Metropolitan Authorities (AMA), Centre for Urban and Regional Studies, School of Public Policy, University of Birmingham, Birmingham.

Clark, G. (1994), *The Single Regeneration Budget, A Handbook for the Community and Voluntary Sectors*, NVCO Publications, London.

Clark, G. (1997), 'Learning from the Experience of North America – The Good, the Bad and the Ugly', *Local Economy*, May 1997.

Cobb, R. and Elder, C.D. (1972), *Participation in American Politics, The Dynamics of Agenda Building*, Allymand Bacon, Boston.

Commission of the European Communities (CEC) (1976), *First Annual Report on the European Regional Development Fund*, Office for Official Publications of the European Communities, Luxembourg.

Commission of the European Communities (CEC) (1988), *Official Journal of the European Communities*, 1988, Council Regulation (EEC) No. 2052/88 of 24 June 1988.

Commission of the European Communities (CEC) (1988), *Official Journal of the European Communities*, 1988, No. L185, 15 July.

Commission of the European Communities (CEC) (1989), *Guide to the Reform of the Community's Structural Funds*, Office for Official Publications of the European Communities, Luxembourg.

Commission of the European Communities (CEC), DG XVI (1990), *Europe 2000. Outlook for the Development of the Community's Territory*, Office for Official Publications of the European Communities, Luxembourg.

Commission of the European Communities (CEC) (1991), *Guide to the Community Initiatives*, Office for Official Publications of the European Communities, Luxembourg.

Commission of the European Communities (CEC) (1993a), *Community Structural Funds, 1994-9. Revised Regulations and Comments*, Office for Official Publications of the European Communities, Luxembourg.

Commission of the European Communities (CEC) (1993b), Green Paper, *The Future of Community Initiatives under the Structural Funds*, July 1993, Brussels/Luxembourg.

Commission of the European Communities (CEC) (1993c), *Urbanisation and the Functions of Cities in the European Community*, European Commission, Brussels.

Commission of the European Communities (CEC) (1993d) *The London Initiative, A report to the European Commission on the operation of the pilot programme of urban regeneration projects in London, undertaken under Article 10 of Council Regulation (EEC) No. 4254/88.*

Commission of the European Communities (CEC) (1994a), *Guide to the Community Initiatives, 1994-1999*, Office for Official Publications of the European Communities, Luxembourg.

Commission of the European Communities (CEC) (1994b), DG XVI, *Urban Pilot Projects*, Office for Official Publications of the European Communities, Luxembourg.

Commission of the European Communities (CEC) (1994c), *Competitiveness and Cohesion: Trends in the Regions. Fifth Periodic Report on the Social and Economic Situation and the Development of the Regions of the European Community*, Office for Official Publications of the European Communities, Luxembourg.

Commission of the European Communities (CEC) (1994d), 'Single Programming Document, 1994-1999', No. ERDF: 94.09.13.00. No. ARINCO: 94.UK.16001, Merseyside Objective 1 Region', DG XVI, Brussels.

Commission of the European Communities (CEC) (1994e), COM (94) 46 25, March 1994, European Communities, Brussels.

Commission of the European Communities (CEC) (1994f), CEC, 1994, COM (94) 46 final 2, 25 March 1994, European Communities, Brussels.

Commission of the European Communities (CEC) (1994g), 'Document Unique de Programmation, 1994-6, Décision de la Commission portant approbation du document unique de programmation pour les interventions structurelles communautaires dans la région Provence-Alpes-Côte d'Azur concernée par l'objectif no.2 en France, No. FEDER: 94.03.13.042, No. Arinco: 94.FR.16.019', DG XVI, Brussels.

Commission of the European Communities (CEC) (1995a), *Bulletin of the European Union*, Supplement 2/95, European Commission, Brussels.

Commission of the European Communities (CEC) (1995b), 'Barcelona Declaration', Adopted at the Euro-Mediterranean Conference, 27 and 28 November, 1995, European Commission, DG 1B, Brussels.

Commission of the European Communities (CEC) (1996a), SEC (96) 85 I final/1, Bruxelles, le 8 mai 1996, 'Communication aux États Membres fixant les orientations pour les programme opérationnels que les États membres sont invités à établir dans le cadre d'une initiative communautaire concernant les zones urbaines'.

Commission of the European Communities (CEC) (1996b), DG XVI, *Social and economic inclusion through regional development. The Community Economic Development priority in Structural Funds Programmes in Great Britain*, DG XVI, Brussels.

Commission of the European Communities (CEC) (1996c), 'Heart of the East End URBAN Initiative Operational Programme', DG XVI, Brussels.

Commission of the European Communities (CEC) (1996d), 'Park Royal URBAN Initiative Operational Programme', DGXVI, Brussels.

Commission of the European Communities (CEC) (1996e), C (96) 644, 'Décision de la Commission du 12.03.1996, relative a l'octroi d'un concours du Fonds Européen de Développement Régional (FEDER) et du Fonds Social Européen (FSE) en faveur pour un programme opérationnel au titre de l'initiative communautaire URBAN en faveur de certains quartiers de Marseille dans la région Provence- Alpes-Côte d'Azur, partiellement éligibles à l'objectif no. 2 en France, No. Feder: 94:03:10.048. No. Arinco: 94. FR. 16.052', Operational Programme Document for URBAN in Marseille, DG XVI, Brussels.

Commission of the European Communities (CEC) (1997a), 'Towards an urban agenda in the European Union', COM (97) 197 final, European Communities, Brussels, 06.05.1997.

Commission of the European Communities (CEC) (1997b), 'Promoting the role of Voluntary Organisations and foundations in Europe', COM (97) 241 final, European Communities, Brussels, 6 June 1997.

Commission of the European Communities (CEC) (1997c), *Community Involvement in urban regeneration: added values and changing values*, DG XVI, Brussels).

Commission of the European Communities (CEC) (1997d), C (97) 3051, Bruxelles 21.10.97 'Décision de la Commission modifiant la décision C (96) 644 du 12 mars 1996 et du Fonds Social Européen (FSE) en faveur pour un programme opérationnel au titre de l'initiative communautaire URBAN en faveur de certains quartiers de Marseille dans la région Provence- Alpes-Côte d'Azur, partiellement éligibles à l'objectif no. 2 en France, No. Feder: 94: 03: 10. 048. No. Arinco: 94. FR. 16. 052', Amended Programme Document for URBAN in Marseille, DG XVI, Brussels.

Commission of the European Communities (CEC) (1997e), 'Décision de la Commission portant approbation du document unique de programmation pour les interventions structurelles communautaires dans la région Provence-Alpes-Côte d'Azur concernée par l'objectif no.2 en France', No. Feder: 97.03.13.018, No. Arinco: 97.FR.16.018', DG XVI, Brussels.

Commission of the European Communities (CEC) (1997f) 'Single Programming Document for Community structural assistance in the region of East London and the Lee Valley concerned by Objective 2 in the United Kingdom, ERDF:97.09.13.001, ARINCO: 97.UK.16.001 Text of 7 May C (97) 1126', DG XVI, Brussels.

Commission of the European Communities (CEC) (1998a), *Guide to the Community Initiatives*, *Volume 2*, Office for Official Publications of the European Communities, Luxembourg.

Commission of the European Communities (CEC) (1998b), 'Sustainable Urban Development in the European Union: A Framework for Action', COM (Q8) 605, adopted 28.10.98, European Communities, Brussels.

Committee of the Regions (1995), 'Opinion on Urban Development', CdR, 235/95, Brussels 19-20 July.

Community Development Foundation (1997), *Regeneration and the Community: Guidelines to the community involvement aspect of the SRB Challenge Fund*, 1997 edition, Community Development Foundation, London.

Deakin, N. and Edwards, J. (1993), *The enterprise culture and the inner city*, Routledge, London.

Délégation Interministerielle à la Ville et au Développement Social Urbain (DIV) (1996), 'La co-opération internationale dans l'Initiative URBAN France, propositions d'action', Internal discussion paper, DIV, Paris.

Department of the Environment (DoE) (1992), 'Working partnerships: City Challenge implementing agencies and advisory note', DoE, London.

Department of the Environment Transport and Regions (DETR) (1997a), 'EC Structural Fund programmes in England: Action Plans for European Regional Development Fund and European Social Fund, Guidance Note 1', DETR, London, June 1997.

Department of the Environment Transport and Regions (DETR) (1997b), 'EC Structural Fund programmes in England: Action Plans for European Regional Development Fund and European Social Fund, Guidance Note 2', DETR, London, September 1997.

Diagonal, Bimestrielle des Équipes d'Urbanisme (1995), Issue no. 116, December 1995.

Donnelly, M. (1993), 'The Structure of the European Commission and the Policy Formation Process', in Mazey, S., and Richardson, J. (Eds) *Lobbying in the European Community*, Oxford University Press, Oxford, pp.74-92.

Donzelot, J. and Estèbe, P. (1994), *L'État animateur, essai sur la politique de la ville*, Editions Esprit, Paris.

Douence, J. (1995) 'The Evolution of the 1982 Reforms: An Overview', in Loughlin, J. and Mazey, S. (Eds), *The End of the French Unitary State? Ten Years of Regionalisation in France (1982-1992)*, Frank Cass, London.

Elazar, D., J., and Greilsammer, I. (1986), 'Federal Democracy: The USA and Europe Compared – A Political Science Perspective' in Cappelletti, Seccombe and Weiler (Eds), *Integration Through Law. Europe and the American Federal Experience, Volume I, A Political Legal and Economic Overview*, Walter de Gruyter, Berlin.

Elazar, D. (1984), *American Federalism: A View From the States*, 3rd edition, Thomas Crowell Co., New York.

Eurocities (1997), *Eurocities Regional Centres, Tenth Annual Conference, 23-24 October 1999*, Rotterdam, Rotterdam City Development Corporation, Rotterdam.

Euroméditerranée Public Agency (1997a), 'La stratégie économique et de marketing d'Euroméditerranée', Internal document, Euroméditerranée Public Agency, Marseille.

Euroméditerranée Public Agency (1997b), 'Marseille, Euroméditerranée', pamphlet produced by Euroméditerranée Public Agency, Marseille.

European Parliament (1993), 'Resolution of 28 October 1993, PE 176. 537'.

Eurostat (1992), *Europe in Figures*, 3rd edition, Office for the Official Publications of the European Communities, Luxembourg.

Financial Times (1993), Monday July 12, London.

Garmise, S., Grote, J. and Leonardi, R. (1992), 'Regional Governance in a European Environment: The Increasing Role of the Region for Functional and Territorial Interest Intermediation,' Paper presented at the IPSA-SOG conference on Levels of Government and 1992, Montpellier, France, 1992.

Goldsmith, M. (1993), 'Local Government', *Urban Studies*, vol. 29, Nos. 3/5, pp. 393-410.

Greenblatt (1976), *Intergovernmental Administration*.

Greenwich Communications Unit (1993), 'The Case for East London's Objective 2 Status. A Joint Submission', pamphlet, Centurion Press, Greenwich.

Grémion, C. (1987), 'Decentralization in France. A Historical Perspective', in Ross, G., Hoffmann, S. and Malzaher, S. (Eds), *The Mitterrand Experiment*.

Grodzins, M. (1966), 'The American System: A New View of Government in the United States' in Elazar, D. (Ed.), *The American System*, Rand McNally, Chicago.

Haas, E. B. (1958), *The Uniting of Europe: Political, Social and Economic Forces*, Stevens & Sons, London.

Haas, E. B. (1975), *The Obsolescence of Regionalist Theory*, Institute of International Affairs, Berkeley.

Habitat (1997), 'Politique de la ville, 20 ans de procédures et de débats', *Cahiers de l'Iaurif, supplement, Habitat*, Issue no. 17, April 1997.

Hall, P. A. (1999), 'Social Capital in Britain', *British Journal of Political Science*, vol. 29, pp. 417-461.

Heart of the East End Urban Partnership Group (1998), 'Heart of the East End, URBAN Action Plan 1997-1999', draft URBAN Action Plan, Urban Initiative Development Unit, London.

Hebbert, M. and Travers, T. (1988), *London Government Handbook*, Cassells, London.

Heclo, H., (1978), 'Issue Networks and the Executive' in King, A., *The New American Political System*, American Enterprise for Public Policy Research, Washington, pp. 87-124.

Hoffmann, S. (1966), 'Obstinate or Obsolete? The Fate of the Nation State and the Case of Western Europe', *Daedalus*, no.95, pp.862-915.

Hoffmann, S. (1963), 'Paradoxes of the French Political Community' in Hoffmann, S., Kindleberger, C. and Wylie et al. (Eds), *In Search of France*.

Hooghe, L. and Keating, M. (1994), 'The politics of EU regional policy', *Journal of Public Policy*, vol. 1.3, pp. 367-93.

Hooghe, L. (1995), 'Subnational Mobilisation in the EU', *West European Politics*, vol. 18, *Special Issue on The Crisis of Representation in Europe*, p.178.

Hooghe, L. (Ed.), (1996) *Cohesion Policy and European Integration: Building Multi-level Governance*, Oxford University Press, Oxford.

Hunter, L. A. and Oakerson, R. J., 'An Intellectual Crisis in American Federalism', *Publius* 16, pp.33-50.

Jacobs, J. (1997), 'Streamlining the Structural Funds. Government Reviews Administration in England', *European Information Service*, Issue 177, February 1997.

Kantor, P. (1995), *The Dependent City Revisited. The Political Economy of Urban Development and Social Policy*, Westview Press, Oxford.

Kaplan, I. and Marshall (1990) 'National Urban Policy: Where Are We Now?' in Kaplan, I., Marshall, James and Franklin (Eds), *The Future of National Urban Policy*, Duke University Press.

Keating, M. (1998), in Le Galès, P., and Lequesne, C. (Eds), *Regions in Europe*, Routledge, London.

Keating, M. and Hainsworth, P. (1986), *Decentralisation in contemporary France*, Gower, Aldershot.

Kempf and Toinet (1984), 'La fin du féderalisme aux Etats-Unis?' *Revue Française de Science Politique*, 30.

King, D. (1993), 'Local Government and Urban Politics', in Dunleavy, P., Gamble, A., Holliday, I. and Peele, G. (Eds), *Developments in British Politics 4*, Macmillan, London.

Knill, C. (1997), 'Implementing European Policies: The Impact of National Administrative Traditions', Florence: EUI Working Papers, RSC No. 97/56).

Laffan, B. (1997), 'From Policy Entrepreneur to Policy Manager: the Challenge Facing the European Commission', *Journal of European Public Policy*, 4.3, pp.422-38.

Lagrange, R. (1996) 'French Policy perspectives' in Bachtler, J. and Turok (Eds), *The Coherence of European Regional Policy*, Jessica Kingsley, London, pp.330-336.

Le Galès, P. and Mawson, J. (1994), *Management innovations in urban policy, lessons from France*, Local Government Management Board (LGMB), Luton.

Le Galès, P. (1995), 'Politique de la Ville en France et en Grande Bretagne: voluntarisme et ambiguités de l'État', *Sociologie du travail*, 2/95.

Le Méridional, Edition of 8 March 1996.

Le Monde, Editions of 11 May 1995, 3 February 1996, 14 March 1996, 16 March 1996, 16 April 1996, 19 June 1996, 25 February 1997, 20 February 1999.

Leach, Richard, H. (1970), *American Federalism*, Norton, New York.

Lelévrier, C. (1997), 'Politique de la Ville: 20 ans de procédures et de débats', *Cahiers de l'IAURIF, supplément Habitat*, no.17, avril 1997.

Leonardi, R. (1995), *Convergence, Cohesion and Integration in the European Union*, Frank Cass, London.

Lindberg, L. N. and Scheingold, S. (1970), *Europe's Would-Be Polity*, Prentice Hall, Englewood Cliffs, NJ.

McAleavey, P. (1992), 'The Politics of the European Regional Development Policy: The European Commission's RECHAR Initiative and the Concept of Additionality', *Strathclyde Papers on Government and Politics*, 88, University of Strathclyde, Glasgow.

McAleavey, P. (1993), 'The Politics of the European Regional Development Policy: Additionality in the Scottish Coalfields', *Regional Politics and Policy*, 3.2, pp.88-107.

McAleavey (1995), 'Policy Implementation as Incomplete Contracting: The European Regional Development Fund', Unpublished PhD thesis, European University Institute, Florence.

McAleavey. P., and de Rynck, S. (1997), 'Regional or Local? The EU's Future Partners in Cohesion Policy', EUI Working Paper RSC no.97/55, Florence.

Marin, B. (Ed.) (1990), *Governance and generalized exchange: self organizing policy networks in action*, Westview Press, Boulder, Colorado.

Marin, B., and Mayntz (Eds) (1991), *Policy Networks, Empirical Evidence and Theoretical Considerations*, Westview Press, Boulder, Colorado.

Marin, B., and Mayntz, R. (1991), 'Introduction: Studying Policy Networks', in Marin, B. and Mayntz (Eds), *Policy Networks, Empirical Evidence and Theoretical Considerations*, Westview Press, Boulder, Colorado.

Marks, G. (1992), 'Structural Policy in the European Community' in Sbragia, A. (Ed.), *Europolitics: Institutions and Policy-Making in the 'New European Community'*, Washington, DC, Brookings Institution.

Marks, G. (1993), 'Structural Policy and Multilevel Governance' in Cafruny, A. and Rosenthal, G. (Eds), *The State of the European Community, Volume 2: The Maastricht Debates and Beyond*, Longman, Harlow, p.392.

Marks, G. (1996), 'Exploring and Explaining Variation in EU Cohesion Policy', in Hooghe, L., (Ed.), *Cohesion Policy and European Integration: Building Multi-Level Governance*, Oxford University Press, Oxford.

Marsh, D. and Rhodes, R.A.W. (1992), 'Policy Communities and Issue Networks: Beyond Typology', in Marsh and Rhodes (Eds) *Policy Networks in British Government*, Oxford University Press, Oxford, pp.249-68.

Mazey, S. (1987), 'Decentralisation: la grande affaire du septennat?' in Mazey, S., and Newmann, M., (Eds.), *Mitterrand's France*, Croom Helm, London.

Mazey, S. (1992), 'Power Outside Paris' in *Developments in French Politics*, Hall, P.A., Hayward, J. and Machin, H. (Eds), Macmillan, London.

Mazey, S. and Richardson, J. (Eds) (1993), *Lobbying in the European Community*, Oxford University Press, Oxford.

Mazey, S. (1995), 'French Regions and the European Union' in *The End of the French Unitary State? Ten Years of Regionalisation in France (1982-1992)*, Loughlin, J. and Mazey, S. (Eds), Frank Cass, London.

Mény, Y. (1982), 'Should the Community Regional Policy be scrapped?' *Common Market Law Review,* vol.19, no.3.

Mény, Y. (1983), *Centres et périphérie, le partage du Pouvoir*, Economica, Paris.

Mény, Y., and Thoenig, J.C. (1989), *Politiques Publiques*, Universitaires de France, Paris.

Mény, Y. (1992), *La Corruption de la République*, Fayard, Paris.

Mény, Y. (1998), 'Les groupes d'intérêt en France ou l'introuvable pluralisme?' Working Paper, European University Institute, Florence.

Mény, Muller and Quermonne (1996), *Adjusting to Europe, the impact of the European Union on national institutions and policies*, Routledge, London.

Ministère de l'Aménagement du Territoire, de la Ville et de l'Intégration, 'Conference de Presse de Jean-Claude Gaudin, Ministre de l'Aménagement du Territoire et Eric Raoult, Ministre Délegué à la Ville et a l'Intégration', jeudi 28 mars 1996.

Mohl, Raymond A. (1993), 'Shifting Patterns of American Urban Policy since 1900' in *Urban Policy in Twentieth-Century America*, Rutgers University Press, pp.1-45.

Moravscik, A. (1991), 'Negotiating the Single European Act' in Keohane, R., O. and Hoffmann, S. (Eds), *The New European Community: Decision-making and Institutional Change*, Westview Press, Oxford.

Moravscik, A. (1993), 'Preferences and Power in the European Community: A Liberal Intergovernmentalist Approach', *Journal of Common Market Studies*, 33.4, pp.473-519.

National Journal, 8 December 1989, Washington DC.

National Journal, Washington DC, 1973.

Nugent, N. (1994), *The Government and Politics of the European Union*, Macmillan, London.

OECD (1998), *Integrating Distressed Urban Areas*, OECD, Paris.

Orlebeke, Charles, J. (1990), 'Chasing Urban Policy: a Critical Retrospect', in Kaplan and James (Eds), *The Future of National Urban Policy*, pp.185-201.

Paddington Development Trust (1999), 'Memorandum of Association', draft, Paddington, London.

Parliamentary Review, March 1999.

Peters, B. G. (1992), 'Bureaucratic Politics and the Institutions of the European Community' in Sbragia, A. (Ed.), *Euro-politics*, Brooking Institution, Washington, pp.75-122.

Peterson, J. (1995), 'Policy Networks and European Policy-Making: A Reply to Kassim', *West European Politics*, vol.18, no.2.

Pollack, M. (1994), 'Creeping Competence: The Expanding Agenda of the European Community', *Journal of Public Policy*, 14.2, pp.95-145.

Pollack, M. (1995), 'Regional Actors in an Intergovernmental Play: The Making and Implementation of EC Structural Policy', in Rhodes and Mazey (Eds) 1995, pp.361-90.

Pollack, M. (1996), 'The New Institutionalism and EC Governance: The Promise and Limits of Institutional Analysis', *Governance*, 9.4, pp.429-58.

Putnam, R. (1993), *Making Democracy Work: Civic Traditions in Italy*, Princeton University Press, Princeton, NJ.

Queen's Park Urban Partnership Group (1998), 'Queen's Park Urban Action Plan', Internal document, draft, Queen's Park, London.

RECITE Office (1995), 'Urban Pilot Projects. Second Interim Report of Urban Pilot Projects funded by the European Regional Development Fund', published on behalf of DG XVI by ECOTEC Research and Consulting Limited, Brussels.

RECITE Office (1997), *Urban Pilot Projects*, newsletter published on behalf of DG XVI by ECOTEC Research and Consulting Limited, Brussels.

Reischauer, Robert, D. (1990), 'The Rise and Fall of National Urban Policy: The Fiscal Dimension', in Kaplan and James and Franklin, *The Future of National Urban Policy*, Duke University Press, pp.225-249.

Rhodes, C., and Mazey, S. (Eds), *The State of the European Union: III. Building a European Polity?* Boulder, Colorado, Lynne Riener; Longman, Harlow.

Rhodes, R.A.W. (1988), *Beyond Westminster and Whitehall. The Sub-Central Governments of Britain*, Routledge, London.

Rhodes, R.A.W., Bache, I. and George, S. (1996), 'Policy Networks and Policy Making in the European Union' in Hooghe (Ed.) *European Integration,*

Cohesion Policy and Subnational Mobilisation, Oxford University Press, Oxford, pp.367-387.

Riker, W. (1964), *Federalism: Origin, Operation, Significance*, Little Brown, Boston.

Ronnier, M. 'How the Community Went into Public Health', Centre for International Affairs, Harvard University.

Sandholtz, W. and Zysman, J. (1989), 'Recasting the European Bargain', *World Politics*, vol.42, October, pp.95-128.

Scharpf, F.W. (1988), 'The Joint Decision Trap: Lessons from German Federalism and European Integration', *Public Administration*, vol.66, Autumn, pp.239-278.

Scharpf, F. W. (1994), 'Community and Autonomy. Multilevel Policy-Making in the European Union', Working Paper, European University Institute, Florence.

Scharpf, F. (1998), *Governing in Europe. Effective and Democratic*, Oxford University Press, Oxford.

Schmidt, V.A. (1990), *Democratizing France: The Political and Administrative History of Decentralization*, Cambridge University Press, Cambridge.

Schneider, V. and Kenis, P. (1991) 'Policy Networks and Policy Analysis: Scrutinizing a New Analytical Toolbox', in Marin, B., and Mayntz (Eds), *Policy Networks, Empirical Evidence and Theoretical Considerations*, Westview Press, Boulder, Colorado.

Secrétariat Général pour les Affaires Régionales, Préfecture de la Région Provence-Alpes-Côte d'Azur (SGAR) (1995), 'Vade-mecum de gestion des programmes communautaires en Provence-Alpes-Côte d'Azur, co-financés par les fonds structurels européens. Génération 1994-1999', Regional Prefecture, Marseille.

Secrétariat Général pour les Affaires Régionales, Préfecture de la Région Provence-Alpes-Côte d'Azur.(SGAR) (1997a), 'Dispositions de mise en oeuvre DOCUP PIC URBAN 1995-1999', Internal Document, Regional Prefecture, Marseille, 16 June 1997.

Secrétariat Général pour les Affaires Régionales, Préfecture de la Région Provence-Alpes-Côte d'Azur (SGAR) (1997b), 'Relevé de conclusions du Comité de Suivi du 9 juillet, 1997', Internal Document, Regional Prefecture, Marseille.

Secrétariat Général pour les Affaires Régionales, Préfecture de la Région Provence-Alpes-Côte d'Azur (SGAR) (1998), 'Relevé de conclusions du Comité de Suivi du 9 juillet, 1998', Internal Document, Regional Prefecture, Marseille.

South Kilburn Urban Partnership Group (1998), 'South Kilburn Urban Action Plan' (Carlton Ward)', draft, South Kilburn UPG, London.

Stoker, G. (1991), *The Politics of Local Government*, Macmillan, London.

Sueur Jean-Pierre, maire d'Orleans (1998), 'Demain la Ville', Rapport présenté à Martine Aubry, ministre de l'emploi et de la solidarité, Dossier de presse, 13 février 1998.'

Tofarides, M. (1994), 'Sub-National Actors in the European Union: A Case Study of Local Government in East London', 1990-1994, Unpublished MSc thesis, London School of Economics, London.

Tofarides, M. (1997), 'Cities and the European Union: An Unforeseen Alliance?' Human Capital and Mobility Network, The European Policy Process, Occasional Paper No.30, European University Institute, Florence.

Tofarides, M. (2003), 'Community-Led Regeneration Strategies: Lessons from the URBAN Programmes in Sheffield and London', Paper presented at the Venice University Institute of Architecture, Department of Planning Workshop: 'Urban Policies under the European Union: are they European?' (Forthcoming, Venice University Institute of Architecture Press).

Travers, T. (1989), 'The threat to the autonomy of elected local government' in Crouch, C. and Marquand, D. (Eds), *The New Centralism: Britain out of step in Europe*? Basil Blackwell, Oxford.

Urban Initiative Development Unit (1998), 'Heart of the East End Urban Initiative Newsletter', Issue 1, January 1998, London.

Ville de Marseille (1995), 'Délégations Accordées par M. le Maire', Code des communes – ART.L.122-11', Secrétariat du Conseil Municipal, Marseille.

Ville de Marseille (1993), 'Projet Pilote, Fonds Européens de développement regional, rapport final, situation du 31/12/93'. Final report on Urban Pilot Projects, 31/12/93, Municipality of Marseille.

Ville de Marseille (1994), 'XI ème Plan, Contrat de Plan, État/Region Provence-Alpes-Côte d'Azur, Politique de la Ville, Contrat de Ville de Marseille'.

Ville de Marseille (1998), 'Rapport au Conseil Municipal, Programme d'Initiative Communautaire "URBAN" Rapport d'étape, 9 juillet 1998', Mission des programmes privés et européens (MIPPE), Municipality of Marseille.

Wallace, H. (1977), 'The Establishment of the Regional Development Fund: Common Policy or Pork Barrel?' in Wallace, H., Wallace, W. and Webb, C., (Eds), *Policy-making in the European Community*, First Edition, John Wiley and Sons, Chichester.

Wallace, H. (1983), 'Distributional Politics: Dividing up the Community Cake', in Wallace, H., Wallace, W. and Webb, C., (Eds), (1983), *Policy-making in the European Community*, Second Edition, John Wiley and Sons, Chichester.

Webb, C. (1983), 'Theoretical Perspectives and Problems', in Wallace, H., Wallace, W. and Webb, C. (Eds), *Policy-making in the European Community*, Second Edition, John Wiley and Sons, Chichester.

White City, Shepherds Bush and Edward Woods, Urban Partnership Group (UPG), 'Annual Report' (1997), Opportunities Centre, Shepherds Bush, London.

White City, Shepherds Bush, Edward Woods Urban Partnership Group (UPG), (1998), 'URBAN Action Plan, 1999-2001', Opportunities Centre, Shepherds Bush, London.

Wishlade, F. G. (1994), 'Achieving Coherence in European Community. Approaches to Area Designation,' *Regional Studies*, vol.28, 1, pp.79-97.

Wishlade, F. G. (1996), 'EU Cohesion Policy: Facts, Figures and Issues' in Hooghe, L. (Ed.) *Cohesion Policy and European Integration: Building Multi-level Governance*, Oxford University Press, Oxford. pp.27-58.
Worms, J.P. (1966), 'Le Préfet et ses notables', *Sociologie du Travail*, July-September.
Wright, Deil Spencer (1988), *Understanding Intergovernmental Relations*, Brooks Cole, Pacific Grove, California.
Wright, V. (1989), *The Government and Politics of France*, Third Edition, Routledge, London.

Interviews

The names and dates listed below are the individual interviews conducted for the purposes of this research. A number of interviews were taped but the cassette was switched off at sensitive moments if requested. In addition to this were other informal discussions during the course of my training period with DG XVI officials and others involved in this policy field.

European Commission

Amblard, Patrick; DG XVI, D.3, informal discussions March to July 1997.
Berkowitz, Peter; official DG XVI, D.3, numerous informal discussions duing the period of the stage, March to July 1997. Other interviews, 16 October 1996, May 12 1998.
Boheri, Jocelyne; *Commission Européenne, Représentation à Marseille* (European Commission, Permanent Representation in Marseille), 3 August 1998.
Curzi, Vittorio; Head of Unit, DG XVI D.3, numerous informal discussions during the period of the stage, March to July 1997. Additional interview, 9 May 1998.
Gallagher, Mark; official, DG XVI, D.3, informal discussions, March to July 1997.
Harding, Richard; official, DG XVI D.3, informal discussions, March to July 1997.
Johnson, Abigail; official, DG V, 22 July 1997.
Kastrissianakis, Antonis; Head of Unit, DG XVI, A.1 and former member of Commissioner Millan's cabinet, 11 May 1998.
Laperrousaz, Michelle; official, DG XVI, Directorate D.2, Regional interventions in France, 8 May 1998.
Lennon, Theodius; former member of Bruce Millan's cabinet, 11 May 1998.

Maes, Marc; *Chef Adjoint d' Unité, Secrétariat général – Relations avec le Comité des Régions* (Assistant Head of Unit, Secretariat General, with responsibility for relations with the Committee of the Regions). Informal discussions on the role of the Committee of the Regions during the stage, March to July 1997. Facilitated access to plenary sessions of the Committee of the Regions during this period and during a mission to Brussels in May 1998.

Mairate, Andrea; DG XVI, G.2, numerous informal discussions and exchange of ideas during my training period at the European Commission, March to July 1997.

Meadows, Graham; Director DG XVI, Directorate D., 30 July 1997, 9 May 1998. Additional informal discussions during my training period at the European Commission, March to July 1997.

Millan, Bruce; DG XVI, former Commissioner for Regional Policies 1989-1993, 12 January 1999.

Mitsos, Achilleas; Director, DG X II, informal discussions, Brussels and EUI, 1997, 1998.

Ojha, Girish; official, DG XVI D.3, informal discussions March to July 1997.

Pyke, Belinda; member of cabinet of former Commissioner Bruce Millan, 22 July 1997.

Ramsden, Peter; Head of Brussels Office, Enterprise plc, former official DG XVI, 29 July 1997, 13 May 1998.

de Rynck, Stefaan; official, DG XVI A.1, 15 October 1996, 6 May 1998, as well as numerous informal discussions.

Roma, Marcello; *chef adjoint d'unité* (Head of Unit), DG XVI A.1, 10 July 1997.

Stahl, Gerhard; member of cabinet of Commissioner Wulf-Mathies, 23 July 1997.

Venineaux, Jean-Marc; official, DG XVI, Directorate D.2, Regional interventions in France, 8 May 1998.

Wendt, Catherine; official, DG XVI D.3, informal discussions March to July 1997.

Westcott, Jackie; official, DG XVI D.3, informal discussions, March to July 1997.

Whiting, Glynis; Detached National Expert, DG XVI, A.1, 13 May 1998. Numerous informal discussions, March to July 1997.

Central Government, United Kingdom

Fraser, Gay; Department of the Environment Transport and Regions official, former member of the European Regeneration Policy Division, Department of the Environment, 22 January 1999.

Ghosh, Helen; Director Regeneration East, Government Office for London, 26 September 1997.

Hampson, David; European Department, Government Office for London, 13 January 1999.

John, Malcolm; Head of European Department, Government Office for London, 23 January 1997, 26 September 1997.

Laforce, Tony; European Department, Government Office for London, 13 January 1999.

Lawlor, Anne-Marie; United Kingdom Permanent Representation to the European Communities, First Secretary Regional Policy, numerous informal discussions between March and July 1997. Additional interview, Brussels, 7 May 1998.

Sturrock, Sarah; Community Initiatives Manager, Government Office for London, September 1996.

Turner, Sally; Department of the Environment Transport and Regions official, 13 April 1999.

Central Government, France

Crepet, Monsieur; official, *Direction Départementale de l'Équipement*, DDE (Field services of the state dealing with infrastructure), 7 August 1998.

Ferrero, Madame; *Direction Régionale du Travail, de l'Emploi et de la Formation Professionelle*, DRTEFP (Field services of the state dealing with regional employment and training), 31 July 1998.

Pichot, Jean; *Secrétariat Général des Affaires Régionales*, SGAR, *Chargé de mission, Affaires Européennes Préfecture de la Région Provence-Alpes-Côte d'Azur* (Secretariat General for Regional Affairs, official with responsibility for European Affairs, Prefecture of the Provence-Alpes-Côte d'Azur Region), 16 July 1998.

Sibertin-Blanc, Rémi; SGAR, *Chargé de Mission Développement Social et Culturel, Préfecture de la Région Provence-Alpes-Côte d'Azur* (Secretariat General for Regional Affairs, official with responsibility for social and cultural development), 20 July 1998.

Veron, Yves; SGAR, *Chargé de mission, Affaires Européennes, Préfecture de la Région Provence-Alpes-Côte d'Azur*, Secretariat General for Regional Affairs, official with responsibility for European Affairs, Prefecture of the Provence-Alpes-Côte d'Azur region), 3 August 1998.

Vrignaud, Monsieur; *Chargé de Mission pour la politique de la ville, Préfecture des Bouches du Rhône* (Official with responsibility for urban policy, Prefecture of the Department of Bouches-du-Rhône), 23 July 1998.

Local Government and Organisations of Local Government (Case Study of Marseille, France)

Besançon, Henri; *Mission Ville, Chef de Projet, Site 15ème sud* (Project Leader, *15ème sud* district of Marseille).

Blum, Roland; *Conseiller Délégué aux Affaires Sociales, au Centre Communal d'Action Social*, CCAS, *aux Centres Aeres, aux Centres Sociaux, à la jeunesse et la vie associative, au Développement Social Urbain*, DSU, *et à la prévention de la délinquance* (Councillor with responsibility for the communal centre for social action, CCAS, day holiday centres, social centres, youth and associational life, urban and social development, DSU, and the prevention of delinquency).

Boyadjan Marie-France; *Mission Ville, Chef de Projet Centre-Ville* (Project Leader, central area of the city of Marseille), 28 July 1998.

Debrenne, Pierre Yves; *Directeur, Ville de Marseille, Politique de la Ville* (DSU, CCPD, *Toxicomanie, Sida* (Director of Department of the Municipality of Marseille dealing with urban and social policy), 21 July 1998.

Ginouvès, Dominique; *Mission Ville, Chef de Projet, Site Saint Antoine Est* (Project Leader, Saint Antoine East of Marseille), 21 July 1998.

Leccia, Bernard; *Adjoint Délégué à la politique de la ville, aux relations avec les organismes d'Habitiations à Loyer Modéré et au Grand Projet Urbain* (Councillor with responsibility for urban policy, relations with representative bodies of public housing (HLM) and the *Grand Projet Urbain* infrastructure programme), 22 July 1998.

de Leusse, Christian; *Conseil Régional Provence-Alpes-Côte d'Azur*, (Official of Regional Council of Provence-Alpes-Côte d'Azur, with responsibility for co-ordination of policy of planning contracts (*Contrat de Plan, Contrat de Ville*).

Mandrille, Henri; official, *Atelier Champ Social*, former Project Leader in St. Mauront district and central area of Marseille (*Centre-Ville*), 3 August 1998.

Meguenni, Zoubida; *Mission Ville*, Assistant to Project Leader in St Mauront district, 23 July 1998.

Meric, Monsieur, *Ville de Marseille, Direction Générale de l'Urbanisme et de l'Habitat, Promotion et Amélioration de l'Habitat* (Official of department of the Municipality of Marseille dealing with town planning and housing, the promotion and improvement of housing), 27 July 1998.

Perrin, Geneviève; *chargée de mission cellule europe, Ville de Marseille, Mission des programmes privés et européens*, MIPPE (Official with responsibility for European Affairs in the MIPPE, department of the Municipality of Marseille dealing with private and European programmes), 20 July 1998.

Planidis, Angèle; *Mission Ville* (Official responsible for Marseille's participation in the *Quartiers en Crise*. 'Neighbourhoods in Crisis' Network), 21 July 1998.

Raoust, Pascal; *Mission Ville*, Assistant to Project Leader in the central area of Marseille), 24 July 1998.

Reymund, Pierre-Emmanuel; Operational Marketing Manager, Euroméditerannée Public Agency, 29 July 1998.

Schauss, Liliane; *Office de la Culture de Marseille, Échanges Culturels Internationaux* (Official from the Office of Culture, Marseille, with responsibility for international cultural exchanges), 22 July 1998.

Schudel, Arnold, *chargé de mission aménagement urbain, Ville de Marseille, Mission des programmes privés et européens*, MIPPE (Official with responsibility for urban development in the department of the municipality of Marseille dealing with private and European programmes, MIPPE), 20 July 1998.

Local Government Organisations (Case Study of London, United Kingdom)

Hughes, Dawn; Association of London Government, seconded to the Government Office for London; previously European Officer for the London Borough of Greenwich, 25 September 1996.

Hughes, Ian; European Policy Officer, London Study Project Manager, 14 January 1997 as well as other informal discussions during observations of events relating to the London Study.

Kitt, Richard; Head of Brussels office, Local Government International Bureau, 19 October 1996.

Warner, Elaine; Head of Association of London Government Brussels Office, 29 July 1997, 7 May 1998.

Welfare, Damien; Assistant Secretary Parliamentary and European Affairs, Association of Metropolitan Authorities, 1 October 1996.

Implementation of URBAN in the Heart of the East End

Casaguana, Mike; member of interim Urban Partnership Group, local resident of targeted area, representative for East London at UK network meetings, 29 January 1998, 20 January 1999.

Esiquiel, Linda; newly appointed Manager, URBAN Initiative Development Unit, member of URBAN Management Committee, 06 February 1998, 9 April 1999.

Islam, Badrul; Community Development Officer, URBAN Initiative Development Unit, 06 February 1998, 11 January 1999.

Potter, Hilary; European Resources Officer, Hackney 2000, 16 September 1996.

Richardson, David; former European Officer, subsequently Regeneration Manager and member of URBAN Management Committee, London Borough of Tower Hamlets, 02 February 1998, 20 January 1999.

Tarifa, Grisel; Community Development Officer, URBAN Initiative Development Unit, 06 February 1998.

Van de Merwe, Karine; Hoxton Trust, member of URBAN Management Committee, 06 February 1998.

Woolford, Andrea; Chair of interim Urban Partnership Group, member of Hoxton Trust and local resident of designated URBAN area, 27 January 1998, 20 January 1999.

Implementation of URBAN in Park Royal: White City, Shepherds Bush, Edward Woods

Bird, Nick; Community Networks, 3 February 1998.

Bray, Bill; Edward Woods Residents Association, 5 February 1998.

McCechrane, Marlene; Edward Woods Development Worker, member of Urban Partnership Group, 2 February 1998, 13 January 1999.

Diamond, Stephen; Regeneration Policy Officer, London Borough of Hammersmith and Fulham, member of URBAN Management

Committee, Urban Partnership Group and Urban Advisory Board, September 1996, 15 April 1999.

Hayes, Pat; Regeneration Policy Officer, London Borough of Hammersmith and Fulham, September 1996.

Keenan, Gordon; former European Officer, London Borough of Hammersmith and Fulham, subsequently URBAN Programme Manager, member of URBAN Management Group, Urban Partnership Group and Urban Advisory Board, September 1997, 18 January 1999.

Powell, Sally; Councillor, London Borough of Hammersmith and Fulham, Chair of Environment Committee, Wormholt Ward. Also, London representative on the Committee of the Regions during the period of this study and member of White City, Shepherds Bush, Edward Woods Urban Partnership Group, 25 September 1997.

Sharpe, Andy; Chair, White City, Shepherds Bush, Edward Woods Urban Partnership Group, 14 January 1999.

Implementation of URBAN in Park Royal, Queen's Park

Daly, Julian; Voluntary Action Westminster, 14 January 1999.

Forde, Dave; Age Concern Westminster, member of Voluntary and Community Sector Forum and Queen's Park Urban Partnership Group, 16 January 1998, 18 January 1999.

Hall, Neil; Head of Regeneration and External Funding, informal discussions after URBAN Management Committee meetings observed.

Shaw, Steve; Director, Paddington Arts, member of Voluntary and Community Sector Forum and Queen's Park Urban Partnership Group, 16 January 1998.

Thomas, Grantley; local resident and member of Queen's Park Urban Partnership Group, 21 January 1998.

Torquati, Marco; Community Development Officer, City of Westminster and Urban Partnership Group member, 9 February 1998, 13 January 1999.

Implementation of URBAN in Park Royal: South Kilburn

Filsjean, Emmanuelle; European Development Officer, member of URBAN Management Committee, 20 September 1996.

Mackie, Carol; Community Projects Officer and Member of South Kilburn Urban Partnership Group, 4 February 1998, 19 January 1999, 14 April 1999.

Nimblette, Debbie; Chair of South Kilburn Urban Partnership Group, 22 January 1999.

O'Brien, Professor; College of North West London, member of South Kilburn Urban Partnership Group, 19 January 1999.

Miscellaneous

Adams-Singh, Laurie; UK URBAN Network, informal discussion by telephone, January 1999 and at DETR conference, 16 April 1999.

Burridge, Diane; officer London Voluntary Sector Training Consortium (LVSTC), 22 January 1997. The LVSTC had some involvement with URBAN, particularly with the early stages of the South Kilburn URBAN programme. LVSTC was not, however, involved in any of the formal management structures for the implementation of URBAN in any of the London programmes.

Chanan, Gabriel; Community Development Foundation, 15 January 1999. Coordinator of study, (CEC, 1997c), *Community Involvement in urban regeneration: added values and changing values*, 15 January 1999.

Clark, Greg; Director, Greater London Enterprise, GLE Regeneration Strategies, informal discussions relating to the case study of London, September 1996, May 1997.

Deason, Barbara; LVSTC officer dealing specifically with URBAN, 23 September 1997.

Eden, Gill; Europe and Research Officer, London Borough of Barnet, 12 September 1996.

Gill, Kathy; European Officer, London Borough of Newham, 24 September 1996.

Jeffrey, Paul; ECOTEC Research and Consulting Ltd., informal discussion at Urban Pilots Project Conference, ECOTEC/DG XVI, 12 May 1998.

de Lange, Chris; Head of European Community Affairs, Rotterdam City Development Corporation, informal discussion and exchange of ideas at London Study presentation, London 25 September 1997, Committee of the Regions plenary session, 13 May 1998.

Laurance, Bolaji; London TEC Council, 20 January 1997.

Löffler, Peter; European Sustainable Cities and Towns Campaign, informal discussion relating to urban issues, 11 May 1998.

Maragall, Pasquall; former Mayor of Barcelona and President of the EU Committee of the Regions, informal discussion relating to urban matters, 2 June 1998, European University Institute, Florence.

Marianou, Eleni; Director, Programmes and Communities, Eurocities, Brussels, 11 May 1998.

Marsh, Pete; European Officer, London Borough of Haringey, 30 August 1996.

Payne, Anthony; European Sustainable Cities & Towns Campaign, informal discussion relating to urban matters, 11 May 1998.

Skarvelis, Efharis; Associate Director, ECOTEC Research and Consulting Limited, Brussels, 18 July 1997.

Stevenson, Drew; Professor of Urban Regeneration, University of East London, 24 September 1997, 20 January 1999.

Swash, Tony; European Officer, Urban Regeneration Unit, Islington Council, 18 September 1996.

Williams, Hugh, ECOTEC Research and Consulting Ltd., Brussels, 1 June 1997.

Selected List of Meetings Observed

URBAN Management Committee Meetings (London)

Park Royal URBAN Management Committee, 16 June 1997.
Park Royal URBAN Management Committee, 9 September 1997.
Heart of the East End URBAN Management Committee, 27 January 1998.

Urban Partnership Group Meetings (London)

Queen's Park Urban Partnership Group, Urban Action Plan strategy day, 16 September 1997.

Queen's Park Urban Partnership Group, Urban Action Plan strategy day, 21 January 1998.

Heart of the East End Urban Partnership Group, 22 January 1998.

White City, Shepherds Bush, Edward Woods Urban Partnership Group, Quality of Life and Community Capacity Building Focus Group, 20 January 1998.

White City, Shepherds Bush, Edward Woods Urban Partnership Group, 3 February 1998.

South Kilburn Urban Partnership Group, Urban Action Plan Strategy Day, 4 February 1998.

Central Government/European Commission

Meeting between officials from the Government Office for London and DG XVI, Brussels, 18 March 1997.

Government Office for London, 'Awayday Conference' for the Park Royal URBAN Programme, Hendon, 29 May 1998.

Meeting between officials from the Department of the Environment Transport and Regions, the Department for Education and Employment and URBAN officers from various programmes in the UK, London, 16 April 1999.

Other meetings between DG XVI officials regarding other UK URBAN programmes were observed in the period March to July 1997. Some of these included DG XVI meetings with local partners in Brussels.

Marseille

Comité de Suivi (Meeting of the Monitoring Committee for the implementation of URBAN in Marseille) including technical meeting prior to this organised by the *Secrétariat Général des Affaires Régionales* (SGAR) *Préfecture de la Région Provence-Alpes-Côte d'Azur* (Secretariat General for Regional Affairs, official with responsibility for European Affairs, Prefecture of the Provence-Alpes-Côte d'Azur region), 9 July 1998.

Visit to *Friche la Belle-de Mai, un projet culturel pour un projet urbain* (Cultural project relating to an urban project for the area), 9 July 1998, afternoon following the meeting of the Monitoring Committee. Project partly financed by the urban dimension to the Objective 2 programme for the Provence-Alpes-Côte d'Azur, 1996-2001, 9 July 1998 (afternoon).

Visit to the *Mission Ville* team (Department of the Municipality of Marseille dealing with urban and social policy) based in the Bellevue estate, Saint Mauront, selected for the URBAN programme, 23 July 1998 (morning observation and interviews on site). Other areas designated for the state's infrastructure programme, *Grand Projet Urbain* (GPU), also eligible for some aspects of URBAN funding were visited as part of the interviewing process in July 1998.

Miscellaneous

Committee of the Regions, 30 May 1997, committee meeting dealing with urban matters.

Committee of the Regions, Plenary sessions, 11 June, 1997, 13 May 1998.
European Summit of Regions and Cities, Amsterdam, 16 May 1997.
European Parliament, presentation of *Agenda 2000* proposals to the European Parliament, Strasbourg, 16 July 1997, by Jacques Santer, President of the European Commission.

Index of Authors